ASPECTS OF DEVON HISTORY
PEOPLE, PLACES AND LANDSCAPES

ASPECTS OF DEVON HISTORY
PEOPLE, PLACES AND LANDSCAPES

The Devon History Society Fortieth Anniversary Book

Edited by

Jane Bliss, Christopher Jago and Elizabeth Maycock

First published 2012 by
The Devon History Society

Copyright © The Devon History Society
and the individual contributors 2012

British Library Cataloguing in Publication Data
A catalogue record of this book is available from the British Library

ISBN 978-0-903766-02-9

Typeset Kestrel Data, Exeter
Cover design by Delphine Jones

Printed and bound in Great Britain by
Short Run Press Ltd, Exeter

Contents

Contents

Editors and Contributors

Editors

Jane Bliss read History at the University of Plymouth following a career in nursing, health visiting and teaching. She completed an MRes in History at the University of Southampton in 2004. She lives in North Devon, where she has served on the Mortehoe Museum committee, and is currently Programme Secretary of the Devon History Society.

Christopher Jago developed an interest in local history, following retirement from the Civil Service. He studied Village and Parish History and British History 1450–1970 in the Department of Lifelong Learning at the University of Exeter and the Advanced Diploma in Local History in the Department of Continuing Education, University of Oxford. He is a council member of the Devon History Society.

Elizabeth Maycock has lived in Exmouth for many years and was educated there at Southlands School. After working at the War Office and in administration, she was a company director. She is a life member of Devon Gardens Trust and of the Devon History Society.

Contributors

Ann Bond has until recently been a senior manager within the NHS. She gained an honours degree in Historical Studies with the University of Exeter as a mature student and her main historical research interest is nineteenth-century social reform. She has lived in Kenton for twelve years and is the owner – or rather the current custodian – of one of the properties discussed in her article.

Peter Bowers is a retired insurance company official, who has been Chairman of The Sampford Peverell Society since its inception in 2003 and has been actively involved in many of the projects undertaken by the Society.

Nicky Campbell researched the history of her house in East Devon, which led to her interest in the village of Combpyne and the neighbouring village of Rousdon, where the Peek family had owned a large estate. She became intrigued by Sir Henry Peek's practical philanthropy, and its profound effect on the locality. She is currently writing a book on his social 'experiment' at Rousdon.

Rachel Cutts graduated in Sociology from Goldsmiths College London and has always maintained a keen interest in social history. Following a varied career which included working in Papua New Guinea, and in the prison service, she is currently a lecturer in sociology at Petroc in Tiverton, Devon.

Arthur Dark is a retired LEA Educational Advisor and was educated at Bideford Grammar School, Devonport High School and University College, Exeter. His interest in Parkham originated in his investigation into the history of his own family who are traceable in Parkham back to the middle of the seventeenth century.

Sue Dymond has lived in East Devon for thirty-seven years. Her interests include industrial archaeology, social history, and changes to the historical landscape. Recognising the importance of recording the memories of older people in society, she has been involved in oral history projects and in local history projects in schools.

Greg Finch is a self-employed corporate financial planning consultant. He was born in Devon, where his interest in history developed under the teaching of Robin Stanes at Exmouth School. His doctoral thesis of 1984 explored the economic history of Devon during the Industrial Revolution. He now lives in Northumberland, where his research interests focus mainly on the early modern landscape and economic history of the Tyne Valley.

Mary Freeman, otherwise Mary Whitear, retired as Reader in Zoology at University College London in 1989. She returned to her native county to live at Tavistock, developed an interest in local history, and is a member of the Tavistock Subscription Library.

Todd Gray is Honorary Research Fellow at Exeter University, Chairman of the Friends of Devon's Archives and of the Devon and Cornwall Record Society, and President of the Devon Family History Society. He has written widely on the history of Devon.

Eve Higgs retired to Thorncombe in 1998 following a varied career. A chance encounter with the Thorncombe 1684 Conventicle at the Devon Record Office took her on a new journey into academe via the Open University and Exeter University's Village and Parish History course. She completed the Oxford University Advanced Diploma in Local History in 2009.

Christopher Holdsworth became a medieval historian while an undergraduate at Cambridge (1950–53), taught at University College London (1956–77) and finally at Exeter (1977–91). He has published largely on monastic, especially Cistercian, history, and is still writing. He plays the cello and enjoys gardening.

Andrew Jackson has been the Editor of *The Devon Historian*, the journal of the Devon History Society, since 2005. He is a historian and geographer with a particular interest in twentieth-century change and local and regional history. Following ten years at the University of Exeter, he currently teaches at Bishop Grosseteste University College Lincoln.

Jeanne James has lived in Devon since 1969. She read History at the University of Exeter and completed her MPhil there, supervised by Professor Nicholas Orme, with an analysis of 'Medieval Chapels in Devon'. She identified some 1,300 from documentary evidence, many of which have disappeared without trace. It is an ongoing project to find the sites of medieval chapels with her husband Matthew as photographer.

Paddy Nash has a degree in Fine Art, and an Open University degree in Philosophy and History. She has lived in Devon since 1970. She is the author of three local history books which trace the history of the Devon Valley paper mill at Hele. The title of her forthcoming book is *George West: Papermaker to Congressman*.

Julia Neville is a research fellow at the Centre for Medical History at the University of Exeter, and has a continuing interest in the history of Devon's communities in the twentieth century. She has recently worked with Exeter Civic Society on *Exeter and the Trams, 1882–1931*, and with Honiton Senior Council over the life and times of Mrs Phillips, Mayor, Alderman and Freeman of the Borough and first woman county councillor in Devon.

Michael Nix was formerly Research Manager for Transport and Technology at Glasgow Museums. In 1991, he completed a PhD with the Department of English Local History, Leicester University, researching the ports of Bideford and Barnstaple between 1786 and 1841. Before working professionally in a number of West Country museums, he co-founded a private maritime museum at Hartland Quay in North Devon.

Nicholas Orme taught history at Exeter University from 1964 to 2007, and is the author of over twenty books on aspects of national and local history. His most recent works include *Exeter Cathedral: the first thousand years* (2009) and *The Victoria County History of Cornwall*, volume 2 (2010). He has been elected president of the Devon History Society and the Devonshire Association.

R.H. (Bob) Parker is Emeritus Professor of Accounting at the University of Exeter. He is the author of many books and articles. He is a member of the Devon History Society and a former treasurer of the Devon and Exeter Institution. He continues to be an active researcher, especially into the history of the accountancy profession: in Devon, in the United Kingdom, and throughout the world.

Colin Passey is a retired civil servant. He joined the Sampford Peverell Society in 2003 and has been involved in many of its activities ever since.

Eric Preston is a member of the Dartmouth History Research Group and a keen local historian. He is also Vice Chairman of the Dartmouth Museum and Vice President of the Dartmouth and Kingswear Society (environmental group). He has written three short booklets on local history. He is a graduate of Cambridge and London Universities and before retirement worked as a computer manager.

Sue Price was born in Devon, and taught in Devon schools until she retired from her post as Headteacher at Widecombe in the Moor. She is currently Programme Secretary of Chagford Local History Society. The George Henry Reed of her article is her great-great-grandfather and his son George Spencer Reed who continued his work, her grandfather.

Jean Rhodes has lived in Chagford for forty-five years. Her interest in local history was fostered by working for a degree with the Open University in the 1990s, which focused on history, and included an oral history project. She is the Secretary of Chagford Local History Society.

Ivan Roots is Professor Emeritus at the University of Exeter, where he taught history from 1947 to 1986. He also held one year teaching posts at University College, Cardiff, and at Lafayette College, Pennsylvania. He is a past President of the Cromwell Association.

Charles Scott-Fox is the eldest son of the eminent archaeologists Sir Cyril Fox, whose biography he wrote in 2002, and Lady Aileen Fox. He served in the Royal Navy from 1952 to 1985, and was subsequently a partner in a family business that ran the Hell Bay Hotel in the Isles of Scilly. His interest now lies in writing and publishing books on the history of Devon buildings and the people with whom they are associated.

Gillian Selley moved to Woodbury in 1991 and became fascinated with the history of the parish. In 1994 she started a two year Local and Regional History Course run by the University of Exeter, and at the same time founded the Woodbury Local History Society. Her research concerns all aspects of the history of Woodbury, though she has written about people and events from other parts of the county.

Tony Simpson was a social worker and community activist in the Welsh valleys. He taught at University of Wales, Cardiff and the Open University for seventeen years. In retirement he helped to establish the Senior Council for Honiton and became the organising secretary. He is interested in the contemporary relevance of social history, a topic on which he writes and gives talks.

Sue Spurr researched nineteenth-century church restoration in Devon as part of her degree in Humanities at Exeter University's Department of Lifelong Learning in 2009. She works part-time as copy-editor of *Vernacular Architecture*.

Geoff Squire retired as Senior Lecturer in Geography Education at Reading University in 1995. Born in Branscombe, he attended Branscombe School and Colyton Grammar School, later graduating from the Universities of Cambridge and Reading. He was an Open University tutor in geography and social science for many years.

Mark Stoyle is Professor of early modern History at the University of Southampton. He has written many books and articles on the English Civil War and on the history of South West England during the Tudor and early Stuart periods. Professor Stoyle's latest book – *The Black Legend of Prince Rupert's Dog: Witchcraft and Propaganda during the English Civil War* – was published by the University of Exeter in May 2011.

John Torrance, retired Lecturer in Politics at the University of Oxford, is an Emeritus Fellow of Hertford College, Oxford. Now living in Beer, he participates in the Branscombe Project for oral and local history and researches topics on the history of East Devon.

Christopher Wakefield trained as an art teacher, but spent nearly all his working life as a designer and illustrator. He joined Walter Minchinton's Exeter Industrial Archaeology Group, and later the Devon Archaeological Society and the Devon History Society as his interests broadened. He is a founder member and trustee of Ottery St Mary Heritage Society, and edits their Journal.

Retha M. Warnicke is Professor of History at Arizona State University, Tempe, Arizona. Her best known publication is *The Rise and Fall of Anne Boleyn: Family Politics at the Court of Henry VIII*, published by Cambridge University Press, in 1989 and 1991. Her most recent book is *Mary Queen of Scots*, published by Routledge in 2006.

Val Weller was involved in social work for thirty years and maintains a strong interest in social and local history as a result.

Margaret Wilson (nee Toyne) was raised in Devon and returned to the county with her husband Michael to live in retirement. She has recently served as secretary of the Woodbury Local History Society. Her many publications include *Norumbega Navigators*, and *A Woodbury Triumph*, which resulted from her father's long campaign in 1972 to save Woodbury Common from the development of two golf courses.

Michael Wilson returned to Woodbury following retirement from his post as a Consultant Anaesthetist, and has recently served as chairman of Woodbury Local History Society. He and his wife Margaret are currently researching the history of the *Virginia*, the first wooden boat to be built in America and sail back to England (probably to Topsham, Devon).

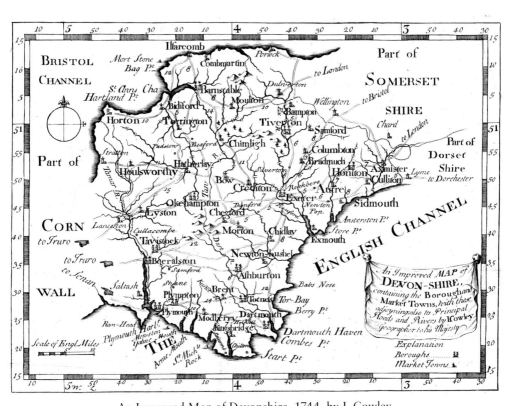

An Improved Map of Devonshire, 1744, by J. Cowley.
Reproduced courtesy of Westcountry Studies Library, Devon Libraries.

Abbreviations

BL	British Library
DAT	*Devonshire Association Transactions*
DCNQ	*Devon and Cornwall Notes and Queries*
DCRS	Devon and Cornwall Record Society
DEI	Devon and Exeter Institution
DHC	Dorset History Centre
DNB	*Dictionary of National Biography*
DRO	Devon Record Office
ECA	Exeter Cathedral Archive
EUL	Exeter University Library
HER	Historic Environment Record
MERL	Museum of English Rural Life, University of Reading
NDMM	North Devon Maritime Museum
NDRO	North Devon Record Office
OS	Ordnance Survey
PWDRO	Plymouth and West Devon Record Office
SDNQ	*Somerset and Dorset Notes and Queries*
SHC	Somerset Heritage Centre
TAVSM	Tavistock Museum Collection
TDH	*The Devon Historian*
TEDAS	*Transactions of the Exeter Diocesan Architectural Society*
TNA	The National Archives
WCSL	Westcountry Studies Library, Exeter

Preface

The main purpose of this volume is to celebrate the first forty years of the Devon History Society. We wanted to encourage new research into Devon's history and to provide a publishing opportunity for writers who had not previously thought of publishing their work. Contributions from both members and non-members of the Society were welcomed. The wide-ranging subtitle of this celebratory volume, 'people, places and landscapes', reflects the diverse range of topics covered in the following chapters. We hope that, at a time when the study of local history is receiving less formal support than it once had, the book will stimulate and encourage future research.

There are many people who have assisted during the production of this volume. The editors would particularly like to thank Professor Christopher Holdsworth, President of the Devon History Society, for providing the Foreword and Dr Todd Gray for writing the Introduction. Their scholarly advice and generous assistance at all stages of the project has been much appreciated. The Chairman, Mrs Shirley Purves has encouraged the project from the outset and council members have been supportive throughout. Our thanks also go to Mr Philippe Planel and Dr Graham Bliss for devoting much time and energy at various stages of the production process, and to Dr Andrew Jackson for his timely advice. Thanks are also due to the staffs of the Devon Record Office and the Westcountry Studies Library, and to Delphine Jones for her excellent cover design.

Finally, we must thank all the authors who responded to our call for papers, and for their patient co-operation during the editorial process. Without them, of course, there would be no book.

Jane Bliss
Christopher Jago
Elizabeth Maycock

Foreword

This book marks the wish of the Devon History Society to celebrate the first forty years of its life and to stimulate and aid the many individuals and groups who are interested in the history of the county. The range of papers collected here is helpfully summed up in the last words of its title, '*People, Places and Landscapes.*' The chronological range emerges from the papers themselves, none of them tackles a subject before the tenth century: the centre lies in the modern or post-Reformation period. Nearly all the papers are written by people who, if not Devonians by birth, are so by present habitation, and some of whom are members of groups concentrating on one, or more, local communities, as Branscombe, Chagford, Dartmouth, Sampford Peverell or Woodbury. Some authors address problems on their doorstep, so to say, or involving members of their own families. For my part I profited most about issues which I had never considered before, for example, the use, storage and transport of water involving leats, dew ponds and rams. The inter-Christian struggles in Rose Ash and Woodbury, on the other hand, left a sad impression.

The Society should be congratulated on three features of this large and impressive book. First, that nearly every paper has a proper bibliography and set of notes, which will enable readers to follow up issues which interest them with relative ease. Second, the book is well illustrated, often with rare material which will awaken new questions for many readers. Lastly, unlike many multi-author collections, this one comes with a proper index. The labour for the three editors in producing such a volume of over 400 pages with so many contributions must have been considerable. They deserve the warmest thanks from all their readers.

Christopher Holdsworth

Introduction

Todd Gray

The span of forty years is no time in Devon's long history but these last forty, since the Devon History Society was formed, have seen tremendous changes in the way in which its history has been researched, constructed and disseminated. The chapters in this volume celebrating the first forty years of the society are a reflection of this. The nature of the contributions are in themselves also telling of the role that the society has played in Devon's history community.

When the society began in 1969 the study of Devon was dominated by the work of W.G. Hoskins, our first President. His monograph on the county was then relatively newly-written and more than a generation later it remains the definitive history. The society was largely the creation of two Exeter University historians, Professors Joyce Youings and Walter Minchinton. They remained dominant figures for the following twenty years. The society began as the Standing Conference for Devon History and it was inspired by the national Standing Conference for History. That body was succeeded by the British Association for Local History and the Devon History Society renamed itself in 1980. From the start the aims were to further the study of Devon's history, to bring together those interested in its history, to hold regular meetings and to disseminate knowledge of what has been written and what work was in progress.[1] The founders' vision was that individual local history societies needed to be linked. Devon's local societies have flourished since then. Their numbers, and members, have increased beyond any expectations. There are few parts of the county which do not have a local society. Devon is a county not only of a great number of museums but also of a greater number of history societies. Many of the chapters in this volume began with lines of enquiry developed as a result of attendance at meetings of these local groups.

New county-wide societies have sprung up since 1969 including the Devon Historic Churches Trust in 1971, the Devon Historic Buildings Trust in 1973, the Devon Family History Society in 1976, the Devon Buildings Group in 1986, the Devon Gardens Trust in 1989 and the Friends of Devon's Archives in 1998. Of these more recent bodies, the most influential has been the Devon Family History Society. Its membership dwarfs all the other county societies and it has become the advocate of what is the largest single historical interest in our archives and libraries. It is also the most active of all the county history societies. Each group has responded to new interests amongst historians and the general public. In the years since 1969 Devon's historians have followed those lines of research which were little discussed or haphazardly organised beforehand. Examples of these interests will be found throughout *The Devon Historian* as well as amongst the following pages.

Volunteers have been the mainstay of Devon's history societies. Their contributions are seldom recognised but without that work these societies would cease. Future historians will note the role of hundreds of volunteers who have brought forward the study of Devon's past. The contributions in this book are just another example of this public service. We have paid archivists, curators and librarians concerned only with Devon but no such equivalent amongst our historians. We rely upon volunteer labour.

Not every recent historical initiative in Devon has succeeded. During these last forty years the Centre for South Western Historical Studies, based at the University of Exeter, was formed, thrived and then has dwindled away. Most of the older county societies have seen significant falls in membership albeit local history has never been more popular. Television in particular has vigorously engaged in and promoted local history. Devon's past is constantly being investigated by local and national programmes. With each one the appetite of the public is whetted but the focus of local studies has more recently concentrated on community and not county studies. It could be said that the result is that the peripheries of Devon studies are stronger than the centre. The chapters in this book reflect an increasing interest in more localised studies.

It was largely because of the pursuit of family history, and the many thousands of genealogists in Devon and of those living further afield, that we have a new archive building in Exeter. It will be because of them that we will hopefully have a new office in Plymouth. Our archives remain our most valuable historical resource in Devon and arguably this county has the greatest archive collection outside London. This year we will have also new facilities at Exeter Cathedral. The records there continue to be listed as have been tens of thousands of other documents elsewhere in Devon over these last forty years. Manuscript material continues to be deposited, catalogued and made available to researchers. This has made the pursuit of Devon's history easier and more straightforward than it ever has been. Our resources would be the envy of the historians who have come before us.

The undertaking of research has been transformed in these forty years. Typewriters have been replaced by computers, index cards have been largely overtaken by online catalogues and digital cameras have usurped the photocopying of documents. The internet was unknown in 1969 and it has since become the greatest tool in researching Devon's past. Many thousands of researchers work only from websites and electronic resources without visiting the county. This would have been unimaginable in 1969.

Nevertheless, one of our greatest problems remains largely as it was forty years ago. The county is too big. We still have a gap in interests not just between Exeter and Plymouth but North, East, South and West Devon remain largely indifferent to one another. They retain different cultural traditions and identities with the result that county studies remain fragmented. The establishment of a university at Plymouth and, more to the point, of its thriving history department there, will help to support local studies in and around South West Devon. Perhaps this will balance the impact which has radiated out from Exeter, for nearly a hundred years, to communities within its reach. Devon, like all other parts of the country, suffered in the 1990s and in the first decade of this century when national funding for British university historians discriminated against local studies. In 1969 university staff led Devon's history research but lately the majority of work has come from local societies. Since the mid-1990s few full-time university historians have written monographs on Devon and the last decade has not seen the landmark publications of previous years, such as *The New Maritime History of Devon* or The *Historical Atlas of South-West England*. More work is now being done by those retired from their jobs who feel able to research and write without any university constraints but it has been local historians, working on a part-time basis, voluntarily and largely untrained, who have taken the initiative. Archaeology in Devon, outside the remit of this Society, has fared better although the recession has restricted the financial input from land developers with the catastrophic reduction of council-supported archaeology in Exeter and Plymouth.

The winners of this society's Devon Book of the Year reflects the significant work which has been published. Over the last thirteen years, since the award began, academics have generally received this accolade but it has also been won by untrained historians and by groups of local historians based in Chudleigh and Instow. It is they who not only fill our archive search rooms and local history libraries but publish the majority of Devon's history.

The three auto-biographical pieces commissioned for this volume will make each reader pause and reflect on what they have previously read. Professors Christopher Holdsworth, Ivan Roots and Mark Stoyle, three of our most respected scholars working on Devon, each describe how they became historians. Their chapters provide insights into the forces that shape a historian's work. Each has a passion for their subject which becomes self-evident but all three are too modest to describe the painstaking efforts they take to pursue their craft. These three pieces will illuminate the individual behind the printed or spoken word which is already familiar to many across Devon.

The subtitle for this celebratory volume, 'people, places and landscapes', indicates the diversity of research interests set within our large county. It does not attempt to be comprehensive in any way; it is merely a collection of twenty-nine disparate articles ranging in date from the early medieval period through to recent times. Diverse parts of the county are looked at although there is more on the eastern part than on the far west. It is the range of subjects that make this a delight to those who enjoy a varied diet. The writers themselves are also a varied group: the contributors include well-known academics to untrained local historians who are published in these pages for the first time.

Discussions of religion, poverty, industry and migration will be found. It is not possible to comment on each contribution but what comes out from each and every one is the diversity of communities within Devon and that each has its own particular history. A comparison between two separate contributions on Rose Ash and Woodbury demonstrates the ways in which differences in religious belief could manifest themselves and the importance of personalities in village life. Other chapters centre on individuals who are looked at in great detail: Piers Courtenay, the county's sheriff at the time of the Prayer Book Rebellion, the Bradninch-born George West who went to America to find his fortune and the rural life enthusiast E.W. Martin are just some of those who emerge from the past in the following pages. Each tells part of the many stories of Devon's history. The chapter on Victorian emigration opens up another view of Devon's people: it reminds us that certain areas of the county contributed to populating other parts of the world. These Devonians found themselves living in other counties in Britain as well as much further afield. Generations later many of their descendants search through Devon's archives for their ancestral roots.

Branscombe, Chagford, Dartmouth, Kenton, Ottery St Mary, Parkham, Rose Ash, Rousdon, Sampford Peverell, Tavistock, Thorncombe and Woodbury are some of the communities which are discussed. Many others are included in a more general sense in a discussion on North Devon's shipping history and in an examination of the coastal landmarks that were Devon's medieval chapels. It will be an unusual reader who does not find the introduction of electricity in Chagford illuminating in several ways. The consequence of the great fire at Kenton also brings light to a subject little discussed in Devon. The examination of the medieval landscape at Branscombe should raise questions for those interested in comparing it to their part of the county. In other chapters there are tantalising glimpses of still wider histories. No doubt the appeal of each contribution will rest with the interest of the reader.

This book indicates the successes that have come from the creation of the Devon History Society. In the earliest years *The Devon Historian* was intended to introduce historical sources to local historians and discuss how to research and write history. This is no longer the case. Where do we go from here? The two annual meetings are still held in different parts of the county and there are few places that the society has not met in or near. Our journal continues to act as a medium for publication and discussion. This book shows that the greatest success story in Devon's history community has been the formation of local history groups. This society has nurtured that development and the essays in this volume are a real celebration not just of the society but of local history groups, of their historians and of the pursuit of Devon's past.

Notes and References

1.   'Editorial', (1978), *TDH*, 16, 2.

Delving in the Dark Corners of the Land: reflections on a historical apprenticeship

Mark Stoyle

'If you want to understand the history, first understand the historian': this is an aphorism which certainly holds true in my own case.[1] I have been fascinated by the past for as long as I can remember, and I have no doubt that this fascination reflects my own family background. My father is a Devon man, descended from that long line of Stoyles who have been living and working in the parishes around the fringes of Dartmoor for at least four centuries, and it is from him and from my grandfather that I have inherited that deep sense of physical 'rootedness' which has influenced – even, perhaps, dictated – the whole course of my adult life. I grew up knowing that we, as a family, had lived in Devon for time out of mind and that knowledge, in its turn, has encouraged me to look back on Devon's history as a past that is peculiarly my own. I was fascinated by the Devon landscape as a child, not least because I saw it as a tangible link with my forebears. I knew that the local fields had been worked by them; that the local lanes had been trudged by them; that the local churchyards still held their mortal remains. I knew that my ancestors had helped to shape the physical world in which I had my own being, in other words – and that it was even possible to hear a faint echo of their voices in the Devonshire accents which rose and fell about me.

But if the Stoyles' tenacious familial attachment to a particular locality – combined with the physical survival of ancient buildings, field patterns, dialect and so on – could sometimes make me feel that our forebears were remarkably close, then the sheer 'unknowability' of the past – particularly where ordinary rural families are concerned – could often make me feel that they were almost impossibly remote, too. Edmund Blunden captured something of this feeling in his poem 'Forefathers':

> 'Unrecorded, un-renowned,
> Men from whom my ways begin,
> Here I know you by your ground,
> But I know you not within –
> There is silence, there survives,
> Not a moment of your lives'.[2]

The desire to break through this wall of 'silence' – to learn more about the thoughts and the inner lives of the men and women who once inhabited the countryside where I myself grew up – is one which has been with me since my earliest days.

If my father's Devon roots impelled me to look back to the past, then so did my mother's Irish ones. My mother belongs to an Anglo-Irish family who had lived in County Wexford in some style during the eighteenth and nineteenth centuries, before prudently retiring to the North. Not surprisingly, perhaps, my mother's older relatives regarded Georgian Ireland as a land of lost content and treasured the heirlooms which they had retained from those days as relics of a grander and more spacious age. From them, I learnt that my family's past on my mother's side had been filled with alarums and excursions and this undoubtedly reinforced my conviction that the past was a thrilling and exciting place with which I possessed a close personal connection. As a child, I felt a deeper sense of affinity with my Devonian ancestors than with my Anglo-Irish ones. Nevertheless, it is the fusion of a Devon family with an Anglo-Irish family which has made me who I am – and this fusion has had a deep influence upon the kind of history which I have gone on to write, ensuring that my gaze has always been drawn towards peripheral varieties of 'Britishness', rather than towards the up-country world of London and the Home Counties. During the early modern period, zealous English

Protestants scathingly referred to the remote parts of the kingdom where godly reformation had failed to penetrate – the North, Wales, Cornwall and Devon – as 'the dark corners of the land'.[3] It is from these same 'dark corners' that I myself have sprung, and therefore it is the histories of these peripheral regions which I have always found the most alluring.

What first aroused my interest in the English Civil War is hard to say, but I do remember, when I was very young, browsing through a collection of papers which my father had borrowed from his friend John Uglow, who shared Dad's passion for the history of the village in which we lived. Among these papers was a photograph of the ancient gate-arch at Culm John, near Killerton House, with a note underneath stating that the mansion-house itself – now long vanished – had been garrisoned for the king during the Civil War. Soon afterwards, my parents took me and my sister to a firework display at Killerton, and as we drove over Culm John bridge on that dark autumn night I recall gazing towards the gate-arch and imagining troops of shadowy horsemen riding up the lane. From that day onwards, if not before, I always dreamt that I might one day find a job which would allow me to immerse myself in the study of the past, and when I left school, in 1984, I decided to spend my gap-year working as a digger with Exeter Museum's Archaeological Field Unit. During that bitter winter I worked as hard as I have ever done in my life, labouring alongside dozens of others to uncover the foundations of the Roman city wall. Gradually I got to know the late Chris Henderson – the Director of the Field Unit and a man who had made the historic defences of Exeter his life-long study. Realising that I was more adept with a book than a shovel, Chris eventually suggested that I should leave the trenches and transfer my activities to Exeter's rich civic archives instead.

Over the next few months, I was introduced to a treasure-trove of documents, a treasure-trove from which – to my surprise and delight – I was actually paid to dig out extracts relating to the city walls and, more particularly, to the destruction of the city suburbs during the Civil War. Those eight months of research were some of the happiest of my life – and, in retrospect, I can see that it was during those same months that my future course was set. If delving into the earth was one way of pursuing the past, I now realised, then delving into the archives was another one – and one which was much better suited to my own particular talents. Thus I started to make the shift from archaeologist to historian even before I had left Exeter, a shift which was finally made official a few months later when I transferred from Combined Honours History and Archaeology to Single Honours History during my first year at University.

Soon afterwards, my tutor, George Bernard, introduced me to David Underdown's wonderful book *Revel, Riot and Rebellion,* which explores the connections between Civil War allegiance and pre-existing cultural and religious patterns in Dorset, Somerset and Wiltshire. Underdown's book was a revelation to me because it showed that research which was primarily focused on just one part of the kingdom could be used to put forward arguments which had the potential to transform our understanding of the early modern period as a whole. I now had a model on which to build, and during the following year I wrote an undergraduate dissertation on popular allegiance in Devon during the Civil War, a dissertation which served, in its turn, as a springboard for my postgraduate work on the same subject at Oxford, and – eventually – for my first monograph. That book was entitled *Loyalty and Locality: Popular Allegiance in Devon during the English Civil War.* I chose this title to reflect the book's central argument that the particular districts in which early Stuart Devonians had lived had had a direct bearing upon their wartime allegiance, with those who came from regions in which puritans had been most active before the war tending to support the Parliament, and those who came from the more religiously conservative areas of the county – the 'dark' parts of Devon – tending to support the king. Yet, at the same time, the title of the book was a private nod to my own world-view, to that passionate sense of loyalty to my own particular locality which I had always felt – and indeed, which I still feel today.

A series of other books followed, and as I look back on them now, I feel extraordinarily privileged to have been given the opportunity to write them. As George Orwell observed, 'writing a book is an exhausting struggle' – but it is a struggle which confers enormous benefits on the author. My books have allowed me to go to all sorts of places where I would never otherwise have gone and to meet all sorts of fascinating and remarkable people whom I would never otherwise have met. They have enriched my existence and at the same time they have ensured that some of my own thoughts and feelings will, I hope, endure, in contrast to the many generations of my Devon forebears whose 'inner lives' went down into silence – and whom I have consequently been pursuing ever since I was a child.

Notes and References

1. Hutton 2004, p. 1.
2. Blunden 1957.
3. For Devon as one of the 'dark corners' of the land, see Dr Williams's Library, London, J. Quick, 'Icones Sacrae Anglicanae', vol. I, part I, p. 51.

Bibliography

Blunden E. (1957) *Poems of Many Years*, London: Collins.

Hutton R. (2004) *Debates in Stuart History*, Basingstoke: Palgrave Macmillan.

Orwell, G. (1946) 'Why I Write', *Gangrel*, summer edition.

Stoyle, M. (2003) *Circled with Stone: Exeter's city walls, 1485–1660*, Exeter: Exeter University Press.

Stoyle, M. (1994) *Loyalty and Locality: popular allegiance in Devon during the English Civil War*, Exeter: Exeter University Press.

Underdown, D. (1987) *Revel, Riot and Rebellion: popular politics and culture in England, 1603–60*, Oxford: Oxford University Press.

How I Became a Historian

Christopher Holdsworth

Many aspects of life aroused my interest in the past, among which were the two houses in which I lived, my boarding school and then university. I early became aware of the large, detached, red brick house where I was born, and soon learnt that it had been built by my paternal grandparents around the turn of the nineteenth and twentieth centuries. Its spacious rooms looked out onto a garden, while on the north-east, in a derelict quarry, a distant relative had created two shale tennis-courts. Victoria Road lay on the north-western edge of Bolton, lined with houses like ours, all needing living-in servants to win the constant daily battle against the soot showering down from the industries dominating the town. The house stood on a raised platform, so from the upper floors one could count on clear days two hundred mill chimneys stretching from Bolton to Manchester.

Havercroft, our house, was a product of the town's most significant industry, cotton, for my great grandfather had become partner in a mill in the eighteen-forties, when he was in his twenties. Thus far the house was typical: but it was distinguished from all its neighbours because our family were Quakers, and had been so since my great grandfather's father, who had been joiner, cabinet maker and furniture broker in Wakefield, had become one. I grasped this in my teens, but belonging to a small, yet economically successful community, was enough to stimulate my imagination, while my father's stories whetted my appetite to learn more about long-dead forebears.

We left Bolton in 1943 for Wensleydale, where the small farm, bought by my grandfather before 1914 as a retirement hobby, needed someone to run it, while the mill where my father had worked had closed. Bear Park, a low stone structure, probably 500 years old, lay on a sheltered ledge looking across the river Ure to Aysgarth, with the great bulk of hills beyond, while behind the house, the lane led up to Carperby where my paternal grandmother had been born. Built into the north wall, overlooking the farmyard, was a late medieval altar front, possibly from Coverham Abbey, eight or so miles to the east, while very old beams in the oak panelled dining room supported its ceiling. Soon we learnt from guide books and family stories, that the place had belonged to Marrick Priory, in Swaledale, the next valley to the north, and that Bear Park had nothing to do with bears, but rather with it being the nuns' favourite manor, Beau Repaire, a nice place to be. We learnt that a distant relative had bought the farm in the 1880s, restored the house and created a glorious garden, whose slopes were brightened with alpine flowers and shrubs. The garden indeed had cost so much to make that, to the horror of his family, the farm had to be sold when he died, since his wealth, amassed as a leather merchant in Liverpool, had vanished.

Moving to Yorkshire also meant a move to Bootham, then a small Quaker boys' school in York, lying a few hundred yards west of Bootham Bar. Despite the war, we were allowed extraordinary freedom: every boy had a bicycle, so we explored the countryside, looked at churches (then all left open), or pursued interests like botany and ornithology. The city too drew our attention, especially its Minster, visible from many parts of the school. At thirteen I took part in an excavation in St Mary's Abbey, and later worked in the Yorkshire Museum cataloguing small portable Roman lamps. Once in the sixth form I knew I wanted to read history, even though, in School Certificate I did best in science and mathematics. We had a fine history teacher, who encouraged us to read and argue. None of my family had been to university, and we followed advice that I should try to get into Clare College, Cambridge, where Bootham boys regularly went. To my intense surprise I won a minor scholarship.

Next came twenty months with a Quaker organisation in London, instead of doing national service in the army. The first ten months passed sorting parcels of clothes being shipped to Germany by Oxfam for displaced people and others. A year as cashier was easier on the legs, and much cleaner, but I was raring to go when I got to Cambridge.

In my first year, I read essays to Geoffrey Elton, whose lectures on sixteenth and seventeenth century English history I attended. He was formidable, and sometimes could be very sharp with sloppy thinking or expression, but he was to prove a most helpful adviser. The next year I was exposed to medieval history, sitting at the feet of David Knowles, one of the great historians of the century, and reading essays on medieval English constitutional history to Marjorie Chibnall. She was in her thirties and was sometimes rather nervous, but, my goodness, how well she helped me to see new sides of every question, and helped me to argue with the ancient Bishop Stubbs. Dom David spoke on the religious orders in a slight, but always audible voice. Those lectures were models of clarity, enlivened from time to time by thumbnail sketches of scholars of an earlier age which could be both sharp and funny. Unfortunately he did not offer a special subject in my third year, and not feeling learned enough to manage a year with Walter Ullmann on papal government, chose instead a subject about the French Revolution and its effects on England. But Knowles that year lectured upon what became his book *The Evolution of Medieval Thought* (1962: Longman), and he really made the third year for me, while Marjorie again read my essays, and I began to realise how little I knew.

When I graduated with a first, and a beautiful silver cup as a college prize, I was not entirely sure whether academic life was right for me, while my father made it clear further support would only be for one more year. The first half I spent at a Quaker study centre in Bournville, reading widely in theology, learning some New Testament Greek, and beginning to realise that I had to pursue medieval history. Once that emerged, knowing that I would need to read German, I found a job in a social centre in Germany at Wuppertal where I spoke it for the whole time.

Back in Cambridge, Knowles took me on, and my work gradually centred on some English Cistercians, active in the second half of the twelfth century, whose works, often still in manuscript, had been little studied. The most significant was a commentary on the last part of the Song of Songs by John, Abbot of Forde, which became the centre of my work. I shall never forget my first sight of Forde, where the Roper family welcomed me most hospitably as I tried to read the

Abbey's cartulary. I was becoming engrossed by the material, but the year was difficult. I was the only first year postgraduate in medieval history, and there were no available seminars, while Knowles saw me about once a month. By the summer I asked whether I might spend a year in Oxford, on the excuse that John of Forde's commentary was at Balliol. Knowles was rather puzzled, pointing out that Balliol would have loaned their manuscript to the Cambridge library. When he agreed, Oriel, sister college of Clare, gave me a base, while Richard Hunt, Keeper of Western Manuscripts in the Bodleian, agreed to become my supervisor. So began the most extraordinary year of my life.

Suddenly I was part of a group of some twenty postgraduates, for whom seminars in palaeography, diplomatic and other useful things existed. We often worked in Duke Humfrey, one of the oldest parts of the Bodleian, where we helped each other with a difficult hand, or an unfamiliar abbreviation. Richard Hunt, a great scholar in intellectual history, was incredibly helpful, regularly passing on titles of books or articles which he thought I should read. I also got to know and admire Beryl Smalley, the greatest English scholar of medieval commentaries on the Bible. I was becoming hooked.

Then unexpectedly, in the spring of 1956, Knowles wrote that University College, London was looking for a junior medievalist: would I like to be recommended? My immediate reaction was that it was too soon, and I wrote to tell him so. Most fortunately I also wrote to Elton who replied by return, 'You would be mad if you turned this chance down.' So I found myself being interviewed, with others, by a bevy of scholars of whom the most terrifying was the remarkable ancient historian Arnaldo Momigliano, who succeeded in rousing me by exclaiming: 'Why are you working on such a ridiculous subject?' Somehow I must have fitted UCL's bill, and started there that autumn. When my thesis was finished in 1960, I turned parts of it into articles, and then began to edit a large collection of charters connected with Rufford Abbey, in Nottinghamshire, a daughter house of Rievaulx in Yorkshire. The first parts appeared in 1972 and 1974 and must have helped me make the move to Exeter in 1977. There I found myself in the county where some of 'my' Cistercian writers had lived, and close to the cathedral where one of them had been a clerk. I easily made room for them in my regular lectures, and began to publish about them again. I also widened my sights beyond the Cistercians to all the different kinds of religious, and the church at large, writing, for example, about St Boniface, Hartland and Tavistock Abbeys. Now I hope I shall have enough energy in my eighties to go on reading and writing, especially about Bernard of Clairvaux, and even to produce an account of early Quakers in Devon, a subject about which little yet has been written, although the sources are voluminous.

Achieving Devon

Ivan Roots

Can I really claim to be a Devon historian? Perhaps not, though I have lived here for half my lifetime. I am, in fact, a man of Kent, born in 1921, and brought up in the historic county town of Maidstone – the Peasants' Revolt, a Second Civil War battle, Christopher Smart, William Hazlitt, Disraeli's first parliamentary seat, and dancer Ann Widdecombe's last. To an early curiosity about local history, I added in my teens an awareness of current national and international issues – the Great Depression, the rise of Hitler, Mosley's Blackshirts, the Spanish Civil War and the Popular Front. Already a bookish boy, by then I had moved on from the Robin Hood's Weekly, through G.A. Henty to *The Cloister and the Hearth*. (*Westward Ho!*, I fear, defeated me.) I have since rarely bothered with historical fiction, preferring detective stories – mostly those of the Golden Age between the wars, which are redolent of contemporary values.

At school, I came under the influence of an inspired teacher, 'Beta' Phillips, whose set of notes got everyone through Matriculation. But once in the sixth form, no notes (unless you made your own), no textbooks, but wide reading, use of documents, frequent essays, free discussions in what would nowadays be called seminars. The Higher Schools course – English and European history 1500–1700 with particular reference to England 1625–60, aroused my enthusiasm. It was paralleled in the English and French syllabuses, mingling George Herbert, John Donne and the Metaphysicals, and Andrew Marvell, with Racine, Moliére and Pascal. Gerard Manley Hopkins,

T.S. Eliot, e.e.cummings and W.H. Auden, I found for myself. My first publication appeared in the school magazine in 1937 – an article on the Maidstone witch trials of 1652, part of the European witch craze which would touch Devon, too.

In 1938 I found myself among Christopher Hill's first pupils on his return to Balliol. (I believe that the death of Donald Pennington in 2008 leaves me the last of that privileged group.) War came in 1939. Having introduced us to Gerrard Winstanley, Christopher, with most of the younger dons, was called up. For the Special Subject of Protectorate and Restoration, Donald and I came under the benign supervision of the West Country historian Mary Coate (*Cornwall in the Great Civil War*). She put regional history firmly into the broader context of what has since moved through the English Revolution to the War of the Three Kingdoms, to pause awhile now at the Crisis of the North Atlantic Archipelago. (What next?)

From 1941 to 1945 I was with the Royal Corps of Signals in India and Burma. There I acquired some technical skills which have since deserted me. One sleepless night in the signal office at Maungdaw, I decided that after the war I would become a professional historian, rather than a journalist or publisher. In September 1946 a very nervous assistant lecturer at University College, Cardiff, was confronted by large classes of ex-servicemen (and some women) determined to get their degrees. They were the best students I have ever had. Attendance at lectures was exemplary. Essays, piles of them demanding my assiduous attention, were never late. Shrewd questions demanded serious answers. It was a baptism of fire. I have benefited from it ever since. When the 'veterans' departed, I was more able to get on with my research and writing. Meanwhile, I had met Tegwyn Williams of Cwm, Ebbw Vale, who started in me a whole litany of endearments, which happily has continued into the sixty-sixth year of our marriage. She has been my unfailing support.

In 1955, with Donald Pennington, I edited the Minute-book of the Parliamentary Committee for Staffordshire (*The Committee at Stafford 1643–45*), which reported activity in a politically divided and strategically important county at war. It demonstrated (we believed) that by fuller study of similar evidence, solutions might be found to some controversial problems about local significance during two vital decades, the 1640s and 1650s. At the same time, besides occasional articles for collaborative historical volumes, I wrote inter alia three historical drama-documentaries for the BBC Third Programme.

After a formative year out of routine at Lafayette College, Pennsylvania, I could get on with *The Great Rebellion 1642–60* (1966), still in print, an analytical narrative, the outcome of twenty years of research, reading and teaching, offering what I hoped would be apt answers to questions about an exciting period of which we know at once more, and rather less, than contemporaries did. In 1967 I came to a chair at Exeter University, bringing my questions with me, teaching much the same courses, and as puzzled as I ever was. Aspects of Devon history had already come my way – Drake, Ralegh, Grenville. Now, of course, I would assign more significance to the New Model Army's Devon campaign in 1646 in achieving Parliamentary victory in the First Civil War. Moreover, I think I have become more aware of the shire's peculiarities, which Mark Stoyle has illuminated under the heading *Loyalty and Locality* (1994). Moving on to the Interregnum, I have found the outsider John Disbrowe trying out in Devon the experiment in local government which became 'Cromwell's Major-Generals'.

The 'great debate' in the Commons in June 1657 about the long-disputed disposition of the will of wealthy Devonian Elisius Hele is a prime example of how local (Devon) and national affairs could impinge sharply upon one another even in the midst of a constitutional crisis. The will, in fact, was not executed until after the Restoration – and then somewhat controversially. The Restoration itself was very much the achievement of an enigmatic Devonian, George Monck, Royalist-turned-Parliamentarian-turned Royalist. His reward was the Dukedom of Albemarle and much more. Of the great house he built at his birthplace, Great Potheridge, near Torrington, little remains.

During the late 1970s, with Maurice Goldsmith, Professor of Politics, I devised a Special Subject on the politics and political theory of the Revolution of 1688. Devon was prominent. Blown by 'Protestant winds' to Brixham, William of Orange landed on 5 November 1688 with troops, a printing press, a chest of English money and some reindeer – a man with a mission, into which Devon was accidentally absorbed, and which would lead to the abdication of his wife's father and to permanent changes in relationships and constitutional arrangements across the realm. Great stuff!

My retirement from the University in 1986 was not retirement from history. Of course, I can never have Bill Hoskins's advantage of being born in Devon, but I have had time now to acquire the Devon that I thrust upon myself by coming here over forty years ago. And so I am still pleased to give talks about these things, which may perhaps with my *Cromwellian and Restoration Devon* (2003) justify my election to the Presidency of the Devon History Society (1989–93). Beyond that, always curious about the work of historians in other fields, I have never confined myself to a narrow specialism, and have enjoyed reviewing for many professional and lay publications, such as *The Listener, The Observer* and *The Daily Telegraph*. Lately, work as a historical consultant to the Royal Mint for a set of commemorative medals on the history of the Monarchy from Henry III to Queen Anne has taken me back to medieval history for the first time since my own middle age, and I have continued to publish on the seventeenth century generally. Meanwhile, Sir Walter Ralegh (pronounced *pace* local preference), 'Rawley', a Renaissance man of many parts, diverse and discordant, reviled and revered, a suave rainbow-hued courtier speaking 'broad Devon', still wriggles in my grasp.

Bibliography

Coate, M. (1933) *Cornwall in the Great Civil War and Interregnum*, Oxford: Oxford University Press.

Pennington, D. and Roots, I. (eds) (1957) *The Committee at Stafford 1643–45*, Manchester: Manchester University Press.

Roots, I. (1966) *The Great Rebellion 1642–60*, London: Batsford.

Roots, I. (1828) (1974 edn) Introduction and additional material to the reprint edition: *Diary of Thomas Burton, Esq., Member in the Parliaments of Oliver and Richard Cromwell from 1656 to 1659*, New York: Johnson Reprint Corporation.

Roots, I. (2003) *Cromwellian and Restoration Devon*, The Mint Press: Exeter.

Roots, I. (ed.) (1989) *Speeches of Oliver Cromwell*, London: J.M. Dent.

Stoyle, M. (1994) *Loyalty and Locality: popular allegiance in Devon during the English Civil War*, Exeter: University of Exeter Press.

Ordulf's Shadow in Tavistock

Mary Freeman

The town of Tavistock is situated about half way along the course of the river Tavy between Dartmoor and the Tamar. The Saxon thane Ordulf held a manor there in the tenth century, and founded a Benedictine abbey. This article seeks to enquire if Ordulf's manorial demesne left any trace in the present town. Documents survive from the monastic records and, after 1539, among the estate papers of the Dukes of Bedford.

Worth[1] and Alexander[2] gave accounts of early Tavistock, still largely acceptable except for the unfortunate belief of both gentlemen in the Great Central Trackway (for another opinion on that, see chapter two of Fleming).[3] Although Exeter Street and West Street, in the town, could mark an ancient way towards the Tamar, it was probably not a major trade route. In the last century, a pair of Neolithic stone axeheads were dug up in a garden in Ford Street, on the western side of the town, and a fine bronze celt (now in the Torquay museum) was found near the Trendle, to the north-east.[4] The Trendle is a small Iron Age fort; bronze ornaments found there suggest it may have been inhabited into the Roman period, but it is outside the built-up area of the town. Roman military activity extended along what might be called the Roman A30,[5] but none has been reported near Tavistock. There are post-Roman remains, in the form of inscribed memorial stones, probably sixth century[6] but only one of these came from the town. Mrs Bray quoted at length an account by her husband of how a large stone was removed from the paving in West Street in the

1780s, eventually being taken to his garden when he became vicar.[7] It is still there, standing some two metres tall on the garden path; Mrs Bray published a drawing (also Woods,[8] with photograph). The inscription is in Latin capitals, with reversed Ns, and reads *Neprani fili Conbevi*. It cannot be assumed that the original site was near West Street, but another piece of evidence suggests that it may have been so.

At the top of the hill in West Street was a house called Stoneposts. The last abbot of Tavistock retired there in 1539[9] and it can be identified in a map and fieldbook made in 1752.[10] The name was unchanged in 1803, when it was occupied by the curate and schoolmaster R.V. Willesford.[11] Later it was completely rebuilt as 59 West Street, but the name was revived by J.J. Alexander (also the schoolmaster) who lived there later.[12] If there were once posts, in the plural, could the Nepranus memorial have stood in a burial ground on a shelf of the rocky valley side? If so, was there a settlement nearby? It would have been a suitable place to live, by a road above the wooded valley bottom, with the well that is now contained in Brown's Hotel providing a generous source of water.

If there was such a British settlement, its name is unknown and it may have been abandoned. Evidence from oak tree-rings shows that there was environmental deterioration in the decade AD 536 to 545,[13] causing famine, followed by plagues that spread from the Mediter-ranean across Europe as far as Ireland. Geoffrey of Monmouth wrote that Cadwallader, the last British king, emigrated to Brittany as a result of the plague.[14] This would not mean total depopulation, but a decrease of Britons may have made it easier for the Saxons to colonise Devon, or Dumnonia as it was then.[15] Most of the place names around Tavistock, except for the rivers, are Saxon in origin.[16] However, if there was a village in West Street, as postulated, it was not at the same centre as the Saxon settlement that followed two or three hundred years later.

A settlement on the site of Tavistock before the foundation of the abbey was assumed by Worth.[17] Radford stated that the abbey was older than the town, but this applies only to the Borough, not to other lay habitation.[18] The Saxons had penetrated West Devon in the eighth century and it was settled by the ninth century. When King Edgar (reign 959–975) married Elfthryth as his second queen in 964, he appointed her father Ordgar as the ealdorman of the shire. Ordgar's son, Ordulf, held numerous estates in Devon, including a manor of Tavistock situated between the Tavy and the Tamar. Ordulf founded the abbey at Tavistock, under the influence of the monastic revival encouraged by Edgar and his bishops.[19] In the Charter granted by King Ethelred, Ordulf's nephew, in 981, Tavistock is the first in the list of lands given by Ordulf and his wife to the abbey as endowments. The existence of a manor implies the formation of hamlets, or a village, for the dependent peasants.

It is probable that Ordulf lived at Tavistock, at least for part of the year. There was a tradition that, before the building of the abbey, Ordulf and his wife saw a vision of a light shining near the river Tavy, prompting him to build a chapel on the spot. This story is a pious fancy, supposedly the invention of a thirteenth-century monk,[20] and the chapel was probably built before Ordulf's time, to serve the local people. It was near the end of St Matthew Street at a place now covered by the pannier market, and was later used as a house; in 1833 it was in the way and removed.[21] In 1738 the dimensions were given as thirty feet by sixteen feet (but noted as seventeen by thirty-one feet in 1726, perhaps the difference was the thickness of the walls).[22] The size is a good match for other early chapels.[23]

If Ordulf lived in Tavistock, where was his manorial Hall? There are clues, but to follow them one has to go to the nineteenth century and work back. Mrs Bray recorded folk lore of an 'Ordulf's palace'; this is also mentioned by Kempe (although he thought that Ordgar was the founder of the abbey).[24] Mrs Bray married in 1822,[25] and learnt of the local traditions from her husband, who was brought up in Tavistock. He had gathered information from Mary Adams, a lady said to be the depository of every legend connected with the neighbourhood.[26] Miss Adams, who lived in West Street, died 14 May 1823, aged 84, and was buried in the Ladychapel of St Eustachius, with the Rev. Bray officiating.[27] It was Miss Adams who transmitted the story that Ordulf had a palace in Tavistock.[28] The local people thought that this was the house with an archway opening near the foot of Kilworthy Lane, which had belonged to the Glanvill family in the sixteenth and seventeenth centuries. The arch, the only surviving structure of the Glanvill house, can still be seen beside the Ordulph Arms in Pym Street. Mrs Bray was unable to persuade the townspeople that this arch was Tudor in date, not Saxon. However, she also mentioned an older arch nearby in Market Street, that had been pulled down.

This ancient arch may have belonged to a medieval house which is recorded in a fifteenth century rental of Tavistock abbey.[29] The second entry in this rental is for a mansion, Abbot's Court, with five closes of land. One close was called 'by the Sanctuary' which probably indicates that it was near the High Cross, known from other records[30] to have been on the site of the Lower Market House opposite the junction of Market Street with what is now Pym Street (see maps, Figures 1 and 2). Two of the closes were called Portmene, the others Orchard and Le Overmore. In the late fifteenth century John Bronescombe was the tenant here. He also held four acres called Mene on a forty year lease from 1 February 1st Edward IV [1462] at an annual rent of 20s, and three closes called Abbot's Parks, on a forty year lease from Michaelmas 22nd Edward IV [1482] for 26s 8d a year. Each of the three holdings carried a heriot of the best beast. Abbot's Court is likely to have been the house regarded as 'Ordulf's palace'; it is the only dwelling in the Borough described, in the rental, as a mansion, numerous other entries refer to burgage houses only as tenements or messuages. Abbot's Court does not appear in the post-dissolution records, but its land can probably be equated with certain tenures that were mapped in the eighteenth century, and, it is here suggested, with the demesne of Ordulf's manorial hall.

In 1752, the 4th Duke of Bedford owned most of the land in the Borough, but other magnates such as Lord Fortescue and Dennis Rolle had substantial holdings, so did families such as Spry and Edgcombe and others. In Wynne's preliminary fieldbook for the Borough there is an anomaly in the entries for certain properties between Market Street and Exeter Lane: ownership of the land was divided between Bedford, Fortescue, Rolle and Spry, who each paid a fraction of the chief rent.[31] This indicated something odd about the tenure of that area of the borough, which was not explained, although it is probable that the Duke had been buying properties piecemeal as they became available. In the final fieldbook of the survey, there is a list of 'premises purchased of Denys Rolle 1756'.[32]

For clarity, the entries in question are listed below, starting with the northernmost which was on the edge of the Borough. In each entry the ownership of the land was indicated at the bottom corner of the space, this is omitted in the transcription. The punctuation is sparse and capitals erratic, and there were some mistakes in copying.

K9, Two fields called Billingsbear Wood and Meadow under called Vyvyans meadow only about 1/2 of the higher Billingsbear wood and meadow in the Borough the Land is 1/6 his Grace 1/4 Lord Fortescue 1/4 Mr Rolle 1/4 [*sic*] Mr Spry. This pays a Chief Rent to his Grace but is charg'd wth. Broom parks and Hawkins Ley see Letter.

K11, Two Fields called the 2 higher Lease divided as No.8 [*sic*] above . . . NB his Graces 6th part has been in hand ever since 1740 by the death of Vyvyan Spry.

K12, Three Fields called Dinibowle als Pigshill Middle Lease & Lower Lease & a Garden by Kilworthy Lane No15 divided as No 9 & 11 His Graces 6th part fell in hand Mar 3 1752 by the Death of Mrs Bolt.

K15, A Garden called Rack Garden in Lease with Dinibowl als Pigs hill Middle Lease and Lower Lease see No.12 above the Lands of [blank].

K16, A Garden in the Tenure of Thos. Parsons in lease with the Brewhouse.

K27, A Brewhouse etc. being now Divided in 3 Tenements with a Stable and Garden No.96 in the Rentall being divided in the Same Manner as No 9 & 11 of this Division.

K28, Three Gardens at the Lower end of the Leases belonging to the Great House called the Great Garden. L No 4.

L1, A House called Caunters house in the Occupation of Jno. Spry divided as Follows Duke of Bedford one Sixth Part Lord Fortescue one Sixth Dennis Rolle Esqr One Sixth William Spry Esqr one third and John Hutchins 1/6 (Purch. Of Richard Edgcombe) one Sixth. NB. John Hutchin's part is in reality Mr Spry's being Purchd. with his money & its supposed Hutchins has privately conve'd the premis. to him.

L2, Shop now an Apothecarys Shop and Parlour Mr Richard Parsons Tenant. His Grace 1/6 Lord Fortescue 1/4 Mr Rolle 1/4 Mr Spry 1/3 NB the other part of the house which Mr Parsons rents is part of the Great house No. 4.

L3, The shop called Willesfords Shop now divided into two Shops one in the occupation of Widow Langman and the other of Mr B. Carpenter and is divided as the foregoing.

L4, The Great House in the Occupation of Mr Carpenter divided as above with Outhouses Stables and 4 Fields called the Warrens M8 and a Great Garden his Graces 6th part has been in hand ever since the year 1741 by the Death of Mrs Mary Spry. NB All the rooms extending over No 2 and 3 as above belong to the Great house the rooms over No.2 let to Mr Parson and those over No.3 to Mr Carpenter Lord Fortescue pays a Chief rent to His Grace for the 4 last premises 2d a year Dennis Rolle Esqr Two pence and Wm Spry Esqr Eight pence.

M8, Four Fields in Ditto [Kilworthy Lane] called the Warrens otherwise Broom parks and the Bowling Green in Lease with the Great House L No.4 and divided as that is His Graces 6th part is in hand This with Vyvyans meadow and Hawkins Ley als Broom Parks pays a Chief rent of One Shilling & Sixpence halfpenny Vizt. Five pence halfpenny Lord Fortescue five pence halfpenny by Dennis Rolle Esqr and Seven pence halfpenny by Wm Spry Esqr.

In the figure, the plots in multiple ownership come together as a tract of land north and east of the Great House (L1-4, K28), it does not appear as an entity until mapped. The identifying numbers in the fieldbook are not sequential and are spread over three Divisions, so that the surveyors were apparently unaware of any peculiarity. The four-part ownership of land does not apply to the other houses and gardens bordering the streets. Can this ground be equated with that belonging to Abbot's Court three centuries earlier? The area does not obviously divide into five closes, although if the Lower Lease and the two gardens by Kilworthy Lane (K15 and 16) are separated off they might correspond to one of the Portmenes. The Great House site in the southern corner could match the small close near the market cross. To the east of Kilworthy Lane, Broom Parks and the Warrens (M8) could correspond to Bronescombe's leases Mene and Abbot's Parks. Comparison with the 1905/06 OS map (Figure 2) shows that the Lower Lease area was the sloping land cut through by Drake Road in 1890.[33] The railway interrupted the Kilworthy road, which continued north of the tracks. The railway station and sidings (now disused) were on

Figure 1. Map showing the area discussed, with field names, redrawn from Wynne's Plan of the Borough, 1752. Kilworthy Lane runs north, and Exeter Lane north-east. Labels K9, L1-4, M8 etc. follow the entries in the Tavistock copy of the fieldbook, also dated 1752. Trees are omitted, outlines of buildings are simplified, the Lower Market House is indicated by an arrow. It is supposed that the Saxon manor house demesne was bounded by the Fishlake stream on the west, and by Exeter Lane, an ancient east-west route, south; also that the gardens bordering the roads were taken out of Abbot's Court after the Dissolution.

former Middle Lease and Broom Parks ground. The 1865 reservoir was also in Broom Parks, while the crescent of Trelawny Cottages (1866) crossed the boundary between the Middle and Higher Leases. Part of this boundary, and of other hedges of the Higher Leases, can still be seen from Kilworthy Lane in 2010.

To enquire further, it is necessary to go back to the seventeenth century, when the land in question belonged to the Glanvill family. Judge John Glanvill died intestate in 1600, and his *Inquisition post-mortem* shows that he owned, among much other property, '30 messuages 3 tofts and 30 gardens and 6 acres of land with appurtenances in the town of Tavistock' and also Kilworthy Barton near the town, in free socage by fealty to Edward, 3rd Earl of Bedford,[34] who was still a minor at the time. However, the Judge never owned the Great House and its

29

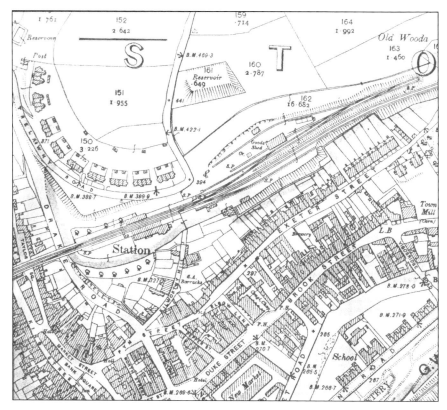

Figure 2. Area corresponding to the southern part of Figure 1, from the OS map of 1905/06, on a slightly different alignment, north to the top. The lower Market House has gone, the site of the Great House is covered by nineteenth century building. Drake Road ran from Bedford Square, was raised where it crosse Pym Street, and cut off the bottom of Kilworthy Lane. The 'S' on the map marks the Higher Leases, with some hedges still as in the eighteenth century. Reproduced courtesy of Plymouth City Library.

demesne lands such as the Leases, those had belonged to his elder brother Nicholas, who died in 1598. There are numerous documents relating to property sales among the Fortescue papers in the DRO (ref.1262M/T) which are not worth citing in detail although some are significant. The Glanvill inheritance was complicated. The Judge's direct male line in Tavistock died out with his grandson Francis in 1658, when the property was split between Francis' sisters, who were not able to inherit until his widow, née Maria Rolle, died.[35] A deed of 1603 shows that the Judge's widow Alice, Lady Godolphin by her second marriage, bought the Great House from Nicholas' widow, her sister-in-law, and her sons.[36] In 1662, one of Francis' sisters, Elizabeth Fowell, sold her share of the inheritance to her sister-in-law Maria, then wife of Sir John Davy by second marriage. A clause in this deed exempts 'the Capitall Mansion house of Tavistock in which the Lady Godolphin did sometimes dwell with the houses shops standings and the Demesnes thereunto belonging called the Leazes Billingbeare Billingbeare Meadow Broomparks alias the Warrens . . .'.[37] This establishes that this land was the demesne of the Great House. It passed from Alice to her son Sir Francis Glanvill and then to his son Francis.[38] Francis' will does not mention the Great House and its lands, which went to his widow Maria, the residual legatee for her life. The inheritance of Kilworthy and the Great House then passed to the judge's grand-daughter Elizabeth Kelly who married Ambrose Manaton in 1674, but died without surviving children. In 1692 Ambrose sold the Great House to William Spry.[39] It was subsequently let in parts and the fields also used by various lessees.

Going back to the late sixteenth century, among the Glanvills of Tavistock were three whose activities have been discussed.[40] John Glanvill the elder and his eldest son Nicholas were merchants, who appear to have been involved in disposing of the fabric of the abbey church, on behalf of the Russells, and to have enjoyed the patronage of Francis Russell, the 2nd Earl of Bedford. Nicholas died in 1598, as owner of the Great House, probably he built it using stone from the abbey church. In 1580 his father John's will divided property between several children (except Nicholas) but left his third son John, later the Judge, 'the lease of the house which I had of Mr Dillington where I now dwell'.[41] This is not located, but the name of Robert Dillington Esquire occurs in at least two of the deeds among the Fortescue papers, mentioned above.[42] It can be supposed that Dillington was an agent for Francis, 2nd Earl of Bedford (and his executors after 1585) concerned with realising the assets of the Bedford inheritance. As Judge John Glanvill held his properties in Tavistock in free socage by fealty (see above) it is probable that this applied also to the other houses concerned, such as Nicholas' sprawling mansion, which probably extended to the east of the gatehouse.

When the lease was transferred to widowed Mary Spry in 1738, two deeds described the premises.[43] The kitchen was separated from

31

the great hall by a paved court, a great parlour was nearby, numerous other named rooms included an oriel and a dining room and there were several staircases. Entrances were from Market Street and by the gatehouse, which contained two rooms; outbuildings were a woodhouse, a stable and a slaughterhouse. Besides the gardens, the Lower Lease, Broomfield and the Warren were included. Miss Adams' account suggests that the ancient premises once extended to the next-door house in Market Street, 'Mrs Rundles' (L5 in Figure 1) which was then the Tavistock Bank.[44]

The Rundle daughter, Elizabeth, described older structure, such as mullioned windows from the abbey, behind the bank's Georgian façade, also gardens that had been made on the slope of the Lower Lease.[45] These houses and probably others further up Market Street such as L9, as part of the 2nd Earl's rebuilding project, could have developed the former Abbot's Court ground. The old mansion may still have been standing, certainly it could have been within living memory at the time, as the 'Ordulf's palace' of folk tradition, built over in the sixteenth century. To explain how the associated land came into the hands of the Glanvills one must admit that they were acquisitive, and sufficiently rich, and it was a prime site. Already in 1574 Nicholas and his brother John were manipulating rights to a house and part of Broom Parks (Hawkins Ley) on condition that their father was not disturbed in his occupation of them; possibly this house was the building east of Kilworthy Lane in Figure 1.[46]

It remains unexplained how or why the demesne retained its integrity for so long after the Dissolution. The abbey church was soon demolished, but other buildings within the precinct, and certain lands associated with the monastery, west of the precinct and across the river, were still distinguished in 1726 as the Abbey Scite and part of the manor of Hurdwick, not of the Borough.[47] Then, they were declared tithe-free, but this ended under the 4th Duke (who was, after all, the Rector and so entitled to tithes). Two of these places, Old Wood and the Common Close, were not adjacent to the abbey but bordered the road east of the Warrens, while the supposed demesne land was not counted as abbey site. In 1726, the divided ownership had included Clinton and Manaton. In the Charter of the abbey provision was made that the gifted lands should stay in possession of the abbey after the death of the Founder.[48] It is significant that neither the abbot, nor anyone else, might sell or exchange 'the lands which have been conceded <u>or are to be conceded</u>'. This can imply that Ordulf reserved a life interest in some part of the endowment.[49] Ordulf could have been living in his Hall until its demesne finally passed to the abbey on his death, which was probably in 1010.[50] What use would successive abbots make of it? It would have been convenient to accommodate important guests and their retinues, who would have been cramped in the house that is thought to have been a monastic guest house in the Court of the precinct.[51] The Saxon Hall itself would not persist, but be repaired and rebuilt many times. By the late fifteenth century, when John Bronescombe (who has not been otherwise identified) rented his mansion, there may have been other accommodation available.

There has been a recent archaeological survey of the Glanvill's Great House site but it was found that much of the land had been quarried away or covered with spoil during nineteenth century-developments.[52] Plate 1 shows the course of Drake Road behind the nineteenth-century buildings on the site of the Great House, it crossed near the Tudor garden (K28 in Figure 1) and the gardens behind the Bank (L5).

The speculative parts of the preceding argument need to bridge the time immediately after the dissolution, and other periods after the death of Ordulf and before the Saxon settlement. There are probably relevant documents from the sixteenth century yet to be identified; for the eleventh century and earlier, this is less likely. Nevertheless I contend that a ghostly outline of Ordulf's manor house demesne can be discerned in the present landscape of Tavistock.

Acknowledgments

Thanks to the staffs of the Devon Record Office and the Plymouth and West Devon Record Office for their courtesy when giving access to documents, to the Tavistock Museum for the use of records held there, to R.J. Glanvill for the texts of his ancestors' wills, to S. Carreck for digitising Figure 1 and to Plymouth City Library for providing copy for Figure 2. Also to S.O. Thompson and S.J. Hobbs for their kind permission to reproduce Plate 1.

Notes and References

1. Worth 1889, pp. 132-137.
2. Alexander 1942, pp. 173-202.
3. Fleming 1988, pp. 12-24.
4. Worth 1947, pp. 125-128.
5. Weddell and Reed 1997, p. 113.
6. Okasha 1993, p. 58.
7. Bray 1838, pp. 360-376.
8. Woods 1988, p. 76.
9. Finberg 1969, [1951] *Tavistock Abbey*, p. 268.
10. Wynne, J.V., 1752 Plan of the Borough of Tavistock, DRO, TD273, also <www.tavistock1752.co.uk>, and preliminary fieldbook in Tavistock Museum, TAVSM/1986-26-H-56, or another copy in DRO, TD273.
11. DRO, 1258M/E36a 1803, Borough of Tavistock, Bedford Estate Survey, vol.i, p.5.
12. Census 1901.
13. Baillie 2000, pp. 65-68.
14. Thorpe 1966, p. 281.
15. Higham 2008, p. 43.
16. Alexander 1942, op. cit., p. 182.
17. Worth 1889, op. cit., p. 136.
18. Radford 1929, pp. 55-86.
19. Holdsworth 2003, p. 37.
20. Finberg 1942, p. 56.
21. Wynne, J.V. 1752, op. cit., Plan of the Borough of Tavistock, DRO, TD273.
22. DRO, L1258M/E/SV/B20, fo.32,3. Survey of the Borough of Tavistock 1738-1755 by Robert Butcher.
23. Blair 2005, p. 375.
24. Kempe 1830, p. 116, (or p. 4 in reprint). [Source for many later accounts of the history of Tavistock].
25. Duffy, D. 2009, Personal communication.
26. Bray 1838, op. cit., i, p. 263 note and ii, p. 316 note.
27. DRO, Tavistock Parish Registers.
28. Bray 1838, op. cit., ii, p. 316 and iii, pp. 59-60.
29. Caley, J. 1796, Translation of a rental or survey of the monastery of Tavistock (p. 1), digital copy in Tavistock Museum of PWDRO, accession no.2310. Transcripts also in DRO as Z17/3/15 and T1258M/S21, and in Plymouth City Library Local Studies, photocopy no. 271.
30. Worth 1887, p. 86.
31. Wynne 1752, op. cit., preliminary fieldbook, TAVSM/1986-26-H-56.
32. Wynne 1755-1756, fieldbook of the Borough of Tavistock, DRO, TD273 marked TAVSM/1986-26-H-57 (fo.207-216).
33. Godfrey 2003.

34. TNA, C142/271 item 158 (1602). John Glanvyle, 7 July 44 Elizabeth.
35. Vivian 1895, pp. 410-412.
36. DRO, 1262M/T1162 (1603) Deed of sale to Lady Alice Godolphin.
37. DRO, 1262M/T1199 (1662) Deed of sale, Fowell to Davie.
38. TNA-PROB 11/ – (1631); PROB 11/180 fo.209 (1635); PROB 11/289 fo.282-2 (1658). Wills of Dame Alice Godolphine, Sir Francis Glanvill, and Francis Glanvill, respectively.
39. DRO, L1258M/E/SV/B20, op. cit., Butcher Survey, fo.24.
40. Freeman 2003, pp. 59-70.
41. PRO/PROB11/62 sig.7 fo.54 (1580) Will of John Glanvile.
42. DRO, 1262M/T1156 and T1157, Deeds of sale.
43. DRO, L1258M/6/37 (1738) bundle, leases marked No.336 and No.340, to Mary Spry.
44. Bray 1838, op cit., ii, p. 316.
45. Charles 1896, p. 15.
46. DRO, 1262M/T1144, 1574. Deed between John Glanvile of Lincoln's Inn and Nicholas Glanvile of Tavistock.
47. Smith 1726, Hurdwick Survey, TAVMS/1986-26-H-53, and DRO, L1258M/E/SVB5.
48. Holdsworth, op. cit., p. 50.
49. Finberg 1969, op. cit., pp. 280 and 281 note 1.
50. Finberg 1946, p. 271.
51. Wynne 1752, fieldbook TAVSM/1986-26-H-56.
52. Thompson, S.O. and Hobbs, S.J., 2006, *Report on archaeological investigations at land to rear of the Ordulph Arms, Pym Street and Drake Road, Tavistock*, deposited with the Devon County Council Archaeological Service.

Bibliography

Alexander, J.J. (1942) 'The Beginnings of Tavistock', *DAT*, 74, pp. 173-202.
Baillie, M.G.L. (2000) *Exodus to Arthur*, London: Batsford.
Blair, J. (2005) *The Church in Anglo-Saxon Society*, Oxford: University Press.
Bray, A.E. (1838) [1836] *Traditions, Legends, Superstitions, and Sketches of Devonshire on the Borders of the Tamar and the Tavy . . .*, 3 vols, London: Murray.
Charles, E.R. (1896) *Our Seven Homes: autobiographical reminiscences of Mrs Rundle Charles*, London: Murray.
Finberg, H.P.R. (1942) 'The Cartulary of Tavistock', *DCNQ*, 22, pp. 55-61.
Finberg, H.P.R. (1946) 'Childe's Tomb', *DAT*, 78, pp. 265-280.
Finberg, H.R.P. (1969) [1951] *Tavistock Abbey*, Newton Abbot: David and Charles.

Fleming, A. (1988) *The Dartmoor Reaves*, London: Batsford.

Freeman, M. (2003) 'The Stone Masks at Kilworthy, Tavistock', *DAT*, 155, pp. 59-70.

Godfrey, A. (2003) *Old Ordnance Survey Maps, Tavistock 1905*, Consett.

Higham, R. (2008) *Making Anglo-Saxon Devon*, Exeter: Mint Press.

Holdsworth, C. (2003) 'Tavistock Abbey in its Late Tenth Century Context', *DAT*, 135, pp. 31-58.

Kempe, A.J. (1830) 'Notices of Tavistock and its Abbey', *Gentleman's Magazine*, 100, pp. 113-118, 216-221, 409-412, 489-495.

Okasha, E. (1993) *Corpus of Early Christian Inscribed Stones of South-West Britain*, London: Leicester University Press.

Radford, E.L. (1929) Tavistock Abbey, Exeter: Pollard [reprint of *Exeter Diocesan Architectural and Archaeological Society*, vol. 15, pp. 55-86].

Thorpe, L. (ed.) (1966) *Geoffrey of Monmouth, the History of the Kings of Britain*, London: Penguin.

Vivian, J.L. (1895) *The Visitations of the County of Devon Comprising the Heralds' Visitations of 1531, 1564 and 1620*, Exeter.

Weddell, P.J. and Reed, S.J. (1997) 'Excavations at Sourton Down Okehampton 1986–1991: Roman road, deserted medieval hamlet and other landscape features', *Devon Archaeological Society Proceedings*, no. 55, pp. 39-147.

Worth, R.H. (1947) 'Prehistoric Tavistock', *DAT*, 79, pp. 125-128.

Worth, R.N. (1887) *Calendar of the Tavistock Parish Records*, Plymouth.

Worth, R.N. (1889) 'Notes on the Early History of Tavistock', *DAT*, 21, pp. 132-137.

Woods, S.H. (1988) *Dartmoor Stone*, Exeter: Devon Books.

The Landscape of Branscombe in the Early Fourteenth Century: historic landscape characterisation in the light of archival evidence

John Torrance

'The landscape is a fine questioner, but, unaided by written evidence, a poor respondent.' – Harold Fox[1]

Introduction

The village of Branscombe in East Devon will be used to compare the mapping of historical field-types on the Historic Landscape Characterisation (HLC) map of Devon with surviving records of medieval landholding. Both these approaches to landscape history are document-based, one cartographic and the other archival. Beyond both lies the historian's awareness of today's landscape, and the present writer's familiarity with Branscombe has been helpful. Limitation of space makes a detailed comparison impractical, even for one village, so the discussion will concentrate on a few points of interest.

Historical Landscape Characterisation (HLC) is a method of displaying some of the historical layering of landscape, especially rural landscape, on a single map. A typology of characteristically differing field-shapes has been developed, with criteria for assigning them to a few broadly defined historical periods. The typology has then been applied to late-nineteenth-century OS maps, using a specially devised method. A user-friendly HLC map of Devon is on the County Council's website, with explanatory text by its author, Dr Sam Turner.[2] Two layers can be displayed, 'post-medieval' and 'modern'; this discussion relates to the former, which includes the traces of medieval agriculture. The field-types with which this comparison is chiefly concerned are 'medieval enclosures', 'medieval enclosures based on strip fields', 'barton fields' and 'post-medieval enclosures'. These are coloured respectively dull green, grey, pink and bright green on the map in Plate 2, the Branscombe section of the Devon HLC map.

The archival evidence that will be used to engage with the HLC map mainly comes from records of the manor of Branscombe in Exeter Cathedral Archives. The manor, held by the Bishop of Exeter in Domesday, was given to the Dean and Chapter of the cathedral in 1148. They farmed out their manors to individual canons for life, to act as *firmarius* or steward, and from time to time other canons came on visitations from Exeter to report on the manor and the parish, of which the Dean and Chapter were patrons. (At Branscombe, manor and parish boundaries coincided.) Documentation in the cathedral archives is fullest between 1280 and 1340, and this study is limited to that period. The reports of five visitations between 1281 and 1330 are the main source for the manorial demesne.[3] In 1339, after disputes between steward and tenants, two canons were sent to Branscombe to draw up a sworn 'rental and custumal', listing all tenants by name with the size of their holdings, rents payable, and services owed to the manor, and this is the main source for tenant holdings.[4]

An essential intermediary in this comparison, part-cartographic and part-archival, is the 1840 tithe map and accompanying tithe apportionments. Cartographically, the map allows the HLC method to be extended to a period before mid-Victorian enclosures obliterated earlier field boundaries. It can sometimes be extended further by using a manorial estate map of Branscombe, surveyed in detail by Alexander Law in 1793. Archivally, the tithe apportionments list farm names, field names, acreages and types of tenure, sometimes with annotations. They are an essential aid in interpreting the medieval records. The Devon Record Office has placed Devon tithe maps and apportionments and Law's map online.[5] A necessary preliminary is a brief look at Branscombe's historical topography.

Branscombe, the Place

Branscombe parish has the shape of a half-moon truncated at each end. From four miles of straight east-west southern coastline, the boundary curves inland to a maximum of two miles north at the centre. The northern boundary in the Middle Ages, as now, was the highway from Exeter to the Axe. The land is an inclined plateau topped with clay-with-flints, about 560 feet (170 metres) high in the north and about 460 feet (140 metres) high at the coastal cliffs.

At Branscombe Mouth, not far from the eastern boundary, a small river reaches the sea through a shingle-bank, a scene that would have looked very different in the Middle Ages. For the early fourteenth century saw the beginning of 'the Little Ice Age': climatic conditions worsened and great storms began to form the shingle-bank across the river mouth.[6] Before that, and for as long as tides could breach the shingle, there was a small estuary and salt-marsh in the valley, perhaps with salt-pans.

The river flows to Branscombe Mouth through a flood-plain from the confluence, a mile inland, of three streams. These streams rise in the parish and their three valleys – of which the largest, the central valley, has eastern and western branches – dissect the plateau. They meet to form a steep-sided triangular bowl, and the village rambles along its lower slopes. High ground surrounding the village gives shelter from south-westerlies and concealment from sea-raiders, and there is a striking contrast between level uplands and deep secluded valleys.

The three-valley system containing the village occupies the eastern three-fifths of the parish. Beyond it to the west, high ground continues for a mile or more towards the boundary with Salcombe Regis. The land dips to the hamlet of Weston, an old satellite settlement, and from there a stream carries the parish boundary steeply down to the sea at Weston Mouth.

The main village, never nucleated, has four nodes joined by a twisting lane, a settlement pattern already visible by the fourteenth century. The eastern node (called 'Vicarage' in the late nineteenth century and therefore on the HLC map, but now 'the Square') is where the stream from the eastern valley reaches the flood-plain. It was called La Forde in the fourteenth century, so the stream ran across the lane leading east to Beer. The vicarage was here from 1269

39

to 1884, with glebe land extending south behind it beside Parson's Lane. The second node, Bridge, where the larger stream debouches from the central valley, was already called La Brygge. Forerunners of the existing mill and forge were probably nearby. Half a mile up the western valley stand the late-twelfth-century church and a farmhouse which has replaced the medieval manor house. The dwellings here, supplied with spring-water from a chute in the hillside, form a third node known in recent centuries as Church. Almost a mile and a half further up the western valley is the fourth node, the hamlet of Street, with several water-chutes; this was called Dean in the eighteenth century and La Dene ('narrow valley') in the fourteenth.

The valley sides are more wooded now than in the past, when they were used as pasture, orchard and coppice, with meadows and withybeds in the bottoms and on the flood-plain. In post-medieval centuries the valleys were divided among a number of small farms, the farmhouses sited near spring lines where porous layers of chalk and sandstone overlie impermeable clay. Other farms lay further afield. The flat or rolling areas of plateau between and beyond the valleys were the main arable areas in the tithe apportionments of 1840. Fourteenth-century practice cannot be read back from 1840, but in so far as the pattern was due to soil, topography or geology, it probably changed little until market forces began to replace arable by livestock farming in the nineteenth century.

Historic Landscape Characterisation of the Flood-Plain and Western Valley

Medieval features marked on the HLC map of Branscombe relate closely to the topography, and the entire flood-plain south of the village road appears as a medieval agricultural area. 'Watermeadows' from the late Middle Ages follow the river up to the junctions with its eastern and central tributaries, flanked by 'medieval enclosures'. On the slopes each side are 'orchards' and areas of 'other woodland', either 'grown up from scrub' or 'ancient woodland replanted'. In the Middle Ages these wooded areas would have been mostly orchard or pasture, and this is how they still appear on the tithe map.

As the valley floor rises westwards from Bridge, watermeadows give way to 'medieval enclosures' but from the church up to Street there are only 'post-medieval enclosures' on the south side of the lane.[7] Law's map of 1793 shows that these were the southern fields of Pitt Farm, and that the nineteenth-century fields were an amalgamation of several smaller fields of medieval shape. In the eighteenth century, therefore, the flood-plain and the western valley up to Street still presented a field pattern of medieval origin.

The tithe map divides up this whole area between a number of small farms, and these might be thought to explain the medieval enclosures. But the tithe apportionments attach to these farms, and these farms only, the phrase 'barton land'. This raises a question for the archives. For the same phrase appears in the Visitation report of 1307, which states that the steward had granted Thomas de Bromptone 'half a ferling of barton land (*de Bertone*) . . . and another half ferling of native land (*de terra nativa*)'. The distinction between 'barton land' and 'native land' separated the demesne from land let to the villeins or *'nativi'*, and the 'barton' also designated the demesne farm. So it seems these small farms had once been part of the medieval demesne.

The Demesne Farm

The canons' visitation reports contain much information about the demesne farm *(bertona manerii)* in the early fourteenth century. In 1281 the steward built two granges, a byre and a barn, but by 1307 the wain house, two barns, the bakehouse and the bailiff's room needed repair. There was a new barn by 1318 but the granary and the byre were in a bad state. Evidently the cob, timber and thatch of which they were built suffered badly from the wet and stormy weather of these years. By 1330 however a second new barn had been built and the byre, dairy and other buildings were well roofed and maintained. More importantly for our purpose, the reports call the demesne farm La Biry, which identifies it as the modern Berry Barton Farm.

The buildings of La Biry presumably lay where Berry Barton's lie today, on a lane up a branch valley which joins the western valley at Street from the southern, seaward side.[8] In 1840, as now, Berry Barton's land was separated from Branscombe Mouth by land belonging to Manor Mill and Little Seaside Farms, and stretched from there westward along the coast to Littlecombe. Chalk had been quarried and burnt for lime on the ridge between the western valley and the sea-cliffs, marked 'rough ground' on the HLC map, and the fields, like those of the modern farm, lay south and west of the farmhouse where the ridge broadens out into plateau land. Berry Barton's medieval status lingers in the preamble to the 1840 tithe apportionments, which names the Dean and Chapter as 'appropriators of all the tithes arising on Berry Farm, and of all tithes of corn and grain on all other lands', other tithes being reserved for the vicar. This matches the 'extent' or valuation in the visitation report of 1281, which claimed for the Dean and Chapter 'tithe of sheaves £22 with the tithe of the demesne'.

La Biry extended further inland than its modern successor. The nine contiguous farms and meadows designated as 'barton land' in the tithe apportionments stretch from above Street to the sea: Cotte, Deem's, Lower Deane, Pitt, Church Living, Hole Meadow, Withy Beare, Manor Mill and Little Seaside. The last six occupy the flood plain and the inner slopes of the seaward ridge in the western valley, and share between them the landward boundary of Berry Barton. They were clearly once part of the demesne farm and only separated from it later. In fact, a lease of 1463 and a rental list of 1506 shows that this hiving-off of tenant farms from the demesne, no longer worked by serf labour, was in progress from the late fifteenth century.[9]

The demesne farm, therefore, contained all the land between Branscombe Mouth and the lane linking Vicarage (La Forde) with Street (La Dene). With the seaward ridge and plateau land to the west, this amounted to a large compact area of about 500 acres (see Plate 3). The only land south of the lane which did not belong to it was the churchyard and glebe, and they had been carved out of the demesne. The Visitation reports show that the demesne also contained, on the flood-plain, a mill with its leat and a fishpond, probably at Bridge where the name 'Waterlakes' survived within memory.[10]

This raises a question about the HLC's 'medieval enclosures' here: were they created by the farms hived off in the fifteenth century, or were they a response to the farming needs of the demesne? The HLC map enables the floodplain and western valley to be seen as a landscape of pasture, orchards and water-meadow, and hedges would surely have been needed on the demesne for stock management and to stop cattle trampling hayfields and withybeds, fouling the fishpond or damaging the mill leat.

Enclosing the Demesne Arable

Three of the nine 'barton land' farms – Lower Deane, Deem's and the northern fields of Pitt Farm – lie higher in the western valley, above Street. The tithe map shows their land spreading southwards on to the plateau north of Berry Barton, separated from Berry Barton's land by the side-lane from Street. They were once part of the demesne, so this part of La Biry's land surrounded the farm buildings on all sides. This is high ground, where the demesne's arable would have been (Plate 4).

The HLC marks this land as a mixture of 'barton fields' and 'post-medieval enclosures' with a few 'modern enclosures'. The term 'barton fields', is not to be confused with 'barton land', meaning 'demesne land'. In HLC parlance 'barton fields ' means 'relatively large, regular enclosures . . . likely to have been laid out between C15th–C18th'.[11] The implication of the HLC map is that the 'barton fields' of Pitt, Lower Deane and Deem's could be fifteenth-century enclosures, and if so, would date from their hiving-off as tenant farms. Berry Barton itself might have been enclosed at the same date, in which case the medieval demesne's arable would have been a large open expanse surrounding the farmhouse rather than a mosaic of hedged enclosures, and the valley and upland sectors of the demesne would have had sharply contrasted landscapes.

Enclosing the Uplands

Eight free tenants appear in the 1339 custumal. Six had small or medium-sized holdings, mostly in the valleys, but two held large holdings for moderate rents: John de Bittelesgate, a Colyton landowner, had one 'carucate' and John de Bromlegh, a Southleigh landowner, had two 'carucates'.[12] A carucate was a somewhat variable measure which took account of the productivity of the land, but it is usually reckoned at 120 acres. Place-names and archival sources reveal that these holdings were on the uplands, and the HLC gives a pointer to their use.

John de Bittelesgate's holding was at Littlecombe, a name that survives: it is a squarish parcel of land running north from the cliffs west of Berry Barton. It provides an example of how the history of a free holding can often be followed through deeds, for deeds in the Devon Record Office show it passed from the Bittelesgates to the Knollys and then to Earl Rivers.[13] It belonged to the Marquis of Dorset in 1506, then to the Petres, who in 1591 leased to William Pole of Shute 'a parcel of land called Littlecombe containing 140 acres'.[14] This was still a distinct freehold on the tithe map, which gave its area as 136 acres, with nine acres of beach. This implies that in 1339 Bittelesgate's carucate was about 140 acres (Plate 3).

John de Bromlegh rented two carucates 'at La Dene'. La Dene was the western valley containing Street, and beyond Street it shallows gradually westwards across the upland. In the eighteenth century, when Street was called Dean, this area was Higher Dean. Deeds locate Bromlegh's holding more precisely, for 'Deane', along with Luggesmore and Bromepark (Plate 3) belonged to the Marquis of Dorset in 1506 and to the Petres thereafter, like Littlecombe. A Petre lease of 1606 refers to 'five closes called Deane Lands containing seventy acres', and shows that it adjoined Littlecombe to the north. [15] This block of fields is also distinct on the tithe map, with an area of seventy-one acres.

Adjacent to Higher Deane to the north and west are two blocks of fields bounded on the OS map by 'Lugmoor Lane'; these are 'closes called Luggesmoore containing sixty-three acres' referred to in a 1560 lease.[16] In the 1840 apportionments they totalled seventy-one acres, so the Marquis of Dorset's estates of Deane and Luggesmoor, both freeholds by 1840, added up to about 140 acres. If a carucate was 140 acres, it looks as if these two estates had made up one of Bromlegh's two carucates 'at La Dene' in 1339.

So were Branscombe carucates 140 acres? This might decide the size of villein holdings, for the 1339 custumal reckons them in ferlings, and a ferling was one-sixteenth of a carucate. At 140 acres to the carucate, the typical villein's holding of one ferling would be about 8.75 acres, but at the conventional rate of 120 acres, only 7.5 acres.[17] However these particular upland carucates might have been counted at 140 acres because they were poor quality land, in which case they might not provide a standard for villein holdings.

The land rented by Bittelesgate and Bromlegh was part of a belt of high ground running from the sea-cliff to the northern parish boundary, separating Weston from the main village. The HLC map divides Littlecombe into 'rough grazing' near the cliff and seven 'post-medieval enclosures'. These lack the 'surveyed straight boundaries' characteristic of eighteenth-and nineteenth-century fields, so could well date back to the sixteenth or seventeenth century. Higher Deane and the eastern half of Lugmoor are 'barton fields' on the HLC map, consistent with sixteenth-century enclosure by the Marquis of Dorset or the Petres. It seems likely, then, that in the fourteenth century Bittelesgate and Bromleghe, lacking the serf labour that enabled the manor to cultivate an extensive upland farm, used these large but quite cheap holdings as unenclosed sheepwalks. There is a glimpse of the unimproved, and perhaps still unenclosed, character of Littlecombe in the 1606 Petre lease of Deane, where a clause allowed John Ham 'to dig marl and sand . . . and to take lops, tops and shrouds of trees on land called Littlecombe'. Perhaps, indeed, Littlecombe and Deane had been common land belonging to the manor and used by the villeins until rented to Bittelesgate and Bromleghe.

An Encloser of Strip Fields?

The western half of Bromleghe's estate at Lugmoor tells a different story. It is near Weston and the HLC map divides it into two 'post-medieval enclosures' and one 'medieval enclosure based on a strip field' (see Plate 5). The tithe map however shows fifteen enclosures, many of them long, thin and sometimes sinuous, which look like the result of enclosing an open field of already consolidated strips. It would seem that the 'post-medieval enclosures' were Mid-Victorian, and obliterated an earlier enclosure of part of a strip field system surrounding Weston. So perhaps it was Bromleghe who enclosed these strip-fields and sub-let them.

Bromleghe's second carucate probably became the Marquis of Dorset's holding of 'Bromepark', which possibly preserved Bromleghe's name. Without going into detail, it seems likely that Bromepark eventually became three small farms, Ashton, Higher Bulstone and Lower Bulstone, which border Lugmoor to the north. They had a combined area of 135 acres in 1840. Half of Ashton and the greater part of the Bulstone farms are marked 'medieval enclosures based on strip fields' on the HLC map, and here again the question arises whether Bromleghe was the encloser, and if so, how the land was used.

Identifying Strip Fields

The Bulstone strip field is one of several which the HLC map shows surrounding the village on the plateau (see Plate 2). To the east it connects with a long spur north of the western valley marked 'medieval enclosures based on strip fields', and to the north with a tongue of land between the two branches of the central valley, similarly marked. This may be an area called 'Norton' in the custumal, largely enclosed by free tenants in 1339. (There may once have been an associated small hamlet called Norton, the northern equivalent of Weston lying to the south-west.[18]) Another spur of upland ran from the highway south to Castle Hill, between the central and eastern valleys, and high ground continued round the head of the eastern valley and on south to Stockham's Hill, with the eastern parish boundary running along it to the coast. Nearly all of this is 'medieval enclosures based on strip fields' on the HLC map, and there is nothing in the custumal to suggest that any of it, east of 'Norton', was enclosed in 1339. So if the HLC label is correct many of the seventy-five villeins named in the custumal still held part of their land in arable strips.

But is there archival evidence that positively identifies strip fields? The custumal contains neither of the diagnostic terms often 'encountered in descriptions of subdivided arable in East Devon . . . *campus* (field) and *cultura* (furlong)'.[19] But the concept of *campus* may have survived in field names in the tithe apportionments. The common names used there for an enclosure are 'close' and 'park'; 'field' is rare, and may be a relic of strip cultivation, as two examples will suggest.[20]

'Northern Fields' in Taylor's Farm are on the spur running eastwards from Bulstone and this 'field' name might be a relic of the strip farming which, according to the HLC, preceded medieval enclosure there. In 1840 Taylor's was one of four narrow parallel copyhold farms, all between nine and twenty-one acres, laid out north-south across the spur, so that each included a section of arable hilltop, coppiced slope, orchard, valley meadow and stream (Plate 6 shows the same area on Alexander Law's map of 1793).[21] Many of the closes, whether marked 'medieval enclosures based on strip fields', 'medieval enclosures' or 'other woodland' on the HLC map, have the shape of strip enclosures on the tithe map. The twelve acres called 'Taylor's Farm' in 1793 might even have been part of the two ferlings possessed by John le Taylor 'above Northedon' in 1339, already enclosed from strips. Another of these farms was called Northern Edge, and Northern Lane runs nearby, so Northedon (North Down) may well have been the medieval name of this area. [22]

At Weston the name 'Dean's Field' looks like a relic of strip farming, all the more so because neighbouring fields are called 'Dean's Little Moor', 'Dean's Titherland', 'Lower Dean's Titherland' and Dean's Two, Four, Six and Seven Acres. [23] These eight names may all commemorate the enclosure of an open field, perhaps known as the Dean's Field, and farmed in strips by the inhabitants of Weston. On the HLC map they are part of an area of 'medieval enclosures based on strip fields', which also implies a former open field system surrounding Weston (see Plate 5). Except for western Lugmoor, enclosure had not taken place here by 1339.

The fourteenth-century landscape of Branscombe was clearly in transition from open fields to hedged farms, but open arable fields still covered much of the high ground despite encroachment by enclosers. Evidence from the custumal which is not included in this article shows that both free and villein holdings in the valleys were becoming enclosed homesteads, but the valleys were not yet divided up between farms. So villeins with upland arable strips could still have acquired pasture in the valleys for animals, and valley farmers specialising in livestock could have rented arable strips on the plateau.

Rights of Common?

Plentiful though the supply of land may seem, the average villein family had to live off less than eight or nine acres. So did villeins benefit from rights of common? Archival sources mention only in one visitation report a common sheep pasture. In general, it was the 'commons and waste' lying beyond the village fields that would have been prized, to the extent that villeins could use them for grazing and for timber and firewood, sand and marl, bracken for animal litter, and so forth.

There does seem to have been a fair amount of unoccupied land. The area of the parish in the 1840 apportionments was about 2,700 acres,[24] so the 500 acres in demesne was less than a fifth. The holdings of villeins in the 1339 custumal amounted to 716 acres,[25] between a quarter and a third of the total. A guesstimate for freely tenanted land (for some of which measures are not given) might be 664 acres, just under a quarter. So occupied land might have totalled nearly 1900 acres, leaving about 800 acres of commons or waste, somewhat under a third. These acres had to be shared with free tenants under the Statute of Merton of 1235, and their use by the villeins was dependent on custom.

The HLC map labels as 'post-medieval enclosures' a swathe of northern upland bordering the highway (Plate 2). In the fourteenth century this, like Kingsdown Common across the road[26] or Beer Common to the east, would have been an open heath – rough grazing with trees, scrub and bracken. Its enclosure, long after 1339 but probably well before 1728, when a sketch-map of the highway shows enclosures along the Branscombe side,[27] would surely have dealt a blow to the traditional village economy.

Conclusion

This comparison of the HLC map with archival sources has found a fairly good match, especially when the tithe map and Law's map are used to extend the cartographical range. Comparison of tenants' holdings in the valleys, not included here, confirms this agreement. Details of the demesne farm culled from the archives have added depth and specificity to the HLC map's labelling of its land. By studying only the period 1280–1340 it has been possible to refine, in some cases, the local application of the HLC map's broad category of 'medieval enclosures', while reference to some later archives has suggested similar refinements to the local application of 'barton lands' and 'post-medieval enclosures'. Comparing deeds for large upland holdings with the HLC map suggests that less productive parts of the manor may have been rented to local sheep-farmers. The medieval enclosure of some strip fields, indicated on the HLC map, has been tentatively assigned to a fourteenth-century tenant, and field-name clues to the location of former strip fields match inferences on the HLC map. Combining cartographical and archival approaches therefore has provided a fuller conception of medieval Branscombe and insight into the making and appearance of its landscape. Many of the findings are inferential, but they raise important new questions.

Acknowledgements

I received many helpful suggestions for this study from Barbara Farquharson, and encouragement from Philippe Planel. Dr Sam Turner commented on an earlier version. To them, and to Sean Goddard for the map in Plate 3, I am very grateful.

Notes and References

1.   Fox 1972, p. 82. Fox also considered that 'we need detailed studies of individual villages', and Branscombe was not among the manors studied in his seminal article on field-systems in East Devon.

2.   See <http://gis.devon.gov.uk/basedata/viewer.asp?DCCService=hlc>.

3.   Visitation of 1281, DC 3672a (trans. R. Bass in ECA); of 1301 and 1307, Hingeston-Randolph 1892, pp. 193-196, with English paraphrase in Hingeston-Randolph 1890; of 1318, DC 2850 (trans. R. Bass in ECA); of 1330, Hingeston-Randolph 1894–1899, part I, p. 574.

4.   WCSL, DC 3683, MS transcription by J.Y.A. Morshead (Branscombe 'scrapboook').

5.   Branscombe tithe map is at <www.eastdevonaonb.org.uk/dro/index.html>. Law's estate map is at <www.branscombeproject.org.uk>.

6.   Morshead 1903, p. 153; Parkinson 1985, pp. 24-5 and pp. 40-41. According to Steven Reed of the Devon County Council's Historical Environment Record, the shingle bank at Seaton appeared with a major storm in 1377. The Branscombe Tithe Map shows four acres called 'The Moor' (i.e. marsh) where the beach carpark is now.

7.   Some of these were irrigated catch meadows in later centuries.

8.   The farmhouse was rebuilt after a fire in the 1880s, but there are old cob outbuildings. Law's survey still called Berry Barton a 'mansion house'. By the eighteenth century the collection of tithes was leased for a third of their yearly value to the lessee of Berry Barton, and a barn stands where the OS map marks 'tithe barn'.

9.   DC 6017/2, DC 3684 (MS transcription by J.Y.A. Morshead in the WSCL, Branscombe 'scrapbook').

10. Chick 1906, p. 26. W. Carpenter, personal communication.

11. The two usages are connected, in that such enclosures often occurred on the land of former bartons, as is the case in Branscombe.

12. John de Bittelesgate complained at a visitation of Colyton in 1330 that the church had meddled in the affairs of his wife, who had died intestate. Hingeston-Randolph 1894–99, part I, p. 573. He may have given his name to Buddleshayes Farm north of Branscombe, in a former outlier of Colyton parish. John de Bromleghe died shortly before the 1339 custumal, and his holding was then in the hands of his heirs.

13. DRO, 123M/ TB 472.

14. DRO, 123M/L 768.
15. DRO, 123M/L 1284.
16. DRO, 123M/L 1280.
17. In either case, villein holdings in Branscombe were scarcely enough to sustain a peasant family without extra resources, which has implications for how the manorial economy worked.
18. Norton means 'north settlement'. I owe this suggestion to Peter Herring.
19. Fox 1972, p. 96.
20. A 1582 estate map of Smallborough, Norfolk, in the British Library (hung in the 2011 Tate Britain exhibition 'Watercolour') supports this reading. It shows enclosures scattered among fields of strips, the former all named 'Close', the latter 'Field'.
21. These farms' layout was drawn to my attention by Philippe Planel.
22. Peter Herring's suggestion.
23. The 'Titherland' names come from Law's 1793 map, and apparently refer to tithes. 'Dean' here has no connection with La Dene or Higher Deane further east.
24. Some 216 acres of cliff and beach have been deducted from the total of about 2,900. Raising crops in small landslip plots on the sea-cliff 'cliff plats' provided a significant addition to labourers' incomes from the 18th to the 20th century, but there is no evidence of this in the Middle Ages.
25. For these rough calculations, one ferling is counted as 8.75 acres.
26. Then an outlier of the parish of Colyton, now in Southleigh.
27. Torrance 2009, p. 241.

Bibliography

Chick E. (1906) *A Short Sketch of the History of the Parish and Church of Branscombe*, Exeter: W.J. Southwood & Co.

Fox, H.S.A. (1972) 'Field Systems of East and South Devon. Part I: East Devon', *DAT*, 104, pp. 81-135.

Hingeston-Randolph F.C. (ed.) (1892) *The Register of Walter de Stapledon, Bishop of Exeter*, London & Exeter: Bell.

Hingeston-Randolph, F.C. (1890) 'The Manor and the Parish 600 Years Ago', *Newbery House Magazine*, February-March.

Morshead J.Y.A. (1903) 'Our Four Manors', *DAT*, 35, pp. 146-155.

Parkinson M. (1985) 'The Axe Estuary and its Marshes', *DAT*, 117, pp. 19-62.

Torrance, J. (2009) 'Raddis Lane: politics and landscape', *DAT*, 141, pp. 237-268.

People and Places in Fourteenth-Century Ottery St Mary

Christopher Wakefield

Understanding the detail of what life was like in any historical period is not easy, but the Middle Ages are the most challenging to our imaginations because the records either do not exist, as in the early post-Roman period, or where they do exist they are difficult to read and interpret. The Lay Subsidies of 1327 and 1332 are something of an exception however, they are simply lists of personal names of a selected group of people owning what was termed 'moveable' property above a certain base value.[1] Deciding what was, or was not, 'moveable' was not an easy matter, and advice from the authorities was often misunderstood or misapplied by local tax assessors. The difficulty here was just one among many faced by the assessors trying to arrive at a valuation figure. In consequence, the Subsidy records usually arrive with a health warning about the proportion of the population which appears there.[2] Even so, they are an eminently useful and very popular resource for local historians, and on close examination they can offer a fascinating glimpse of fourteenth-century life at close quarters.

The 1332 Lay Subsidy records for Devon are already easily available in the Devon and Cornwall Record Society publication of 1968.[3] Of the seventeen subsidies levied between 1290 and 1334, that of 1332 is favoured by historians because it was annotated to show settlements below hundred level, setting out more fertile ground for comparative analysis across localities and regions.

To squeeze the maximum social and economic history from these records demands that they should be understood in their proper historical context, but even without that context we can see to some extent who was wealthy and who poorer, and how the local economy of one area was performing in comparison with another. Where a single locality is in view, as here for Ottery St Mary, there is the option of tracing its journey through a consecutive series of returns to see what can be discovered about its economic and social development. Also, if we read the records in conjunction with a large scale map, we can see an outline picture of the medieval landscape.

In 1061 the parish of Ottery St Mary was given by Edward the Confessor to the Cathedral at Rouen in northern France. The charter recording this event includes the territorial bounds of Ottery which are still recognisable as the modern parish boundary.[4] The King's gift is described as the 'villa' of Ottery,[5] a term which describes a taxable asset, rather than a specifically urban or rural entity. In Ottery's case it refers to the whole estate rather than just the town area (even if such existed in 1061). The fact that a very large parish and a very small town share the same name has led to a misconception about Ottery's historic economic significance. In league tables compiled from the 1334 returns it is boosted to fifth most important contributor in the South West, well above Truro (sixteenth) and Taunton (nineteenth), a quite unwarranted elevation, due partly to the sheer size and character of the estate – 10,000 acres and mostly rural (which is noted) – but also because of the sudden leap in tax that Ottery had to bear between 1327 and 1334 (which is not noted).[6] In fact the tax for 1334 was too much for twenty-five Ottery tenants, who simply abandoned their tenancies unable to pay rent and subsidies.[7] As a guide to the character of the parish at this period, it is probably best not to attach too much significance to the rankings.

For some reason, Ottery escaped devolution into a series of smaller parishes that was a characteristic development of old Saxon estates during the tenth and eleventh centuries.[8] Ottery remained with its French overlords, who seemed hesitant to allow it economic independence of the kind which was developing elsewhere in Devon. A market charter was granted in 1226 – probably due to an already thriving local exchange; an assize of Bread and Ale in 1280, and privilege of Gallows the same year,[9] but Ottery was never to become a borough – the Dean and Chapter of Rouen clearly considered Ottregians sufficiently troublesome without giving them an even greater say in local economic affairs.[10]

In many respects the 1327 and 1332 returns, both literally and metaphorically, cover the same ground.[11] They are only a few years apart and it is likely that they reflect a broadly similar social and economic situation. The lowering of the allowance threshold to 6s in 1332 means we should expect to see an increase in the number of taxpayers. This patently did not happen. The number of taxpayers in 1332 is four per cent below the figure for 1327 (144 in 1327; 138 in 1332) and only eighty-seven of those paying in 1327 appear in the list for 1332 (sixty per cent). The reasons for this dramatic change are not easy to discover. A number of factors could have played a part: the frequency of tax demands, which would have the effect of encouraging evasion; economic uncertainty following a series of disastrous harvests between 1315 and 1318 (bad enough to cause a famine);[12] or landlords perhaps demanding extortionate rents and fines, which could cause rapid changes in property holding if poorer peasants were not able to meet the demands, and sold out to their more fortunate neighbours.

In the absence of any firm evidence for dramatic upheavals in the property market or large rent rises in the decade prior to 1334, the most likely cause is the erratic process of local tax assessment and collection. Add to this the fact that the assessors would be neighbours in your parish, inevitably with personal agendas extending far beyond the actual requirements of the job, there would be fertile ground for mischief. It seems highly probable that in their efforts to be objective and dispassionate, crown employees were put under tremendous strain in the mesh of local personal relations in which they were embedded. The problem was a widespread one, in the aftermath of the 1332 levy there was a nationwide furore about corruption and fraud, aimed mainly at the highly questionable behaviour of local assessors.[13] The disturbances resulted in a new system of assessment for the next levy, just two years later in 1334.

Notwithstanding the changes between the two lists, the situation on the ground (the actual infrastructure of houses, farms and fields), would have changed very little over the five years between 1327 and 1332. The two lists can be compared for insights into Ottery society at the time, and can be added together for a better picture of the landscape. It will not be a perfect picture; deciding how many people were genuinely not eligible to pay tax, and how many were exempt or able to make a deal with the assessors is very difficult to calculate.[14] The two levies taken together overcome this problem to some extent, as long as we understand the implications of such an addition, which in turn requires a look at the practical implications of tax assessment and collection routines.

The County Assessors were appointed by the King's court in London, and given some management training to help them with operations in their own counties. When the Devon assessors returned, they appointed local assessors for each hundred. Every householder in each hundred, except the clergy (the laity only, hence the unofficial title 'Lay' Subsidy) was eligible for assessment, but in practice the local assessors would have a reasonable insight into who was likely to be taxable simply because of their local knowledge. In Ottery the assessors were Thomas de la Thorne and Ralph atte Burghe, easily identifiable as the occupiers respectively of Thorne and Burrow Hill Farms.[15] Their job was to visit each householder and value their moveables, then calculate the due sum if the value exceeded a basic allowance. Allowances in Ottery had been set at 10s in 1327 and 6s in 1332,[16] and the fraction taken in tax was a twentieth in 1327 and a tenth in 1332. The doubling of the tax rate in 1332 was due to a reclassification of Ottery's status from rural hundred to Ancient Demesne (which was taxed at the same rate as a borough). There was a requirement also for assessors to make a written inventory of household moveables, to a pro forma advised by the county assessors, but these records have not survived in any quantity and unfortunately Ottery's are not among them.

Since taxes were at least as unpopular in the 1300s as they are now, election to the position of tax assessor/collector could easily affect their standing in the community. One advantage though, was that they could set their own assessment at a comfortably low level. Ralph atte Burghe appears in the 1327 return assessed at 2s. His election in 1332 as an assessor would suggest no significant change in his situation as a respectable farmer, yet he assessed himself at 8d. Thomas de la Thorne, another substantial farmer, is similarly assessed at 8d. Awarding yourself a low tax assessment was just one among a number of semi-official rewards for the job. The assessors were not paid for their work and they were expected to cover any personal expenses out of their own pockets, except for one or two gratuities along the lines of the tax reduction mentioned above. These were mostly gifts of food or drink, which were in any case acts of habitual courtesy in the Middle Ages. On the other hand, assessors had to be mindful of their reputations and longer term relations with their neighbours, so any sign of undue influence had to be guarded against. They could usually give favours to parishioners as long as they were prudent in their assessments. These two certainly appear to have done what they could to minimise the impact of a doubling of the tax rate in 1332 by tinkering with the assessed value of moveables. By fair means or foul then, the assessors came up with lists of those due to pay and how much each of them owed. The total assessments were £11 (in 1327) and £15 11s 10d (in 1332), putting Ottery among the most expensive places to live in Devon for a taxpayer.[17]

Turning to the substance of the returns – particularly the names[18] – it is immediately obvious that the settlement pattern is partially reflected in the locational surnames on the lists. There are also occupational names there which offer a view of the conditions of Ottery's town life at the time. We need now to pinpoint these observations to see what picture emerges of the local landscape, the process of tax assessment and Ottery society in general. First though, we have to accept the limitations of surnames as a source of evidence and take care not to make unwarranted assumptions. A few notes of caution are therefore required before looking at the names in detail.

By the twelfth century, christian names alone were no longer sufficient, even in relatively small settlements, to identify an individual for tax or other administrative purposes. The addition of a second name based on their place of residence, their occupation, their father's name, or even on a striking personal characteristic, was therefore used to ease the problem. By the fourteenth century surnames were fairly well established, some of them already two or three generations old. We may no longer assume, that in 1330, John Dyer was necessarily a dyer, it may have been his great grandfather that was named for his occupation and the name stuck to his offspring, especially if they continued in the family trade. The general fluidity of all types of surnames in the fourteenth century poses some problems for those wishing to extrapolate from the data. Many place names were first given for the person or people in occupation of a particular site. For example, the farm belonging to the British farmer Cada became known by later Saxon settlers as Cada's hege or Cadhay. Later on, the reverse process can occur and the occupant takes a surname from his or her location or holding. Hence we have Thomas de Cadhay (Thomas of/ from Cadhay). With the development of inheritance customs, the history and origin of family members became crucially important, so people would carry their place name-surname away from its original location to wherever they were living, which is why in 1332 we find a John de Cadhay in Broadhembury rather than Ottery St Mary. So we should not assume that all the de Cadhays in Ottery are living at Cadhay itself. They may be elsewhere in the parish (although they do appear consecutively on the 1332 return).

Another common group of locational surnames are identified by the preposition 'atte' or alternatively 'in the'. There is also a single 'by' (or 'beneath') element. This group identifies the individual by reference to a local landmark or well known topographical feature. So we have John in the Lane or Henry atte Stone. The problem here is that specific locations may not be easy to pinpoint from the term Lane, Stone, Wood, Well or the other common 'atte' surnames, unless a modern farm or settlement exists of the same name. In fact we often find a place name surname which has no identifiable equivalent in the modern landscape. This could indicate a lost or subsequently renamed settlement or farm, or it could, as we noted above, be a migrant occupier whose original home base, and surname origin, lies elsewhere outside the parish or hundred.

Finally, as mentioned at the start of the surname discussion, occupational surnames such as fletcher, baker or carpenter, and personal characteristic surnames, for example, longshanks or whitehead, must be treated with the same care as those deriving from place names. In all cases the first holder of any particular surname is the only truly authentic holder, where the name does have some real personal significance. In the space of a generation or two the situation will have changed, and the surname evidence, although still useful, is much harder to fathom. Some names will have been carried forward through several generations, whereas others will be newly minted for the individual concerned. The proportion of each of these types in any particular list of medieval names will depend mainly on the date of the list. Between 1100 and 1400, as increasing numbers of peasant households acquired the right to pass on property to their children, so family based surnames became more important and permanent.

Place Name Surnames

Of the 198 surnames in the two returns, fifty-three are specific Ottery placenames relating to thirty-six farms, hamlets or locally recognisable landmarks. These are denoted by the prefix 'de' (French 'of'), or 'atte' (Old English 'at' or 'at the'). The French version was probably the more refined of the two, so you would be, for example, Thomas de Cadhay, de Aishe or de Knightstone, whereas you would be Henry atte Coombe, atte Pitte or atte Wood, the 'atte' descriptor referring more often to a local landmark close to the location of your dwelling rather than to a ready-named settlement or farm. Not all the surname locations are identifiable as surviving farms or hamlets, but those that are strongly suggest that the land usage in 1330 (except in the area of Ottery town) was not vastly different to what we see today. Waxway and Blacklake, both substantial farms whose names suggest early origins, do not appear in either list, and that is not easy to explain unless they have been renamed at some point or were occupied by inveterate tax dodgers. The Anglo-Saxon personal name Wacca, which appears at a proximate location to the modern Waxway Farm in the 1061 description of the bounds (Wacca's tree), presents us with a plausible origin of the modern name (Wacca's Way).[19] The Charter also includes reference to Straightgate, but the majority of the boundary names recorded here in 1061 are on the high ground to the west and east of the parish, unattractive in the main as locations for settlement. Another problem with the data occurs in Fluxton Tithing, though this may have something to do with the episcopal residence there (now Bishop's Court), which may have claimed exemption from the tax.[20]

Table 1. Place Name Surnames from the 1327 and 1332 Lay Subsidies

SEPO stands for Surname of Extra Parochial Origin. TM refers to the Tithe Map and Apportionment of 1843. Ordnance Survey references are included where appropriate.

Personal Name	Place Name
John atte Thorne, Thomas de la Thorne	Thorne Farm (SY 0886 9558)
Richard de Stre'yete, William atte Yete	Straightgate Farm (SY 0700 9564). Streteyete is mentioned in the 1061 Charter
John atte Furse	No Furze Farm exists today, but a likely farmhouse, now demolished, stood on New Street, close to the Furzebrook on the east of Ottery.[21]
Christine de Cadeheie, Richard de Cadeheie, Thomas de Cadehaie	Cadhay Farm, on the site of or near to the present Cadhay House. (SY 0879 9625)
Geoffrey atte Pitte	Pitt Farm near Taleford (SY 0889 9670)
Walter de Taleford	Taleford Farm (SY 0906 9701)
Robert de Wonnyngescomb, Richard de Wonnyngiscombe, John de Wonnyngiscombe, Henry de Wonnygiscomb	Later called Winscombe Farm,[22] near Wiggaton. Also referred to as Woolscombe. Now possibly Lower Wolston Farm (SY 0961 9375).
Henry de Cada	De Cada is a surname found in other East Devon parishes. This is probably a SEPO.
Adam de HoleWeye	Holloway or Holway. Either a lost / renamed farm or SEPO.
William de Aysshe, Wymark de Aishe, Joan de Ayshe	Ash Farm on the old A30 (SY 1020 9796)
Henry de Kyclyue (Ketclyue)	Cutcliff. Either a lost/renamed farm or SEPO. TM has plot 1442 in Alfington tithing called Cutliffs, and the surname Cutcliffe survived in Ottery until 1795.[23] There is also a possible link with the borsten clyve mentioned in the 1061 charter.

Amelia de Holecomb	Higher Holcombe Farm (SY 1191 9645)
Robert de Wolcome	This possibly refers to Lower Wolston Farm (SY 0961 9375) in Wiggaton, earlier called Woolscombe or Winscombe (see also above – Wonnygiscombe).
William de Wodeford, Henry de Wodeford	Woodford Farm by the river Otter (SY 1021 9705)
John de Foghelhulle, Walter de Foghelhull	The surname appears later as Foulehill (Devon Feet of Fines ref. 1423, also in the Subsidy returns of 1581). A lost or renamed farm.
William atte Were	Ware Farm on East Hill (SY 1236 9583)
Richard atte Wille, John atte Wille, Matilda atte Wille	There are plenty of atte Wille names in Devon, but Ottery has two old established farms with 'Well' as part of their names: Littlewell (SY 1100 9580), also called Northwell, and Great Well (SY 1097 9547).[24]
Isabella atte Slade	Slade is a common topographical name meaning 'hillside'. This refers to Slade Farm (SY 1141 9486) on the east side of Ottery town.
Roger de Morcome, Stephen de Morcome	Moorcombe hamlet or farm is no longer recorded on OS maps. TM has a field named Murcombs (plot 3819) located close to Beatlands Farm (SY 0783 9195).
Richard de Hembry	Hembury. Either a lost/renamed farm or SEPO.
Thomas de Borcome	Burcombe Manor Farm in Wiggaton (SY 0972 9332)
Thomas atte Leueran	Leafren/Leveran (?). This may be derived from Leofan dune mentioned in the 1061 charter. Nothing similar exists in TM but the will of Robert Haydon 1627 (TNA Prob/11/152) mentions a property called Leah Pill in Rill tithing. Now lost or renamed.

John atte Lane, Richard atte Lane	No Lane Farm survives to be mapped, so this refers to a notable Lane in Ottery. There are several to choose from.
Agnes de Pirieslade	Possibly Purslake – the name of the stream that runs though Alfington. TM 1407 and 1408 also contain the name. This could refer to one of a number of farms that exist there.
Steven de Cobbestrete	Cobbe or Cobbeton or Cobthorn Farm somewhere near Thorne Farm. Now lost or renamed. Oliver transcribed Goveton as Cobeton in his summary of an Ottery rental from 1381,[25] but later references confirm its location as near to Thorne Farm (SY 0882 9564).
Adam atte Hurne	No Hurne Farm survives to be mapped so this refers simply to a habitation enclosed by a bend in the river or a small corner of land. The surname 'Hearn' survived in Ottery until the 1870s. See census data at <www.ancestry.co.uk>.
William de Lancercomb	Lancercombe Farm (SY 0967 9283)
Henry atte Stone	Stone Farm/hamlet. Either lost or renamed. TM has a number of 'Stone' element names in Rill tithing clustered around Burrow Wood. The name here suggests a landmark stone worthy of particular note.
Agnes atte Heigheis	Hayne Barton Farm in Tipton St John (SY 0914 9173)
William atte Brigg	There is no Bridge Farm surviving to be mapped, and 'atte Brigg' occurs elsewhere in East Devon. This indicates a residence close to Ottery's first bridge – (probably St Saviour's).
Richard de Yicheton/Wyggaton	Wiggaton Farm is now lost among the residential dwellings in Wiggaton.

Anne atte Burghe, Ralph atte Burghe	Burrow Hill Farm (SY 1095 9366)
Alice atte Wode	Wood Farm (SY 1022 9102)
Alice de Knyghteston, Joseph de Knightiston	Knightstone Farm (SY 1063 9425)
Walter de Comb, Henry de Come	Higher Coombe Farm (SY 0983 9202)

Source: Erskine 1968; TNA, E179/95/6: Details from Devonshire Lay Subsidy of 1327 transcribed by C. Wakefield.

Occupation Surnames

The range of occupations represented in this list of surnames tells us something of the level of urbanisation that we could expect to find in Ottery St Mary town. Most, but not all of the surnames probably refer to active craftsmen and women, and the presence of 'le' or 'the' before the surname strengthens that assumption. The average tax payment for this group was 20d in 1327, rising sharply to 32.3d in 1332, well in excess of the average rise. This gives rise to the suspicion that artisan townspeople were somewhat discriminated against by the local tax assessors facing the problem of a doubling of the tax demand in successive royal levies (Table 3).

The presence of 'cook' is a sign that there is rooming accommodation in the town for labourers, servants and others without sufficient land or resources on which to survive. Some of these men and women lived in houses rented out by wealthier townsmen. Sometimes they would lodge in purpose built tenement houses (often church funded). In either case there would be no cooking facilities available, so they would need to buy meals from a cookshop, where pies and other hot food would be served. Cooks appear in both tax returns for Ottery indicating that they did a brisk trade in the town.

Water was often unfit to drink in an urban setting, and ale was the staple for use at home and for sale in the marketplace (or illicitly elsewhere and at other times). Brewing was most frequently undertaken by women – alewives and brewsters – and we find the more successful among them with sufficient wealth to appear among the taxpayers. Emma Brewer's moveables were valued at £1 10s in 1327 and £1 11s 8d in 1332, suggesting steady and continuous trade.

The last entry on the 1327 list is Mary Carpenter. The listing of women as craftsmen is not uncommon. If Mary was a widow whose husband was a carpenter with a workshop and possibly an apprentice or two, she may well have carried on her husband's business after his death, including taking on some of the active work.

The presence of hoopers, blacksmiths, potters, tanners, dyers, bakers, soapers and tuckers are all further reminders of the urban character of late-medieval Ottery. These industries were all small scale and domestic – often in the home of the craftsman, but they were sufficient for local demand and some of them may have been producing for wider markets – particularly those engaged in the wool trades. All of them probably also did some farming to make ends meet, and the physical character of the town at that time would have been generally more open with spaces between individual houses, and ready access to farm land. It is even possible that there is some relationship between the enclosed strip fields south of the town and the process of urban development. There is a good deal of work to do here before the character of these fields is fully explained.[26] The list of potential tradespeople is shown in Table 2.

Comparison of the 1327 and 1332 Returns: variations in assessment

There are sixty taxpayers in 1327 who don't appear in 1332 – they are the lower orders of payers – making an average payment of 13.6d (equal to £3 8s 0d lost). There are forty-nine new payers in 1332 – paying an average of 24.3d per payer – thereby providing a welcome influx of new money for the collectors (equal to £4 19s 3d gained). This was essential if Ottery was to meet its escalating tax demand. Without any changes in Ottery's economic situation, its share of the levy in 1332 should have been in excess of £22. In fact it ended up at £15 11s 10d, down at least thirty-two per cent. There were indeed some difficulties in the economy of the early years of the fourteenth century, but it beggars belief that Ottery's fortunes would have dropped so dramatically that the 1332 return delivered only about two-thirds of what might reasonably be expected. The assessors had clearly made an effort to minimise the impact of a doubling of taxes. They achieved this by massaging the assessment figures; increasing

Table 2. Occupational Surnames: 1327 and 1332 Lay Subsidies

Cook	Alice Cok, Robert the cook, William le Cok
Brewer	Emma Brewer
Manservant	John le Gome, Thomas Gome
Fence, hedge and wall maker/mender	John le HayWord
Coopers/Hoopers	John le Hope (two of – one at Salston), Thomas le Hope
Servant	John Sweyn, William Sweyn
Blacksmith	John the Smith
Carpenter	Mary Carpent(er)
Baker	Roger le Pestour, Ona Bakere
Potter	Reginald le Pottere
Tailor	Richard le Taillour
Carder/Teaser (wool trade)	Richard Tissor
Chapman	Roger Chepman
Herder/Shepherd	William the Shepherd, William Flocour,
Dyer	Steven Dire
Boot (boat?) maker	Thomas Botavaint
Moneylender?	Thomas Goldweig
Soaper (wool trade)	Thomas le Sopere
Tanner	Thomas le Tanner
Tucker (wool trade)	Henry le Toker, Thomas Touker
Ford crossing guide	William Fordeman

Source: Erskine 1968; TNA, E179/95/6: Details from Devonshire Lay Subsidy of 1327 transcribed by C. Wakefield.

some (mainly of the artisan classes) and reducing others (mainly the farmers and better off taxpayers). The division of taxpayers in Table 3 is by surname on the assumption that those with occupational surnames are by and large from the artisan class, and are more likely to live in the town, and those with 'de' or 'ate' surnames represent the mainstream farming community and live in the rural hinterland.

Maybe there are signs here of a social division between town and country, where the assessors, as aspiring gentry living in substantial rural farms, regard the town as a place that can afford to pay more, and that charging a greater proportion of the new tax to the urbanites is something that they can manipulate without penalty (even though they probably have substantial dealings with and in the town). The table makes this clear. The artisan class have been hit hardest by the tax rises, their average payment rising sixty-two per cent in real terms. The farmers fared better, their tax rise was about half that of the artisans (thirty-three per cent), in fact their tax in 1332 was, on average, the same as an artisan, whereas in 1327 they had paid quite substantially more. Their assessments were reduced further than were the those of the artisans too, down thirty-four per cent on average as opposed to only twenty per cent reduction for artisans.

The group which is not identifiable as artisans or farmers by surname probably includes a few of each of these classes, but predominantly this group appears to consist of those enjoying the most extreme reductions in assessment and the genuinely borderline payers, who were not lucky enough, or lacking sufficient influence, to avoid being caught in successive tax rounds. Included among the top ten beneficiaries of the most extreme assessment reductions are William Woleward, Henry Basse, John Sot, Peter Batt, John Boueweye, Margery Tudde, Thomas Bealde, Peter Kynrich, Henry Dobyl junior and William Bolle. They all ended up paying less in 1332 than they did in 1327 (I

Table 3. Tax rises for different classes of taxpayer

1327 and 1332. Figures all in pence (d) per taxpayer. Percentages show rise or fall of 1332 versus 1327 figures for taxpayers appearing on both returns.

	1327 (1/20th)		1332 (1/10th)	
	avg. tax due	avg. assessed wealth	avg. tax due	avg. assessed wealth
artisans	20.0	400	32.3 (+62%)	323 (-20%)
farmers	24.5	490	32.2 (+33%)	322 (-34%)
others	18.1	362	22.5 (+24%)	225 (-38%)
all taxpayers	21.2	424	29 (+37%)	290 (-32%)

Source: Erskine 1968; TNA, E179/95/6: Details from Devonshire Lay Subsidy of 1327 transcribed by C. Wakefield.

have not included the two assessors who also enjoyed big reductions). Add this to the genuinely borderline payers who were indeed unlucky to be caught twice, and the figures for 'others' in Table 3 begin to make sense; a mix of genuine low payers and low payers by friendly assessment.

Conclusion

The 1327 and the 1332 lay subsidies taken together, offer a much better insight into the economic and social environment of early fourteenth-century Ottery St Mary than either return considered separately. The five year gap is short enough to allow an assumption of only small-scale economic and social change, and the new intake of taxpayers in 1332 simply brings into view more of what was there before. The differences between the lists are not representative of an overheated property market, or rapid rise and fall of personal fortunes. More than anything else, it appears to provide a snapshot of a community struggling with the compulsory and universally unpopular process of tax collection. This is played out in the behaviour of the assessors as they negotiate their way around the parish, dealing with all classes of people, some their inferiors, some their superiors and all known to them personally. The assessors are trying to make sure they collect enough tax to appear to have fulfilled their obligation to the monarch, trying to remunerate themselves as inconspicuously as possible, and all the time taking care not to annoy their neighbours to the point of damaging their local social standing. Whilst everyone knew their place in the social hierarchy, personal status was mutable according to circumstance. With success the social ladder could be ascended, with failure, the reverse.

A further, more generalised division appears to have developed between town and country, and consequently we find the artisan classes, probably concentrated in the town, at a disadvantage in the influence they can bring to bear on the taxation process. Alongside other evidence, this division further confirms Ottery's urban credentials even in advance of the foundation of Bishop Grandisson's College, which would take place within a decade of the events discussed here, and propel Ottery to a much loftier position among East Devon's market towns. Alongside the unmistakable urban developments in Ottery town, there are a number of substantial agricultural communities in the farms and hamlets scattered throughout the parish. It needs to be remembered that Alfington, Wiggaton, Fluxton and Tipton for example, were all communities which became somewhat frozen in time when seigneurial interest became focussed exclusively on Ottery town as it did after 1061.

The Records

The original 1327 and 1332 returns for Ottery St Mary are part of the Devon county returns held in The National Archive, consisting of hand written text in Latin, in two columns per page on pieces of parchment sewn together at the bottom edges, each forming a roll almost thirty feet long. They are both in good condition. The Ottery sections are included below (see Appendix 1 and 2) in the order and in the columns in which they appear in the original. The reading order of the originals is by row; that is across the two columns as if they were lines of text. The assessed payments are in pre-decimal British currency (before February 1971) expressed in pounds (£), shillings (s) and pence (d). For conversion purposes: there are twelve pence in a shilling and twenty shillings to a pound. So two shillings and sixpence is thirty old pence, equal to about thirteen pence in decimal money.

Notes and References

1. 'Moveable' is a technical term in this context, and refers to household items liable for valuation for taxation purposes. A full discussion of what was considered appropriate for inclusion or exclusion from the tariff appears in Willard 1934, pp. 73-81.
2. Franklin 1995, p.18. He estimates that less than fifty per cent of households were represented on the returns list of 1332.
3. Erskine 1968, pp. 123-124 (from TNA, E179/95/7). The section on Ottery is reprinted in Table 2. The 1327 returns, TNA, E179/95/6, have been transcribed by the author. They have not been previously published.
4. For a discussion of the bounds recorded in this charter see Rose-Troup 1939, pp. 201-220.
5. 'Villa' – the Latin term translates variously, and unhelpfully, as 'farm/ country home/estate; large country residence or seat/villa/village', see <http://users.erols.com/whitaker/words.htm>. The earliest use

occurs in Domesday, where it replaces the OE tun – 'town'. The later distinction between a small *village* and a large *town* was not yet in use in 1086, Morris 1985.

6. Slater 2000, p. 601. Regional Surveys, Table 22.6.

7. Maddicott 1975, p. 15. Where might we be in the rankings if Ottery's tenants had hung on and paid up?

8. For discussion of the development of English parishes see Blair 2005, chapter 8; or Higham 2008, chapter 3, or Pounds 2004, chapter 1.

9. Ottery's market charter is noted in an Inspeximus Canterbury Cathedral Archive – DCc-ChAnt/R/52/. For Privilege of Gallows and Assize of Bread and Ale, see Rose-Troup 1934, p. 213.

10. Ottery was not a settled place in the later 1200s. In 1275, there were rumblings about tithes. A band of locals, unknown, or at least unnamed, had forcibly turned away the Rector – one William of St Gorone, when he came to collect the church's dues. A few years later in 1282, Rouen leased Ottery to Walter de Lechlade, precentor of Exeter Cathedral, whose enthusiasm for extracting income from the parish led to his prompt and gruesome dispatch in Cathedral Close just three months later. Ottregians, including the local vicar, were considered the main culprits. In 1285 there was a raid on the tithe barn in Ottery, again by some locals, one of whom was caught and killed by the Dean's bailiff. All in all, our French landlords must have been relieved when Bishop John Grandisson made an offer to buy the place in the mid 1330s. (See information in Coope 1900, pp. 10-14, Whitham 1984, pp. 13-14 and Calendar of Inquisitions Misc. vol.1, item 1389.)

11. Erskine 1968, pp. 123-124; TNA, E179/95/7.

12. The 1315-1318 famine remains a talking point among historians – see Dyer 1998, p. 110 and pp. 266-7. On medieval crop yields <http://www.cropyields.ac.uk/project.php> is useful. It has been argued that the population decline following the famine took some of the heat out of the economy, allowing a period of relative calm before the much more profound upheaval caused by the plagues later in the century. See Miller and Hatcher 1995, pp. 60-62.

13. Willard 1934, p. 205 *et seq.*

14. Franklin 1995, p. 18.

15. Gover, Mawer, and Stenton 1932, p.605. This is for the 1332 return. No assessors are listed in the roll with the Ottery return for 1327.

16. Allowances for the various subsidies are noted in Willard 1934, p. 88. The change of minimum allowance in Ottery from 10s (1327) to 6s (1332) will (or should) have had an effect on the people who appeared in the tax lists. The main effect that might have been expected, (more people on the list) did not happen, and the 1332 newcomers to the list – forty-nine of them – are not those (or even *mainly* those) assessed as worth between 6s and 10s (and therefore paying between 8d and 12d

in tax). Seventeen of them are paying 2s and upwards, including the mysterious John Bateman (see note 27 below) with his 12s (provided that is not a mistake). Even without Bateman's contribution the average tax demand is 21d in this group. Any clear rationale for including those who are new recruits in 1332 is undetectable.

17. Average payment per taxpayer in Ottery in 1332 was 27.5d. Those paying more than that were all in the urban areas of Devon – Bideford, Barnstaple, Totnes, Plymouth, South Molton, Tavistock or Exeter, which topped the league at 49.8d per taxpayer. Appendix 2, (from Erskine 1968, pp. 130-131).

18. There is a lot of information about surnames on the internet, principally at <http://www.genuki.org.uk/>. For distribution of surnames nationally in 1881 and 1998 see <http://gbnames.publicprofiler.org/Surnames.aspx>. For a more Devon-based discussion see Dr. Max Hooper's contribution at <http://genuki.cs.ncl.ac.uk/DEV/Devon Surnames/>.

19. Rose-Troup 1939.

20. Peter Quivel, Bishop of Exeter (1280–1291) bought the estate of Fluxton from Agnes de Crues in 1281, long before Grandisson acquired Ottery and built the College there. It became a convenient episcopal residence on the journey east from Exeter. Presumably it qualified as church property and thereby avoided taxation. See Reichel, Prideaux and Tapley-Soper 1904, vol 2, p. 21.

21. OS County Series, second edition 1905, Devon Sheet LXX13.

22. Oliver 1846, p. 246.

23. TNA, prob/11/1259. Will of Feder or Federata Cutcliffe, Widow of Ottery Saint Mary, Devon 15 April 1795. The surname is concentrated in East, Mid and North Devon in the 1881 census, see <http://gbnames. publicprofiler.org/Surnames.aspx>., and although Federata was the last Cutcliffe in Ottery, others of the same surname exist later than this in other Devon parishes. See also Devon Wills Project consolidated wills database, [online] Available at: <http://genuki.cs.ncl.ac.uk/DEV/ DevonWillsProject>.

24. There is also a third contender – a 'Wylle' name was associated with Clapperntale Farm in a rental made in the 1680s (Whetham 1913, pp. 86-7). Although they are listed as a pair, and the occupier paid separate reliefs for each, Well Farm was probably aggregated with Clapperntale farm at some point, losing its individual identity. This 'Wylle' may recall the Blind Well included in the 1061 Charter.

25. Oliver 1846, p. 246.

26. Fox 1972, pp. 81-136.

27. John Bateman appears only in the 1332 return with a spectacular due payment of 12s – far above anyone else in East Devon. TNA does not list any other records relating to John Bateman in Devon, yet a Philip

Bateman appears in a record from forty years earlier as the Dean and Chapter of Rouen's bailiff in the town (see note 10 above). This is likely to be an error somewhere, even though the total assessed payment for Ottery as a whole would appear to include Bateman's 12s (in fact the values total only £15 7s 4d). I have assumed that this was originally intended as 12d, and used that value in any calculations I have made.

Bibliography

Beresford, M.W. (1963) *Lay Subsidies and Poll Taxes*, Canterbury: Phillimore & Co Ltd.

Blair, J. (2005) *The Church in Anglo Saxon Society*, Oxford: Oxford University Press.

Calendarium Inquisitionum Post Mortem sive Escaetarum (1806) London: Public Records Commission.

Coope, F.E. (1900) *Thurlestone Church and Parish*, Kingsbridge, Devon: Published by the author.

Dalton, J.N. (1917) *The Collegiate Church of Ottery St Mary*, Cambridge: Cambridge University Press.

Dyer, C. (1998) *Standards of Living in the Later Middle Ages*, Cambridge: Cambridge University Press.

Erskine, A.M. (1968) *Devonshire Lay Subsidy of 1332*, Exeter: DCRS, 14.

Fox, H.S.A. (1972) 'Field Systems of East and South Devon', *DAT*, 104, pp. 81-136.

Franklin, P. (1995) 'Gloucestershire's Medieval Taxpayers', *Local Population Studies Society*, 54, pp. 16-27.

Goldberg, P.J.P. (2004) *Medieval England: a social history, 1250–1550*, London: Hodder Arnold.

Gover, J.E.B., Mawer A., and Stenton F.M. (1932) *Place Names of Devon*, London. English Place Name Society.

Higham, R.A. (ed.) (1989) *Landscape and Townscape in the Southwest*, Exeter: University of Exeter.

Higham, R.A. (2008) *Making Anglo Saxon Devon*, Exeter: The Mint Press.

Kowaleski, M. (1995) *Local Markets and Regional Trade in Medieval Exeter*, Cambridge: Cambridge University Press.

Kowaleski, M., and Goldberg P.J.P. (eds) (2008) *Medieval Domesticity*, Cambridge: Cambridge University Press.

Maddicott, J.R. (1975) 'The English Peasantry and the Demands of the Crown 1294–1341', *Past and Present. Supplements*, 1. Oxford: The Past and Present Society.

Miller, E., and Hatcher J. (1995) *Medieval England: towns, commerce and crafts*, New York: Longman.

Morris, J. (ed.) (1985) *Domesday Book: Devon*, Chichester: Phillimore & Co. Ltd.

Oliver, G. (1846) *Monasticon Diocesis Exoniensis*, Exeter: P.A. Hannaford.

Palliser, D. (ed.) (2000) *Cambridge Urban History of Britain*, Cambridge: Cambridge University Press.

Pounds, N.J.G (2004) *The History of the English Parish*, Cambridge: Cambridge University Press.

Reichel, O.J., Prideaux, H.B., and Tapley Soper, H. (1912–1939) *Devon Feet of Fines*, Exeter: DCRS.

Rose-Troup, F. (1934) 'Medieval Customs and Tenures in the Manor of Ottery St. Mary', *DAT*, 66, pp. 211-233.

Rose-Troup, F. (1939) 'The Anglo-Saxon Charter of Ottery St. Mary', *DAT*, 71, pp. 201-220.

Saul, N. (1997) *Oxford Illustrated History of Medieval England*, Oxford: Oxford University Press.

Slater, T.R. (2000) 'The South-West of England, 600-1540', in Palliser, D. M, (ed.) *The Cambridge Urban History of Britain*, vol. 1, Cambridge: Cambridge University Press.

Turner, S. (ed.) (2006) *Medieval Devon and Cornwall*, Macclesfield: Windgather Press.

Turner, S. (2006) *Making a Christian Landscape*, Exeter: Exeter University Press.

Whetham, C.D. (1913) *A Manor Book of Ottery*, London: Longmans, Green and Co.

Whitham, J. (1984) *Ottery St Mary*, Chichester: Phillimore & Co Ltd.

Willard, J.F. (1934) *Parliamentary Taxes on Personal Property, 1290 to 1334*, Cambridge, Massachusetts: Medieval Academy of America.

Appendix 1

The Lay Subsidy List for Ottery St Mary, 1327

* = taxpayers who also appear in the 1332 returns

John le Hope*	2s	Stephen Cobbe*	2s
John atte Thorne*	6d	Elena Wyne	12d
Richard de Stre'yete*	3s	Reginald le Pottere*	12d
Walter Charde	12d	John atte Furse	12d
Cristine de Cadeheie*	12d	Richard de Cadeheie*	12d
Geoffrey atte Pitte*	3s	Roger Berd*	18d
Walter de Taleford*	2s	William Cole*	2s
Adam de HoleWeye	8d	William Dobyl*	2s 6d
John Aylmer*	2s	Richard Spene*	20d
William Fordeman*	2s	William Cole de Gosford	2s
William Sweyn	18d	William de Aysshe	16d
Richard Markere*	2s	Richard Chard de Aysshe*	6d
William Ilberd	2s	William Frenshe de Aysshe	12d
Henry de Kyclyue*	2s	Henry Chote	6d
John Gerueys*	12d	William Seger*	12d
Peter Kynrich*	2s	William Gerueys	12d
John Symeon*	18d	Richard Symeon*	2s
Roger Pistor*	12d	William Kynrich	12d
John Isaac*	2s	Richard Kynrich*	18d
William Frenshe*	18d	Thomas Bealde*	18d
Henry Mortimer*	16d	Robert the Cook*	16d
Amelia de Holecomb	16d	William Hughe	18d
William Gopil	6d	William Bassecot	2s 6d
Robert de Wolcome*	18d	John le Hope*	12d
Michael Dobyl	12d	Henry Dobyl*	3s
Emma Brewer*	18d	Henry de Wodeford*	3s
William de Wodeford*	12d	John de Foghelhulle*	3s
John Frenshe*	2s	Henry Basse*	3s
William atte Were*	2s	Henry Dobyl Jun*	18d

John BouetheWay*	2s	John atte Wille	2s
Isabella atte Slade*	18s	William Flocour	18d
Richard atte Wille*	12d	Thomas Goldweig	6d
Roger Ok	6d	William le Cok	6d
Richard Coleman	6d	Thomas Clappe*	18d
William Aleyn	6d	Thomas Botavaint	18d
Henry Killy*	18d	Thomas le Tanner*	12d
Roger de Morcome	2s 6d	Thomas Broun*	18d
Richard Tissor	6d	William atte Yete (Straightgate)	12d
Richard de Hembry	6d	John le HayWord	8d
William Geffrai	6d	Robert Broun*	18d
Roger Honte	12d	Thomas Gome	6d
Thomas Bernard	12d	John Slake*	6d
Ralph Gaudichoun*	2s	John Hughe	2s
Thomas Mone'	18d	John Slake Jun	12d
John Sot*	4s	Ona Bakere	6d
William le Kyne*	2s	Serlo Bolle*	12d
John Sweyn*	12d	Thomas de Borcome*	2s
John de Wonnyngiscombe*	2s 6d	Henry de Cad	2s 6d
Roger Mahoun*	6d	William Valyntyn	16d
Richard de Wonnyngiscombe	18d	Ralph Harg'*	18d
Margery Tudde*	3s	John Turpyn	3s
Ralph atte Burghe*	2s	Anne atte Burghe	12d
Alice atte Wode*	2s 6d	Joseph de Knightiston*	2s
Matilda Hayghe	18d	John Isaac*	18d
Henry de Come	15d	John Ilberd*	16d
Roger Chepman*	2s	Thomas le Hope*	2s
Richard de Yicheton	2s	John le Gome*	2s
William Garson*	2s	William Bolle*	3s
William Woldward*	3s	Henry Ilberd*	12d
John Swete*	18d	Henry atte Stone*	18d

Roger Dauy*	12d	Agnes atte Heigheis*	3s
William atte Brigg*	3s	Thomas atte Leueran*	18d
Peter le Bat*	3s	Alice Cok*	3s
William Ste'ygge*	2s	Stephen de Morcome*	2s
John atte Lane	12d	Richard atte Lane	2s 6d
Henry le Toker	18d	Henry Russel*	2s
Walter de Foghelhull	12d	Henry Aunger	9d
Robert de Wonnyngescomb	6d	Wymark Yordan	10d
Geoffrey Bolle*	10d	Joabell Bouewode	6d
William Ilberd	6d	Thomas Touker	6d
Alice Bynitheweye*	6d	Ralph Toly* (Hoye?)	8d
Robert le Bat	6d	John Horlok	6d
John Pykeney*	6d	Celia Kempe	6d
Mary Carpent(er)	6d		

Total: £11 0s 0d.

Source: TNA, E179/95/6: Details from the Devonshire Lay Subsidy of 1327 transcribed by C. Wakefield.

Appendix 2

The Lay Subsidy List for Ottery St Mary, 1332

Henry de Ketclyue	2s 6d	Agnes de Pirieslade	2s 6d
John Geruays	20d	William Seger	22d
Peter Kynrich	20d	Henry Inthelane	18d
Joan Gerueys	22d	John Symyon	19d
Richard Symyon	4s 6d	Richard Kynrich	20d
John Isaac	2s 6d	Juliana Russel	12d
Roger le Pestour	3s 6d	Henry Dobil senior	5s 6d
John Foghille	3s 6d	Emma Brewere	3s 2d
William de Wodeford	12d	Henry de Wodeford	8s 0d
John Poyer	2s 0d	Henry Mortimer	2s 1d
Robert the cook	2s 0d	Thomas Hughe	20d
Emma Gopil	16d	Robert de Wolcomb	2s 0d
William Baystok	3s 6d	John le Hopere	2s 0d
Isabel Frensch	18d	John Frensch	4s 6d
William atte Were	3s 6d	Henry Basse	8d
Henry Killy	20d	Isabel Hughe	3s 0d
John Slake	8d	Ralph Gaudechun	4s 6d
John the Smith	8d	Serlo Bolle	18d
Steven Thornborn	8d	Richard atte Wille	8d
Roger Hok	10d	Thomas Clappe	20d
Thomas le Tannere	16d	Richard le B . . . more	20d
Thomas Broun	20d	Robert Broun	18d
Thomas Bealde	8d	Henry Bollok	3s 4d
Richard Tudde	18d	Roger Hounte	12d
Matilda atte Wille	18d	Henry Dobyl junior	12d
John Boueweye	18d	Alice de Knyghteston	3s 4d
William the Shepherd	4s 0d	Joseph de Knyghteston	3s 6d
Alice atte Wode	4s 6d	Richard Ballard	8d
Margery Tudde	3s 6d	Ralph Harrug	22d
Agnes Turpyn	18d	John Pynkeny	8d
Richard de Wyggaton	12d	Roger Mayhoun	18d

John de Wonnygiscombe	3s 6d	Henry de Wonnygiscomb	3s 6d
Thomas de Borcome	22d	John Sweyn	12d
Ralph Hoye	15d	William Coppe	15d
John Isaak	18d	Walter de Comb	20d
John Ilberd	13d	Roger Horrig	3s 6d
Roger Chepman	3s 0d	Thomas de Hopere	2s 6d
Richard Nitherton	18d	Thomas de Cadehaie	2s 0d
Christine de Cadehaie	12d	Richard de Cadehaie	2s 0d
John le Gome	4s 0d	Geoffrey Bolle	20d
William Woleward	2s 0d	William atte Brigge	3s 6d
Henry atte Stone	12d	Agnes atte Heghen	4s 6d
Roger Dauy	18d	Henry Ilberd	18d
William Bolle	4s 0d	William Garsoun	3s 6d
Steven de Morecome	2s 0d	Richard Inthe Lane	2s 6d
William Skarige	2s 6d	Peter Batt	3s 0d
Alice Cok	3s 0d	Steven Kynrich	15d
Katherine Aunger	2s 6d	John Sot	8d
Henry Russel	3s 8d	John Goue	3s 4d
John le Hopere de Salfynistone	3s 6d	Richard Cole	20d
Steven de Cobbestrete	2s 0d	John atte Thorne	2s 6d
Richard de Stretyate	6s 0d	Reginald le Pottere	16d
Geoffrey atte Pitte	5s 0d	Walter de Taleford	2s 6d
Roger Berd	18d	William Cole	3s 0d
William de Aishe	2s 0d	Wymark de Aishe	2s 0d
John Mayou	12d	Richard Charde	2s 0d
Joan de Ayshe	8d	Richard Markere	3s 6d
William Fordeman	3s 0d	John Aylmere	2s 6d
Edith Cole	20d	Richard Spene	3s 6d
William Dobil	3s 6d	Adam atte Hurne	18d
William Frensh	20d	Thomas le Sopere	15d
John Bateman[27]	12s 0d	William Kyng	4s 0d
Isabel atte Slade	12d	John Swete	2s 0d
Steven Dire	12d	William de Lancercomb	21d
Thomas atte Leuren	20d	Alice Bynytheweie	18d ?

| Richard Wyne | 2s 6d | Cecilia Ware | 18d |
| Thomas Persoun | 12d | Richard le Taillour | 18d |

Assessors:

| Thomas de la Thorne | 8d | Ralph atte Burghe | 8d |

Total: £15 11s 10d.

Source: Erskine 1968.

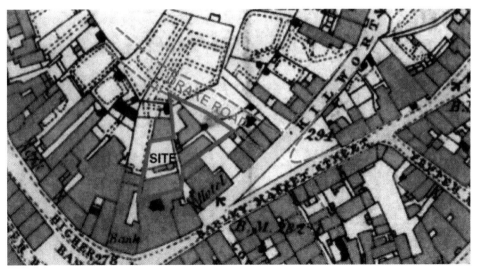

Plate 1. Site of the former Great House as in 1885, with the route of Drake Road (1890) overlaid in blue (from Thompson and Hobbs, 2006).
Reproduced courtesy of S.O. Thompson and S.J. Hobbs.

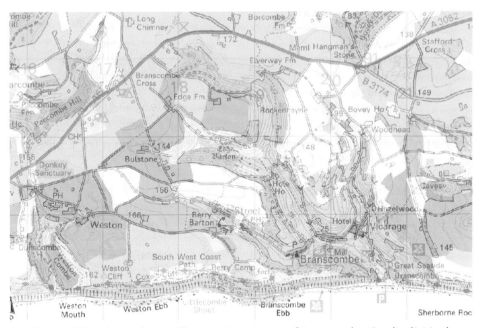

Plate 2. Historic Landscape Characterisation map of Branscombe. On the digitised map more detail can be found by zooming in on particular places.
With grateful acknowledgement to Devon County Council.

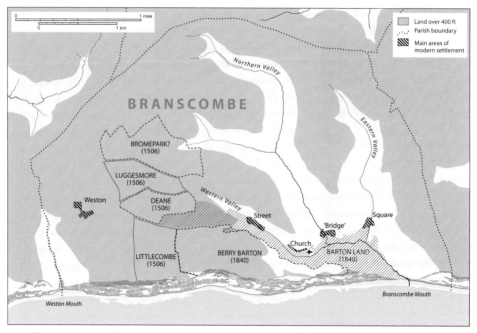

Plate 3. La Biry, the demesne farm, showing 'barton land' hived off in 15th century and estates belonging to the Marquis of Dorset in 1506 as successor to John de Bittelesgate and John de Bromlegh. Map by Sean Goddard.

Plate 4. Tithe map section showing Berry Barton with surrounding 'barton land'. Reproduced courtesy of Devon Record Office.

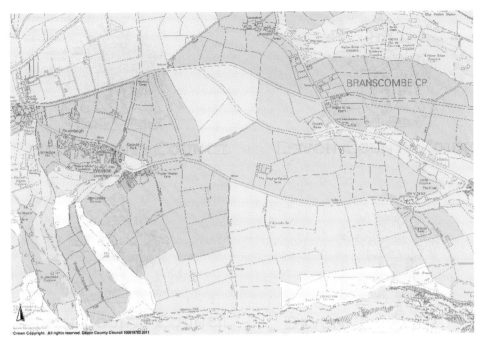

Plate 5. HLC map of uplands, showing 'post-medieval enclosures' at Littlecombe and Lugmoor; 'barton fields' at Higher Dean (Cox's Farm), Lower Dean and Berry Barton; and 'medieval enclosures based on strip fields' at Weston, western Lugmoor, Ashton, Bulstone and Taylor's Farm.
Devon County HLC reproduced by permission of Devon County Council.

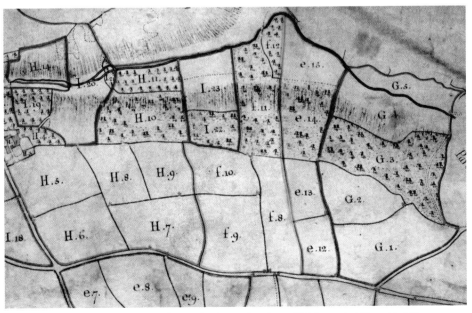

Plate 6. Probable site of 'Northedon'. Northern Fields are 'e12' and 'e13'.
Reproduced courtesy of Devon Record Office.

Plate 7. St Michael's Chapel, Braunton.
Photograph: Matthew James.

Plate 8. Sidmouth, tablet
identifying site of St Peter's
chapel Sidmouth and part
of its walls.
Photograph: Matthew James.

Plate 9. Donn's map showing St Anne's Braunton and unused chapel at Appledore. Reproduced courtesy of Westcountry Studies Library, Devon Libraries.

Plate 10. St Petroc Dartmouth.
© Photograph Bryan Southward with grateful acknowledgement.

Plate 11. John Hawley, MP 1390.
Reproduced by courtesy of St Saviour's Parish Church, Dartmouth.

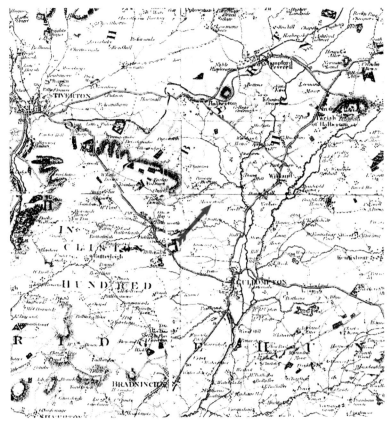

Plate 12. Extract from Greenwoods Map of the County of Devon, 1827.
(*Moorstone indicated by arrow*).
Reproduced courtesy of Devon Record Office.

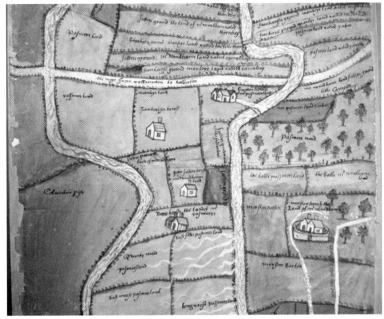

Plate 13. The 'Halberton Map', DRO Reference: DSCF0869.
Reproduced courtesy of Devon Record Office.

Plate 14. Blackdown Hill, Thorncombe, seen from the unrecorded byway.
Photograph: Eve Higgs.

Plate 15. Blind Lane, Thorncombe.
Photograph: Eve Higgs.

Devon's Medieval Chapels as Coastal Landmarks

Jeanne James

In medieval society, the Church played a greater role than it does today. It supported public works and services, partly by encouraging donations for remission of all or part of a penance for sins by means of indulgences and pilgrimages. As Nicholas Orme has shown, in the diocese of Exeter up to 1536, the greatest number of indulgences recorded was for public works (71), followed by chapels (64), below which were parish churches (54).[1] In Devon, one branch of public service was protection along the coast where landmarks included medieval chapels on prominent island and coastal sites, a few of them staffed by hermits. These chapels would have guided mariners from afar, giving bearings or identifying stages in a voyage; served fishermen as chapels of ease, perhaps also for bearings; or marked dangerous passages. Some played a part in defence; a few at ferry points were used for funding and prayers and as harbour lights or marks. Many chapels were associated with cults of particular saints who were believed to intercede on behalf of certain groups of people.[2] The Church's role in coastal public services changed after 1514 when Trinity House was incorporated by royal charter and became the authority for lighthouses and pilotage.[3] From around 1520, there was a fundamental change in theology, promulgated particularly by Martin Luther, that penance and forgiveness were through faith and divine grace not through works or payment of money. This led to the end of the practice of indulgences at the Reformation. Furthermore, abuses had occurred in the later Middle Ages in the unrestricted sale of indulgences by professional 'pardoners', whose activities were to be prohibited in 1567 by Pope Pius V.[4] In 1536 and 1538, Henry VIII issued injunctions against aspects of medieval worship including images of saints, pilgrimages and praying for souls, thus reducing funding of public services associated with churches and chapels.[5] At the Reformation chantries (an endowment for a priest to say Mass for identified deceased people) were dissolved; many chapels fell into disuse, some used as dwellings or farm buildings; others became parish churches.[6] Yet, despite such radical changes, there is continuity in that some of Devon's former medieval chapels near the coast are still landmarks for seafarers; furthermore, anecdotal glimpses into their history reveal some issues that are recognisable today.

However, before embarking on discussion and historical examples, an outline of the general background of medieval chapels is appropriate. The period considered dates from the mid eleventh century to the Reformation of the mid sixteenth, when chapels and oratories were still within the structure of the Catholic Church. In effect, the first chapels were Anglo-Saxon field churches the need for which grew out of increased population in land distant from the parish church.[7] In the twelfth and thirteenth centuries legislation decreed that new chapels were to be licensed by the bishop and be subordinate to the parish church, to which oblations were paid.[8] There were chapels of ease, licensed on account of distance or difficult terrain, and domestic chapels or oratories.[9] Oratories, or 'praying places', were associated with hermit cells but could also be a room in a house or monastery. Institutions such as hospitals and craftsmen's guilds often had their own chapels. References to chapels appear in early charters; the registers of the bishops of Exeter (the main source); surveys of church property; and the writings of antiquaries up to the nineteenth century. These sources did not record all chapels; maps, archaeological evidence and place-names have identified some.[10] By the Reformation there had been about 1,300 chapels in Devon, some of which already had ceased to function, whilst a few had become churches, or *vice versa*. The purpose of all chapels and oratories was primarily for celebration of divine service, but many were situated so that they could provide service to the public.[11] Amongst these were coastal chapels, the choice of sites for many being as landmarks for navigation.

David W. Waters noted that until the late-sixteenth century most English seamen were small shipmen, specialising in various carrying trades. The literate had a 'rutter', a small pocket book. The earliest one surviving – dating from the early fifteenth century but believed to be based on much older lore – includes landmarks such as parish steeples and shows that English seamen sailed from landmark to landmark. A statute of 1565 recorded that certain steeples and other marks on the main shores had served as beacons and marks 'from ancient time' to save seafarers and ships from danger, and prohibited the destruction of steeples used as recognised beacons. Some had been destroyed and removed in the early-sixteenth century because the French had used them to advantage in time of war, with the resulting loss of ships and people returning to England and Wales.[12]

Such landmarks along the north and south coastlines of Devon included over forty identified medieval chapels (Appendix). Whilst there are few pre-Reformation references to their secular use, it may be inferred because some of them, or their sites, are still used to guide seafarers. This survey begins with examples of prominent medieval chapels serving as landmarks on islands and high ground, starting with Lundy Island, Abbotsham and Croyde. Lundy was perhaps a similar spiritual outpost to Farne Island, where St Cuthbert sought solitude in the seventh century and where in the twelfth century fishermen and seamen visited a hermit, taking counsel on their ships and souls, and receiving hospitality.[13] Charles Thomas argued that the only convincing explanation for two of the early memorial stones on the island is that Lundy was, from a little before AD 500, a small outlying monastic establishment in a naturally isolated position. Beacon Hill on Lundy was an early burial ground and Thomas suggested that the likely date for the foundation of the small 'chapel' there was the twelfth or thirteenth century.[14] The earliest documentary evidence for a 'church' is in 1244, by 1254 dedicated to St Mary, but between 1325 and 1364 recorded as St *Elena, Helena and Elene*; it appears to have fallen into disuse after the Reformation.[15] By 1630 Thomas Westcote referred to 'relics of a chapel dedicated to St Helen'. The ruins were near to the old lighthouse built in 1819; James Coulter quoted a reference of 1925 when they could still be traced without difficulty.[16] Such continuity on the same site indicates its use as an important landmark for sea traffic for centuries. Nearby, chapels at

Abbotsham and Croyde were dedicated to St Helen. Abbotsham's was formerly a church, called a chapel after the parish church was relocated and rebuilt.[17] The original church was assigned to the sacristan of Tavistock between 1168 and 1173 for lights in the abbey church.[18] Its dedication was to St *Helene* in 1193 and *Elene* in 1284.[19] The 'new' church, also St Helen, apparently dates from the thirteenth century but its Norman font was presumably from the old church. In reply to a questionnaire to parishes by Dean Jeremiah Milles in 1755-6, the latter was described as a ruin with walls of the south porch still standing 'on ye north side of ye parish (on high ground) near ye sea'.[20] W.G. Hoskins described the location, discovered when a bungalow was built, noting that it commanded a wide view of Barnstaple Bay with Lundy Island and also the cliffs near Croyde in full view. The Croyde site was examined and measured in 1954, when an exterior scratch dial was noted. The building was dated as fourteenth century, the scratch dial wall possibly earlier.[21] Coulter drew attention to the discovery in the 1950s of an Ogham stone on the site, which suggested the possibility of a much earlier Celtic foundation since Ogham was a form of writing originating in fourth-century Ireland, from whence came some of the early Christian missionaries.[22] Hoskins suggested that the dedication to St Helen at Lundy, Abbotsham and Croyde meant the early Celtic saint, *Endelienta* or *Elen*, not St Helen the Empress, mainly on the grounds that Abbotsham belonged to Tavistock Abbey where the Calendar mentions St Elen's feast as 25 August whereas that of St Helen Empress, whose feast is 18 August, is not mentioned. Nevertheless, Orme considers it equally likely that the dedication referred to the Roman (Empress) Helen, mother of Constantine.[23] To add to the confusion, at St Helen's on the Isles of Scilly, where traces remain of a Celtic monastery probably of the sixth century, the twelfth-century dedication to *Sancti Elidii* refers to *Elid* or *Lyde*, a male saint.[24] Dedication aside, evidence suggests early use of all three chapels in Devon as coastal landmarks.

Not far from Croyde at Braunton, and also on the south coast at Burgh Island, Sidbury and Torbay were chapels dedicated to St Michael (the archangel). He is often associated with religious buildings on summits or high ground.[25] North-east of Braunton parish church, a late Perpendicular ruin remains of St Michael's on Chapel Hill, a conspicuous landmark from the sea (see Plate 7).[26] There is little doubt about its dedication, despite legends.[27] Its funding was increased by donations from pilgrims, in return for a grant of indulgence for penance in 1435.[28] Milles noted that the chapel, a ruin by 1755–6, was unendowed; and J.F. Chanter described it as a votive chapel for sailors and fishermen.[29] According to tradition, prayers were offered there for sailors, and watch kept for fishermen.[30] On the south coast, Burgh Island had on its summit the chapel of St Michael first mentioned in 1411 in the will of the Rector of Bigbury. Captain Greenvile Collins' chart of 1693 shows the chapel; a ruin now stands on its site, but the island is still used as a landmark.[31] At Sidbury, St Michael's chapel was granted licence for celebration of divine service in 1426. It was situated at the north-east of the 'castle' but in ruin by the mid eighteenth century.[32] The site would have been clearly visible when approaching Sidmouth, being situated below Castle Hill House at a place formerly known as 'St Michael's Green'. High above Torbay the chapel of St Michael on Chapel Hill, in 1960 at least, was clearly visible from southern parts of the Bay and still stands as an ancient monument.[33] It

Figure 1. Torre Chapel. DRO Reference: 564M/6/64.
Reproduced courtesy of Devon Record Office.

is a single-celled, stone-roofed chapel, probably of fourteenth-century date.[34] George Oliver suggested that a hermit might have occupied the west end.[35] An engraving of Torre Abbey dated 1662 identifies St Marie's Chapel, perhaps erroneously.[36] In 1822, the Lysons brothers (one a clergyman, the other keeper of the king's records), referred to it as St Michael.[37] Reverend John Swete illustrated the chapel in 1793 (Figure 1).

He noted that it 'hath never been desecrated, or even applied to the uses of the reformed church it hath not infrequently been visited by the Roman Catholic crews of ships'.[38] This custom continued to the late nineteenth century.[39]

Also on the south coast on high ground at Exmouth and Kingswear two chapels dedicated to the Holy Trinity served as conspicuous landmarks. That at Exmouth, first mentioned in 1412, stood on Chapel Hill to the north east of Beacon Place. Commanding the entrance to the Exe, the former chapel was sited as a landmark, lookout point and chapel of ease, rebuilt as a church in the eighteenth, nineteenth and early twentieth centuries and still serving as a coastal landmark.[40] On the Kingswear side of Dartmouth Haven, John Leland (in travels authorised by Henry VIII to search the libraries of monasteries and colleges for ancient books between 1538 and 1543) noticed a chapel on 'a great hilly point caullid Doune', half a mile farther in to the sea than the west point of the haven.[41] An early Tudor coastal map shows the ruined tower of a chapel (Figure 2).

Saxton's map of 1575, Speed's of 1610 and Camden's of 1695 name Trinity Chapel, Trinity being the name adopted by the authority for lighthouses and pilotage (see note 3).[42] The location shown on the later maps corresponds approximately with two fields named Lower and Higher Chapel Park on the Tithe Apportionment and Map of Brixham, east of Coleton Farm.[43] Members of the Fishacre family held the manor of Coleton between 1285 and 1346; in the thirteenth century, Prior Nicholas of Totnes granted a chantry in the chapel of Martin of Coleton, presumably Martin Fishacre who held Coleton in 1294.[44] Just south of Coleton Farm buildings near the site of the former manor house, part of the wall of the chapel is believed to remain – presumably the one noted by Leland. It was probably not at the site of the nearby Admiralty signal station of 1800 and the radar station of 1939–1945 as Percy Russell suggested. The chapel would

Figure 2. Early Tudor coastal map showing entrance to the river
Dart and chapel on Kingswear side (Lysons, i, p. 51).
Reproduced courtesy of Westcountry Studies Library, Devon Libraries.

have been clearly visible to seafarers, perhaps used as a landmark until the Day Beacon was built in 1864 on a more conspicuous site.[45]

Another conspicuous site, Prawle Point in Chivelstone parish, is a former Lloyd's signal station and Admiralty Coast Guard station, now manned by National Coastwatch Institution volunteers. Hoskins and others assumed that the chapel of St Brendon at *Southpralle*, licensed in 1421 and 1425, was situated here.[46] However, Milles' questionnaire of 1755-6 recorded a ruined chapel at East Prawle at a place called Chapel Green, converted by that time to dwelling houses, and the Tithe Apportionment and Map for Chivelstone of *c*.1840 shows three adjoining fields with 'Chapel' names on the south-west edge of the village.[47] According to local tradition, the chapel was at the site of cottages adjoining the north sides of two of the 'Chapel' fields. A building here would not have been visible to seafarers as would be expected of a chapel dedicated to St Brendan 'The Navigator', unless Prawle Point itself obviated the need for a conspicuous chapel. Research indicates that the chapel was founded close to the time of the first licence, and that it served as a chapel of ease for a growing community in East Prawle of farmers and fishermen.[48]

Other chapels on the south coast served as chapels of ease for fishermen, perhaps also for taking bearings, and as landmarks for those sailing along the coast. They included Revelstoke and Sidmouth, both dedicated to St Peter, a fisherman and leader of the apostles.[49] The chapel at Revelstoke (Noss Mayo) was first mentioned between 1224 and 1244 as a chapelry of Yealmpton and by name in 1269; it appears to incorporate part of an Anglo-Saxon cross, suggesting a much earlier history (Figure 3).[50]

Figure 3. Part of an Anglo-Saxon Cross incorporated into the fabric of a former chapel at Revelstoke? Photograph: Matthew James.

By around 1432 it was a chapel of ease for fishermen and labourers, who petitioned for the right of burial to avoid funeral journeys to the mother church of Yealmpton because – apart from the tides, danger-ous river Yealm and fear of attack from the King's enemies – they could not afford, and neither could the general economy sustain, such long absences from work.[51] Sidmouth, according to G.H. Gibbens, had before the time of Edward III (1327–1377) become a moderate port, but the question of its location later gave rise to arguments. The matter was settled by the finding of a document of 1322, concerning a dispute over the boundary of Sidmouth and Salcombe Regis when six men from the priory of Otterton appeared for Sidmouth and six from the chapter of Exeter for Salcombe Regis, as recorded by Oliver. They used as a starting point for their measurements the 'Chapel of the Blessed Peter'.[52] Richard Polwhele, a clergyman, drew attention to a house near the beach known by an anchor sign and said to have been a chapel of ease dependent on Otterton Priory. The thick walls and doorway arch were of stone; human bones had been dug there.[53] A tablet identifies part of its walls, incorporated into the café near the sea on the west side of Church Street (see Plate 8). That fishing took place at Sidmouth by the mid sixteenth century is known from Leland.[54]

Fishing was clearly important along the South Devon coast where Harold Fox described the transition from early cellar settlements to the fishing villages of the fifteenth century.[55] Hallsands, on the coast of Stokenham manor, had been a watching place for fish as early as the fourteenth century. Fox quoted from the Stokenham custumals of about 1346, which decreed that Joanna, the widow of Gervase, 'shall sit upon the seashore at *le Hole* [from 2 February until the second Tuesday after Easter] expecting the coming of the mullet and, with the men of Frittiscombe, she will catch the said fish and they shall have two-thirds and the lord one-third'.[56] In 1505–6, an indulgence was granted to the chapel of St Mary of *Stert* in Stokenham parish; and in 1540 licence to celebrate in the chapel of St Mary *de holisande* (Hallsand).[57] Hallsands and Start are so close that these chapels were probably one and the same. Fox suggested that the chapel would have been built around the time of the indulgence and thereafter a permanently occupied village developed.[58] The chapel was still used in 1547, when the churchwardens of Stokenham were to pay 12d for a chapel and associated building near Hallsands; but its use in about 1559 is questionable when 'Thomas Gyffey who held a building called Halsande Chapel is dead; his widow is admitted to the premises'. Almost two hundred years later it was a ruin, its site unidentified.[59]

Fox also found that on the North Devon coast in the 1340s there was a stall 'next to the strand at Appledore' where fish was almost certainly sold and perhaps salt as well. Even before fishing villages were established, there is evidence during the fourteenth and fifteenth centuries for migration towards the coast, including from Hartland to Northam, the parish to which the minor port of Appledore belonged.[60] A fair dedicated to St John the Baptist had been held in the parish since 1252. In 1400, Bishop Stafford licensed a chapel at Northam dedicated to St John, perhaps that at Appledore, desecrated and in ruin by the mid eighteenth century.[61] On Benjamin Donn's map of 1765, an unused chapel is shown at Northam Burrows at the north east point at Appledore, on the curve of the river (see Plate 9).[62] The quays for fishing were post-Reformation at Hartland, Clovelly and Bucks Mills.[63] There is less medieval evidence of fishing on the coast of North Devon than on the south, probably because the coastline is shorter but more especially because of the dangerous rocks.

On the rocky Atlantic coast south of Hartland Quay is St Catherine's Point where stood the former chapel of St Catherine.[64] The dedication is popular for chapels on hills near the sea; according to tradition, the body of St Catherine of Alexandria was miraculously translated to Mount Sinai in the ninth century.[65] Tiles of fourteenth or fifteenth century date were discovered on the site in the nineteenth century.[66] Unlike several medieval chapels at Hartland, St Catherine's is omitted in the bishop's registers and Hartland Abbey records. It might have been the same as St Michael at Kernstone licensed in 1400, although that could have been a domestic chapel.[67] On the south coast, the dangerous passage across Wembury Bay was described and 'Church Ledge' or 'Blackstone Rocks' illustrated by Montagu Evans (Figure 4).[68]

The church of Wembury, first mentioned in 1335 as a chapelry of Plympton Priory, stands alone on the edge of the cliff and has a 'striking' fourteenth-century tower.[69] It is still an important landmark for the avoidance of the above-mentioned rocks.[70]

Other chapels guarded against a different kind of danger and helped to defend the vulnerable shores of the south coast, as at Teignmouth where the French burnt part of the town in 1340. St Michael's at East Teignmouth, situated directly above the beach, had a defensive as well as religious appearance (Figure 5).[71]

First mentioned in a boundary charter of 1044 as a church, by 1282 it was a chapel dependent on Dawlish parish church.[72] The tower of St James in Teignmouth, a chapel before 1275, was also supposedly part of the town defences.[73] The Hundred Years War against the French

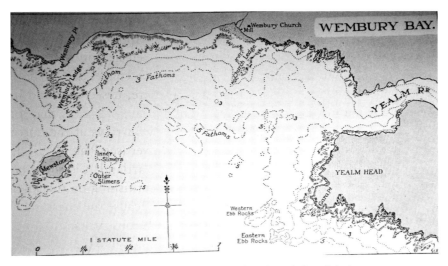

Figure 4. Wembury, showing church and church ledge.
From H. Montague Evans, see note 68.
Reproduced courtesy of The Devonshire Association.

continued from 1337, with intermissions, until 1453.[74] Edward III, who died in 1377, ordered special measures for the defence of the strategic port of Dartmouth against attack from the sea, but it was not until 1388 that John Hawley began the building of a *fortalice* at the entrance to the harbour and the tower of Dartmouth Castle was not begun until 1481. The chapel of St Petroc, said in 1332 to have been a building 'from antiquity', probably served as a watch place even then.[75] Strife was evident when, in 1427, a sea captain of Dartmouth offered up in the chapel the standard with the arms of the king of Scotland, that he had plundered from a Scottish ship off the French coast.[76] The Church supported the chapel's construction, repair and maintenance by granting an indulgence in 1438, before the castle was built.[77] Both still mark the entrance to Dartmouth harbour (see Plate 10).[78]

At Exmouth there was strife of a more local nature, concerning a ferry from *Pratteshide* to Starcross. Robin Bush noted that the mayor and corporation of Exeter, who possessed all rights over the river estuary, moved the ferry site here after a dispute in 1267 (ending in their favour) with the abbot of Sherborne, who owned Littleham and all rights appertaining to that ferry (and was thereafter granted free

Figure 5. St Michael Teignmouth, from 'A History of Teignmouth', see note 71.

transport). Bush described the location of the quay and the passage-house as west of Glenorchy chapel, about two-thirds of a mile from high water mark. In 1329, licence was granted for a chapel at *Pratteshide*, and in 1381 for that of St Margaret at Exmouth, almost certainly one and the same and later converted to domestic use, at the junction of Chapel and Margaret Streets.[79] Chapels at ferry points were important marks for safe passage for the ferryman and for travellers over land for prayers for safety or thanksgiving, together with offerings to help fund the ferry service. On the north coast, St Anne's chapel near the south point of Braunton Burrows marked the crossing of the estuary to Appledore. It is first identified on Saxton's map of 1575, that also appears to show the chapel at Appledore; both are shown on Donn's map (Plate 9).[80] By 1755–6 there were small remains yet it must have had a dual role in public service, marking a channel for navigation and being situated at the end of a ferry since, by the early nineteenth century, two lighthouses had been erected nearby for the security of coastal mariners and those crossing the Barnstaple bar in the Taw estuary.[81] Coulter quoted notes about a linhay constructed from remains of the old chapel incorporating in its west wall two 'slit' windows and a sandstone arch.[82]

The building remains at Ifracombe where Bishop Veysey himself confirmed in 1522 that vessels were guided into safe port by the light on St Nicholas's chapel.[83] Its lantern still leads mariners (Figure 6).[84]

The chapel was first mentioned early in 1416; in 1436, Bishop Lacy granted indulgences to pilgrims and benefactors and, in 1439, licence for services in St Nicholas *supra portum maris*.[85] In 1522, Bishop Veysey granted another indulgence, thus emphasising the official support of the Church. He verified the social use of the chapel, referring to its light shining at night year by year throughout the winter like a star, guiding vessels into the safety of the port.[86] St Nicholas, Bishop of Myra in the fourth century, is one of the patron saints of sailors and travellers.[87] On the south coast, the chapel of St Nicholas at Ringmore on the west side of the river Teign dates from the thirteenth century and has a Norman font. In 1445 the rector of Haccombe made a bequest for keeping a light there.[88] Near the chapel is a dwelling called 'The Hermitage'. According to tradition, a hermit tended the light to mark the entrance to the Teign.[89] Medieval mariners would have been guided into port at Plymouth by landmarks including a chapel on St Nicholas Island, now known as Drake's Island. The Close Rolls of 1396 recorded 'St Nicholas' island, and a Plymouth record of 1573 mentioned *Sent Nicholas Ilond*, the assumption being that the island

Figure 6. St Nicholas Chapel Ilfracombe. Photograph: Matthew James.

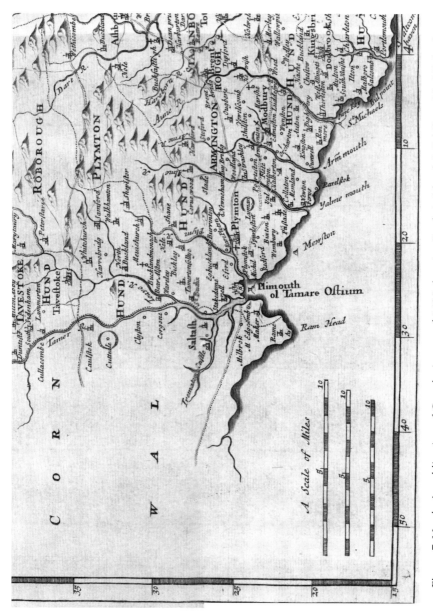

Figure 7. Norden's publication of Camden's map of 1695 showing Drake's Island (Michil) and St Michael on Burgh Island. Reproduced courtesy of Westcountry Studies Library, Devon Libraries.

was named on account of the dedication of its chapel.[90] Confusion arises because Lysons quoted references to the Island of St Nicholas and chapel of St Michael: firstly, a letter dated 28 March 1548 to the mayor of Plymouth and his brethren, 'mervelinge of their unwillingness to proceede in the fortifyinge of St Michaelles chapelle to be made a bulwarke . . .' (indicating reluctance to deface their chapel after the Reformation); and secondly, Camden's map (1695) where the island seems to be named *Michil* (Figure 7).[91]

Lysons reproduced an early Tudor map of Plymouth showing St Nicholas Island surmounted by the chapel before it was fortified against the French (Figure 8).[92]

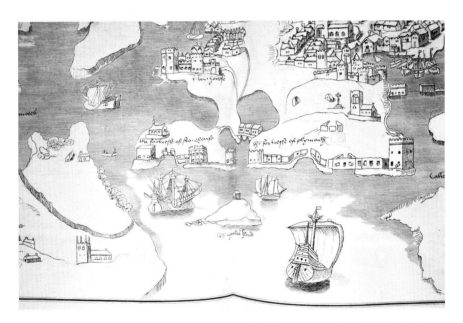

Figure 8. Early Tudor coastal map showing St Nicholas Island, and St Katherine, Plymouth (Lysons, i, opposite p. 399).

The island is shown on Greenvile Collins' charts of 1693 and is still used as a landmark.[93] Further into the port stood the chapel of St. Katherine on the Hoe on its elevated site, mentioned in licences to celebrate in 1370–1, 1375, 1381 and 1388.[94] By 1413, St Katherine's chapel, 'built for God's honour and commonly attended by large numbers of people', had become dilapidated; Bishop Stafford granted an indulgence, extended over five years, to the faithful who should contribute to its repair.[95] Bishop Lacy granted another indulgence in 1425, this time widening it to visitors for devotion or pilgrimage, with the customary stipulation 'that they be penitent and have confessed their sins'.[96] In 1511–12 a tile was 'broken with the gunne'; for its repair the corporation of Plymouth, not the Church, paid a hermit 4d.[97] The significance of the chapel of St Katherine on the Hoe can be inferred from these references and the illustration of it with a cross nearby on the early Tudor coastal map (Figure 8).[98] The building was replaced on a different site in 1668 and light beacons now guide seafarers, including one on the Hoe.[99]

Examples have shown that, through donations for indulgences for remission of penance, pilgrimages and the cults of saints, the Church supported medieval chapels on coastal sites that served the seafaring community. Anecdotal glimpses of economic hardship, disputes between different groups of people and external threat reveal issues recognisable today. Despite changes at the Reformation, it has been shown that some former medieval chapels, or their sites, still serve as landmarks for seafarers. If not altogether surprising since the coastline has changed little, it does demonstrate that medieval seafarers were astute in their positioning of landmarks. Their continued use also emphasises the significance of the role of the Church in medieval society in this particular branch of public service.

Acknowledgements

Thanks to my husband Matthew for producing the illustrations and accompanying me on site visits. Thanks also to staff at the Devon Record Office and Westcountry Studies Library, Exeter, for their continuing help and for giving permission to use copyright material. Local people who kindly helped in the identification of sites have been acknowledged in the appropriate endnotes. Thanks are also due to a resident of Turnchapel who directed us to the site of St Anne's, and to Mrs Jean Trevaskus for helpful discussion about the location of the former medieval chapel of St Lawrence at Stonehouse, Plymouth (both chapels are listed in the Appendix).

Notes and References

1. Orme 1988, p. 16; Orme 1992, pp. 152, 154-6.
2. James 1997, pp. 135-149.

3. London, Guildhall Library, Aldermanbury, Keeper of Manuscripts leaflet, 'Records of the Corporation of Trinity House'.
4. Cross 1997, pp. 829, 830, 1073, 1007, 1008; Koenigsberger and Mosse 1968, p. 117.
5. Frere and Kennedy 1910, pp. 5-6, 37-9.
6   James 1997, pp. 242-3.
7. Powicke, Whitelock, Brett and Brooke 1981, i, 97-8, 210, 217, 390.
8. Powicke and Cheney 1981, I, ii, 676, 680; II, i, 766, 2 vols, (by the Canons of the Legatine Council at St Paul's, London, 1268).
9. Powicke and Cheney, II, i, p. 1005.
10. James 1997, pp. 26-59.
11. These also included chapels on inland hills or beacon sites; fords, bridges and main roads; marking boundaries of towns, estates or parishes; and near wells for water supply, baptism or healing.
12. Waters 1958, pp. 10-12, 435.
13. Clay 1914, p. 50; Colgrave and Mynors 1969, 434-7.
14. Thomas 1992, pp. 43-45.
15. Orme 1996, p. 179; Hingeston-Randolph 1892, p. 232; Blackwell 1960, pp. 89, 90, 92.
16. Westcote 1845, p. 343; Russell 1955, p. 292; Coulter 1993, p. 48.
17. Hoskins 1954b, pp. 101-2. The chapel site is below the brow of the hill so it is unlikely that the cliffs at Croyde would have been visible, unless from a tower.
18. Finberg 1947, p. 361; Finberg 1951, p. 21.
19. Orme 1996, p. 126.
20. Cherry and Pevsner 1989, p. 123; Oxford, Bodleian Library, MSS Milles, 22754-5 MSS Top. Devon, 'Queries for the County of Devon', b.1. 1.
21. Crowley 1954, pp. 166-172.
22. Coulter 1993, pp. 33, 71 n.
23. Hoskins 1954b, p. 102; Orme 1996, pp. 126, 179.
24. Orme 1996, p. 115; Pevsner 1951, p. 191.
25. Orme 1996, p. 33.
26. Cherry and Pevsner 1989, pp. 208-9.
27. Coulter 1993, pp. 25-6.
28. Dunstan 1963, i, 300.
29. Milles, MSS Top. Devon, b.1-2, b.1, 82; Chanter 1908, p. 9.
30. Chanter 1908, p. 9.
31. WCSL, LM B/PLY/1720/COL, Collins, Greenvile 1693 *Great Britain's Coasting Pilot* 'Coast of Devon from Newton Ferry [*sic*] to Exmouth; Hingeston-Randolph 1886, pp. 403-4; Coles, 1971, pp. 135-6; see also Figure 7.
32. Dunstan 1963, i, 185; Lysons 1822, p. 445; Milles, MSS Top. Devon b.2, 157. Thanks to Mr Andrew Webb of Castle Hill House and Mrs

Barbara Softly, local historian, for information and for helping to identify the site.

33. Russell 1960, p. 13; Fox, A. 1952, p. 240.
34. Exeter, County Hall, Property Department, HER, SX96NW – 014.
35. Oliver 1846, p. 170.
36. HER, SX96NW-014; White 1878, engraving facing page 32, p. 85.
37. Lysons 1822, p. 525.
38. DRO, Revd John Swete, 564M/6/64, 72 (1793); 564 M/F 4, vol. 6, 63-67.
39. Russell 1960, p. 13, also Figure 4, p. 51; Page 1895, p. 366.
40. Hingeston-Randolph 1886, p. 100; Bush 1978, p. 96; Cherry and Pevsner 1989, p. 443; *Channel Pilot* 1984, p. 133.
41. Smith 1906-10, i, part iii, pp. ix, 223.
42. Lysons, i, p. 51; Exeter University: Rare Books, Constable maps 11, Christopher Saxton's map of Devonshire (*c*.1575); WCSL, OM WES, Speed, John 1610, Map of Devonshire, Morden, Robert 1695, The County Maps from William Camden's, *Britannia: Devonshire*.
43. DRO, Tithe Apportionment and Map (TA and M) (*c*.1840), Brixham: Coleton Farm, 232 Lower Chapel Park, 270 Higher Chapel Park.
44. Reichel 1908, pp. 110-137, p. 126; Watkin 1911, pp. 164-5.
45. Thanks to the farmer at Coleton, who does not wish to be acknowledged personally, for helpful discussion and for giving permission to visit the site; Russell and Yorke 1953, pp. 73-4; Russell 1955, p. 295 .
46. Dunstan 1963, i, 34, 144; Hoskins 1954a, pp. 12, 222, 365; Russell 1955, p. 294; Born 1986, p. 23.
47. MSS Milles, Top. Devon, b.1, 136; DRO, TA and M (*c*.1840), Chivelstone.
48. James 2009, pp. 136-147.
49. Farmer 1987, p. 344.
50. Hingeston-Randolph 1889, pp. 6 and 193; James 1997, p. 13, Plate 1.
51. Dunstan 1971, iv, 314-8.
52. Gibbens 1950, p. 222; Oliver, *Monasticon, Additional Supplement*, p. 22.
53. Polwhele 1793-1806, ii, p. 235.
54. Smith, i, p. 243; 80.
55. Fox, H. 2001, pp. 145-175.
56. Fox, H. 2001, pp. 123, 129-30, 136, 149.
57. DRO, Chanter XIII, The Register of Bishop Hugh Oldham 1504–1519, f.139; Chanter XV, The Register of Bishop John Veysey 1519–1551, f. 84.
58. Fox, H. 2001, p. 149.
59. Roberts 1980, p. 9; personal correspondence from the late Dr Harold Fox, reference to: DRO, Cary MSS, Court of Sept., 26 Eliz. Stokenham Manor; Court Roll printed in Roberts 1984; Milles, MSS Top. Devon,

b.2, 165; the TA and M for Stokenham name no 'Chapel' fields at Hallsands or Start Point that would have indicated the chapel's location.

60. Fox, H. 2001, pp. 89, 162.
61. Orme 1996, p. 187; Hingeston-Randolph 1886, p. 265; Milles, MSS Top. Devon, b.2, 78.
62. Donn 1765, sheet 1b.
63. Fox, H. 2001, p. 16.
64. Hoskins 1954a, Plate 22; HER, SS22NW/2.
65. Farmer 1987, p. 77.
66. Chope 1940, p. 7; Gregory 1949, p. 14 (booklet).
67. Oliver 1846, p. 205; HER, SS22SW/5.
68. Evans 1909, pp. 264-5.
69. Hingeston-Randolph 1894-99, ii, 775-6; Hoskins 1954a, p. 512.
70. Coles 1971, pp. 140-2; *Channel Pilot* 1984, p. 112; the medieval dedication is not known, Orme 1996, p. 214.
71. DRO, MSS, Palmer, F.W, Morton (*c*.1919), compiler, A History of Teignmouth, comprising 'Notes on Old Teignmouth', by H. Parry, p. 94.
72. ECA, archives of the Dean and Chapter, 2526, transcribed by Hooke 1994, pp. 203-5; Hingeston-Randolph 1889, pp. 323, 352; Davidson 1881, pp. 114-6, illustration p. 15; Lake 1890, p. 113.
73. Hingeston-Randolph 1889, p. 213; Cherry and Pevsner 1989, p. 796.
74. Koenigsberger 1987, p. 304.
75. Hoskins 1954a, p. 385; Hingeston-Randolph 1894–99, ii, 653.
76. Gardiner 1976, pp. 26-7.
77. Dunstan 1966, ii, 107.
78. Coles (1971), illustration p. 129; *Channel Pilot* 1984, p. 122.
79. Bush 1966, pp. 72-3; Bush 1978, p. 95; Hingeston-Randolph 1894–99, i, 508; Hingeston-Randolph 1901–06, i, 453; Reichel 1902, pp. 716-7, noting that the name of Exmouth is not used for *Pratteshide* before 1348.
80. WCSL, OM WES, Saxton, Christopher *c*.1575, Map of Devonshire; Donn 1765, sheet 1b.
81. Milles, MSS Top. Devon, b.1, 82; Lysons, ii, p. 66.
82. Hoskins 1954a, p. 346; Coulter 1993, pp. 26-8.
83. DRO, Chanter XV, f. 13.
84. HER, SS54NW/5: D'Oliveira and Featherstone 1995, p. 555.
85. Hingeston Randolph, (1886), p. 140; Dunstan 1966, ii, 25, 146.
86. Chanter, XV, f. 13.
87. Hall 1974, p. 223.
88. Cherry and Pevsner 1989, p. 797; Dunstan 1971, iv, 48-50, although entered under Ringmore, the reference to nearby Haccombe surely indicates Ringmore at Shaldon, not the parish of Ringmore.
89. Russell 1955, p. 295.

90. Gover, Mawer and Stenton 1931–2, vol. i, p. 236, quoting Close Rolls, unprinted (TNA).
91. WCSL, OM WES, *The County Maps from William Camden's Britannia, 1695: Devonshire.*
92. Lysons 1822, i, opposite p. 399; Russell 1955, p. 274; Woodward 1991, p. 4.
93. WCSL, LM B/PLY/1720/COL: Collins, *Great Britain's Coasting Pilot* 'A new and correct large draught of Plymouth Sound Catt-Water and Ham-Owse, 1693, 1720 edn; Coles 1971, p. 147.
94. Hingeston-Randolph 1901, i, pp. 238, 362, 450; 1906, ii, p. 659.
95. Hingeston-Randolph (1886), p. 295.
96. Dunstan 1963, i, 107.
97. Worth 1882, (quoting accounts of the receivers of the borough of Plymouth), p. 610
98. Map reproduced by Lysons, i, opposite p. 399; Bill Horner considered, 1992, that it is probably mis-located on the map: HER, SX45SE/121.
99. Copeland 1947–8 and 1948–9, pp. 120-1; *Channel Pilot* 1984, p. 100.

Bibliography

Blackwell, A.E. (1960) 'Lundy's Ecclesiastical History', *DAT*, 92, pp. 88-100.

Born, A. (1986) *A History of Kingsbridge and Salcombe*, Chichester: Phillimore.

Bush, R. (1978) *The Book of Exmouth*, Buckingham: Barracuda Books.

Bush, R.J.E. (1966) 'The Origins of Exmouth', *DAT*, 98, pp. 71-4.

Channel Pilot (1984) (revised edn) published by the Hydrographer of the Navy.

Chanter, J.F. (1908) *The Church of St Brannock, Braunton*, Exeter: James Townsend.

Cherry, B., and Pevsner, N. (1989) *The Buildings of England: Devon*, (2nd edn), Harmondsworth: Penguin.

Chope, R. Pearse (1940) *The Book of Hartland*, Torquay: The Devonshire Press.

Clay, R.M. (1914) *The Hermits and Anchorites of England*, London: Methuen and Co.

Coles, K.A. (1968) (repr. with present title 1971) *The Shell Pilot to the South Coast Harbours*, London: Faber.

Colgrave, B. and Mynors, R.A.B. (eds) (1969) *Bede's Ecclesiastical History of the English People*, Oxford: Clarendon Press.

Copeland, G.W. (1947–8 and 1948–9) 'Presidential Address', *Transactions of the Plymouth Institution*, XXI, pp. 99-123.

Coulter, J. (1993) *The Ancient Chapels of North Devon*, Barnstaple: J. Coulter.

Cross, F.L. (ed.) (1997) *The Oxford Dictionary of the Christian Church*, (3rd edn), Livingstone, E.A., Oxford: Oxford University Press.

Crowley, J.M. (1954) 'Notes on the Ruined Chapel of St Helen at Croyde, in the Parish of Georgeham', *DAT*, 86, pp. 166-172.

Davidson, J. Bridge (1881) 'On the Early History of Dawlish', *DAT*, 13, pp. 106-30.

D'Oliveira, B. and Featherstone, N.L. (eds) (1995) *The Macmillan and Silk Cut Nautical Almanac, incorporating Reed's*, held at Exeter, County Hall, Property Department, 'Historic Environment Record', S54NW/5.

Donn, B. (1795) *A Map of the County of Devon with the City and County of Exeter.*

Dunstan, G.R. (ed.) (1963–72) *The Register of Edmund Lacy, Bishop of Exeter . . . (1420–1455)*, Registrum Commune, 5 vols, (Canterbury and York Society 60; 61; 62; 63; 66) DCRS, new series, 7; 10; 13; 16; 18, Torquay: The Devon Press Ltd.

Evans, M.H. (1909) 'Wembury: its bay, church and parish', *DAT*, 41, pp. 264-289.

Farmer, D.H. (1987) *The Oxford Dictionary of Saints*, (2nd edn), Oxford: Oxford University Press.

Finberg, H.P.R. (1947) 'Some Early Tavistock Charters', *The English Historical Review*, LXII, pp. 352-377.

Finberg, H.P.R. (1951) *Tavistock Abbey*, Cambridge: Cambridge University Press.

Fox, A. (1952) '21st Report on Ancient Monuments', *DAT*, 84, p. 240.

Fox, H. (2001) *The Evolution of the Fishing Village: landscape and society along the South Devon coast, 1086–1550*, Oxford: Leopards Head Press.

Frere, W.H. and Kennedy, W. McC. (1910) *Visitation Articles and Injunctions of the Period of the Reformation, 1536-1558*, London: Longman, Green and Co.

Gardiner, D.M. (1976) (ed.) *A Calendar of Early Chancery Proceedings relating to West Country Shipping 1388-1493*, DCRS, New Series, 21.

Gibbens, G.H. (1950) 'A Short History of Sidmouth', *DAT*, 82, pp. 217-224.

Gover, J.E.B., Mawer, A. and Stenton, F.M. (1931–2) *The Place-Names of Devon*, 2 vols, viii, Nottingham: English Place-Name Society, ix, Cambridge: Cambridge University Press.

Gregory, I.L. (1949) *Hartland: coast and quay*, booklet.

Hall, J. (1974) *Dictionary of Subjects and Symbols in Art*, London: J. Murray.

Hingeston-Randolph, F.C. (ed.) (1889) *The Registers of Walter Bronescombe*

(1257–1280), and Peter Quinel (1280–1291), Bishops of Exeter, London: G. Bell and Sons.

Hingeston-Randolph, F.C. (ed.) (1892) *The Register of Walter de Stapeldon, Bishop of Exeter (1307–1326)* London: G. Bell.

Hingeston-Randolph, F.C. (ed.) (1894–99), *The Register of John de Grandisson, Bishop of Exeter (1327–1369)*, 3 vols, London: G. Bell.

Hingeston-Randolph, F.C. (ed.) (1901–06) *The Register of Thomas Brantingham, Bishop of Exeter (1370–1394)* 2 vols, London: G. Bell.

Hingeston-Randolph, F.C. (ed.) (1886) *The Register of Edmund Stafford, Bishop of Exeter (1395–1419)*, London: G. Bell.

Hooke, D. (ed.) (1994) *Pre-Conquest Charter Bounds of Devon and Cornwall*, Exeter Cathedral Archives, archives of the Dean and Chapter, 2526.

Hoskins, W.G. (1954a) (1972 edn) *Devon*, Newton Abbot: David and Charles.

Hoskins, W.G. (1954b) 'Devon Parish Notes', *DCNQ*, 26, pp. 101-2.

James, J. (1997) 'The Medieval Chapels of Devon', unpublished MPhil dissertation, University of Exeter.

James, J. (2009) 'The Medieval Chapel at Prawle, formerly in the Manor and Parish of Stokenham, Devon', *DCNQ*, vol. XL-Part V, pp. 136-147.

Koenigsberger, H.G. and Mosse, G.L. (1968) *A General History of Europe in the Sixteenth Century*, London: Longman.

Koenigsberger, H.G. (1987) *Medieval Europe 400–1500*, Harlow: Longman.

Lake, W.C. (1890) 'The Origin of the Streets of Teignmouth', *DAT*, 22, pp. 111-28.

Lysons, D. and Lysons, S. (1822) M*agna Britannia*, vol. vi, *Topographical and Historical Account of Devonshire*, 2 vols, [online] Available at <http://www.british-history.ac.uk> (Accessed)

Oliver, G. (1846) *Monasticon Diocesis Exoniensis* with supplement, Exeter: P.A. Hannaford.

Orme, N. (1988) 'Indulgences in the Diocese of Exeter 1100–1536', *DAT*, 120, pp. 15-32.

Orme, N. (1992) 'Indulgences in Medieval Cornwall', *Journal of the Royal Institute of Cornwall*, New series II, vol. i, part 2, pp. 149-70.

Orme, N. (1996) *English Church Dedications*, Exeter: University of Exeter Press.

Page, J.L.W. (1895) *The Coasts of Devon and Lundy Island*, London: Horace Cox.

Pevsner, N. (1951) *The Buildings of England: Cornwall*, Harmondsworth: Penguin Books.

Polwhele, R. (1793–1806) *The History of Devonshire*, 3 vols, Exeter: Trewman and Co.

Powicke, F.M. and Cheney, C.R., (eds) (1964), *Councils and Synods with*

Other Documents Relating to the English Church, II: 1205–1313, 2 vols, Part i, 1205–1313, Oxford: Clarendon Press.

Powicke, F.M., Whitelock, D., Brett M. and Brooke, C.N.L., (eds) (1981) *Councils and Synods with Other Documents Relating to the English Church, I: 871–1204*, 2 vols, Part ii, 1066–1204 Oxford: Clarendon Press.

Reichel, O.J. (1902), 'The Devonshire "Domesday" VI some notes on part I of "Domesday" identifications', *DAT*, 34, pp. 715-731.

Reichel, O.J. (1908), 'The Hundred of Haytor in the time of "Testa de Nevil" AD 1244', *DAT*, 40, pp. 110-137.

Roberts, W.A. (1980) *Stokenham Occasional Papers* 1, 'Queen Katherine's Rental: 1547', Kingsbridge: W.A. Roberts.

Roberts, W.A. (1984), Elizabethan Court Rolls of Stokenham Manor, Kingsbridge: W.A. Roberts.

Russell, P. and Yorke, G. (1953) 'Kingswear and Neighbourhood', *DAT*, 85, pp. 56-85.

Russell, P. (1955), 'Fire Beacons in Devon', *DAT*, 87, pp. 250-302.

Russell, P. (1960) *A History of Torquay*, Torquay Natural History Society.

Smith, L.T. (ed.) (1906–10) *The Itinerary of John Leland in or about the years 1535–1543*, 5 vols, London: Bell.

Thomas, C. (1992) 'Beacon Hill Re-Visited', *Annual Report of the Lundy Field Society*, 42, pp. 43-54.

Waters, D.W. (1958) *The Art of Navigation in England in Elizabethan and Early Stuart Times*, London: Hollis and Carter.

Watkin, H.R. (1911) 'The Foundation and Early History of Dartmouth and Kingswear Churches', *DAT*, 43, pp. 149-65.

Westcote, Thomas (1845) *Devonshire in 1630*.

White, J.T. (1878) *The History of Torquay*, Torquay: Printed at the Directory Office.

Whitelock, D., Brett, M. and Brooke, C.N.L. (eds) (1989) *Councils and Synods with Other Documents Relating to the English Church, I: 871–1204*, 2 vols.

Woodward, F.W. (1991) *Drake's Island*, Devon Archaeology, 5, Exeter: Exeter Archaeological Society.

Worth, R.N. (1882) 'Men and Manners in Tudor Plymouth', *DAT*, 14, pp. 603-630.

Appendix

Devon's Medieval Chapels as Coastal Landmarks

Civil parish	Name	Dedication	Site	Remains	OS reference
Abbotsham		St Helen	Hill	Tithe Map: Chapel Field	SS426283
Barnstaple		SS Mary and Nicholas	Harbour	None documented	SS557331
Beer			Coast	Church on site of chapel	SY229894
Bigbury	Burgh Island	St Michael	Island	Later ruin on site	SX646438
Braunton	Burrows	St Anne	Estuary	None on site	SS463331
Braunton		St Michael	Hill	Late Perpendicular ruin	SS491373
Chivelstone	East Prawle (not visible?)	St Brendon	High Ground	Tithe Map (T.M.): 3 'Chapel Park' fields	?SX779364
Dartmouth	Hardnesse	St Clare	Harbour	Dwellings on site	SX875514
Dartmouth	Clifton	St Petroc	Estuary	Church: Norman font	SX886503
Dartmouth		Trinity or St Saviour	Harbour	Church: early tower	SX877513
East Portlemouth			Estuary	T.M.: Chapel Park field	SX752388
Exmouth	Checkstone	St Saviour	Estuary	None found	
Exmouth	Beacon Hill	Holy Trinity	Hill	Rebuilt on site	SY002806
Exmouth	Pratteshide	St Margaret	Estuary	House demolished 1961	SY002809
Georgeham	Croyde	St Helen	Coast	14th-century remains	SS443389
Hartland	Kernstone	St Catherine	Cliff	14th- or 15th-century tiles.	?SS225241
Holbeton		St Anecorite	Coast	'St Anker' field; rock	?SX591472
Ilfracombe		St Nicholas	Harbour	Building remains	SS526479
Kingswear		St Thomas Martyr	Harbour	Church: medieval tower	SX882510
Lundy	Beacon Hill	St Mary then St Helen	Island	None documented	SS132442
Malborough	Soar		Coast	Steeple Cove	?SX705369
Malborough		St Peter	High Ground	Church: Norman font, 13th-c. tower arch	SX706397

Civil parish	Name	Dedication	Site	Remains	OS reference
Newton and Noss	Revelstoke	St Peter	Coast	Ruin	SX548475
Northam	Appledore	St John the Baptist	Estuary	T.M: Chapel Field T.M.: Chapel Plot	SS464306 SS460301
Plymouth	Drake's Island	St Nicholas or St Michael	Island	None documented	SX469528
Plymouth	Hoe	St Katherine	Harbour	None documented	SX480537
Plymouth	Stonehouse	St Lawrence	Harbour	Demolished	SX460535
Plymouth	Turnchapel	St Anne	Harbour	House on site	SX493525
Plymouth	Warren Point	Holy Trinity	Estuary	None documented	?SX45160-
Plymouth	St Budeaux	St Budeaux	High Ground	Remains in church	SX454592
Salcombe		St John the Baptist	Harbour	None found	SX740391
Sidbury	Castle Hill	St Michael	Hill	None found	SY131911
Sidmouth		St Peter	Coast	Part of wall exposed	SY126872
Stoke Fleming	Black Pole		Coast	T.M.: Chapel Down	SX859478
Stoke Fleming			Estuary	T.M.: Chapel Park	SX876509
Stokenham	Hallsands	St Mary	Coast	None found	
Stokenham	Start	St Mary	Coast	None found	
Stokenham	Torcross Point		Coast	T.M.: 'Chapel' field	SX823419
Teignmouth		St James	Estuary	Church: 13th-c. tower	SX939731
Teignmouth		St Michael	Coast	Church: Norman doorway	SX943730
Teignmouth	Ringmore	St Nicholas	Estuary	Chapel: Norman font	SX923723
Torbay	Coleton Fishacre	Trinity	Coast	Part of wall?	SX906509
Torbay	Ilsham Grange		Coast	Building remains	SX937642
Torbay	Torre	St Michael	Hill	Ancient monument	SX903650
Wembury			Coast	Church: 14th-c. tower	SX518485

A Chronology of Dartmouth's Members of Parliament

Eric Preston

Dartmouth's representation in Parliament has a long history. From 1298 until 1832 Dartmouth was a Parliamentary Borough entitled to elect two Members of Parliament. Following the 1832 Reform Act Dartmouth was restricted to one MP, until the constituency was abolished in 1868 (after the 1867 Reform Act). Since then the town has been included in a variety of larger constituencies, the most recent being Totnes. While little is known about most of the early Members for Dartmouth there have been several who became celebrities. More recent Members may be better known, and their Party allegiances have been recorded.

The earliest known reference to Dartmouth MPs is in 1298, soon after King Edward I's visit to Dartmouth in 1286 when he gave permission for the building of St Saviour's Church. The two members sent to the Parliament at York in April 1298 were known as 'John le Bakere' and 'William atte Fosse' (William at the Fosse) who was believed to be a smith.[1] This Parliament was one of the first to call for elected representatives of boroughs and counties; the first with such representation was Simon de Montfort's Parliament of January 1265. Before that only knights of each 'shire' were called by the King to meetings of the 'Curia Regis'. While most Parliaments were held at Westminster, a few were arranged elsewhere, including York, Shrewsbury, Oxford and Leicester. The journeys on horseback between Dartmouth and

York, or even Westminster, must have been uncomfortable and time-consuming in those days.

The next reference to MPs from 'Clifton Dartmouth' is in 1351 when Mayor, merchant and privateer William Smale, and lawyer Nicholas Whiting were the chosen members, the latter sitting simultaneously for Devonshire, Exeter and Dartmouth. William Smale had been Dartmouth Mayor in 1346, and probably helped to fund a chapel at St Petrox. Thereafter, in the records of members, the only significant gap occurs during and after the Wars of the Roses, between 1478 and 1529. The Dartmouth MPs up to 1868 were listed in 1911 by J.J. Alexander.[2] It is likely that members were chosen by the County Court in Exeter during the fourteenth and fifteenth centuries, and were not necessarily Dartmouth men. After 1689 however, they were chosen by the Mayor and Magistrates ('Masters'), together with the freemen of the town. They were usually lawyers or soldiers in these early days, and later merchants or county magnates. Parliaments were called by the King in most years, but only sat for a few weeks. Interestingly, in 1413 a law was passed requiring members to be resident in their own constituencies – this of course is no longer the case!

The most well-known of the early members was John Hawley (Plate 11), returned in 1390, 1393, 1394 and 1402, followed by his sons John and Thomas Hawley in 1410–1432. John Hawley (*c*.1340–1408) was a wealthy Dartmouth merchant and Mayor of Dartmouth fourteen times. He built the first fort at the entrance to the river Dart between 1388 and 1400, following orders from Edward III and Richard II, and helped to enlarge St Saviour's Church, where a fine brass shows him in full armour with his two wives (see Plate 11). During 1370–1390 he was active in the wars with France, using Richard II's licence as a privateer to 'attack and destroy the King's enemies' – to his own advantage as well as the King's.

In this respect he and his friends have been thought to be models for Chaucer's 'Schipman from Dertemouthe' in his Prologue to *The Canterbury Tales* (1373). Later he not only attacked French ships but also those of allies and neutrals, so straining relations with the new King Henry IV who instructed him to return merchandise wrongfully taken. Hawley did not comply and consequently in 1406 spent time in the Tower until he agreed to do so. However only two years earlier he had been a hero at Court after his victory over a Breton force of 2,000 men and 300 ships at the battle of Blackpool, near Stoke Fleming. The French force had tried to attack Dartmouth from the land by circumventing the river fortifications, which included a protective chain stretched across the Dart from Hawley's fort to a small fort on the other side.

Other Dartmouth mayors and MPs who acted as privateers, using licenses from the King to capture French and other ships during the Hundred Years War were William Smale (MP in 1351) and Robert Wenyngtone (MP in 1449). Both of these men added to Dartmouth's wealth by bringing in captured ships, although they sometimes evoked the King's displeasure by taking non-French ships that were not at war with England. Another well-known early Member for Dartmouth was Nicholas Bacon (1509–1579, MP from 1545–1553), later Elizabeth I's Chancellor, and father of Francis Bacon the essayist and philosopher. Nicholas Bacon was called to the bar in 1533, and as a leading Protestant was fortunate to survive through Queen Mary's reign. In 1558 he became Keeper of the Privy Seal having married Lord Burghley's sister-in-law, and in 1559 became Lord Chancellor.

The two members in Charles I's Long Parliament were Roger Mathew and John Upton, merchants of Dartmouth. Mathew sided at first with Parliament, along with most Dartmouth merchants, but later seems to have supported the King against Parliament, and therefore, in 1646 he was 'disabled' and replaced by Thomas Boone. The new member was a keen Parliamentarian who survived Colonel Pride's 'purge' of 1648 but refused to sit as one of Charles' judges. Upton and his successor Samuel Browne were moderate Parliamentarians, supporters of John Pym, but Browne was excluded by Colonel Pride from the Rump Parliament, probably considered politically unreliable. Thomas Boone (*c.*1609–1679, MP 1646–60) was a keen supporter of Oliver Cromwell and one of the only two Devon MPs allowed to sit in the Rump Parliament. From humble beginnings as a Dartmouth butcher's son he rose to become Cromwell's Ambassador to Russia, and in 1659 acted as a sequestrator of Royalist estates. He thus became wealthy and joined the gentry as Thomas Boone of Mount Boone mansion, Dartmouth. He only had one eye, but was said 'to see more clearly with that than did most of his colleagues with two eyes'. His refusal to act as one of Charles I's judges stood him in good stead after the Restoration, and his son Charles became MP (a Whig) in 1689.

After the Restoration in 1660 there was keen competition between the Whigs and the Tories, who were evenly balanced in Dartmouth, and many disputed elections. Between 1659 and 1722 there were no less than nine election petitions to Parliament by losing candidates, disputing the legality of the vote. The petitions against elected members were based on questions of who were qualified to vote, such as the few freemen, who were usually Government employees appointed by the Corporation. There was a great temptation to bribe the freemen or create more freemen as required, and results depended largely on the politics of the local landowners. Most were supporters of the Government at the time.

In 1689 the election of George Booth (Whig) was disputed by Joseph Herne (Tory) who succeeded in replacing him in November 1689. The House of Commons decided that the Dartmouth Mayor, John Whitrow had created twenty five new freemen to vote for Booth after the election writ was issued. From 1689 until 1722 the Tory Herne family were in control, and a number of petitions against them were rejected by the Tory Governments. In 1701 there were two rival mayors, Joseph Bully (Whig) and Thomas Floud (Tory), who each put forward rival MPs based on the vote of the mayor and some of the magistrates. A Tory Government decided in favour of Floud's nominees, Frederick and Nathaniel Herne! Surprisingly, the rules for election of a mayor were not clear: Bully nominated himself, while some of the masters nominated Floud. The rules for electing a mayor and for making freemen were clarified by a local agreement in 1706. Following a judgment at Exeter assizes and the intervention of the Town Clerk, only a majority of the magistrates could elect a mayor or make freemen.[4]

From 1722 to 1780 Dartmouth became a 'Treasury Borough', returning one member proposed by the Treasury and one by the Admiralty – and then nominated by the mayor and masters. Consequently Dartmouth members generally supported the government of the day, usually Whig at this time, and often accepted salaried government appointments necessitating by-elections.

The most distinguished of the Dartmouth members in this period was Richard Howe, later Admiral Earl Howe, KG (1726–1799), MP from 1757 to 1782 when he was called to the House of Lords. Howe had a long career in the Navy, with active service in the Seven

Years War, the American War of Independence and the French Revolutionary Wars. He was the son of the second Viscount Howe, Governor of Barbados, and Charlotte, half-sister of George I. This may have helped him to rise to post-captain in 1746 at the age of twenty, and later to the Admiralty as Treasurer of the Navy, First Lord of the Admiralty and Admiral of the Fleet. His sailors called him 'Black Dick', owing to his dark complexion. He helped to win the vital battle of Quiberon Bay (1759) and later took command at the 'Glorious First of June' victory 300 miles west of Brittany (1794). Finally in 1797 he was able to pacify the Spithead mutineers, thanks to the respect he had from the sailors. He was made a Knight of the Garter by the King in 1797, the first awarded for naval services, in spite of opposition from Government ministers.

From 1780 to 1832 the control of Dartmouth was shared mainly between the local Holdsworth and Bastard families. Between 1715 and 1830 a Holdsworth was Mayor for forty nine years, and if related families are included, for seventy six years. In 1780 Arthur Holdsworth arranged for Howe to be re-elected together with himself, defying the Whig Government as they both voted with the Opposition against various taxation and regulation Bills. Arthur's son, Arthur Howe Holdsworth (1781–1860) was MP from 1802 to 1820 and from

Figure 1. Richard Howe, MP 1757.
Reproduced by courtesy of Dartmouth Museum.

Figure 2. Arthur Howe Holdsworth.
Reproduced courtesy of Dartmouth Museum.

1829 to 1832. He was a merchant, prominent in the Newfoundland fishing trade, and he encouraged trade with Portugal, the Baltic and West Indies. He became wealthy thanks to his ability to levy tolls on all goods landed between Salcombe and Torbay. He and his family ran the Dartmouth Corporation and in 1809, in common with his Holdsworth ancestors, he was appointed Governor of Dartmouth Castle. Like many other boroughs at this time Dartmouth was a 'Rotten Borough' (it had parliamentary representatives elected by a very few voters, unlike other places such as Torquay with 15,000 voters but no MPs), and a 'Pocket Borough' (in the 'pocket' of one or two patrons). This all changed in 1832.

The 1832 Reform Act extended the franchise from about fifty to 300 in Dartmouth, and reduced the two members to one. The new voters voted against the old oligarchy, and consequently Sir John Seale of Mount Boone defeated the Holdsworths and sat as a Whig MP until his death in 1844. Later the seat changed allegiance between Whigs and Tories at each election until 1868. Notably one Whig member, James Caird was a maverick, and helped defeat both Palmerston's Whig Government and Lord Derby's Tory Government, before being

Figure 3. John Henry Seale MP 1832.
Reproduced courtesy of Dartmouth Museum.

voted out in 1859. Bribery and corruption still went on, but did not always succeed, as evidenced by the unseating in 1859 of Edward Schenley (Liberal) for bribing the freemen.

The 1867 Reform Act finally disenfranchised the Borough of Dartmouth, and in 1868 the Borough formed part of the new constituency of South Devon, one of three Devon seats which elected two MPs each. The South Devon MPs were all Conservatives, including Sir Massey Lopes, Bart, until this constituency was abolished in 1885. From 1885 until 1948 Dartmouth was part of the Torquay constituency; the only part that was west of the River Dart, returning one MP. (The other part of South Devon became the Totnes constituency.) With this arrangement there were alternating Conservative and Liberal members, generally following the national trend. The MP for Torquay from 1924 to 1948 was Charles Williams, Conservative.[5]

Then in 1948 the boundaries were again re-drawn and Dartmouth joined the Totnes constituency, leaving Torquay to cover the area east of the Dart. The Totnes MP from 1948–1955 was Ralph Rayner, Conservative, who had been MP for Totnes since 1935. From 1955 to 1983 Raymond Mawby, Conservative, was Totnes and thus Dartmouth's MP for twenty-eight years, the longest unbroken period that any Dartmouth member has served. Mr Mawby served as Assistant Postmaster-General from 1963–4.

In 1983 the Totnes seat was abolished and a new constituency of South Hams created. The MP elected was Anthony Steen, Conservative, who retained the seat throughout the rest of the Thatcher era from 1983 until 1997. Then the South Hams constituency was abolished again and Dartmouth became part of the Totnes constituency once more, as it still is. Mr Steen was MP for Totnes from 1997 to 2010, when he stood down after twenty seven years. Prior to the General Election in 2010, Totnes Conservative Party held a 'Primary' election by postal ballot of all registered electors to select a candidate – the one and only time that such an election has been held to date. The selected candidate was Sarah Wollaston, a general practitioner from Chagford, who was duly elected as MP for Totnes constituency on 6 May 2010.

This short history of Dartmouth's MPs illustrates not only the rich history of Dartmouth and its significance over the centuries in connection with national politics, but also the many twists and turns that parliamentary government has undergone. Dartmouth's MPs have seen, and sometimes suffered from, royal patronage, the French wars, civil war, party politics, democratic reforms of voting rights, boundary changes, and sadly, in the past much bribery and corruption. Nevertheless they have generally acquitted themselves well in representing Dartmouth's various interests over the years, including merchant shipping, ship-building, the Royal Navy, fishing, farming and, more recently, the environment and tourism.

Notes and References

1. Freeman 2007, p. 24.
2. Alexander 1911, pp. 350-370.
3. Connors 2008, p. 120.
4. Russell 1982. Gives details of change of rules for electing a mayor and making freemen in 1706, pp. 138-144.

5.　Wikipedia, 2009, Dartmouth (UK Parliament Constituency), South Devon (UK Parliamentary Constituency), Torquay (UK Parliament Constituency), Totnes (UK Parliament Constituency), South Hams (UK Parliament Constituency) [Online] Available at: <http://en.wikipedia.org/wiki/>. (Accessed 10 March 2009).

Bibliography

Alexander, J.J. (1911) 'Dartmouth as a Parliamentary Borough', *DAT*, 43, pp. 350-70.

Connors, M. (2008) *John Hawley, Merchant, Mayor and Privateer*, Dartmouth: Richard Webb.

Freeman, R. (2007 edn) *Dartmouth and its Neighbours: a history of the port and its people*, Dartmouth: Richard Webb.

Russell, P. (1982 edn) *Dartmouth, a History of the Port and Town*, Callington, Cornwall: Penwell Ltd.

Appendix

A List of Dartmouth's Members of Parliament

Year	Month	First Member	Second Member
		EDWARD I	
1298	April	John le Bakere	William atte Fosse
		EDWARD III	
1351	Feb	William Smale #	Nicholas Whytyng
1352	Jan	Nicholas Whytyng	William Smale #
1358	Feb	John Wyncaultone	John Henry
1360	May	John Wyncaultone	William Henry #
1361	Jan	John Wynkaultone	Nicholas Whytyng
1362	Oct	John Wynkaultone	John Hylle
1363	Oct	John Wyncaultone	John Clerke #
1365	Jan	John Astone	Thomas More
1366	May	John Potel	John Coplestone
1368	May	Richard Whitelegh	Giles Prideaux
1369	June	John Sampson	William Stabba
1370	Feb	John Pasford	??
1371	June	John Pasford	(only one member)
1372	June	John Copilstone	Robert Hulle, jun.
1373	Nov	John Clerk	William Henry
1377	Jan	Thomas Asshendene	John Brasyuter #
		RICHARD II	
1377	Oct	John Copleston	Thomas Reymond
1378	Oct	John Passe	William Caunton
1380	Jan	John Brasuter #	John Lecche
1381	Sept	Richard Henry #	John Lacche
1382	Oct	William Burlestone	John Lecche
1383	Feb	John Lecche	William Burlestone
1384	April	Richard Coplestone	William Ryke
	Nov	Thomas Assheldene	William Borlestone
1385	Oct	William Burlestone	Thomas Ayshendene
1386	Oct	Richard Whiteleghe	Robert ate More
1388	Feb	William Burlestone	John Lacche
	Sept	William Bast	Roger Skos
1389	Jan	Thomas Aysshenden	John Hawley #
1391	Nov	John Brasutere #	John Willeam
1393	Jan	John Hawley #	John Ellemede
1394	Jan	John Hawley #	William Damyet #
1395	Jan	John Bosoun	Edmund Arnalde
1397	Jan	John Bosone	William Glovere.

112

HENRY IV

1402	Sept	John Hawley #	Ralph North
1406	Feb	John Foxley	John White
1407	Oct	Henry Bremelere	John Pille
1410	Jan	John Hawley, jun.	Edmund Arnolde #
1411	Nov	John Hawley, jun.	John Corpe.

HENRY V

1413	May	John Hawley	John Corpe
1414	Nov	John Hawley	Edmunde Arnolde
1420	Dec	Thomas Asshendene	Walter Wodelonde
1421	May	John Hawley	Thomas Hawley
1421	Dec	John Burley	Henry Sadeller

HENRY VI

1422	Nov	John Hawley	Thomas Ayssheldone
1423	Oct	John Hawley	John Rede
1425	April	John Hawley	Thomas Lanoy
1426	Feb	John Gaynecote	William Notefelde
1427	Oct	John Hawley	John More #
1429	Sept	John Hawley	Thomas Ayssheldone
1431	Jan	John Hawley	Thomas Hawley
1432	May	John Hawley	Nicholas Stybbynge #
1433	July	Thomas Gille	Hugh Yone or Thomas Asshenden
1435	Oct	Thomas Gylle	John More #
1437	Jan	Thomas Ayssheldone	John Walshe #
1442	Jan	Thomas Gille, sen.	Nicholas Stebbynge #
1447	Feb	Thomas Gylle	Robert Steven #
1449	Feb	Nicholas Stybbinge #	Robert Wenyngtone #
	Nov	Robert Wenyngtone #	Thomas Gylle, sen.
1450	Nov	John Brussheforde #	Stephen Ussher
1453	Mar	Nicholas Stebbynge #	John Brussheforde #
1455	July	Thomas Gill, sen.	Nicholas Stebbynge #

EDWARD IV

1467	May	Thomas Gill	Thomas Gale #
1472	Oct	Thomas Gale #	Miles Metcalf
1478	Jan	Thomas Gale #	Thomas Grayston

HENRY VIII

1529	Oct	John Trevanyan #	William Hollande #
1545	Jan	Nicholas Bacon	John Ridgeway.

EDWARD VI

1553	Feb	Nicholas Adams	Gilbert Roope #

MARY

1553	Sept	Nicholas Adams	Nicholas Roope (?)
1554	Mar	Edmund Sture	Nicholas Adams
	Nov	John Peter	Nicholas Adams (?)
1555	Oct	Sir John St Leger	James Courteney
1558	Jan	George Huckmore(?)	Thomas Gourney.

ELIZABETH I

1562	Dec	Sir John More	John Lovell
1571	Mar	John Vaughan	Thomas Gourney #
1572	April	William Cardynall	Thomas Gourney #
	? *		William Lyster (vice Gourney dec.)
1584	Nov	Thomas Ridgeway	Hugh Vaughan
1586	Sept/Oct	Robert Petre	George Carey
1588	Oct	Roger Papworth	Richard Drew #
1593	Jan/Feb	Nicholas Hayman #	Thomas Holland
1601	Oct	John Treherne	William Bastard

JAMES I

1604	Feb	Thomas Holland	Thomas Gourney (jun.) #
1614	Mar	Thomas Howard	Thomas Gourney #
1620	Dec	William Nyell	Roger Mathew #
1624	Jan	William Plumleigh #	William Nyell
	? *		Roger Mathew # (vice Nyell)

CHARLES I

1625	Apr	John Upton	Roger Mathew #
1626	Jan	John Upton	Roger Mathew #
1628	Feb	John Upton	Roger Mathew #

From 1629–1640 no Parliament was summoned.

1640	Mar	John Upton (Parliament)	Andrew Voysey #
	Oct	Roger Mathew # (Royalist)	Samuel Browne (Parliament)
1646	April *	Thomas Boone (vice Mathew disabled) (Parliament)	
1648	Dec		Browne excluded by 'Pride's Purge'.

COMMONWEALTH

1654	June	Thomas Boone	(only one seat)
1656	Aug?	Edward Hopkins	(only one seat)
1657	*	(name missing) vice Hopkins dec.	
1659	Jan	Robert Thompson (?)	Col. John Clarke
	OR	Thomas Boone (probably)	Col. John Clarke (double return)

CHARLES II

1660	Mar	John Hale	John Frederick
1661	April	William Harbord	Thomas Southcote
1664	April *		Thomas Kendall (vice Southcote dec.)
1667	Jan *		Sir Walter Yonge, Bart (vice Kendall dec.)
1670	Dec *		William Gould (vice Yonge dec.)
1673	Feb *		Josiah Childe (vice Gould dec.)
1679	Feb	Sir Nathaniel Herne	John Upton
1681	Feb	Edward Yard	John Upton.

JAMES II

1685	April	Roger Pomeroy	Arthur Farwell.

WILLIAM III AND MARY

1689	Jan	Charles Boone (Whig)	William Hayne
	Sept *	George Booth (vice Boone dec'd)	
1689	Nov	Joseph Herne (Tory, vice Booth unseated after petition)	
1690	Mar	Joseph Herne	William Hayne
1695	Oct	Sir Joseph Herne	William Hayne
1698	July	Sir Joseph Herne	Frederick Herne
1699	Dec *	Rowland Holt, Nathaniel Herne (vice Joseph Herne dec'd)	
1701	Jan	Frederick Herne (Tory)	Nathaniel Herne (Tory)

ANNE

1702	July	Nathaniel Herne	Frederick Herne
1705	May	Nathaniel Herne	Frederick Herne
1708	May	Nathaniel Herne	Frederick Herne
1710	Oct	Nathaniel Herne	Frederick Herne
1713	Sept	Sir William Drake, bart.	Frederick Herne
1714	Mar *		John Fownes, sen. (vice Herne, appointmt)

GEORGE I

1715	Feb	Joseph Herne	John Fownes, jun.
1722	Mar	George Treby, sen. (Whig)	Thomas Martyn
1726	June *		Thomas Martyn (re-elected after appointmt)

GEORGE II

1727	Aug	George Treby	Walter Cary (Whig)
1729	May *		Walter Cary (re-elected after appointment)
1730	May *	George Treby (re-elected after appointment)	
1734	April	George Treby	Walter Cary
1738	May *		Walter Cary (re-elected after appointment)
1740	Nov *	George Treby (re-elected after appointment)	
1741	May	George Treby	Walter Cary
1742	Mar *	Lord Archibald Hamilton (vice Treby dec.)	
1747	July	Walter Cary	John Jeffreys (Whig)
1754	April	Walter Cary	John Jeffreys
	Dec *		John Jeffreys (re-elected after appointment)
1757	May *	Richard Howe (vice Carey dec.)	

GEORGE III

1761	Mar	Richard Viscount Howe	John Jeffreys
1763	April *	Richard Viscount Howe (re-elected after appointment)	
1765	Dec *	Richard Viscount Howe (re-elected after appointment)	
1766	Feb *		Richard Hopkins (vice Jeffreys dec)
1767	Dec *		Richard Hopkins (re-elected after appointmt)
1768	Mar	Richard Viscount Howe	Richard Hopkins
1780	Sept	Richard Viscount Howe	Arthur Holdsworth #
	Oct	Richard Viscount Howe	Richard Hopkins
1782	April *	Charles Brett (vice Howe, called to Upper House) (Whig)	
1783	Dec *	Charles Brett (re-elected after appointment)	
1784	April	Arthur Holdsworth #	Richard Hopkins
1787	Oct *	Edmund Bastard (vice Holdsworth dec.)	
1790	June	Edmund Bastard	John Charles Villiers
1796	May	Edmund Bastard	John Charles Villiers
1802	July	Edmund Bastard	Arthur Howe Holdsworth #
1806	Nov	Edmund Bastard	Arthur Howe Holdsworth #
1807	May	Edmund Bastard	Arthur Howe Holdsworth #
1812	Oct	Arthur Howe Holdsworth #	Edmund Pollexfen Bastard (Tory)

116

1816	May *		John Bastard (vice Edmund P.Bastard resigned)
1818	June	Arthur Howe Holdsworth #	John Bastard

GEORGE IV

1820	Mar	John Bastard	Charles Milner Ricketts
1822	April *		James Hamilton Stanhope (vice Ricketts resigned)
1825	Mar *		John Hutton Cooper (vice Stanhope dec.)
1826	June	John Bastard	John Hutton Cooper
1829	Jan *		Arthur Howe Holdsworth (vice Cooper dec.)

WILLIAM IV

1830	Aug	Arthur Howe Holdsworth	John Bastard
1831	May	Arthur Howe Holdsworth	John Bastard
1832	Dec	John Henry Seale (Whig) #	
1835	Jan	John Henry Seale #	

VICTORIA

1837	Aug	John Henry Seale #
1841	June	Sir John Henry Seale, Bart #
1844	Dec *	Joseph Somes (vice Seale dec.) (Tory)
1845	July *	George Moffatt (vice Somes dec.) (Whig)
1847	July	George Moffatt
1852	July	Sir Thomas Herbert (Conservative)
1857	Mar	James Caird (Whig)
1859	April	Edward W.H. Schenley (Liberal)
	Aug *	John Dunn (vice Schenley unseated) (Conservative)
1860	Nov *	John Hardy (vice Dunn dec.) (Conservative)
1865	June	John Hardy
1868	Nov.	**BOROUGH DISFRANCHISED**

MPs FOR SOUTH DEVON

VICTORIA

1868		Sir Massey Lopes, Bart (Conservative)	Samuel Kekewich
1873		Sir Massey Lopes, Bart	John Carpenter Garnier (Conservative)
1884		Sir Massey Lopes, Bart	John Tremayne (Conservative)
1885		**CONSTITUENCY ABOLISHED**	

MPs FOR TORQUAY

VICTORIA

1885		Lewis McIver	(Liberal)
1886		Richard Mallock	(Conservative)
1895		Arthur S Philpotts	(Conservative)
1900		Sir Francis Layland-Barratt	(Liberal)

GEORGE V

1910	Dec	Charles Rosdew	(Conservative)
1918		Col. Charles Burn	(Coalition Conservative)
1922		Col. Charles Burn	(Conservative)
1923		Piers Gilchrist Thompson	(Liberal)
1924–1948	Charles Williams		(Conservative)

GEORGE VI

1948   DARTMOUTH TRANSFERRED TO TOTNES
CONSTITUENCY

MPs FOR TOTNES

GEORGE VI

1948–1955	Ralph Herbert Rayner	(Conservative)
	(MP for Totnes since 1935)	

ELIZABETH II

1955–1983	Raymond Llewellyn Mawby	(Conservative)
1983	CONSTITUENCY ABOLISHED	

MPs FOR SOUTH HAMS

ELIZABETH II

1983–1997	Anthony Steen	(Conservative)
1997	CONSTITUENCY ABOLISHED	

MPs FOR TOTNES

1997–2010	Anthony Steen	(Conservative)
2010–	Sarah Wollaston	(Conservative)

* indicates by-election
# indicates an MP who (usually later) became Dartmouth Mayor.

Spelling shown for Dartmouth Borough MPs is as reported in ref. 2.

The Moorstone Leat[1]

Charles Scott-Fox

Introduction

Moorstone Barton is a classic example of a medieval hall-house, parts of which can be attributed to the early fourteenth century. This Grade I listed building remained in the possession of the family, by whom it was built, for well over 500 years. Indeed, if one includes the Saxon/Norman cob and timber farmhouse that almost certainly occupied the same or an immediately adjacent site, this would extend to over 700 years. Situated on the western side of the Spratford Stream, some two miles north of Cullompton, Moorstone Barton is tucked into the north-east slope of a spur from the high ground that separates the Exe from the Culm. From Five Bridges, where the old Turnpike Road (which became the A38 and is now the B3181), crosses the Spratford Stream, a narrow winding lane passes Moorstone Barton on its way to Brithem Bottom, Ash Thomas and Halberton (see plate 12).

Set back some thirty metres from the road, entry to the court-yard in front of the house is by a carriageway through the centre of the eastern block of the nineteenth-century farm buildings that almost enclose the yard. To the south, the steep partially wooded hillside rises for some thirty metres to a high point 102 metres above sea level with a view on a fine day that one could almost believe gives a glimpse of the sea, which extends from the Quantocks, through the ancient settlement of Hembury Hill and the Sidmouth gap, to Woodbury. To the north and east of the house, the land falls some fifteen metres to the fertile fields in the flood-plain of the Spratford Stream, and to a

119

very minor tributary, which skirts Brithem Bottom and heads west to its source in the hills above the nearby Leonard Farm. The springs in these hills are also the source for a medieval watercourse, known as the 'Moorstone Leat', which was constructed to provide a stream of running water for this ancient manor. Now of no commercial or domestic use, being partially filled in and ploughed over, but in 1607 the water rights of this leat were of vital importance to the owners of Moorstone Barton.

According to Domesday, the mesne-tenancy of Linor (Exon) or Limor (Exchequeur) 'which Frawin held T.R.E. [*Tempore Regis Edwardi*] and it paid geld for 3 virgates of land,'[2] extended to about ninety acres.[3] The tenancy was granted to the Norman Knight Morin (or Morey) of Caen by William the Conqueror's sergeants, William the Porter and William the Usher. From Domesday, and the written records of Pole, Risdon, Lysons and Polwhele, it is clearly established that Moorstone was held directly from the King, originally by Morin's descendants and subsequently by the Gambons from Gambuston in Chittlehampton parish near South Molton in Devon. Sir William Pole (1561–1635) states that 'Morston in Halberton parish, had in ye beginnynge of Kinge Henry [as no numeral attached, it infers reference is to King Henry I (1100–1135)] Gilbert de Morston and Roger de Morston after hym.; then Richard Gambon dwelt their; whom successively followed Walter, Walter, Thomas, Walter, John, John and John.'[4]

Polwhele, writing in the early nineteenth century quotes Risdon (1580–1640) 'Morston, now Mowston [*sic*], had the Gambons for its lords from King John's time (1199–1216) to the reign of King Henry VI (1422–1471).'[5] The last of the three John Gambons probably inherited Moorstone *c*.1445 with, what had become by the start of the fifteenth century, an extensive estate of properties in Devon. Contrary to Risdon, he survived almost until the end of the reign of King Edward IV, as a former monument in Halberton Church gave the date of his death as the 18 October 1481.[6] Having no male heir, his estate was left to his eldest daughter Elizabeth, who had been married in 1462 to John Sydenham of Orchard Sydenham near Watchet in Somerset. Some sixty-five years later the combined Sydenham-Gambon estates were inherited jointly by their two grand-daughters, Jane, who was married to Sir Thomas Bryggs (also known as Bruges) of Oxford, and her unmarried younger sister Elizabeth. In 1528 Elizabeth Sydenham was married to John Wyndham, the second son of Sir Thomas Wyndham of Felbrigg in Norfolk, Vice Admiral of England and Knight of the Body to King Henry VIII. In 1529 John Wyndham purchased his sister-in-law's half share and settled in Somerset, renaming his newly acquired property Orchard Wyndham.

Throughout the succeeding near 400 years, this Somerset branch of the Wyndham family were active in both public life and service to the Crown, for which they were rewarded with knighthoods, a baronetcy and peerages. In 1582 John Wyndham was succeeded by his grandson John (1559–1645), who entailed all of his estate to his male heirs, which included the Gambon property, Moorstone and both the neighbouring farms, Five Bridges and Leonard that he had acquired in 1636.[7] Following the death in 1847 of George Wyndham, 4th Earl of Egremont, these entailed properties were inherited by William Wyndham of Dinton, whose successors now live at Orchard Wyndham. After William Wyndham's death in 1914, the trustees of the entailed estate decided to raise funds for death duties and to invest in the Somerset estate by selling most of the properties in Devon. In the spring of 1915 the 1400 acre Cullompton estate, consisting of Moorstone Barton, (which by 1861 had been increased to 273 acres), Leonard, Five Bridges and several other farms and parcels of land, as well as property in Cullompton and the manors of Cullompton and Moorstone, was offered for sale by Nicholl Manisty & Co. of London in co-operation with the Exeter auctioneers Messrs Whitton & Laing. Curiously, although the Devon Record Office file includes a supporting document that provides proof of ownership of these entailed properties,[8] there is no mention of the Moorstone Leat.

Ownership, Rights and Responsibilities

On 15 May 1915, Moorstone Barton (Figure 1) was purchased by Albert Bowden of Sampford Peverell, subject to the necessary assurances from his solicitor. It is assumed that having spoken to the tenant John Clifford Were, Mr Bowden was informed of the work that was needed to maintain the leat[9] and instructed his solicitor to make the necessary additional searches in regard to his rights and responsibilities. In July 1915, before inviting their client to sign the final contract, Messrs Partridge & Cockram of Market Chambers, Tiverton, wrote to the Wyndham Estate solicitors, Nicholl Manisty & Co., to clarify Albert Bowden's responsibility for 'maintenance and cleansing' of the leat and the rights of 'occupiers of property adjacent to Moorstone's land' to a water supply from it. A protracted correspondence over the succeeding five weeks between the solicitors, the Wyndham Estate's agent A.W. Horne and his father A.V. Horne, who had been the agent for the previous fifty years, and the tenant J.C. Were, produced no written evidence and could only state what was 'established practice'. As Mr Horne wrote, in a seemingly exasperated tone, in his letter of 24 August 1915 to Partridge & Cockram: 'I have supplied [you] with all the information I could obtain and regret it is so insufficient. However, it would be well to bear in mind that the Were family have occupied Moorston Barton for several centuries and the present tenant has a very clear knowledge of the rights exercised respecting the Leat.'[10]

Notwithstanding these assertions, it is evident from the corres-pondence that neither the agent nor his tenant was aware of the existence of any estate map, or legal correspondence, which would

Figure 1. Moorstone Barton (from the Sale Brochure 1915). DRO Reference: DSCF0808. Reproduced courtesy of Devon Record Office.

have established the provenance of the Moorstone Leat. The estate solicitors could only confirm that:

[the] leat is an open ditch cut many years ago by Act of Parliament, providing an important water supply to Moorston Barton Farm and, to provide this supply appears to be the chief, if not the only, reason for the Leat. The Leat has . . . been cleaned from time to time <u>throughout</u> by the tenant of Moorston Farm and on several occasions the banks and sides have been repaired at the cost of this estate. About 3 years ago a considerable cut of wall was rebuilt.[11]

With this letter they enclosed a statement by John Greenslade of Leonard Farm, who added that 'the stream is 6 feet wide and the tenant of Moorston claims 3 feet on each side for cleaning. There are three bridges crossing the leat in Leonard Farm. The stream is not used for irrigating Leonard Farm but only for drinking purposes and the tenant of Moorston usually cleans out the leat once a year after harvest.'[12]

Further information from John Greenslade confirmed that:

the tenant of Leonard Farm has no right to Moorston Leat, only for drinking purposes for cattle, but there is a weir in Wyndham's Meadow the overflow of which belongs to that meadow, bought by Mr Heal of Waymill Farm, Halberton. The tenant of Leonard's Farm has voluntarily helped to clean the Leat but is not compelled to do so. [At the end of this letter the agent added the rider] the tenant of Leonard has probably volunteered to clean part of Moorston Leat within the boundary of his farm, in return for the manurial value of the sediment.[13]

The result of this correspondence was that the final version of the conveyance from the trustees of the Wyndham Cullompton Estate to Albert Bowden, which was signed on 9 August 1915, had a rider to state that it was conveyed

together with the benefit of the water supply obtained by means of the Moorstone Leat in the manner and to the extent in and to which the same is now enjoyed by the occupier for the time being of the said hereditaments but subject to the liability to maintain and keep the said Leat in good and substantial repair and properly cleansed.[14]

On the 28 September 1932, the executors of Albert Bowden sold Moorstone Barton to Herbert John Wood, who added some twenty-two acres before selling it to Percy Maunder, grandfather of the current occupant, on 31 December 1941. Although this rider remained as a 'right and responsibility' for both of these subsequent contracts, it would seem from the surviving solicitor's records that no other rights were identified from the searches at that time. Nevertheless, it is clear that Percy Maunder was made aware of the importance of this water supply, and for the need for his tenant to undertake regular maintenance, as a note dated 30 November 1941 from Herbert Wood informed him that: 'about three loads of clay is wanted behind the upright corrugated iron sheets above the masonry walls',[15] but there is no written evidence to establish for how long after the war the leat was kept up to this standard.

The spectacular map (see Plate 13), known as the 'Halberton Map', which was presented to the Devon Record Office in 1934 by Mr William Wyndham and illustrated in the first of the Friends of Devon Archives publications, was prepared

> to provide evidence in a legal dispute in 1603–1608 [Chancery Case between Sir John Wyndham MP (1559–1645) and Abraham Turner] and another [against John Harris] in 1618 concerning rights and control over water supply . . . The houses and cottages, drawn in various ways suggestive of their size and importance, for the most part have their owner's names alongside.[16]

The petitions and rejoinder relating to these disputes are held in the Wyndham archive in the Somerset Heritage Centre, but this map 'shows vividly the importance of water, used here for irrigation and controlled by various sluice gates'[17] and to whom the water was connected.

The map and associated Wyndham documents provide indisputable evidence of the medieval origins of the Moorstone Leat, but sadly there is no discernible statement of authority for its construction. In the deposition dated 4 February 1607[18] Nicholas Turner and Thomas

Rolleston, acting on behalf of Mr Abraham Turner of Halberton, on whose land the initial diversion had been made (now Remberton), and through whose land the leat continued towards Leonard Farm, claimed 'jeopardy' for the illegal retention of the outcome of the water flow. The rejoinder, dated 21 January 1608, signed by John Slade of Halberton for Sir John Wyndham, stated that the leat had been in existence 'in the memory of man'. This phrase was repeated in evidence from other users, including a lengthy section relating to the rights of access for Mr Passmore, the owner of Sutton House (Court). As there were no further proceedings it is presumed that the defence of 'existence of the leat since time immemorial' had prevailed. Some nine years later, in a deposition dated 6 January 1617, John Harris of Halberton complained of the 'undermining of banks' from the flow of the 'Morston Leat',[19] but no rejoinder to this charge survives if one was ever made. It may perhaps be assumed, judging from Mr Herbert Wood's note in 1941, that Moorstone's tenants had always known they were required to repair any banks where erosion threatened.

Despite this apparent recognition by successive tenants of their responsibility for maintaining the channel, it is clear from later correspondence that this duty was never included in the Orchard Wyndham estate office records. As both Moorstone and Leonard farms were Wyndham properties, and no-one else seemed to be aware of any statutory obligation to supply water to the other farms along the route, although from 'time immemorial' this had been the practice, the rights and responsibilities relating to this leat were probably considered to be only of academic interest. The leat was featured in the Ordnance Survey,[20] but again its relevance seems to have been overlooked. As previously mentioned, the 1915 sale particulars for Moorstone made no mention of its water supply: it was only the searches undertaken by Albert Bowden's solicitor that established an apparent ownership of the rights to the leat, and the responsibility of Moorstone's tenants for its upkeep.

In 1964, when Messrs Hole & Pugsley of St Peter Street, Tiverton were instructed by Percy Maunder that provision of a public water supply to Moorstone rendered the leat unnecessary, an additional 'right to a supply of water' was discovered. A typed memorandum, produced by Hole & Pugsley for all the involved parties, states that:

a plan of 1863 shows that a branch had been taken off to supply Sutton and that in 1926 Sutton was conveyed 'together with the right to a supply of water from the leat through a four inch square'. Presumably therefore an agreement must have been made between the owners of Sutton and Moorstone sometime before 1863. No liability appears to have been assumed however by the owner of Sutton for the maintenance and repair of the leat.[21]

Although the existence of the 'Halberton Map' was known within academic circles, until it was analysed by Ravenhill and Rowe at the end of the twentieth century, it was only seen to be a highly decorative estate map. Neither Hole & Pugsley, nor any of the owners of the four farms involved, could possibly have appreciated the importance of the leat as an historic watercourse. All parties accepted the report and on 31 December 1964 the right for Moorstone to receive water from the leat through Leonard Farm, Sutton Barton and Pond Farm was released, together with the owner of Moorstone Barton's responsibility for its maintenance.

The Line and Purpose of Moorstone's Leat

In re-tracing the line of the leat from its source (Figure 2), one cannot fail to be impressed by the scale and complexity of the work. Initially it takes advantage of the original stream bed from Warnicombe, down through Thorne's Wood, to the recently restored holding ponds at Remberton. Below the old farmhouse is the first of many sluices, designed to re-direct the flow from its natural run south-east to join Fulford Water, into the Moorstone Leat. Here, this still active sluice apportions water between a leat that runs through Leonard Farm and the lower fields of Pond Farm to Brithem Bottom, and the original stream bed, which continues down the valley to pass under the road below Crywshayes. A second active sluice allows the stream to continue down the valley when water levels are high, but normally directs the flow into the main line of the leat to Kettlewell.

Today Kettlewell Farm is where it ends, but until 1964 it continued its zigzag route across the fields of Leonard and Sutton Barton farms, to the holding pond at Moorstone. Where possible it followed the contours, crossing and re-crossing the Sutton Barton-Brithembottom

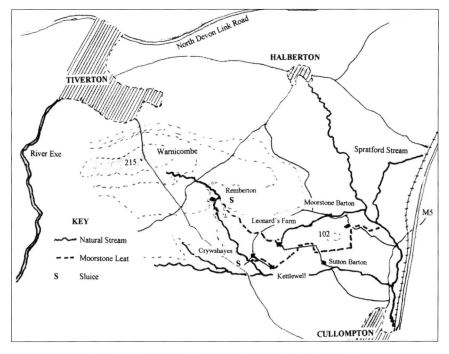

Figure 2. Course of Moorstone Leat. Charles Scott-Fox.

road, with weirs and sluices to provide watering holes for stock and supplies to smallholdings on the way. In two places, below Crywshayes and above Sutton Barton, the leat runs through deep cuttings, the one above Sutton Barton being nearly six metres deep and over six metres across. There are occasional places where the leat still exists as a small pond, but apart from the ditch through Burn Woods above Moorstone, there is virtually nothing to be seen. On Moorstone land, some water drains from the fields into the lower section of the old holding pond, beside the Five Bridges-Brithem Bottom lane, but the sluice gates have been abandoned and the leat is silted up, overgrown and no longer serves any irrigation or water supply purpose.

The 1915 statements by the tenants of Leonard and Moorstone Barton farms seem to infer that the leat was only required for drinking and watering purposes, but it is now known that it was also a contributor to the river that powered the grist and fulling mills at Five Bridges, by adding to the flow of the Spratford Stream, and the sole source of power for the grist mill at Sutton Farm. The flow from the leat was never strong enough to drive a waterwheel, and two holding ponds (both now filled in) were created that could be filled over time, similar to the system provided for the grist mill at Ayshford Court,[22] and used to drive the wheel when required. Although the 'Halberton Map' shows a run off from the leat to the back of the house, it is most unlikely that it was used for Moorstone's drinking water as there was an ample supply provided from at least two wells. As recently as the late 1950s, there was a fully functioning well in the front garden and a relation of the Moorstone Dairy tenants between the wars knew of another at the rear, close to the dairy, in which it is known that 'butter was placed in a bucket and lowered down to keep it from going off in hot weather'.[23] Both of these wells have been capped and covered over, and the actual location of the dairy well is now unknown.

The tithe map of 1843 shows the line of the leat through Leonard Farm and Sutton Barton land to the holding pond above the Five Bridges-Brithembottom lane and on to its junction with the Spratford Stream but nothing to indicate a connection to Moorstone. However, examination of the Maunder family archive, which includes Percy Maunder's annotated copy of the six-inch Ordnance Survey map of 1905 of Moorstone Barton farm land, shows that he had inserted a dotted line from the end of the leat, shortly before it enters the pond, to the road, and from there along the hedge-line and through the Chapel Field to the house. Although difficult to read, the line beside the pond appears to state 'piped drinking water', and the line from the pond to the house 'piped leat water' from which it can be assumed that as recently as the 1950s, the Moorstone Leat was still needed as a primary supply of fresh water for the farm, though whether this was still into the house, which was by this time connected to the public mains, or just for the farm animals, must remain open to doubt.

Conclusion

Desirable though it may have been for all these farms to have had additional access to running water, this cannot be considered to have been the reason for building the leat. Provision of a domestic supply for house and farmyard would not seem to be sufficient justification to construct a near five-mile-long waterway, or the expense of Chancery

Court action to defend its existence. Although the 'Halberton Map' shows that there has always been a connection to Sutton Barton, the use of this stream to run its grist mill was apparently made in the late eighteenth or early nineteenth century. The eighteenth-century grist and fulling mills at Five Bridges were adequately driven by the Spratford Stream, so it seems that water power was a marginal benefit of a much later period. The fees or rent for a supply of fresh water to the other properties, as illustrated in this map, would have been minimal and it therefore follows that the reason for building this leat must primarily have been due to the position of Moorstone's farmland relative to the floodplain. As anyone, who drives up the B3181 knows only too well, the fields at Five Bridges on either side of the Spratford Stream are frequently under water, even in summer. Although this creates a rich pasture, in winter in the Middle Ages this boggy land would have been dangerous for cattle and occasionally inaccessible. There being no springs or other streams running through the farm, this river would have been Moorstone's only supply of drinking water for cattle, requiring frequent movement from pastures on higher ground in summer or water from the well in winter.

Though it has not been possible to determine the date of construction of this medieval leat, it can almost certainly be assessed as being fifteenth century or earlier. Therefore, it is clear that for over 500 years, until the advent of the piped mains supply, the Moorstone Leat provided the only all-year-round flow of fresh drinking water for the farm. The loss of this supply could, on occasions, have threatened the very livelihood of Moorstone Barton's tenants and so it is not unreasonable to conclude that in no small measure the survival of this ancient hall-house, which is such an important part of Devon's heritage, can be attributed to the Moorstone Leat.

Notes and References

1. Much of the information for this article was obtained from the private papers of the Maunder family and their solicitor's records, whilst researching the history of Moorstone Barton, for which unrestricted access and publication rights have been granted. See also, G.W. Copeland (undated *c.*1964) 'Notes on Moorstone Barton', Manuscript: Tiverton Library.
2. Barlow 1991, folio 117v.

3. The hide was the principal measure of assessment of geld (tax) rather than acreage and can vary from location to location according to the productivity of the land but is usually calculated at 100-120 acres. The lesser measures were ferlings and virgates, four ferlings to a virgate and four virgates to a hide. The geld rate in 1086 was two shillings requiring Moorstone to pay one shilling and six pence to the Crown.
4. Pole 1791, pp. 196-8.
5. Polwhele, 1793–1806, vol. ii, pp. 361-2.
6. *Devon & Exeter Gazette*, 3 September 1930, report of lecture by the Reverend Charles Sherwin, Rector of Clyst-Hydon to his local Antiquarian Society , who stated that 'there is a monument in Halberton Church, which now seems to have disappeared, with an inscription that commences 'Orate pro anima' (pray for the soul) of John Gambon of Morceston, who died 18 day of October 1481.'
7. SHC, DD/WY Box 17. This document also shows that the 'Lordship of Morston' came with his purchase of Leonard Farm. How it came to be with this farm, instead of remaining with Moorstone, remains a mystery, but it was shown as a separate item when both farms were offered for sale in 1915. In the event it was unsold and was combined with the last lot of the sale, which curiously was Leonard Farm.
8. DRO, 74B/MP72-77.
9. One of the local farmers, now retired, can recall after harvest time seeing a dozen or more men working their way up the leat to keep it clear of silt and weeds.
10. Maunder family records.
11. Mr Peter Pugsley of Hole & Pugsley has informed the author that despite attempts to trace this private Act through the Parliamentary authorities in 1964, nothing could be found and that, if it ever existed, it could have been enacted before the earliest House of Lords records, which start in 1427.
12. Maunder family records.
13. Ibid.
14. Ibid.
15. Ibid.
16. DRO, 6065, p. 29.
17. Ibid.
18. SHC, DD/WY Box 22/1.
19. SHC, DD/WY Box 22/3.
20. Ordnance Survey (old series) 1805–1874.
21. Maunder family records. As just under half a mile of the leat crossed what was Sutton land it is presumed that their free supply of water was negotiated as a 'quid pro quo'.
22. Scott-Fox 2008, p. 28.
23. From an interview by the author with the granddaughter of Frederick

Daniel, the Moorstone dairyman in 1914, recalling the memories of her grandmother Julia of life at Moorstone.

Bibliography

Barlow, F. (1991) 'Introduction', *The Devonshire Domesday*, London: Alecto Historical Editions.

Cherry, B. and Pevsner, N. (1989 edn) *The Buildings of England, Devon*, Harmondsworth: Penguin.

Domesday Folios (1991) *The Devonshire Domesday*, London: Alecto Historical Editions.

Lysons, D. and Lysons, S. (1822) *Magna Britannia* VI: *topographical and historical account of Devonshire*, 2 vols, London: Thomas Cadell.

Page, E.W. (ed.) (1906) *The Victoria History of the Counties of England: a history of Devonshire*, 5 vols, London: University of London.

Pole, Sir W. (1791) *Collections towards a Description of the County of Devon*, 2 vols, London: J. Nichols.

Polwhele, Reverend R. (1793–1806) *The History of Devonshire*, 3 vols, London: Cadell Johnson Dilley.

Ravenhill, M. and Rowe, M. (2000) *Early Devon Maps*, Exeter: Friends of Devon Archives.

Risdon, T. (1811) *The Geographical Description or Survey of the County of Devon*, London: Rees and Curtis (1970 edn), Barnstaple: Porcupine Press.

Scott-Fox, C. (2008) *Ayshford's Heritage*, Willand: Friends of Friendless Churches.

Wyndham, Hon. H.A. (1939 and 1950) *A Family History, the Wyndhams of Somerset, Sussex and Wiltshire*, 2 vols, Oxford: Oxford University Press.

Wyndham, Dr K. (1985) 'Orchard Wyndham Somerset', *Country Life*, March, 21 and 28.

William Worcester in Devon, 1478

Nicholas Orme

On the afternoon of Friday 11 September 1478, a man on horseback rode into Devon along what is now the A38, the old road from Taunton to Exeter. He was aged in his early sixties and, at a time when clothes expressed social rank, he was probably wearing a robe of the kind that indicated a man of middling status. He was in fact a gentleman, although not wealthy or self-conscious enough to bring a servant with him. No portrait of him exists except for a fanciful nineteenth-century one in a window of Bristol Cathedral, and the sole report of his appearance comes from a hostile writer who claimed that he was 'one-eyed, black in colour, and swarthy of face'.[1]

William Worcester is one of the most appealing people of his century: a pioneer, perhaps the pioneer, of English antiquarian history and archaeology. Born in Bristol in 1415, he studied at a grammar school and at Oxford University before marrying and entering the service of a wealthy Norfolk knight, Sir John Fastolf, to whom he acted as secretary and agent. During his employment he kept up a variety of interests: family history (useful in handling lawsuits over property), Latin and French literature, and astrology, among others. He wrote a treatise on nobility, *The Book of Noblesse*, and a translation of Cicero's work on *Old Age*, both in English.

By 1478 Fastolf was dead and William had gained possession of a small estate near Norwich which his master had promised him. He was now, in modern terms, 'retired' and free to give most of his time to his personal hobbies. His visit to Devon in 1478 was part of an expedition to St Michael's Mount, ostensibly on a pilgrimage. The adverb is not intended to question his religious motives: he visited the Mount, heard mass there, entered other churches on his route, and took a particular interest in local saints. But a pilgrimage was an acceptable reason for travelling when people might look suspiciously on strangers asking questions, and William's journey enabled him to satisfy his curiosity about secular matters as well, such as islands, roads, bridges, castles, noble houses, and their families.

Devon featured in his plans only in as far as he had to cross it to reach Cornwall, and he did not spend much time there. He passed his first night in the county at an unidentified place which he could not remember later on when he tried to reconstruct the diary of his movements.[2] Probably it was an inn or house on the way between Wellington and Cullompton.[3] The next day, Saturday, he reached Crediton (perhaps via Thorverton) by midday and Okehampton by evening, where he spent the night.[4] Sunday saw him leave the county near Launceston, a transit of the county that took him just over two days.[5]

On his return, he crossed the Tamar by the ferry at Hatch near Calstock on Monday 21 September and stayed overnight at Tavistock. On Tuesday he probably rode from there to Okehampton, or possibly Crockernwell, before proceeding to Exeter on Wednesday 23rd. The afternoon of Thursday was spent traversing East Devon to Newenham Abbey near Axminster, and on Friday he bade farewell to the county on the road to Chard. This section of his travels lasted about four days, so his total time in Devon was slightly less than one week.[6]

William's notes of his journeys survive in a manuscript in the library of Corpus Christi College, Cambridge, which has probably been there since the late sixteenth century. Unfortunately the manuscript was bound up from a collection of his papers in that century without much regard to their order, and it is difficult now to make sense of how he originally kept them. At least one of his notes may have been written before he set out: this is an account of the staging posts on the way to the Mount made by Thomas Clerk of Ware in 1476, which William may have copied for his own guidance.[7] Other notes were probably made on the journey, and yet others afterwards. His record of his return through Devon is inaccurate in some of its chronology, suggesting that it was compiled from memory some time later.[8]

Nevertheless it is remarkable how much William learnt and recorded during the short period that he passed through the county. Some of what he learnt came from personal observation, but he must have collected a great deal from other sources: certainly what people told him and possibly written sources like Clerk's itinerary. William was good at making acquaintances. In Devon he mentions talking to Thomas Peperelle, a notary public of Tavistock; John Skinner, a minor employee of Exeter Cathedral; John Burges, a Dominican friar of Exeter; and 'Master Cornewayle', one of the clergy of Ottery St Mary.[9] The first three told him things that he noted down.

Pre-eminent among what he recorded was geographical information, especially relating to roads. Travellers generally planned each day in two parts, morning and afternoon, with a stop for midday dinner between them. They had to know where to make this stop, where to spend the night, and the distances between the stops. These distances were in miles: not measured miles like those of today but 'reputed' miles which were generally longer.

William refers to distances and stopping places on three main roads in Devon, not all of which he travelled: Wellington to Exeter, Launceston to Exeter, and Exeter to Axminster. Some of these facts must therefore have been learnt from other people or from writings. Oddly by modern standards, he says little about the places where he slept overnight, and nothing about where he ate at midday. At Exeter he stayed at the Bear Inn on South Street, and at Tavistock and Newenham he lodged in the guest rooms of the abbeys there, but his other accommodations, whether inns or private houses, are not recorded.[10]

Rivers were also prominent in his mind. They had an influence on travel because they had to be crossed, and sometimes one journeyed down them in boats (although William only used a ferry across the Tamar), but they also seem to have been important to him (and to other people) as landscape features. His account of them is remarkably full. He lists all the main rivers of south Devon, which if we put them in order from west to east, encompass the Tamar, Lyd, Tavy, Plym, Yealm, Erme, Dart, Teign, Yeo, Exe, Culm, Otter, and Axe. His knowledge of the northern rivers was less, but included the Torridge, Okement, and Taw. In several cases he noted where rivers rose, how long they were, and where they reached the sea.

Linked with rivers were bridges. He learnt of five across the Tamar: Bridgerule, Polston Bridge at Launceston, Greystone Bridge, Horse Bridge, and Newbridge. On or off the main roads east to west he noted those at Lydford, Okehampton, Crediton, Cowley, Exeter, Ottery, and Axminster. He also heard of Barnstaple and Bideford bridges. Somebody told him that Lydford Bridge, which he did not see, was 'the highest bridge of the whole of England and the narrowest beneath'. And when he was in Exeter, William took the trouble to look at Exe Bridge and to record that it 'has sixteen arches, and I reckon its length at 200 of my steps'.[11]

Finally, he was aware of coastlines although he was travelling far from them. As a native of Bristol, he was familiar with sea-routes and ships, and other parts of his manuscript include information about the Hebrides, the Orkneys, the islands of Ireland, and those of north-west Africa that were just coming to be known in Europe. His Devon notes refer to the 'south sea' (the English Channel), the 'northern sea' or 'Severn water' (the Bristol Channel), and several of the harbours along the Devon shores.[12] These include Plymouth, Dartmouth, Teignmouth, Topsham, Exmouth, Ottermouth, and Seaton on the south coast, and Appledore, Barnstaple, and Ilfracombe on the north. He heard about St Nicholas Island, just off Plymouth Sound, and the Eddystone rock, estimated as fifteen miles further out into the sea. In later notes at Bristol, he mentions Lundy Island.[13]

This information adds up to a considerable knowledge of Devon's dimensions and major physical features, apart from hills which he does not record systematically although he refers to Dartmoor and Exmoor. His data is comparable with that of the famous fourteenth-century 'Gough Map', the most realistic cartographic portrayal of Britain before the later sixteenth century. The Gough Map was in large measure constructed from a similar knowledge of road distances.[14]

William's information would have allowed him to measure Devon from east to west: not accurately by our standards but by those of his day. In some respects he could have done the same from north to south, because he gives a distance of twenty five miles from Exeter to Barnstaple Bridge; one of thirty miles from Exeter to the source of the Exe on Exmoor; and estimates of six miles from Exeter to Exmouth, nine from Ottery St Mary to Ottermouth, and eight from Axminster to Seaton.[15]

In cartographic terms there would have been distortions and a lack of knowledge about the coastline with regard to capes and bays. But William was not making a systematic study of Devon's geography. He was merely picking up information that came to his attention, and a few more enquiries (especially if reinforced by some official rank in the king's service) would have enhanced his resources considerably. The Gough Map is unique today, and may have been unusual when it was made, but the data that it used was evidently widely available.

William does not express an interest in the Devon landscape through which he passed, save for its roads, rivers, and bridges, or in the county's economy. He is less revealing here than John Leland who followed him in the 1530s and 40s. He learnt that there were silver mines at Bere Ferrers, that Brentor church was one of a number of hill-top churches in the South West dedicated to St Michael, and, as we have seen, that Lydford had a high bridge. But his concern with landscape throughout his notes is usually practical rather than picturesque, so for example the cliffs of the Clifton Gorge are mentioned in terms of their height and Gulland Rock near Padstow as a great haunt of seabirds.[16]

Buildings attracted his attention much more, wherever he went, although here again he is more of a Pevsner than a Betjeman: short on the picturesque. He noted castles, two of which he may have seen (Exeter and Okehampton) and others of which he was told (Lydford, Plympton, and Woodbury – the latter really a hill-fort).[17] In Bristol he mentions merchants' houses, but those of Exeter do not seem to have struck him as worth recording. Bridges, as we have seen, figure largely in his notes, and sixteen are mentioned in Devon.

He was fascinated by churches, and is famous in this respect through recording the dimensions of many of them in England, some-times in yards and feet (indicating that he had access to a measuring rod) but frequently in 'steps', a step consisting of the length of his two shoes placed end to end and varying between twenty and twenty-three inches.[18] He does not seem to have visited churches while he was riding – no doubt because of a wish to complete each stage of his travels according to his horse's capability and the available time and light – but he did look at some of those where he stopped for the night.

As a result he gives us measurements of five Devon churches (Crediton, Exeter Cathedral, Newenham Abbey, Tavistock Abbey, and its neighbouring parish church. The dimensions usually include width and length, and are sometimes subdivided into those of chancel (or choir) and nave. Occasionally he goes beyond mere figures. Crediton had 'a beautiful clerestory'. Tavistock Abbey contained the shrine of St Rumon and a new cloister, and a board in either the abbey or the parish church displayed a Latin poem about love, hope, and fear, of which he transcribed five lines. At the cathedral, he admired the 'beautiful lights' of the nave windows (they follow various patterns) and the way that the church was 'vaulted over in the most lovely way'. He visited Bishop Lacy's shrine, the cloister, and the new chapter house, and took notes from another board which contained the main events of the cathedral's history.[19]

These religious interests extended to saints. He frequently copied down their feast-days from church calendars, especially if their names were local and unusual, and he was evidently struck by the large number of such figures in the South West: indeed, an interest in the subject may well have helped draw him to Cornwall. Three people in Devon told him about saints. One was Thomas Peperelle of Tavistock, whom William describes as his 'host': perhaps Peperelle, although a notary public, was also an officer of the abbey and helped entertain its guests. William learnt from him about Tavistock's own saint, Rumon; Brannoc of Braunton, described as 'son of the king of Calabria'; and three saints of west Cornwall: Erth, Euny, and Ia.[20]

A second informant was John Burges, a friar of the Dominican house in Exeter, whom William met either during his Exeter visit or subsequently in the South West. He told of two saints local to Exeter – Sidwell and Walter of Cowick; of Branwalader, commemorated at Milton Abbey in Dorset (but also linked by Burges with Branscombe); and of Wulfric of Haselbury in Somerset.[21] A third person at Newenham Abbey added two further names: Reine, with a chapel near Crewkerne, also in Somerset, and White or Candida, honoured at Whitchurch in Dorset.[22]

The other people who interested William were the nobility and gentry: he wrote a now-lost work about those of Norfolk. It was his practice, where possible, to look at obituary records in churches and to note down the death dates of important men and women recorded there, but he had poor luck in Devon in this respect. The only such record to which he gained access was the martyrology of Newenham

Abbey, from which he transcribed information about the Bonville, Broke, and Mohun families. He also noted the murder of Nicholas Radford at Upcott Barton near Cheriton Fitzpaine in 1455, a notorious event that he would have remembered and which he either asked or was told about as he passed through Crediton.[23]

What was the purpose of this note-making? In the case of Bristol, where he made detailed observations of the streets and principal buildings, including their dimensions, he may have intended to write a work in praise of the city, compile a detailed map of it, or both.[24] Either enterprise would have been unusual at that time, and even in their unfinished state his notes constitute an original and impressive record of Bristol's past. His travels through England, of which notes survive from 1478 to 1480, can hardly have aimed at doing the same for the kingdom. He had no authority to this effect, he was elderly by contemporary standards, and he seems to have been more concerned with his Bristol project than with one any wider.

Probably the notes simply reflect the variety of his interests. The information he gathered may have been gathered to enjoy and reflect on, to help solve historical puzzles, or to share with like-minded friends. William may not have been the only person with such interests or the maker of notes about them. Paper was widely available by the fifteenth century, and literate men often carried a pen and inkhorn on their belts, so that noting things down was easy. It may be that other such note collections once existed and that William's has survived only because it was so comprehensive. It was also lucky to pass fairly quickly from his family in Norwich to an Elizabethan cleric and schoolmaster in the city, and thence to Corpus Christi College.

For west-country historians, William's importance lies in him being the first private visitor to the region to leave both a diary of his movements and notes on what he saw and heard at the time.[25] He is the only known visitor before the Reformation, apart from John Leland who left a short account of a visit to Cornwall in 1533.[26] But Leland's most substantial exploration of the South West took place in 1542 when the monasteries had been dissolved and shrines and pilgrimages had mostly been abolished.[27]

William in contrast experienced Westcountry religion when it was still flourishing in its late-medieval Catholic state. Although he says much more about it in Cornwall than in Devon, he gives us valuable information about two of the uncanonised but venerated saints of Exeter, Walter of Cowick and Edmund Lacy, and about the appearance and dimensions of five churches. He also reveals, more clearly than other sources, the extent of knowledge that people had about their regional geography.

Others in later centuries were to spend more time on topographical and antiquarian research than was available to William, and, after 1600, to produce county histories, but he anticipated most of the topics they wrote about. He is truly the first of the long line of antiquaries leading down to the present day, a man deserving to be praised and remembered.

Notes and References

1. Davis 1971–76, ii. On Worcester's life and writings, see the present author's article in the *Oxford Dictionary of National Biography*; McFarlane 1981, pp. 199-230; and William Worcester, *Itineraries*, ed. J. H. Harvey 1969, pp. ix-xxii.
2. Harvey 1969, *Itineraries*, pp. 38-9.
3. William does not mention Tiverton in his notes, which makes it unlikely that he stayed there or even passed through it.
4. Harvey's edition of the *Itineraries* translates Worcester's verb *jantare* as 'breakfast' at Crediton, but here and later at Taunton (ibid. pp. 40-1) the distance travelled suggests a mid-day meal.
5. Ibid. pp. 38-9.
6. Ibid. pp. 38-41.
7. Ibid. pp. 12-13.
8. Ibid. pp. 38-41.
9. Ibid. pp. 38-9, 114-15, 116-17, 124-5.
10. Ibid. pp. 38-9 (compare pp. 114-15), 116-17.
11. Ibid. pp. 28-9 (Lydford), 116-17 (Exe Bridge).
12. Ibid. pp. 26-7, 28-9, 110-11.
13. Ibid. pp. 110-11 (St Nicholas, Eddystone), 302-3 (Lundy). The reference on pp. 30-1 is to Cornwall not Lundy.
14. On the Gough map, see N. Millea 2007.
15. *Itineraries*, pp. 16-17, 18-19.
16. Ibid. pp. 110-11, 262-3.
17. Ibid. pp. 16-17, 18-19, 28-9, 124-5.
18. Ibid. p. xv.
19. Ibid. pp. 80-1, 114-15, 116-17, 124-5. On Worcester's visit to Exeter, see also N. Orme, *The Cathedral Cat* (Exeter, 2008), pp. 73-9.
20. *Itineraries*, pp. 114-15.

21. Ibid. pp. 124-5.
22. Ibid. pp. 122-3.
23. Ibid. pp. 82-3. For the murder, see Storey 1966, pp. 168-71.
24. Worcester's materials on Bristol are printed in *William Worcestre: The Topography of Medieval Bristol*, ed. F. Neale, Bristol Record Society, 51 (2000).
25. There are, of course, earlier records of itineraries by kings and bishops, such as that of Edward I in 1297 (J. Good and N. Orme, 'Edward I and the Churches of Devon, 1297', *TDH*, 67 (2003), pp. 3-9).
26. Leland 1907–10, i, 315-26.
27. Ibid. i, 169-244.

Bibliography

Davis, N. (ed.) (1971–6) *Paston Letters and Papers of the Fifteenth Century*, 2 vols, Oxford: Oxford University Press.

Good, J. and Orme, N. (2003) 'Edward I and the Churches of Devon, 1297', *TDH*, 67, pp. 3-9.

Leland, John (1907–10) *The Itinerary of John Leland*, ed. Toulmin Smith, 5 vols, London: Bell (repr. London: Centaur Press, 1964).

Millea, N. (2007) *The Gough Map: the earliest road map of Great Britain*, Oxford: Bodleian Library.

McFarlane, K.B. (1981) *England in the Fifteenth Century*, London: Hambledon Press.

Orme, Nicholas, 'William Worcester' (2003) *The Oxford Dictionary of National Biography*, ed. C. Matthew and B. Harrison, 60 vols, Oxford: Oxford University Press; updated electronic edition: <http://www.oxforddnb.com>.

Parsons, E.J. (1958) *The Map of Great Britain Circa A.D. 1330 Known as the Gough Map: an introduction to the facsimile*, Oxford: Oxford University Press.

Storey, R.L. (1966) *The End of the House of Lancaster*, London: Barrie and Rockcliff.

Worcester, William (1969) *Itineraries*, Harvey, J.H. (ed.) (1969) Oxford: Oxford University Press.

Worcester, William (2000) *The Topography of Medieval Bristol*, Neale, F. (ed.) Bristol Record Society, 51, Bristol: Bristol Record Society.

Sheriff Courtenay and the Western Rising of 1549

Retha M. Warnicke

In contemporary documents concerning the Western Rising of 1549, some references were made to Piers Courtenay, sheriff of Devon, but neither John Hooker, who wrote about the siege of Exeter nor Sir Peter Carew, vice-admiral of Devon, who was sent to investigate the rebellion, referred to his imprisonment. Notice of it survives only in the funeral sermon for Courtenay's wife, published in 1606.

Piers was the second son of Sir William Courtenay of Powderham Castle and Margaret, daughter of Sir Richard Edgecombe of Cotehele. Belonging to one of the four great feudal families of Devon, the Courtenays were descendants of Edward I. Before 1537, when his oldest child was born, Piers was married to Elizabeth, daughter of Robert Shilston of Bridestow. At Michaelmas 1548, he was appointed sheriff of Devon, thus becoming responsible for putting down riots or insurrections and breaking up illegal gatherings, specifically the Western Rising in 1549.[1]

By the Tudor period, parliamentary statutes had greatly diminished the sheriff's judicial and financial powers. He continued, nevertheless, to be recognised as the king's 'Chief Minister and Officer' in his county, and important royal notices were forwarded to him for proclamation 'by sound of trumpet and beat of drum.' At the end of parliamentary sessions, copies of the new statutes were also sent to be displayed in his shire court.[2]

Because of the heavy expense of holding this one-year office, the men selected for it belonged to the 'cream of the gentry.' On the day of his appointment, the sheriff placed his securities at the Exchequer, took the oath of office and the oath of supremacy, obtained his patent, his predecessor's writ of discharge, and appointed attorneys to represent him in the royal courts since he was forbidden to leave the shire during his term except to be discharged by the Exchequer. He had personally to pay the wages of an undersheriff, four bailiffs, and a clerk; the undersheriff, usually a lawyer, alone might require as much as three hundred pounds sterling. In addition, he owed the crown forty pounds sterling for the privilege of holding the office and the Exchequer fifty pounds for his writ of discharge. There were other expenses, such as entertaining justices of assize, important visitors, and sometimes even the monarch, himself. Irene Gladwin pointed out in 1974: 'The ability to meet these charges out of his own pocket, without skimping, was the basic qualification required of any gentleman selected to be sheriff.' His major compensation was an enhanced reputation, since holding the office gave him a 'grand opportunity for the display of family prestige and wealth'.[3]

What is known about Sheriff Courtenay's role in suppressing the Western Rising is very little. The agitation against the Book of Common Prayer, authorised by the First Statute of Uniformity, started in Cornwall around Easter 1549. Rebels marching under the banner of the Five Wounds of Christ defeated gentry loyal to the crown at St Michael's Mount. The rebel grievances here and later in Devon were a combination of mistrust of the gentry, hostility toward religious changes, and concern about rising costs and unemployment. In early June, the Cornish rebels invaded Devon, and Sheriff Courtenay did not have the forces to impede their progress.[4]

On 10 June, an independent rising broke out in the Devon village of Sampford Courtenay. Sir Hugh Pollard and other local gentry tried but failed to negotiate with the rebels, who shortly afterwards, joined with the Cornish insurgents. Meanwhile, the royal council decided to send Sir Peter Carew, vice admiral of Devon, and his uncle, Sir Gawain Carew, to pacify the shire. The Carews possessed a proclamation promising pardons to all who ceased their defiance. When they reached Exeter about 21 June, they met with the Devonshire Justices of the Peace and Sheriff Courtenay. Apparently leaving Courtenay at Exeter, the Carews and their associates attempted but failed to negotiate with the rebels at the village of Crediton.

A further rising took place at Clyst St Mary, a village belonging to John, Lord Russell. On 23 June, the rebels fortified a position in Clyst St Mary where Sir Hugh Pollard and his associates succeeded in negotiating with them but complicated matters by promising the rebels, at least temporarily, to suspend the new religious laws. When informed about these concessions, Sir Peter Carew, supported by Sheriff Courtenay, reacted with outrage. They 'sharply' criticised these 'sinister . . . dealings.' Pollard and his associates should have 'suppressed their outrages' rather than 'maintaining their follies.'[5]

On 2 July, the rebels began a siege of Exeter, which was to last five weeks, and established a circuit of fortified places around the city. Although there were social and religious divisions at Exeter, which was still mainly Catholic, the governing elite retained control of the city. Sheriff Courtenay was said to have criticised some of its inhabitants who were sympathetic to the rebels, deploring their 'lukewarm attitude and lack of active support' for the civic leaders.[6] In response to the inability of local officials to subdue the Rising, the royal council ordered Lord Russell to take armed forces to pacify the shire. On 6 August, the siege was raised and on 16 August, the rebels were defeated at Clyst St Mary.

Meanwhile, Sheriff Courtenay's whereabouts remained undisclosed in documents until his widow died in 1605. John Hooker noted 'sundry gentleman' who left Exeter for their 'appointed places' were held captive in prison and 'many of them kept . . . the whole time of the commotion and abode great hardness, and were in peril of life and limb.' Among them Hooker named Walter Raleigh, who was kept in the Tower of St Sidwell's without the east gate of Exeter and was 'many times threatened to be executed to death.'[7] Hooker also identified some gentlemen who remained in Exeter, including John Courtenay, Piers's younger half-brother. Had Sheriff Courtenay stayed at Exeter, surely Hooker would have noted his presence.

After the rebellion ended, Courtenay seems to have been rewarded for his loyalty, acquiring a knighthood and Ugbrooke Park in 1549. He was only the second lay possessor of the park which was attached to the precentorship of Exeter Cathedral until 1547, when Bishop John Veysey granted a lease for ninety-nine years of the manor, park, and palace to Edward Seymour, Duke of Somerset, King Edward VI's lord protector. Courtenay obtained the park while the manor went to an Oxfordshire resident.

In 1551, Sir Piers escaped the fatal sweating sickness that swept through Devon but died in May of the next year. He was buried at St Martin's and St Mary's Church in Chudleigh Parish, and his will, dated 23 May, was later proved by Dr Miles Coverdale, Bishop of Exeter. The church's most prominent memorial, which can be found on the north wall of the chancel, is of members of Sir Piers's family. It honors him and his wife Elizabeth, names their seven children, and identifies their daughters' husbands. It was erected in 1607 by Sir Piers' grandchild, Thomas, the son of Anne Courtenay and Anthony Clifford, whose descendants still possess Ugbrooke.[8]

Sir Piers's widow would survive him by fifty-three years during which time she remained unmarried. She died on 8 November 1605, and, according to Robert Wolcombe, the vicar of Chudleigh who preached her funeral sermon, all seven of her children predeceased her as well as her husband. Extolling her piety, Wolcombe referred briefly to her religious patience that was challenged by Sheriff Courtenay's imprisonment in 1549:

> This patience was shaken by the captivity of her husband, an honorable and worthy gentleman; who being sheriff of this county was taken prisoner, and in extreme peril to be cruelly handled by the rebels in the Western Commotion, in the reign of Edward VI: again, by the death of her aforesaid husband, within a few years after . . .[9]

In his sermon elsewhere, Wolcombe indicated he was quite familiar with the personal details of her life and those of her family. As her pastor, he seemed to have developed a good relationship with her, since she trusted him enough to ask him to write portions of her will.

It is extraordinary that neither Hooker nor Peter Carew reported the rebels' capture of the king's sheriff. However, Hooker's focus was on Exeter and both Carews departed that city momentarily to report to the royal council on the conditions in Devon.[10] While the first evidence of the sheriff's imprisonment was not written down until 1605, there seems no reason to disallow the testimony of the preacher, who was well acquainted with Lady Courtenay's personal life and that of the members of her family.

Notes and References

1. For details of the Courtenay family, see William Harwood 'The Courtenay Family in the Politics of Region and Nation in the Later-Fifteenth and Early-Sixteenth Centuries,' Unpublished PhD thesis, University of Cambridge, 1978.
2. Gladwin 1974, pp. 269-76.
3. Ibid, p. 277 and pp. 286-7.
4. The most detailed modern account of the rebellion remains Frances Rose-Troup, *The Western Rebellion of 1549: an account of the insurrection in Devonshire and Cornwall against religious innovations in the Reign of Edward VI*, London: Smith, Elder & Co., 1913.
5. Hooker 1765. The text was printed in 1587.
6. Gladwin 1974, p. 272. This is not in Hooker and Gladwin gave no source for it.
7. Hooker 1765, p. 42 and p. 46. This Walter Raleigh was the father of the more famous Elizabethan courtier, explorer, and author, Sir Walter Raleigh.
8. Crockett 1985, p. 22, Jones p. 83.
9. Wolcombe 1606, repr. 2009, pp. 73-4. Although Wolcombe was spelled with an 'e' on this printed funeral sermon, it is usually spelled without the 'e'.
10. Maclean 1857, pp. 47-53.

Bibliography

Crockett, A. (1985) *Chudleigh: a chronicle*, Exeter: Devon Books.

Gladwin, I. (1974) *The Sheriff: the man and his office*, London: Victor Gollancz, Ltd.

Hooker, J., The *Antique Description and Account of the City of Exeter in Three Parts*, Exeter. 1765. Eighteenth Century Collections Online. http//find.galegroup.com (Accessed 1 September 2009). The text was printed in 1587. See 'The Holinshed Texts', The Holinshed Project <http://www.english.ox.ac.uk/holinshed/> (Accessed 22 September 2009).

Jones, Mary (1875) *The History of Chudleigh, Devon*, revised 2nd edn by William W. Snell, Chudleigh: G.E. Searle.

Maclean, J. (1857) *The Life and Times of Sir Peter Carew, Kt. With a Historical Introduction and Elucidatory Notes*, London: Bell & Daldy.

Rose-Troup, F. (1913) *The Western Rebellion of 1549: an account of the insurrection in Devonshire and Cornwall against religious innovations in the reign of Edward VI*, London: Smith, Elder & Co..

Wolcombe, R. (1606) (rept 2009) *The State of the Godly Both in This Life and in the Life to Come*, Doebler B.A. and Warnicke R.M. (eds) Ann Arbor, Michigan: Scholars' Facsimiles & Reprints.

A Thorncombe Byway: an investigation

Eve Higgs

'Every object in the landscape tells us something, though we are not always sure what it is really saying.'

W.G. Hoskins[1]

Introduction

Set in the West Dorset Area of Outstanding Beauty, the parish of Thorncombe is a secluded rural settlement nestling in the Axe Valley beneath Blackdown Hill in the Dorset borderlands, abutting East Devon and South Somerset (see Plate 14). The nearest towns are Axminster, Chard and Crewkerne, each being just over seven miles away. Until the 1844 parliamentary boundary changes Thorncombe was in Devon, and part of the Axminster Hundred. Its population rose from approximately 945 in 1674 to 1,425 in 1841.[2] Surviving wills paint a picture of a community supporting itself through a combination of agriculture and the various processes associated with wool production.[3]

The 4,896 acre parish which currently has a population of around 700, retains its historic form with habitation concentrated around the village, radiating outwards from the church at its centre. Its two gentry seats, Forde Abbey and Sadborow Hall, are isolated from the parish nucleus. Whilst their owners remain major local landholders, dispersal of their estates began in the late nineteenth century and continued piecemeal during the economic depression which preceded World War

149

II, so with the exception of a small proportion of public housing, most of the houses in the parish are privately owned.

Pockets of concentrated habitation are also found in the outlying hamlets of Hewood and Holditch. Elsewhere in the parish, isolated farms and houses are scattered across the open countryside. Land use echoes the mid eighteenth century; crops grown mainly for fodder, cattle husbandry, milk production and lamb breeding. The landscape is characterised by areas of woodland, wet valley bottoms with rough pasture, a patchwork of small enclosed fields, trimmed hedgerows and an intricate network of public footpaths and tracks of which one in particular invites further investigation.

An unassuming rutted grass track, it appears to be an alternative byway of some antiquity for travellers wishing to avoid the centre of the village. Examination of the surrounding landscape yields several clues suggesting one of its possible functions. A highly visible Scots pine marks another footpath along the skyline of Blackdown Hill to its north-east. Other trees define the line of Causeway Hill. These evergreen trees with their distinctive silhouettes, are said to have been traditional waymarkers for drovers.[4]

Droving, the herding of large numbers of cattle and sheep in search of new pastures, dates back to the Neolithic. With the growth in commerce during the Middle Ages the drover became a familiar figure at cattle markets. Trade reached its peak during the eighteenth century with the expansion of urban populations, and died away during middle of the nineteenth century with the introduction of the railways, finally disappearing during the early years of the twentieth century. The Irish, Scots and Welsh trade is well documented but published material on the history of English drovers, particularly in the South West is fragmentary. The last known drover, Edward Know died in South Croydon, in 1961 aged 100. But Walter Scott's fictional drover Rob Roy still lives on in folk memory and continues to stalk the speculative landscape of a wayfarer's romantic imagination.[5]

As well as Scots pines there are other physical indicators of possible regular drover traffic in Thorncombe, in the network of roads connecting to the track. What appear to be overgrown drifts line the road between Forde Abbey and Birdsmoorgate, one of the main arteries running through the parish. Drifts are wide parallel tracks tracing thoroughfares providing drovers with alternatives for driving herds.

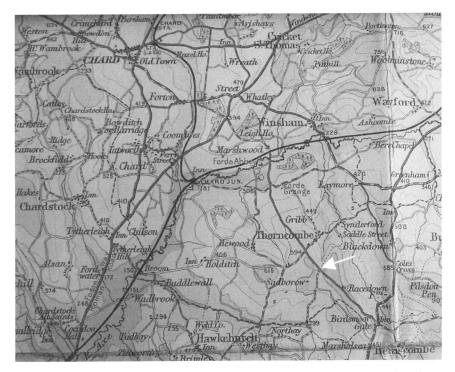

Figure 1. Bartholomew's Reduced Ordnance Survey Map for Tourists and Cyclists *c.*1897–1903 showing Sadborow Pound, Thorncombe and the track leading to Saddle Street. Dorset History Centre, Shelfmark 912.4233. Reproduced by kind permission of Dorset History Centre.

This road crosses the south-west end of the track, at a junction called Sadborow Pound (Figure 1) which could relate in some way to the track and the drifts. The pound survives here amongst the undergrowth. So there is strong circumstantial evidence that significant numbers of drovers passed through Thorncombe during its history.

Eight other tracks in Thorncombe are registered as monuments and categorised as medieval drove roads by English Heritage. This particular track remains unrecorded, except as a bridleway on the current Definitive Footpath Map and as part of a long distance footpath, The Monarch Way. What follows is an account of an investigation exploring why this track hasn't been recorded and whether there is sufficient evidence to make a case for its inclusion in the Dorset Historic Environment Record database as a drove road.[6]

Measuring up to four metres wide in places, the track is reached

through a farm gate opposite Sadborow Pound from the aforementioned
metalled road at its south-west end. It curves along the north-west
perimeter of four hedged and gated arable fields, initially following
the course of Stonelake Brook, before veering towards what was once
the farmyard for Yew Tree Farm and becoming a metalled road at
Saddle Street which meets the main access road into the village from
the north-east. While still used by agricultural vehicles, the track is
now mainly frequented by walkers and horse riders.

Cartographic evidence

The earliest traceable record of the track is as a minor road, identified
as having potential military use, on the 1806 Ordnance Surveyor's
hand-drawn map of Beaminster. The map is one of a series drawn

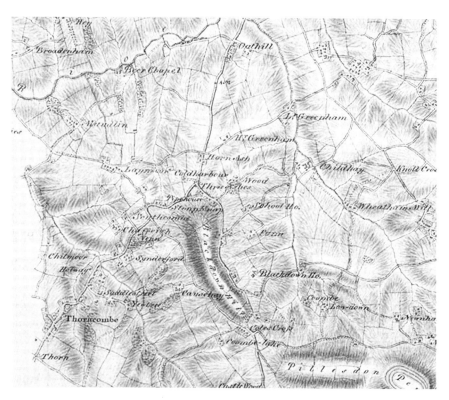

Figure 2. Budgen's 1806 drawing, extracted from the Ordnance Survey hill
sketches, also showing the track. © British Library Board. Reference: BL
Shelfmark: Maps Reference: Z.5a.(5).

up in anticipation of possible invasion along the southern seaboard. Surveyor C. Budgen's drawings which formed the basis of the first 1809 OS map for the area (two inches to the mile), appear to offer the earliest detailed depiction of Thorncombe's road network (see Figure 2).[7] The track provides an alternative route to Sadborow Hall, formerly Thorncombe Manor, from the north-west avoiding the centre of the village. Until its dissolution in 1544, Thorncombe Manor was part of the Forde Abbey estate.

The oft quoted Mr Good speculates that the track is part of the route from Axminster to Yeovil, on Speed's 1662 map of Dorsetshire, but this is unlikely given the medieval King's Highway went through the middle of the village providing a direct route for travellers.[8] Although there is a possibility, given its configuration, that the track could once have been a main thoroughfare skirting Thorncombe Manor's medieval parkland and that the road running from Thorn to Sadborow Pound is a later addition to Thorncombe's infrastructure. However, no documents have come to light to support this hypothesis. Nor is there any evidence to support Good's theory suggesting the footpaths leading to Causeway Lane from Yew Tree Farm were part of the Axminster to Yeovil route.

PREHISTORIC AND MEDIEVAL EVIDENCE

Archaeology

Motorised farm vehicles and mechanised ploughing along its edges have much altered the track. Its provenance could well stretch back into prehistory, given its inclusion in Grundy's Dorset network of prehistoric ridgeways.[9] However, despite the proximity of the Iron Age hill forts of Pilsdon Pen, Lambert's Castle and Coney's Castle, no formal archaeological investigations have been undertaken in the vicinity, nor have any finds of objects been recorded near the track.[10] So while there is circumstantial evidence, whether or not the track dates back to the Stone Age is uncertain.[11]

Hedgerows

According to Hooper's Rule hedgerows can be dated accurately by counting the number of species of indigenous shrubs and trees in a sample thirty yard (twenty-eight metre) stretch, each species representing 100 years.[12] Applying the rule to the hedge along the track's perimeter and the pound in August 2010, suggested a date of around 1000. Ash, blackthorn, dogwood, elder, hazel, holly, oak, hawthorn, briar rose and sycamore, were recorded. However an eighteenth-century document found among papers from the parish of Cruwys Morchard in the Devon Record Office describing the construction of a Devon hedgebank casts doubt on Hooper's hedge dating method. The evidence is that mixed species were planted on new Devon hedgebanks during this period, so self seeding may not necessarily be a valid argument to support his rule.[13] In his considerations on Hooper's preliminary results, Hoskins also pointed out that if the number of species vary from county to county and given those limitations, a hedgebank could be older than numbers indicate, so he was not convinced by Hooper's Rule either.[14]

Nevertheless, documentary evidence of one of Thorncombe's listed medieval drove roads, Blind Lane, supports its application. Another rutted track, hedge banked on both sides, it follows the route of the old Winsham Road from Chard Street, opposite Gribb View (see Plate 15). A 1549 charter describes land belonging to John Chydley abutting a tenement 'in the lane called Blynd lane' belonging to 'John Veer', Earl of Oxford.[15] Hedge dating in Blind Lane in September 2010 identified elder, holly, hawthorn, hazel and sycamore in a specimen thirty yard stretch. This indicated an estimated age of 500 years, suggesting that the hedge was planted around the time of the 1549 charter, which puts it just outside the English Heritage medieval listing timeframe of 1066-1539 and supports the veracity of Hooper's Rule.

Drifts

Hoskins identified roads converging on 'recognised cattle markets' and running parallel with main roads as drifts or droveways.[16] Tree lined channels, marked on the 1889 OS map which could be drifts, still shadow the road on both sides in places, running from Forde Abbey to Birdsmoorgate. They vary in width between two metres and four metres. One, which runs from the gateway towards Birdsmoorgate yielded five species growing on its hedgebanks which according to Hooper's Rule dates it to around 1500, while four species recorded along those running down Horseshoe Lane from Forde Abbey date it 100 years later. Large crowned hazels lining these routes are possible witnesses to generations of Sadborow and Forde Abbey tenants exploiting their ancient *estover* rights of fire and *hedge botes* and coppicing over the centuries.[17] The channels could also have been dug for drainage purposes, the roads in question being subject to torrents of water and flooding during heavy rain. Or they could been alternative thoroughfares for travellers when the road was congested with pack horses, the principal means of conveying goods through the steep narrow muddy roads in Devon until turnpiking began in the mid eighteenth century. In view of their other possible functions, and given their restricted width in places, whether these parallel channels are drifts is uncertain.

Dorset Historic Environment Record

In the Dorset Historic Environment Record the eight roads are 'green lanes . . . old unpaved thoroughfare[s] with hedges and banks on either side'.[18] The roads were included in the English Heritage Monuments Record in 1979 following a 'Countryside Treasures' Survey which was carried out by local volunteers. Their recommendations have never been substantiated by listings officers. Medieval Drove Road was the closest available category, hence the nature of their listed status.

Market Charter

None of the readily available material relating to Thorncombe for this period proved useful during this investigation, apart from the 1313 market charter granted to the Abbot and Convent of Forde Abbey by Edward I. The terms of the charter are 'a weekly market on Wednesday at their manor of Thorncombe . . . and a yearly fair there On Tuesday in Easter Week and the five days following', but no evidence has come to light that it was a cattle market during the Middle Ages.[19] Therefore while, according to Grundy, there are some grounds for claiming that the track dates back to the tenth century, there are insufficient grounds for claiming that the track was part of a network of medieval drove roads serving Thorncombe's cattle market.

EARLY MODERN EVIDENCE

Antiquarian

Antiquarians often include market town status in their gazetteers. While he includes the value of Thorncombe's tithe in his list of Devon parishes, there is no separate entry in Elizabethan Devon antiquarian John Hooker's *c*.1600 manuscript, nor does he mention Thorncombe in his list of market towns.[20] Westcote writing around 1630 does not include Thorncombe at all and Pole writing around the same time, focuses on Thorncombe's history of land ownership. The earliest description of Thorncombe is found in Risdon's 1630 *Chorographical Survey . . . of Devon*, but he does not refer to a weekly market or an annual fair either. Risdon identifies thirty-three other market towns in Devon, but in his introduction states there are thirty-seven, so it is possible Thorncombe was excluded in error, his arithmetic was poor or perhaps the market closed following the dissolution of Forde Abbey?[21] There are no records of butchers' licences or prosecutions for short-selling for example, in the Devon Quarter Sessions papers for Thorncombe for the period spanning the sixteenth and seventeenth centuries, which might support this theory.

However, evidence of an eighteenth-century market is found in two nineteenth-century topographies. In the Devon volume of *Magna Britannia* published in 1822, Samuel Lysons includes brief details of Thorncombe's market and fair, adding that the market ceased trading in the 1770s.[22] Further evidence of cattle being brought to Thorncombe on a regular basis is found in Pulman's 1854 *Book of the Axe*.[23] As well as mentioning Thorncombe's annual cattle fair, Pulman also adds that meat was sold weekly in 'a large market house'.

Questionnaires

Unpublished documents yield further evidence. 'Sheep & horned cattle' were sold at Thorncombe's weekly market and annual fair according to answers to a questionnaire sent to Thorncombe's parish priest Samuel Hood by Jeremiah Milles, Dean of Exeter, who researched Devon agriculture between 1762 and 1784.[24] Hood's questionnaire is undated but was completed in 1767 or thereabouts. Despite lack of evidence relating to the Middle Ages, Milles's evidence suggests that

Thorncombe's weekly market and annual fair may have been revived sometime during the second half of the eighteenth century.

Answers in Hood's questionnaire relating to the market are corroborated in a letter dated 1821 by another Thorncombe parish priest, Charles Etherington, support Pulman's assertion.[25] Etherington's letter is addressed to Samuel Lysons, who like Milles, used parish priests as scouts for his *Magna Brittania*. In response to a request for further information about Thorncombe's market, Etherington reports back the results of his inquiries made among older residents 'who state there was a very pretty market place for grain and meat, & had [some] little shops [permanent stalls] for other wants'.[26] Hood says that cattle bred in the parish are mainly for 'the pail' (milkers) and for grazing (fattening up), so as well as sheep, cattle for slaughter could have been brought into the market by drovers on a weekly and annual basis.

Tithe Map and Apportionment

Charles Etherington's letter enabled identification of the site of Thorncombe's market hall, when cross-referenced with the 1839 Tithe Map and the Apportionment.[27] The market place was '. . . enclosed with a wall and folding gates . . . it stood on the north side of the road a little away from it at the higher extremity of the village and that now forms part of a larger field called Pinney's Close'.[28] Plot 872 on the Apportionment is Great Pinneys Close and abuts plot 956, an open piece of ground located on the north side of High Street which is on a steep hill leading up to Thorncombe Thorn. There is a closed rectangular opening against the road, which suggests a gate. Here the road is wider than further down the hill, an indicator that there may also have been stalls along the street on market days. Plot 956 is therefore, the most likely location of Thorncombe's market place.

Field names in the Tithe Apportionment signpost Thorncombe's meat trade. Plot 1349 at the south-west end of the track is called Starve Acre which supports the theory that sheep and cattle were brought up the track from Saddle Street via Yew Tree Farm to avoid the main thoroughfare through the village. Animals due for slaughter were starved overnight and only allowed water to enable easier removal of the intestines. Synderford Brook is easily accessible from the meadow.

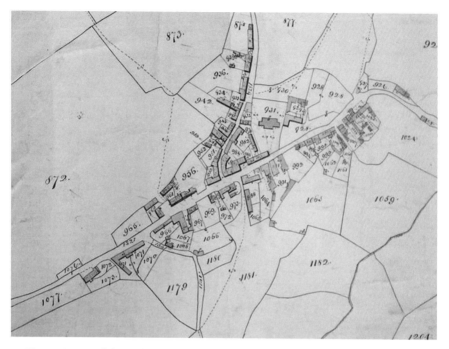

Figure 3. Detail from the Assize copy of the 1840 Tithe Map of Thorncombe.
Reproduced courtesy of Devon Record Office.

It runs along the perimeter of the track leading up to the road. From here there is a logical progression to the market. An enclosed footpath following the gorge through which the brook flows is a natural pen. It is still known today as 'The Dungeon'. Perhaps given the fate of the animals, this is an example of butchers' black humour? The path continues beyond The Dungeon, across to a field identified on the Tithe Map as Back Lears. Lairage means cattle enclosure which suggests that this is the site of the cattle auctions which took place at the annual Easter fair and were advertised in *Trewman's Exeter Flying Post* up to 1856.[29] No other information relating to the fair has been discovered to date during the course of this investigation.

Buildings

There is an illegible word in the Hood document which could be 'fodder' and refers to the sale of oats at the market. In his letter Charles Etherington also cites the sale of grain. Reverend Hood says that oats, barley and wheat were grown in the parish. Oats were fed to horses and cattle. Barley was either used for bread or malted to make beer. Selling by sample was established practice by 1750. The contents of a small bag of grain formed the basis of the transaction between buyer and vendor and took place away from the market place and auction. As was customary, deals were often struck in a pub over a glass of ale.[30]

The Golden Lion (now a private house) is conveniently situated for the cattle market at the top of Wittey's Lane. It connects the High Street with the footpath leading from Back Lears. Surviving wills of innkeepers William Hallet (1690) and Susan Follet (1767) show that the Golden Lion was open for business during the known lifetime of the market.[31] Of Thorncombe's two other pubs, the Royal Oak and The Crown, there is no evidence that they date back to the late eighteenth century. Oral tradition has it that there was a slaughterhouse behind the Golden Lion. But no records appear to have survived to support the suggestion that this is in some way connected to the Saturday market. In the 1841 census, eight butchers and one jobber in cattle are listed. It is therefore more likely that the hearsay refers to the nineteenth century rather than the eighteenth century.

Notebooks

Like Milles and Lysons, William Chapple also sent out questionnaires to parish priests in or around 1773. His plan was to revise and update Risdon but alas he died in 1781 before he could complete his task and only managed to publish a revised introduction to Risdon which does not include Thorncombe.[32] Chapple's papers were traced to private hands, enquiries were made and it is understood that neither the completed questionnaire nor any other relevant information relating to Thorncombe's market has survived.[33] Etherington puts the date of the market's closure at 'about 50 years ago' which corroborates a manuscript note also found among Lyson's notebooks. On a scrap of paper is a transcription of a list of Devon markets which apparently closed between 1772 and 1773, attributed to Chapple, which includes Thorncombe. Cross-referencing against an unattributed printed list of Fairs and Markets dated 1821 on the next page of Lyson's notebook confirms the supposition that Lysons used Chapples' list in his appendix of markets.[34] Etherington found that, 'many who could perfectly remember [the market, but] none can at all recollect the time of its removal. They account for their large [forgetfulness] upon this point by saying that after a gradual [declination] of the market, it entirely stopped for some time & then again was revived for a short time, & again ceasing the buildings were at last pulled down'.[35]

Chartres in Havinden suggests factors which influenced the decline of rural markets included road improvements, loss of trade to larger neighbours, and cattle disease.[36]

Turnpike Acts

By 1772/3 the main arteries from Axminster, Crewkerne and Chard linking to Thorncombe's approach roads were turnpiked.[37] A parliamentary act passed in 1770 enabled the Lyme Regis Crewkerne Trust to turnpike the road running between Hawkchurch and Thorncombe via Easthay and Schoolhouse through the village past the market place, which meant that traders and customers from outside the parish were subject to tolls from whichever direction they approached. The Trust levied twenty pence for every score of cattle or oxen and ten pence for every twenty sheep, calves or lambs. Wagons paid between four pence and two shillings depending on the number of horses, while horses were charged two pence each.[38]

Markets and Fairs

In 1767 Hood in answer to the Milles' question regarding where locally bred cattle were sold, answered, '[At] neighbouring fairs in Devon, Dorset and Somerset'. Thorncombe's Saturday market and annual Easter fair had stiff local competition. Axminster had a Saturday market and fairs in April, June and October. Crewkerne had a Saturday market and a cattle fair in September.[39] Chard had a Monday market and cattle markets in December, January, February and March.[40] Cricket St Thomas's annual Whitsun Whitedown Fair which attracted customers from within a forty-five mile radius, devoted Whit Tuesday to the sale of sheep, bullocks and other cattle.[41]

Cattle disease

From 1769 onwards cattle disease contracted as a result of imports from Holland spread sporadically through mainland Britain. Symptoms were similar to anthrax. An outbreak of cattle disease reached Southampton in 1770. In 1771, following wholesale slaughter, the epidemic died out but further measures were passed by parliament in December 1772 to 'prevent the further spreading of the Contagious disorder among Horned Cattle in Great Britain'.[42] While there is no evidence to suggest that the area around Thorncombe was affected, national movement of cattle was restricted by legislation during this period, which may account for the market's irregular trading pattern during the early 1770s before it closed for good, as recalled by older parishioners and reported to Samuel Lysons by Charles Etherington.

Conclusion

Between 1755 and 1812 five local butchers are recorded in Thorncombe and Hawkchurch's marriage registers but that is not enough to justify the theory that drovers brought large herds of animals for sale at Thorncombe market.[43] Of course butchers may have come from outside Thorncombe to trade but the area allocated to the market is not sufficient to accommodate significant numbers. So whatever the reason for its demise it is unlikely that Thorncombe's market was large enough to attract drovers in sufficient numbers to justify applying to the Dorset Environment Record to upgrade the status of the track as an early modern drove road.

The investigation failed to identify the byway linking Sadborow Pound with Saddle Street, as a drovers' road. There is circumstantial evidence in Grundy that the track's provenance may date back to the Neolithic, but this theory founders on lack of archaeological proof. No evidence has come to light to support the theory that it delineated the perimeter of Thorncombe Manor's park and pre-dates the road which connects Sadborow to what is now the crossroad at Thorncombe Thorn. Lack of medieval records also means that the physical clues in the landscape, the Scots pine waymarkers along the horizon of Blackdown Hill overlooking the track, hedge dating the boundary and the proximity of cattle pound are unsupported. Furthermore, as in other parts of Devon, the pines have been planted by nineteenth-century landlords. Informed speculation into the various possible functions of the rows of parallel trees lining overgrown channels along one of Thorncombe's main thoroughfares, while superficially resembling drifts, raises further doubts. English Heritage listings of medieval drover's roads elsewhere in the parish are unsubstantiated. Although it cannot be entirely ruled out that they are not part of a wider network of regional drove roads.

The investigation has uncovered new material regarding Thorncombe's early modern market and its annual fair. Linkage of parish records and secondary sources identified a small community of butchers, but not large enough to attract drovers herding large numbers of animals. Taking into account the stiff competition from neighbouring market towns, it would seem that Thorncombe's eighteenth-century Saturday market and annual Easter fair were not sufficiently significant to attract drovers. Therefore despite several physical indicators in the landscape, available supporting evidence suggests that the byway which has been the subject of this investigation, is not a missing element in Thorncombe's network of drovers' roads, medieval or otherwise.

Notes and References

1. Hoskins 1969, p. 32.
2. Stoate 1982, pp. 14-15; *Census of Great Britain* 1841.
3. <http://www.opcdorset.org/ThorncombeFiles/ThorncombeWills.htm>.
4. Mabey 1998, pp. 115-120.
5. Bonser 1970, pp. 17-20, 29-33, 223-229.
6. South Somerset District Council 1993, *Liberty Trail*, Stage 5.
7. Budgen's drawing can be viewed on the British Library website: www.imagesonline.bl.uk. Ordnance Survey Hill Sketches, OSD 54, Beaminster (1806) [online] Available at: <http://www.bl.uk/onlinegallery/onlineex/ordsurvdraw>. The 1809 ordnance survey map for Thorncombe can be viewed [online] Available at: <www.visionofbritain.org>.
8. Good 1996, p. 59.
9. Grundy 1975, pp. 278-280.
10. Cumulative index to The Proceedings of The Dorset Natural History and Archaeological Society.
11. Hoskins 1988, p. 191.
12. Rackham 1986, pp. 194-204.
13. Stanes 2008, pp. 139-149.

14. Hoskins 1969, pp. 128-129.
15. Anon. 1935, p. 243-244.
16. Hoskins 1969, p. 145.
17. Blackstone 1832, p. 27.
18. <www.heritagegateway.org.uk>.
19. Maxwell 1908, p. 240
20. DRO, Z/19/18/9, pp. 73, 223, 225 and 339-341.
21. Risdon 1811, pp. 15-17.
22. Lysons 1822, pp. 496-520.
23. Pulman 1854, pp. 211-226.
24. WCSL, [microfiche], Milles, *Questionnaires*, 1767–1784. Thorncombe.
25. BL, Add. MS 9427, p. 116.
26. Ibid.
27. DHC, PC/THO, Thorncombe Tithe Map and Apportionment (1839).
28. Ibid.
29. <http://www.oed.com>.
30. Mingay 1989, pp. 128-131; 238-240.
31. TNA, PROB/11/638; PROB11/934.
32. DRO, 3590.
33. TNA, NRA 39274.
34. WCSL, [microfiche] Lysons, D. & S. (*c*.1807) *Notebook*, pp. 67-70.
35. Ibid.
36. Havinden 1973, pp. 65-66.
37. 31 Geo. II *c*.43 (1757), p. 8.
38. 10 Geo. III *c*.59 (1770), pp. 124-125, 127.
39. Dunning 1978, pp. 4-38.
40. Owen 1816, pp. 16, 60.
41. Dunning 1978, pp. 133-141.
42. Spinage 2003, pp .138-139,706.
43. <http://www.opcdorset.org/ThorncombeFiles/Thorncombe Mars2.htm>; <http://www.opcdorset.org/HawkchurchFiles/ HawkchurchMars.htm>.

Bibliography

Anon. (1935) 'Thorncombe Thorn', *SDNQ*, 21, p. 243-244.

Blackstone, Sir W. (1832) *Commentaries on the Laws of England in Four Books: with analysis of the work*, Archer Ryland, vol. 1, J.B. Lippincott & Co., [online] Available at: <http://books.google.co.uk/ books> (Accessed 17 December 2010).

Bonser, K.J. (1972) *The Drovers: who they were and how they went: an epic of the English countryside*, Newton Abbot: Country Book Club.

Brayshay, M. (ed.) (1996) *Topographical Writers in South-West England*, Exeter: University of Exeter Press.

Census of Great Britain 1841. [online] Available at: <http://www.opcdorset.org/Thorncombe> (Accessed 17 December 2011).

Dorset Historic Environment Record, [online] Available at: <www.heritagegateway.org.uk> (Accessed 3 December 2010).

Dorset Natural History and Archaeological Society, Cumulative Index to the *Proceedings*, [online] Available at: <http://research.dorsetcountymuseum.org/> (Accessed on 2 December 2010).

Dunning, R.W. (ed.) (1978) *Victoria County History: a history of the county of Somerset*: vol. 4, [online] Available at: <http://www.british-history.ac.uk> (Accessed 20 December 2010).

Good, R. (1966) *The Old Roads of Dorset*, Bournemouth: Horace G. Commin.

Grundy, G.B. (1975) 'The Ancient Highways of Dorset, Somerset and South-West England', *Archaeological Journal*, 94, pp. 257-290.

Havinden, M. (ed.) (1973) *Husbandry and Marketing in the South-West 1500–1800* Exeter: University of Exeter.

Hobbs, S. (ed.) (1998) *Cartulary of Forde Abbey*, (Series), 85, Taunton: Somerset Record Society.

Hooker, J. (1599) A discourse on Devon, with blasom of armes etc, the bishops of Exeter, the revenews of the deaneries and pastonages and other gentlemen, microfiche, WCSL, Exeter.

Hoskins, W.G. (1969) *Fieldwork in Local History*, London: Faber & Faber.

Hoskins, W.G. (1988) *The Making of the English Landscape with an Introduction and Commentary by Christopher Taylor*, London: Hodder & Stoughton.

South Somerset District Council (1993) *Liberty Trail*, Stage 5, Thorncombe to Wootton Fitzpaine, South Somerset District Council.

Lysons, S. & D. (1822) *Magna Britannia*, vol. 6, [online] Available at: <http://www.british-history.ac.uk> (Accessed 21 December 2010).

Mabey, R. (1998) *Flora Britannica, the concise edition*, London: Chatto & Windus.

Maxwell H.C. et al. (1908) *Calendar of the Charter Rolls Preserved in the Public Record Office*, vol. 3, London: HMSO, [online] Available at: <http://www.archive.org> (Accessed 6 December 2010).

Mingay, G.E. (ed.) (1989) *Agrarian History of England and Wales*, vol. 6, 1750–1850, Cambridge: Cambridge University Press.

Oliver, G. & Jones P. (eds) (1845) *A View of Devonshire in 1630, T. Westcote*, Exeter: W. Roberts.

Ordance Survey Hill Sketches, OSD 54, Beaminster (1806), [online] Available at: <http://www.bl.uk/onlinegallery/onlineex/ordsurvdraw> (Accessed 7 December 2010).

Ordnance Survey Old Series, Sheet 21 (1809) [online] Available at: <www. visionofbritain.org.uk> (Accessed 7 December 2010).

Owen, W., (1816) *Owen's New Book of Fairs, being a complete and authentic account of all the fairs in England and Wales*, London: Scatherd & Latterman et al, [online] Available at: <http://www.archive. org> (Accessed 23 December 2010).

Oxford English Dictionary, [on-line] Available at: <http://www.oed.com> (Accessed 20 December 2010).

Pole, Sir W. (1791) *Collections Towards a Description of the County of Devon by Sir William Pole – (who died A.D. 1635)*, London: J. Nicholls [on-line] Available at: <http://books.google.co.uk/books> (Accessed 7 December 2010).

Pulman, G. (1854) *Book of the Axe*, [on-line] Available at: <http://books. google.co.uk/books > (Accessed 7 December 2010).

Rackham, O. (1986) *The History of the Countryside: the classic history of Britain's landscape, flora and fauna*, London: Phoenix Press.

Risdon T. (1811) *The Chorographical Description or Survey of the County of Devon*, London: Rees & Curtis, pp. 15-17. [online] Available at: <http://books.google.co.uk/books> (Accessed 16 December 2010).

Spinage, C. (2003) *Cattle Plague: a history* (New York: Springer) [online] Available at: <http://books.google.co.uk/books> (Accessed 20 December 2010).

Stanes, R., Jewell, A. & Bass, R. (2008) *The Husbandry of Devon and Cornwall*, Exeter: Stanes.

Stoate, T. (ed.) (1982) *Devon Hearth Tax Return, Lady Day 1674*, Bristol: Stoate.

The North Devon Shipping Industry c.1650–1850: war, Wales, and the Bristol Channel dynamic

Michael Nix

Ten years after the signing of the Treaty of Versailles in 1783 Britain was again at war with France resulting in a dramatic contraction of overseas markets. The conflict and structural changes brought about by increased industrial and agricultural production combined to stimulate demand for more shipping resources at a time of great tonnage shortages. In addition to this, large numbers of merchant ships were needed for government transports or lost to enemy action. The pressures on shipping capacity applied by the volume of trade in the Bristol Channel mounted as new inland transport infrastructures in South Wales helped to accelerate the exploitation of vast reserves of coal for outward shipment. Cornish mine owners also capitalised on the Welsh demand for copper and tin ores. It seems natural to assume that the ripple effect of these powerful interactive forces would have stimulated all of the North Devon shipping industry, but this was not to be the case.

At the end of the seventeenth century the merchants and shipowners of Bideford and Barnstaple enjoyed the confidence and increasing prosperity generated by the English Atlantic trades, especially from the import and re-export of tobacco and the Newfoundland cod fisheries. As the only receiving ports in the county, they benefitted too from the carriage of Irish wool to manufacturing centres such as Tiverton

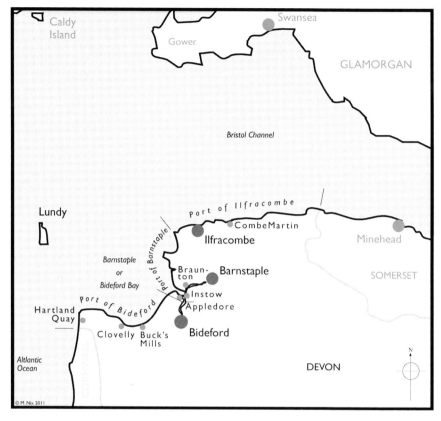

Figure 1. The Customs ports, port boundaries, creeks and some landing places in North Devon before 1814.

and Ashburton. Evidence of the buoyant economy during this period is reflected in local landmarks. Notable examples are Nathaniel Gascoyne's handsome brick houses in Bideford, and the colonnaded Exchange (sixty-seven feet in length) in Barnstaple known as Queen Anne's Walk. However, during the eighteenth century, North Devon's merchants could not absorb the disruptions of recurrent warfare and its attendant fluctuating economic cycles. Neither could they avoid the consequences of the South West's diminishing wool trade. Their problems were compounded by the fact that they were unable to compete on equal terms with the vigorous and expanding port of Bristol. Acting as the focal point for coastal and river traffic, the city imposed considerable demands on the agricultural and industrial output of counties along the Bristol Channel, although much of the coastal shipping remained in the hands of owners living in ports within the commercial ambit of the metropolis.[1]

Following the American Revolutionary War, Barnstaple, although commercially damaged, emerged from the conflict with some of its once extensive overseas connections still intact. Its vessels employed in carrying goods between both Britain and Europe, and North America and the West Indies, directly imported wines and fruit from southern Europe, cod-fish from Newfoundland and timber and naval stores from the Baltic.[2] During the course of the century, Bideford proved less resilient. A plea made on behalf of some inhabitants of the town during proceedings in the Court of Exchequer in 1766, incorporated the belief that their present pecuniary problems dated to the war years at the turn of the century. Looking back from a standpoint of 'a now decayed Town' to the days of 'a once flourishing' port they concluded, after combing through official records, that the year 1693 possessed a special significance: then sixty-four 'sail of ships' traded 'to foreign ports'.[3] The petitioners complained of the loss of the Newfoundland fishery and the wool trade and drew attention to the Custom House records which showed that in 1765 only seven craft were employed overseas and just one, a 'small vessel', imported tobacco.[4]

The ports of North Devon (Figure 1) entered the nineteenth century primarily engaged in the coasting trades whose carrier routes were geared to the needs of a predominantly agrarian society. Geographically, trading networks were confined predominantly to the western half of the British Isles, from South Devon to the Firth of Clyde in Scotland, and to Ireland. The ports of the South West peninsular (including Bristol) and South Wales were significant to both Bideford and Barnstaple. Barnstaple also benefitted from important trading links embracing a number of Irish ports, notably Dublin.[5]

South Wales supplied North Devon with large quantities of coal, culm and limestone, used for either industrial or domestic consumption.[6] The development of the Rolle Canal between Langport and Rosemoor, and branches of the Bude Canal near Holsworthy, considerably enlarged the region's agricultural hinterland accessible from the sea and created increased demand for limestone and culm supplied through Bideford and Bude. In 1818 a Swansea outport letter book reported 40,000 tons of limestone shipped from Wales to the North Devon coast in twenty coasters aggregating 800 voyages per year.[7] Other goods including building materials such as Delabole slate and timber and naval stores for shipbuilding were also brought into the region coastwise.[8]

The relatively small quantities of agricultural goods reported in newspaper shipping arrivals lists – including malt from Swansea, clover seed from Bridgwater and Irish livestock – suggests a degree of self-sufficiency, with produce supplied to satisfy occasional needs, or in response to periods of dearth. Merchandise from Bristol, and to a lesser extent from London, consisted of a profusion of articles. With rare exception, the variety was usually lost in the all embracing term 'sundry'. However, the surviving papers and accounts of the Barnstaple quay master John Milton provide an invaluable source for studying the distribution and collection of such goods in the North Devon area. In late November 1811, for example, 'country' goods unloaded from the Barnstaple-Bristol regular trader *Resolution* included, amongst other things, bags of nails, plough share moulds, bar iron, rum and cheese. Earlier in the month the carrier between Barnstaple and South Molton delivered goods from another vessel comprising bags of dye, half a ton of hemp for a rope-maker, five casks of currants, two chests of soap, one box of tobacco, hardware, pots, nails, paint, oil, pitch, rock lead, coffee, candles, sugar, fudge and leather. Other cargoes included a rocking horse, malt and chaffing mills and a harpsichord.[9]

The market for North Devon's abundant timber supplies included shipbuilding centres, particularly Greenock, Port Glasgow and Plymouth. Another source of revenue for the wooded estates of the region was derived from the sale of oak bark to Scottish and Irish leather tanners. Other returns came from town and village potteries which shipped their products to ports mainly in South Wales, Devon and Cornwall. Key markets were located in Swansea, Carmarthen, Pembroke, Plymouth and Bristol. Most cargoes of malt went to Swansea, Newport and Tenby, whilst Bideford, Ilfracombe and Hartland Quay were noted for the large amounts of corn sent to Bristol in particular. Dubliners favoured Barnstaple beer. Apples were occasionally dispatched with oak bark to Scotland and with earthenware to South Wales. Similarly, cheese, fish, live cattle, reed, wheat flour, cider, potatoes and wool were sent on an irregular basis to various ports. Other products – from guns and bricks, to lampblack and copper ore, to ochre and paint, to iron ore and silver-lead ore from a Combe Martin mine – were similarly distributed coastwise.[10]

In the year before the outbreak of war in 1793 Barnstaple received nineteen overseas cargoes. The diverse range of goods consisted of fish from Newfoundland, rice from North Carolina, raisins from Bayonne, wine from Cadiz, fruit and wine from Malaga, and timber and naval stores from the Baltic. The seven overseas inward cargoes for Bideford consisted mostly of timber and lumber from the Baltic.[11] In 1792, the Bideford cleric John Watkins reported that although 'at the present time, Bideford enjoys no foreign commercial consequence, at least not worth mentioning' he noted a revival in trade with the United States and British North America in the previous two or three years following the importation 'of a few occasional cargoes of timber, pine, plank, and tar from the Massachusets [*sic*] and Nova Scotia'.[12] Later, following the imposition of Napoleon's Continental Blockade in 1807, national shortages of timber forced a redirection of trade towards British North America. In 1818, one entrepreneurial Bideford merchant, Thomas Burnard, sent experienced shipwrights to establish a new enterprise at New Bideford, Prince Edward's Island. There they constructed the 342 ton *Mars* which sailed to Bideford carrying lumber, the opening of a new trade.[13]

An examination of the overall tonnage owned in Bideford and the tonnage of vessels regularly trading coastwise with the home port reveal a marked difference between the two. During 1806, for instance, a total of 458 vessels arrived at Bideford quay, of which 351 carried cargoes (seven came from abroad). Thirty-three of the eighty-two vessels (7,326 tons) registered in Bideford, aggregating more than half the port's tonnage, did not visit the port at any time during the year. If the arbitrary figure of four arrivals is used to define a 'constant' trader then sixty-one (just over 6,000 tons) of the vessels did not use the port on a regular basis. Allowing for some craft operating in and out of Clovelly and Hartland Quay, as well as those that arrived with a cargo before laying up for the winter, a very high proportion of Bideford's tonnage (perhaps as much as five or six-sevenths of the total) did not consistently engage in the home trade.[14]

Although the expanding North American trade in ships and timber offered new possibilities and promising returns, a new dynamic in waters closer to North Devon presented commercial opportunities for the region's ship owners. During the late eighteenth and early nineteenth centuries the volume of trade in the Bristol Channel grew rapidly, intensifying pressures on existing shipping capacity. The ports of South Wales were responding to a quickening rhythm in outward shipments of coal and inward movements of mineral ores for smelting. In 1799, over 300,000 tons of coal were dispatched coastwise; within twenty years the figure doubled.[15] The coal-fields were distributed along the Bristol Channel coast. Located at the western end the mines of Pembrokeshire yielded culm for industrial use, in lime and malt-kilns, for example. Moving eastwards the coal types graduated from hard culms to the softer bituminous grades more suited to domestic needs.[16] An area between Llanelli and Neath formed the centre of the industry during the eighteenth century. Miners exploited the coal seams nearest the seaboard, taking advantage of rivers and pills along which small vessels could navigate to load.[17] Beyond Port Talbot the southern fringes of the Culm Basin turn away from the coast where, approximately ten miles inland, the greatest reserves of coal were located. Beyond the reach of cheap transportation, they remained virtually unworked until the second half of the eighteenth century.

The exploitation of these vast reserves of coal accelerated in the 1790s following the construction of a number of canals and iron railways. The uplands of South Wales were connected to the tidewater by navigations completed at Cardiff in 1794, at Neath in 1795, and at Swansea in 1798.[18] Within the Bristol Channel region, Swansea's industrial progress, one of the outstanding economic features of the period, contributed to the waning of Bristol by attracting an increasing proportion of the coasting trade to South Wales.[19] The trend was heavily influenced by the bi-directional trades in Cornish tin and copper ore shipped up the Bristol Channel to the sources of fuel for smelting and refining and coal shipped in the opposite direction. During the 1810s, the author Richard Ayton noted of Hayle in Cornwall that 'there is a considerable trade at this port; the imports consisting principally of Welsh coal for the steam-engines and smelting houses, and the exports of copper'.[20] In 1824, over 100 vessels regularly engaged in Swansea's copper ore and coal trades.[21]

North Devon merchants and traders participated politically in promoting developments across the channel. The mayor and corporation of Barnstaple, for example, petitioned Parliament in favour of the construction of the Swansea Canal in March 1794.[22] By 1829, Devon (a significant consumer of South Wales coal) imported 273,000 tons annually; Cornwall received 163,000 tons. The two figures combined represent over one-tenth of coal imports into all of England's coastal counties.[23]

Thirteen outports lay within the vast geographic triangle of the Bristol Channel (Figure 2). The smaller ports, primarily active in the coasting trades, remained sheltered from the worst vicissitudes of fluctuating foreign markets. Focused on the needs of rural communities, they used shipping routes not readily interrupted by war, although still subject to enemy action. In response to the rapid expansion in the carrying trades resulting from industrialisation and an expanding population, the number of shipping movements in and out of the thirteen Channel ports increased substantially. In 1789, 11,036 movements were reported. Averaging thirty arrivals and departures per day, they aggregated about half a million registered tons. Two-thirds of all movements are attributable to the smaller English and Welsh ports in about equal proportions, while Bristol accounted for the remaining one-third. Seven years later, shipping movements amounted to 14,055, the equivalent of 38.5 movements per day or three-quarters of a million tons overall. Welsh ports now predominated, accounting for one-half of all movements; the other half was more or less evenly divided between Bristol and the other English ports.[24]

The rapid growth of trade in the Bristol Channel coincided with and was stimulated by war which prompted the more intensive use of vessels nationally. Higher productivity and an inelastic supply of shipping meant charging higher freight rates and, through the multiplier effect of more voyages, resulted in greater profit margins.[25] In the Channel the number of vessels sailing uni-directionally with cargoes declined rapidly from 2,630 (twenty-four per cent of all known voyages) in 1789 to 979 (seven per cent) in 1796, a consequence of increasing two-way trade between Cornwall and South Wales. This meant fewer 'subsidised' return voyages in ballast paid for out of the profits earned from carrying goods in one direction only. Another effect of the changing tempo was an increase in the average size of vessel operating in the Channel, from forty-six to fifty-three tons, a noteworthy increment of about thirteen per cent.

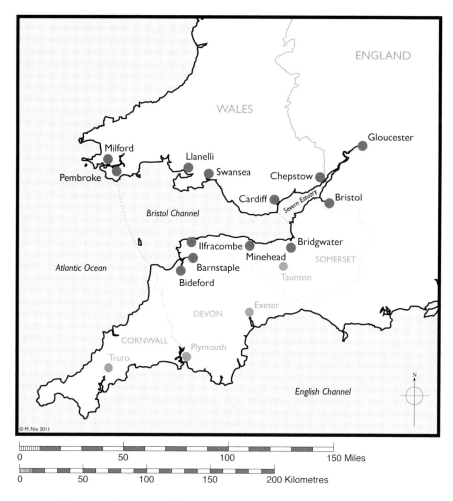

Figure 2. The ports of the Bristol Channel and the Severn Estuary.

The group of graphs (Figure 3) records the registered tonnage of shipping owned in each of the Channel ports between 1789 and 1808. The downturn experienced by several ports in 1793–4 is attributable to the interruption of foreign trade by war. While local factors explain the dramatic expansion of the newly formed port of Milford, initially attributable to the book transfer of shipping from the Pembroke Custom House ship registers. At Gloucester port officials were legally obliged to register trows used on the river Severn for the first time in 1805. In North Devon, it can be seen that Ilfracombe's tonnage

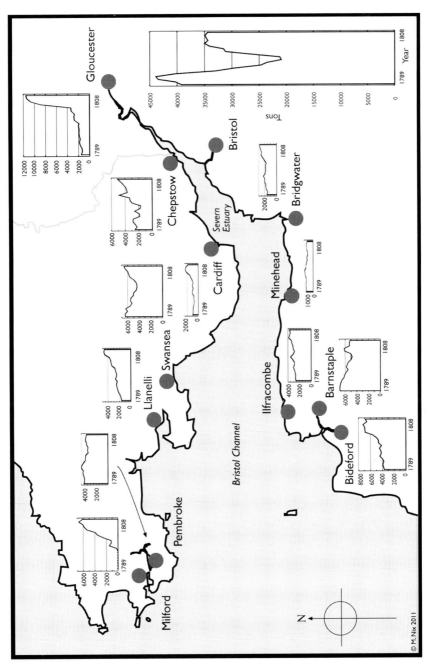

Figure 3. Total measured tonnage of vessels owned in each of the ports of the Bristol Channel between 1789 and 1808. Reference: TNA, CUST 17/11-30.

Figure 4. Barnstaple Quay and Queen Anne's Walk in 1833. Reference: WCSL, SC 87. Reproduced courtesy of Westcountry Studies Library, Devon Libraries.

increased by about one-third, while changes experienced by Barnstaple and Bideford are markedly at variance. While Barnstaple did not make a sustained recovery at the beginning of the century, the shipping stock of Chepstow, Swansea and Bideford expanded. In September 1789, seventy-eight vessels aggregating 6,912 tons were entered in Barnstaple's shipping register; Bideford's register shows fifty-six vessels aggregating 3,670 tons. By the end of 1801 the tonnages of the two ports were about equal. In a twelve year period Barnstaple shed about 2,000 tons of shipping, while Bideford gained about 1,000, a figure set to grow even further. Compared with other ports in the Channel, Bideford's expansion is impressive. In tonnage terms, the port ranked fifth out of the thirteen in 1789, rising to third place in 1803, after Bristol and the newly created port of Milford. Barnstaple ranked second after Bristol, but this declined to fourth equal with Swansea. Ilfracombe fell from sixth to ninth place. Barnstaple's shipping stock declined just when its business community needed to directly engage with the rapidly expanding Welsh economy, which offered the prospect for regular employment for a growing number of ships.

In 1790, of the thirty-three Barnstaple owned vessels listed in *Lloyd's Register of Shipping*, twenty-two traded overseas; for Bideford the figures are seventeen and ten respectively. Venturing vessels in overseas markets was expensive. Goods had to be carried long distances and over long periods of time; capital did not turn over quickly creating potential problems with cash flow.[26] Vessels were usually larger than those in the coasting trade. If the proposition holds that owners of vessels of 100 tons and above generally deployed them in overseas markets,[27] then Barnstaple's problems can, in part, be quantified. In 1787, the Barnstaple fleet consisted of seventy-eight craft of which thirty-four were over 100 tons; by 1808 the number had fallen to fifteen. In the interim shipowners lost more than half of their larger vessels, the majority of which were two-decked and unsuitable for carrying bulk cargoes such as coal and ores in the Bristol Channel. Appledore suffered particularly severely. In 1787 at least twenty-four brigantines and brigs were owned there; by 1814 the figure stood at six.[28]

Although the decline in shipping stock was rapid, some investors attempted to redress the situation by buying smaller craft more suited to the coasting trades. But the port failed to recoup its overall losses even during a period of national recovery around the turn of the nineteenth century. For a port the size of Barnstaple, the breaking of financial and personal links with foreign markets, especially during a protracted war, meant either irretrievable loss of shipping or years of rebuilding a business. The psychological toll following the loss of so many vessels must also have had an effect. Shareholding in a vessel was not solely related to the profit motive: becoming a partner or sole proprietor gave a sense of independence and status.[29] The diminution in the number of larger vessels was compounded by the book transfer of Appledore's fleet to Bideford in 1814. Between 1814 and 1839, when Ilfracombe shipping was transferred to Barnstaple, the number of *de novo* ship registrations averaged only 3.5 per annum. In 1841 Barnstaple owned only forty-four craft (excluding Ilfracombe vessels) aggregated around 2,700 tons, a reduction of nearly fifty per cent in vessels and about sixty per cent in tonnage since 1789.

In 1789, Bideford shipowners possessed ten vessels of over 100 tons

BIDEFORD QUAY. DEVON.

Published by John Wilson, Bideford.

Figure 5. Bideford Quay in about 1820. Reference: WCSL, SC 196.
Reproduced courtesy of Westcountry Studies Library, Devon Libraries.

compared with Barnstaple's thirty-four; by 1808 the figure totalled
twenty-eight and fifteen respectively. Expressed as a ratio, about one in
five vessels on the Bideford register exceeded 100 tons before the war;
soon after the turn of the century the proportion rose to about one in
three. Undoubtedly in peacetime this would have been attributed to
a growth in foreign trade, but the deployment of Bideford's shipping
overseas was at a low ebb. In 1806, for instance, only three vessels out
of thirty-six listed in *Lloyd's Register of Shipping* operated in foreign
or colonial markets. This compares with ten out of seventeen in the
pre-war period.

During the eighteenth century North Devon shipowners established
strong and lasting ties with South Wales which translated into regular
employment for their vessels. In Llanelli, for instance, North Devonian,
Cornish and Irish master mariners and ships predominated in the
carriage of coal. When Sir Thomas Stepney attempted to expand the
trade from the same port in the late 1740s he turned to North Devon

and Cornwall to provide him with experienced masters for his vessels.[30] In 1773, of the 236 vessels loading culm at the Kidwelly Canal, fifty-six hailed from the port of Bideford (Bideford forty-six, Clovelly ten); thirty-one from Barnstaple (Northam fifteen, Appledore fourteen, Barnstaple two); and five from Ilfracombe.[31] Twenty years later, Watkins wrote that the greatest number of Bideford vessels trade 'from Wales, with coals and culm, to different ports of the south coast of Devonshire, and others get freights from one port or another, as best they can'.[32] One Bideford vessel, the *Albion*, is a good example of the South Wales-South Devon link, regularly carrying coal from Cresswell, near Pembroke, to Dartmouth between the 1780s and mid 1800s.[33]

The number of changes of command recorded in the Bideford ship register provides a useful indicator of the deployment of locally owned vessels in Welsh and Westcountry ports. Between 1790 and 1814, sixty-seven registrations were endorsed with ninety-three names. The greatest number, accounting for nearly thirty per cent of the total, are associated with South Wales, and Swansea in particular (then at the centre of the Cornish ore trade). Another fifteen changes were made in South Devon, adding weight to Watkins' statement concerning Bideford's prominent role in the carriage of Welsh coal. Although only one change is recorded in Ireland, the evidence of a considerable number of *Lloyd's* surveys made on Bideford ships in Irish ports indicates that these vessels were playing a part in carrying coal to ports in southern Ireland.[34]

The commercial interconnections between North Devon, Wales and Cornwall are emphasised by Welsh and Cornish investments in several Bideford vessels. Between 1803 and 1808, for example, the Governor and Company of Copper Miners in England (the owners of works in Taibach near Port Talbot, Glamorganshire) bought shares in five vessels. These were the *Beaver*, *Underhill*, *Mary's*, *Cotton* and the appropriately named *Miners*, all brigantines of between fifty-four and 141 tons.[35] Before the firm purchased shares in the *Cotton* in 1808, the vessel was owned by seventeen partners who had bought the vessel new five years earlier. Six of the partners lived in Gwithian, Cornwall, including the miner John Davey, four resided nearby in Phillack, and two in St Clement near Truro. All three places were close to the copper exporting port of Hayle and the metalliferous mining area of West Cornwall. Three other owners were from Swansea, Baglan and Margam, all in Glamorganshire. In North Devon, the owners comprised the Bideford shipbuilder George Crocker (who almost certainly built the *Cotton*), the butcher John Bishop, and the vessel's master William Hockin of Clovelly.[36]

Enjoying the profits made from high freight rates in the Channel and, almost certainly, from the employment of Bideford ships as military transports, shipowners had sufficient surpluses to invest heavily in the industry. From 1799, Bideford shipbuilders responded to and accommodated an accelerating demand for new craft. The fleet increased in number and tonnage while the balance between second-hand and newly constructed vessels changed in favour of the latter. Expenditure on new shipping stock helped modernise the fleet and placed the port, albeit temporarily, as the leading shipbuilder, in terms of tonnage, in the Bristol Channel. After the war, prime registrations in Bideford averaged 9.2 per annum, nearly three times that of Barnstaple or Ilfracombe. By 1841, Bideford owned 136 vessels aggregating 11,581 tons, an average of 85.2 tons per craft. Compared with 1789 this was almost a sixty per cent increase in the number of vessels and almost seventy per cent in tonnage.

In the centuries between *c.*1650 and 1850 we have seen that North Devon was an agricultural region with some craft industries. The economy clearly benefitted from access to a communications network geared to transporting its raw materials and products by land and sea. It has also been seen that a significant shipping industry existed in the region whose carrying capacity far exceeded the volume of trade handled by the three ports. Furthermore, North Devon ship owners, with long standing commercial connections on the opposite shores of the Bristol Channel, were strongly positioned to respond to carrier needs arising from the rapid industrialisation of South Wales. Barnstaple vessels clearly engaged in the new dynamic developing in the Channel, but many of the ship owners active in overseas markets were caught off guard by the outbreak of war and unable to reposition themselves to take advantage of changing conditions. The industry in Bideford, on the other hand, unencumbered by vessels which were not suited to carrying bulk ore and coal, adapted to the escalating demand for hold space and channelled profits into expanding its fleet. Thus, through its shipping industry, rural North Devon directly contributed to the industrialisation of South Wales.

Notes and References

1.   Hussey 2000, pp. 196-201.
2.   Nix 1991, Chapter 3.
3.   Rogers undated, p. 178.
4.   Ibid.
5.   Nix 1991, Chapter 9.
6.   Nix 1991, Chapter 8. Based on shipping arrival and departure lists in *Trewman's Exeter Flying Post*, July 1791 to June 1793, and NDRO, Bideford port book, 1805–13, R2379A/Z8.
7.   NDMM, Limekiln file.
8.   Nix 1991, pp. 269-82.
9.   SHC, Hancock Papers, DD/HC Bx6.
10. Nix 1991, Chapters 5 and 6.
11. Ibid, Tables 9.7 and 9.9.
12. Watkins 1792, p. 74.
13. DRO, 3319 S/1; Greenhill and Giffard 1975, pp. 52-9.
14. Based on an analysis of NDRO, R2379A/Z8, Bideford port book, 1805–13.
15. Johns 1950, p. 114.
16. Nef 1932, pp. 116-17.
17. Symons 1979, p. 241. A pill is a small creek or river inlet.
18. Russell 1971, pp. 116, 125 and 128.
19. Minchinton 1972, p. 58.
20. Ayton and Daniell 1978, p. 15.
21. Stanier 1979, p. 18.
22. *Journals of the House of Commons*, 1803, pp. 310-11.
23. Flinn 1984, pp. 220-21.
24. TNA, CUST 17/11 and 17/18 , 'The state of navigation, commerce and revenues'.
25. Ville 1984, *passim*.
26. Minchinton 1969, p. 44.
27. Jackson 1981, pp. 129 and 134.
28. DRO, 3319 S/1.
29. Craig, 1973, pp. 36-37.
30. Craig, Protheroe Jones and Symons, 2002, pp. 379 and 459.
31. Craig, 1973, p. 33.
32. Watkins, 1792, p. 4.
33. NDRO, R2379A/Z60.
34. Nix 1991, pp. 147-51.
35. DRO, 3319 S/1, entry 10/1805, 2/1806, 7/1806, 9/1809 and 13/1809.
36. DRO, 3319 S/1, entry 8/1803.

Bibliography

Ayton, R. and Daniell, W. (1978) *A voyage round Great Britain Undertaken Between the Years 1813 and 1823 and Commencing from Land's End, Cornwall*, London: Tate Gallery : Scholar Press, vol. 1.

Craig, R.S., 'Shipowning in the South-West in its National Context', in Fisher , H.E.S., and Minchinton, W.E., (eds) (1973) *Transport and Ship- owning in the Westcountry*, Exeter: University of Exeter Press, pp. 33-48.

Craig, R.S., Protheroe Jones, R., & Symons, M.V. (2002) *The Industrial and Maritime History of Llanelli and Burry Port 1750 to 2000*, Carmarthenshire: Carmarthen County Council.

Flinn, M.W. (1984) *The History of the British Coal Industry, vol. 2, 1700–1830: the Industrial Revolution*, Oxford: Clarendon.

Greenhill, B., & Giffard, A. (1975) W*estcountrymen in the Prince Edward's Isle*, Toronto: University of Toronto Press.

Hussey, D. (2000) *Coastal and River Trade in Pre-Industrial England: Bristol and its region, 1680–1730*, Exeter: University of Exeter Press.

Jackson, J. 'Scottish Shipping, 1775–1805', in Cottrell, P.L. & Aldcroft, D.M., (eds) (1981), *Shipping, Trade and Commerce: essays in memory of Ralph Davis*, Leicester: Leicester University Press, pp. 117-36.

Johns, A.H. (1950) *The Industrial Development of South Wales*, Cardiff: University of Wales Press.

Journals of the House of Commons, from January the 21st 1794 to November 25th 1794 (1803) London: House of Commons.

Minchinton, W. 'The port of Bristol in the Eighteenth Century', in MacGrath, P. (ed.) (1972) *Bristol in the Eighteenth Century*, Newton Abbot: David and Charles.

Minchinton, W., (ed.) (1969) *The growth of English Overseas Trade in the Seventeenth and Eighteenth centuries*, London: Methuen.

Nef, J.U. (1932) *The Rise of the British Coal Industry*, London: Routledge, vol. I.

Nix, M. (1991) 'The Maritime History of the Ports of Bideford and Barnstaple, 1786–1841', unpublished PhD thesis, University of Leicester.

Rogers, W.H. (undated) 'Notes on Bideford', vol. I.

Russell, R. (1971) *Lost Canals in England and Wales*, Newton Abbot: David and Charles.

Stanier, P.H., 'The Copper Ore Trade of South West England', *Journal of Transport History*, 3rd series, 5, 1, 1979, pp. 18-35.

Symons, M.V. (1979) *Coal Mining in the Llanelli Area: sixteenth century to 1829*, Llanelli: Lanelli Borough Council, vol. I.

Ville, S. 'The Deployment of English Merchant Shipping: Michael and Joseph Henley of Wapping, shipowners, 1775–1830', *Journal of Transport History*, 3rd Series, 5, 2, 1984, pp. 16-33.

Watkins, J. (1792) *An Essay Towards a History of Bideford in the County of Devon*, Exeter: Printed by E. Grigg.

'The Good' and 'The Needy' of Eighteenth-Century Sampford Peverell

Peter Bowers, Rachel Cutts, Colin Passey and Val Weller

Introduction

With fertile soil suitable both for arable use and pasturage, Sampford – 'Sanforde' as it was known in Saxon times, because of its sandy ford across a stream – was ideal as an agricultural centre. A Saxon charter and Domesday give details of Sampford's agricultural activity.[1] In the Middle Ages, like many parts of England, Sampford was involved in producing woollen materials – kersey and later (from about 1660) serge – often sold to wool merchants based in Tiverton or Exeter. From there they went to the continent where there was a substantial market for them.

Early in the twelfth century, the manor of Sampford was granted to two members of the Peverell family.[2] Arguably the first of Sampford's 'Good', this family retained the manor for nearly 300 years. They oversaw its early growth in size and prosperity, providing the village with a (short-lived) castle, its church and its suffix. They also elevated its status to that of borough, allowing weekly markets and biannual fairs to be held. These attracted outsiders and raised taxes on goods sold. When the last of the Peverells died, Sampford was given by Henry IV to his half brother John Beaufort in about 1400. A century later, Margaret Beaufort, mother of Henry VII, inherited the manor. A generous benefactor, she provided an aisle for the church and a magnificent rectory. When she died, the Crown sold the manor to the Poulett family of Hinton St George, Somerset. The manor remained with the Pouletts until the beginning of the nineteenth century, when it was sold off piecemeal. By the end of the seventeenth century these families had seen Sampford become a self-sufficient, but not isolated community, with a tannery, smithy, mills and inns. Its markets and fairs, and its situation on the road from Wellington to Tiverton, meant drovers and other travellers visited frequently. There was no school, but there were a church and church house, the latter probably used for meetings and celebrations.

While the lords of the manor and their major tenants became wealthy, most inhabitants, 'the Needy', toiled on the land and lived just above subsistence level. They would feel most sharply the impact of changes to the community's economy in the eighteenth century.

The Eighteenth Century

Threats to the wool trade in the first decade of the century led several Devon wool towns, including Sampford, to petition the House of Commons to act on their behalf.[3] They cited losses at sea and also, more significantly, cheaper imports of woollen fabric from Ireland. Separately, Bennet Bobish, a Sampford serge maker, sued a wealthy Tiverton merchant for the balance of money owed him.[4] The merchant was apparently having difficulty in recovering debts from Holland and Flanders, blaming war in Flanders and the death or insolvency of some of the merchants with whom he traded. Nevertheless, the parish's economy still depended heavily on the wool trade for most of the century. Old field names show the location of rack parks where cloth was stretched out on tenterhooks to dry. Most households would have had a loom. However, the continued increase in overseas competition, and the introduction of cotton cloth later in the century, meant that woollen industry profits were badly hit. Cheaper goods made in mechanised mills left virtually no market for traditionally made serge. By the early nineteenth century the local wool industry was in free fall.[5] Other sectors of the village's economy were less turbulent. There was probably an increase in cattle husbandry to offset falling profits from wool. Unlike Tiverton, there were no major fires to affect the economy adversely. Nor does there seem to have been any serious epidemic, although the church burial register shows two years with higher than average death rates, 1747 and 1758, the latter due to smallpox.[6]

'The Good'

The Pouletts, resident in Hinton St George, left running the parish to better-off residents and to the Vestry committee, who were responsible for making appointments to many key roles in the parish. As spiritual head of the community, the rector undertook its moral supervision. He chaired Vestry meetings of churchwardens, constable, waywardens and overseers, in order to determine how ratepayers' funds should be spent. However, in the absence of surviving Vestry minutes or other evidence, we know little about the rector's influence. His answers to the Visitation Queries in 1744 and 1779 show that a curate undertook ecclesiastical duties – sermons twice on Sundays, and communion four times a year.[7] It is not clear if the rector lived in the parish in 1744, but in 1779 he resided in neighbouring Uplowman where he had another benefice.

'The Good' taking on unpaid roles of churchwarden, constable, overseer, waywarden and feoffee of the Poor Lands were mostly gentlemen or yeomen, often holding two or more of these roles in any year. They also acted as assessor for Land Tax, a paid office. We know the trades of some of them: John Cowlen, tallow chandler; William Chave, butcher;[8] Henry Dickenson, serge maker.[9] Others rented out properties and employed labourers to farm their land. Most were eligible for jury service and were therefore named in the annual freeholder lists.[10] All appointees needed a basic education, whilst churchwardens, overseers and feoffees (landholding trustees) had to be able to keep books of accounts. This would have limited the numbers of eligible local people as the parish had no schools; education was at home or boarding school.

The Poor Law Act of 1601 dictated how poor relief operated. The Overseers of the Poor were the churchwardens, plus two or more substantial landowners. In Sampford they were appointed annually on a fifteen year cycle, so that each year two of thirty named properties had to provide an overseer or nominate someone else to do it for them. They collected the poor rate and administered relief to the poor.[11]

They could remove strangers from the parish, and organise and pay for apprenticeships for children of poor families. They could commit paupers to the workhouse, although there is no evidence of this in Sampford . Indeed, like many parishes, Sampford had no workhouse, probably because providing outdoor relief was cheaper.

The Overseers' Accounts for much of the century have survived and record all income and expenditure. Those deemed to qualify received monthly payments. In 1744, when the Visitation Returns identified about 150 households, twenty-four people were receiving monthly payments ranging from 2s to 8s, averaging a little over 3s, a low figure compared with some other years. For example, in 1706, thirty-seven people received relief averaging 4s 6d per month; in 1768 relief to thirty people averaged 4s 8d. Apart from these regular payments, extraordinary payments were made for such expenses as doctors' fees; shoes; removals from the parish; apprenticeships; caring for the sick, and funerals. In 1763, the constable received expenses for holding a reluctant bridegroom, James Morgan, until he could be married to Mary Sanders![12]

Administration costs were quite a high proportion of the overseers' outgoings. Expenses included: meetings from 1s to 14s; making various tax rates and entering them in the accounts (usually 5s a time); apprentice indentures; meetings to choose overseers and waywardens, and nomination warrants for these posts. There were also expenses for travelling to court and associated legal costs; the Constable's costs in dealing with wrongdoers, as well as settlements; the doctor's retainer, and 'entertaining' (most importantly, ale for the parishioners on Easter Monday, at a cost of up to 14s)! Overseers and other officials were chosen at the Easter meeting. Other odd payments include: 9d for a new bag for the parish books; 1s 6d for William Sweetland to buy a violin; 10s 6d for David Webber (by the consent of parishioners) to buy books for the better instruction of the singing in church![13]

During the eighteenth century more legislation was passed to regulate parish officials because, owing to the 'incapacity, negligence or misconduct [of overseers], the sufferings and distress of the poor are grievous'.[14] The only evidence of this in Sampford is a comment made in the accounts of April 1767 that 'what follows was paid by Mr Cowlen through Mr Taylor's ungenerous behaviour in refusing to pay the poor. For Saunders children 7s 6d; several other entries

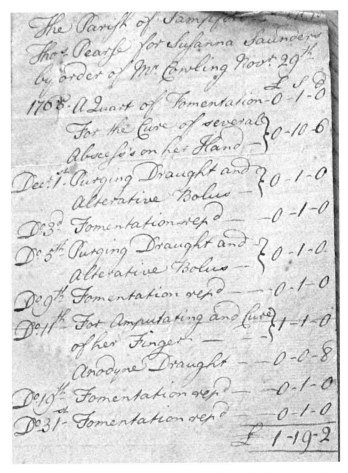

Figure 1. DRO Reference: 1198A-1. Extract from the Overseers Account
Book 1765. Reproduced courtesy of Devon Record Office.

totalling in all £8 10s 7d.' William Cowlen and Francis Taylor were
joint overseers from April 1766 to April 1767.[15]

The parish had Charity Lands to supplement the poor rate support,
donated 'beyond all time of memory'[16] (before 1610, which is the date
of the earliest surviving document[17]), by whom we don't know as 'the
length of time which devoureth all things had eaten out both the name
and the memory of the donor'.[18] At the beginning of the century the
estate comprised ten burgages (tenements). John Lock later gave £100
which the charity used to purchase two more properties, Webber's
and Smoke-alley. The trustees (feoffees) were responsible for letting

them out to tenants. Rents and fines levied on these tenants provided money which the feoffees distributed to poor people not receiving poor relief, especially those considered most in need.

The Charity Lands' trust deed required that the properties be conveyed to sixteen feoffees. When their number had reduced through mortality to four, the properties were conveyed again to another sixteen inhabitants. In 1750, John Cowlen, one of the feoffees, had two wooden tablets made listing the properties owned by the charity and their rental value. They probably hung originally in the church house where, each year, the trustees had to account to the minister, churchwardens, overseers and other principal inhabitants for how monies had been distributed.[19]

Some properties were let to yearly tenants who had to pay the full rent, but not property maintenance. Other properties were mostly let on ninety-nine year leases, determinable on three lives. Rents for these were much lower, but the tenants had to carry out repairs. When a new lease commenced, a 'fine' was payable, often £10 or more. In years when a fine was paid, money available for distribution could easily be double that of a normal year. Typically, the amount for distribution in a year with no fines was £6 to £8. For example, in 1766 the feoffees distributed £7 9s 6d amongst ninety-nine people.[20] Most received 1s but a few, with greater need, got more; Thomas Brice junior received the most at 8s 6d.[21] By contrast, a substantial fine was received in 1789. The feoffees paid out £19 19s to ninety-two people (seventy-nine men and thirteen women).[22] They also paid £10 'towards inoculation of the children'; such a payment was unprecedented and shows how far the 'Good' of Sampford would go to reduce the incidence of smallpox, in view of the risks involved with this comparatively new procedure.[23]

In 1766, ninety-nine people received from the feoffees the small annual payment for the needy, and thirty-one received regular payments from the Overseers of the Poor. The records suggest, and the Charity Lands trust deed allowed, only one payment per family. There were 178 families in 1763[24] and 143 in 1801.[25] Assuming that there were 175 families in 1766, and 130 of those were considered poor or needy, then only about forty-five families were better off; from these 'the Good' were drawn.

A few names recur, from generation to generation. Members of the Cowlen (otherwise Cowling) family were prominent, acquiring more land throughout the century. Benjamin Donn's map of 1765 shows (William) Cowling's name beside 'Sampford Peverell' highlighting his importance.[26] In 1779, William occupied properties amounting to a greater yearly value than anyone else.[27] The Rowe family enjoyed significant economic success, having acquired eleven properties by the end of the century. However, Thomas Rowe's account book for 1728 to 1741 shows that he accumulated the properties gradually and had to borrow from relatives to do so.[28] The Dawbney family lived at a property known as Riverton. They were related to the Dawbneys who held more extensive lands in Misterton and South Petherton, Somerset.[29] Other families, with less valuable land holdings but nonetheless influential, were Ballamy, Saunders and Taylor.

'The Needy'

The Poor Law Acts of the seventeenth century delegated many powers and responsibilities to parishes for the relief and management of needy inhabitants. The Act of 1662 concerning Settlement and Removal was particularly potent as it prevented inhabitants moving out of the village if likely to become a charge on the rates elsewhere, and people from other parishes could not move in without showing sufficient means of support.

The Overseers Accounts show that the requirements were applied, no doubt causing much distress to individuals involved, and at a considerable cost to the parish in examinations before a magistrate, travel to court, and removal expenses.[30] They record just fourteen removals to or from Sampford between 1714 and 1750.[31] Five single persons and seven families were removed from the village, two families removed inwards from elsewhere. From 1750 to 1795 there were forty-two removals. This increase was perhaps due in part to changes in farming practices and poor harvests in the 1790s, leading to a growing number of displaced persons. These years saw twenty-five removals outwards, nine for single people, mainly women, and sixteen for families or couples. They included: an infant of six months, deserted by her mother in 1786, sent to East Stonehouse where she was born, and in 1762 a soldier's wife and her two children. Twelve families and five single people were allowed to settle in Sampford having been removed from elsewhere, usually neighbouring parishes, but some in Somerset or North Devon or even further away.[32] Margaret Baker, aged sixty, widow of William Baker born in Sampford was apprehended as a vagrant in St Martin-in-the-Fields, Westminster, and removed to Sampford in 1761.[33] In 1765 a vagrant pass, and copy of her settlement examination, was issued for 'Elizabeth, widow of John Saunders, late a soldier in the first Regiment of Foot Guards, and her two children, from Willoughby, Warwicks, to 'Stanford' Devon, where her husband served an apprenticeship' which gave him a right to settlement in the parish.[34]

In 1759 Grace Coombes was removed from the village after falling on the parish 'in necessity'.[35] The overseers allowed her 2s, but then applied for a summons (6d) to have her examined before a magistrate.[36] The examination and removal order cost 6s, wagon hire to take her to Bristol 8s, their four days' travelling 4s, and the overseer's expenses for himself and his horse £1 – a total of £2 0s 6s.[37] Costs of 2s 6d were incurred opposing the officers of Thorverton who were keen to remove Mary Davy and her daughters to Sampford Peverell.[38]

Many people found life very difficult and had to suffer the indignity of applying to the overseers for help. The Poor Law Act of 1697 required every pauper, his wife and children to wear a badge on the shoulder of their right sleeve to show they were receiving relief and therefore not allowed to beg. The accounts have several references to buying badges: 2½ dozen in 1758, 1½ dozen in 1762, 1 dozen in 1764.[39] Later in the century people could be excused from wearing the badge on proof of very decent and orderly behaviour. The Poor Law Act of 1697 was repealed in 1810.

The names of people receiving long term relief crop up repeatedly, many getting weekly payments of two or three shillings for as long as they lived. In 1753, for example, thirty-three people were getting regular payments adding up to approximately £6 a month. The parish then often paid the funeral expenses, although the pauper's goods were sometimes seized and sold as reimbursement. Some entries detail short-term relief for sickness and nursing or attendance by a doctor, who was paid approximately £5 a year as a retainer specifically for treatment of the poor. Many entries are for help with clothing, often for a specific item only – from a few pence for a shift to a full outfit of clothes.

Other payments include attendance at childbirth, equipment for

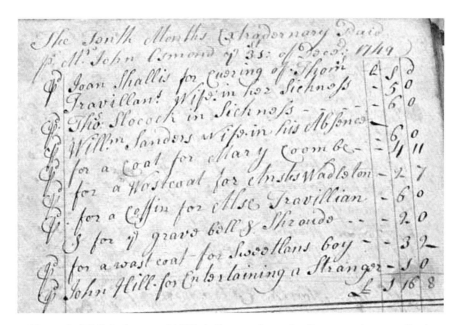

Figure 2. DRO Reference: 1198A-1. Extract from the Overseers Account Book 1749. Courtesy of Devon Record Office.

craftsmen, and so on. As the cloth industry declined, more relief was given to skilled workers such as weavers, woolcombers and serge makers. During an outbreak of smallpox in 1758 affecting four families and twelve children, a total of £2 19s 6d was paid, as well as 6s for the funeral of one of the children.[40] There are instances of payments for travelling to Exeter for ill children seeking specialist advice and for children with serious disabilities such as blindness.

A considerable amount was spent chasing putative fathers for maintenance, 'encouraging' marriages (including the already mentioned James Morgan and Mary Sanders), removing pregnant women to other parishes to give birth so their child had a settlement elsewhere, and supporting single mothers and their children. The 1732 Act required a woman pregnant with an illegitimate child to declare herself and name the father, who could, by agreeing to a bond (lump sum), discharge himself of further responsibility. The accounts have several references to these bonds.[41] A man charged on oath with being the father could be apprehended and committed to gaol until he gave surety to indemnify the parish from expense.

In March 1745 expenses of 7s 6d were incurred at Bampton Sessions for Margaret Kerslake's examination, two orders and summary 'concerning her base child charged on Mr William Chave.' The constable received 1s 'for attending the justice and obtaining an order of Bastardy on the said William Chave.' Margaret received 2s 6d per week. In April she gave birth, her childbed expenses being 10s 6d. She then received 3s 4d per month until August 1749. Thanks to the court order, the parish could recoup these expenses from Mr Chave. As one of the better-off villagers he could hardly avoid it, himself an overseer the following year! In 1760 a woman's marriage expenses of £2 9s were paid and, in 1744, the overseers paid £3 7s 6d to get banns of matrimony between Henry Pullman and Mary Stephens published in the parish churches of Willand and Sampford Peverell.[42]

Apprenticeships were one way of dealing with the problem of poor, orphaned and illegitimate children.[43] There are many records of indentures made and of money paid (usually £1) to parishioners for the maintenance of these children. Between 1700 and 1798, 243 child apprentices, 160 boys and 83 girls, are recorded. They were bound to their 'masters' for many years, but the indenture could be cancelled if the master died. Occasionally apprenticeships were within the family. In 1771, the overseers' accounts record 'William Facey of Taunton St Mary Magdalen, Somerset, by consent, serge weaving endorsed: "John Gillard is the son of Wm Facey's wife – was born before her marriage, she did not swear to the father, but it is supposed to be the said Facey".'[44]

Most apprenticeships were unspecified and so, rather than learning a trade, the children were probably used as domestic servants or agricultural labourers. Specific apprenticeships include four to serge weavers, five to weavers, one to a woolcomber, and one each to a cooper (at Culmstock), a tanner and a tailor. Four were taken on by yeomen, presumably to learn husbandry. The apprentices' ages are not generally recorded. They might have been as young as seven, but some were much older. Sarah Salter, bound to Thomas Row for Lee Ditch in 1762, already had a child and had received relief since 1756.[45] In 1759 Captain William Kerslake was apprenticed,[46] but in 1762 he needed assistance and was granted 2s regularly until his death.[47] We don't know much about the apprentices' fate. In October 1769, Mr Broom was fined 5s 6d for refusing to care for his apprentice.[48] It seems likely that parishioners were reluctant to take these children. Legislation in 1792 provided that masters be punished for ill usage of apprentices.

Maintenance for dependants of serving militiamen included payments between 1779 and 1782 to Mary Carter and one child 'being the wife and child of William Carter of Tiverton, admitted to the second battalion of the Devon Militia as a substitute for Edward Trevelian of Sampford Peverell'.[49] Four further entries for maintenance were recorded, the family having two further children. Payment was made to Henry Brice and Nicholas Curwood who had provided other men to serve in the militia in their place.[50]

Conclusion

From the point of view of 'the Good', taking care of 'the Needy' inhabitants of Sampford must have been a time-consuming, and at times demanding, activity. However, it conferred upon them both power and status within the community, all the more so because there was no resident Lord of the Manor. It was in the collective interest of 'the Good' that 'the Needy' were provided for and kept fit for work, because 'the Good' depended upon them to provide their labour and to be able to pay their rents. We can surmise that the individuals concerned undertook their roles out of a sense of duty, and also as a moral obligation for which they expected to receive their reward in Heaven. From the perspective of 'the Needy', the system provided the security of a safety net in hard times. They would have had to ensure that they showed due deference to all members of 'the Good' so that there was no cause to discriminate against them in their time of need. The price paid for their security was the lack of mobility, both upwards through the social hierarchy, and also geographically by means of restrictions in movement between parishes. Also, for those receiving Parish Relief on a regular basis, there would also have been the social stigma of being labelled 'poor'.

Looking at the system of financial support as a whole, it can be seen as a form of social control, whereby 'the Needy' were kept beholden and dependent upon 'the Good' for their welfare. The targeting of assistance to where it was most needed may have helped to keep the incidence of crime down, because the poor were kept from destitution.

The process of changing the office-holders of Overseer and Feoffee on a rotational basis would have been instrumental in preventing serious and recurring abuse of the funds. Finally, the system appears to have worked, and endured, not just because it was required by Law, but also because there was a strong interdependence between 'the Good' and 'the Needy'.

About the Article

Inspired by Dr Simon Dixon, who was undertaking a two-year research project into eighteenth-century Devon records, the Sampford Peverell Society set up a twelve-member team to undertake the research for this article. Three of the team went on to write it up, and the whole was edited by another member who had not been involved previously. The Society intends to make much of the transcribed research material available on its website <www.sampfordpeverellsociety.com>.

Research team

Peter Bowers, David and Rachel Cutts, David and Mary Hennings, Christine Mason, Anita and Vic Maynard, Guy and Penny Mindelsohn, and Allan and Val Weller.

Notes and References

1. Scott-Fox 2007, p. 3.
2. Ibid, pp. 4-8.
3. *Journal of the House of Commons*, 19 December 1707, p. 476.
4. TNA, C6/482/4.
5. Lysons & Lysons, 1822.
6. DRO, 1198A/PR1-10.
7. *Episcopal Visitation Returns 1744 and 1779.* [Online] Available at: <www.foda.org.uk/visitations> (Accessed 2010).
8. DRO, 1198A-1/PO9-83.
9. Chapman 1978, p. 11.
10. DRO, QS/7/1-57.
11. DRO, 1198A-1/PO548.
12. DRO, 1198A-1/P01, P01a, P02.
13. Ibid.
14. Tate 1989, p. 193.
15. DRO, 1198A-1/P01, P01a, P02.

16. TCL, Local Studies box for the parish of Sampford Peverell. Inquiry into Charity Lands 1910 for Parish of Sampford Peverell, section II, referring to the 1820 inquiry.
17. DRO, 1198A-1/PF6.
18. TCL, Local Studies box for the parish of Sampford Peverell. Inquiry into Charity Lands 1910 for the Parish of Sampford Peverell, section II, referring to the 1820 inquiry.
19. These two boards now hang in the bell-tower of St John the Baptist Church, Sampford Peverell.
20. DRO, 1198A-1/PF6.
21. Ibid.
22. Ibid.
23. Patrick Pead 2008, Wellcome Library. [email] Message to author 7 July 2008, 'Inoculation against smallpox (by the introduction of smallpox matter into the skin with a lancet) was indeed widespread during the last twenty years of the eighteenth century. It continued in some areas into the first few years of the nineteenth century until vaccination (with cow pox) became more accepted'.
24. DRO, 1198A/PR1-10, Bishop Heppel's Visitation, as recorded in the Parish Registers.
25. 1801 Census Return.
26. Donn, B. 1765, *A map of the County of Devon London*, 1765. [Online] Available at <en.wikipedia.org/wiki/Benjamin_Donn> (Accessed July 2008).
27. DRO, 5948B-0/AK, 1779. Values totalled for each individual in a document about the funding of part of the Tiverton Turnpike. Also available by property in Land Tax Returns, DRO, 1198A-1/PC1.
28. DRO, 1044B-0/M/E/1.
29. SHC, DD/BR/hk/4 Will (1750) and Probate (1797) of Henry Daubney Esq.
30. DRO, 1198A-1/P01, P01a, P02.
31. DRO, 1198A-1/PO9/1-83.
32. DRO, 1198A-1/PO106-172.
33. DRO, 1198A-1/PO87/2.
34. DRO, 1198A-1/PO31.
35. DRO, 1198A-1/P0174.
36. DRO, 1198A-1/P01, P01a, P02.
37. Ibid.
38. Ibid.
39. Ibid.
40. DRO, 1198A-1/P01, P01a, P02.
41. DRO, 1198A-1/PO511-547.
42. DRO, 1198A-1/P01, P01a, P02.
43. DRO, 1198A-1/PO190-454.

44. Ibid.
45. DRO, 1198A-1/PO371.
46. DRO, 1198A-1/PO366.
47. DRO, 1198A-1/P01, P01a, P02.
48. Ibid.
49. DRO, 1198A-1/PO183-188.
50. Ibid.

Bibliography

Friar, S. (2004) *The Sutton Companion to Local History*, Stroud: The History Press.

Chapman S.D. (1978) (ed.) *The Devon Cloth Industry in the Eighteenth Century: Sun Fire Office Inventories of merchants' and manufacturers property 1726–1770*, DCRS, New Series, 23, Exeter: DCRS.

Lysons, D. & Lysons, S. (1822) *Magna Britannia*, vol. 6, part 1, Devon, London: Cadell.

Scott-Fox, C. (ed.) (2007) *Sampford Peverell: the village, church, chapels and rectories*, Sampford Peverell: Sampford Peverell Society.

Tate, W.E. (1989) *The Parish Chest*, Andover: Phillimore.

A Nineteenth-Century Ecclesiastical Dispute and a Lost Historic Interior

Sue Spurr

St Peter's church in Rose Ash sits tucked away at the west end of the village green close to the Victorian school.[1] Its appearance is unremarkable. Pevsner says (incorrectly) that it was heavily restored by Edward Ashworth in 1874, and (correctly) that it was largely rebuilt by St Aubyn and Wadling between 1882 and 1892.[2] It now has the air of a typical Devon village church restored in the nineteenth century and well cared for by its parishioners. But for the two hundred or so years before its restoration the interior of the chancel with its many painted texts and unusual colourful decoration was far from typical. And in the second half of the nineteenth century the chancel found itself at the centre of a surprisingly acrimonious dispute between the rector and the rural dean.

In 1848 the rural dean's notebook recorded that the roof was in poor condition, that the screen was dilapidated and should be either removed or repaired, and that the seating was uneven and 'out of repair'.[3] Similar remarks appear fairly regularly in the notebook and a comment in 1856 that 'there appears to be no disposition to carry out last year's recommendation' could apply equally well to many other years. By the 1870s the condition of the chancel in particular had become a bone of contention between William Karslake the rural dean and John Southcomb the rector. The story unfolds following Karslake's visit to inspect St Peter's on 22 April 1874. During his inspection he had damaged some plaster and loosened some of the stone rubble in the chancel. He wrote to let Southcomb know: 'I was at Rose Ash on Wednesday and visited the Church where my eye was caught by a suspicious bulge . . . I procured a ladder and made, as bound to do, an examination of the actual state of things and was horrified at the result . . . There can be no doubt, I fear, that your Chancel roof is in a ruinous condition . . .'[4] He also wrote a detailed report in the rural dean's notebook:

> The Rural Dean is very sorry to report that this Church is, as he fears, in a dangerous state as respects the Roofs and Arcade. At the junction of Nave and Chancel each toe of the Principal is thoroughly decayed, and the North End is pressing the Arcade dangerously towards the North.The Wall plate, Ceiling and Ribs of Chancel Roof are completely rotten, and some of the Principals are defective. The Wall plates of Nave are completely rotten, and some of the Principals are defective. The North Aisle is not so bad but the Wall plates are defective so are the Laths of the Ceiling.[5]

Southcomb, clearly annoyed that he had not been notified of the visit and was not present at the inspection, replied to Karslake that he would give the matter his prompt attention.[6] He then wrote to ask William Gould of Barnstaple, a statuary mason and slate merchant, if he could recommend a good building surveyor to report on the condition of the chancel.[7] (As rector he was responsible only for the chancel. The remainder of the church was the responsibility of the churchwardens and parish.) Two days later he wrote to Gould again: 'Thank you for yours of the 28th. I do not contemplate alteration in the design of the fabric . . . but the placing the present one in a state of thorough repair [sic]. It seems to me that you are just the man I want'.[8] On 5 May he attended a parish meeting at the church to discuss the repairs with Karslake, the churchwardens and three local landowners.[9] Later the same day he met Gould at the church as arranged and two days later he wrote to Karslake with Gould's recommendations – that the church should be thoroughly examined by an architect before trying to repair the chancel roof.[10] Southcomb heard no more from Karslake until 19 May when he received a letter telling him that Edward Ashworth, an architect from Exeter, would be at the church the following day.[11] Despite the short notice he duly met Karslake and Ashworth at the church and the next day he reported back to Gould. Somewhat embarrassed, he explained that Karslake had already consulted Ashworth: 'Mr Ashworth was at Rose Ash accordingly yesterday, and I suppose is there today. I can only say that these proceedings are quite different from what the proceedings at the parish meeting on the 5th ult led me to expect and I trust you will receive my assurance to that effect.'[12]

It seems that following his visits to Rose Ash Ashworth recommended a substantial restoration of the church.[13] It also seems that Southcomb refused to carry out Ashworth's recommendation for the chancel. The contents of Southcomb's letter to Karslake on 1 June suggests that Karslake then proposed to get someone else to deal with the chancel repairs: 'I should wish to have in writing your proposal with respect to the handing over to others (with the funds for the purpose) the execution of any repairs required by the Chancel of Rose Ash Church, and also your reasons for making the proposal.'[14] The proposal was in fact highly irregular, since by law the chancel was Southcomb's responsibility, and it cannot have failed to irritate him. It comes as a surprise after these events to read in Southcomb's diary that he and his wife dined with the Karslakes on 23 June. Perhaps Karslake hoped to smooth ruffled feathers over a good bottle of port. If so, he must have been disappointed.

By the following summer the Archdeacon of Barnstaple had been drawn into the dispute. Southcomb wrote to him in indignation saying:

> I cannot agree with Karslake in his opinion as to the dangerous state of the chancel of Rose Ash church (except as far as he may have caused it). . . . I am at a loss to imagine where he gets his power to knock churches about in an experimental manner . . . his functions being that [sic] of mere inspection – and whilst on this subject I shall feel obliged to Mr Karslake if he will send someone to repair the damage he has occasioned.[15]

The bulge in the chancel, he went on to say, had been there for at least twenty years, and in his view the chancel 'even in its present condition' would stand quite safely for the next two hundred years.[16] Three weeks later, on 30 July 1875, Southcomb made the following *Presentment of the Minister and Churchwardens of the Parish of*

Rose Ash at the Episcopal and Archdiaconal Visitation held at South Molton.

> We present the Church of Rose Ash as reduced to, and left [by] the Dean Rural for the last fifteen months in a most unseemly condition. On the 22 of April 1874 the Dean who had stated on a previous Visitation that he wished that all the Churches in the Deanery were in as good order as the Church of Rose Ash (or words to that effect) without any instruction to us, and in our absence, took a mason to the church, where his (the Dean Rural's) "eye was caught by a very suspicious looking bulge in the plaster" whereupon he proceeded to knock to pieces in other places as well the plaster of the walls and ceiling. This "bulge" had been there in its then state, and without a sign of decadence nor evident a crack for 20 years at the very least and the Dean Rural had filled the office since 1865. The Dean Rural having stated that he was "bound to do" this, and having said to us subsequently "I am answerable for what is done here" we have taken no proceedings herein, but leave it for the Ordinary to deal with.[17]

Two weeks after the Visitation Karslake sent an official complaint about the state of the chancel to Frederick Temple the Bishop of Exeter. This requested that the 'Surveyor of Dilapidations . . . be directed to survey the said chancel of the said Parish of Rose Ash in order that the same may be duly repaired according to Law'.[18] The bishop sent a copy of this to Southcomb. Southcomb responded robustly on 23 September, sending the bishop a copy of the Presentment made at South Molton which he felt would 'modify [his] Lordship's future or further proceedings'.[19] He went on to say:

> It is difficult to understand in a favourable sense the representations of the Dean Rural as to the condition of the Chancel of Rose Ash Church, but I venture to assert that were "the Chancel Roof in the ruinous state" which the Dean Rural estimates, possibly as a tolerable justifica-tion of his wanton proceedings, far less violence than his would have brought it to the ground. And assuming for an instant that a new Roof were required, it would be more than injudicious to place one [sic] (as the Dean Rural is well aware) with the Nave and Aisle in their present condition'.[20]

He concluded by saying that he trusted that Temple's influence would induce Karslake to repair 'without further delay the mischief which he has so irregularly done'.[21] Temple either declined to use his influence over Karslake, or his influence was ineffectual, for Karslake's damage remained unrepaired.

Karslake's official complaint, however, had set diocesan wheels in motion, albeit rather slowly, and in November the following year the archdiaconal surveyor made his inspection of the chancel.[22] On receiving the resulting report Southcomb produced an immensely detailed thirteen page reply rebutting much of the content. He sent this to Temple. In it he admitted that 'from an artistic or aesthetic point of view' the rough cast walls could be called defective, but he insisted that there were no bulges, cracks or signs of settlement in them. The problem was, he said, that rough cast was 'an eyesore to the Dean Rural – Hinc illæ lacrymæ'. Southcomb complained that the surveyor had 'no authority to order rough cast walls to be replaced by pointed masonry'. And he said he had examined the roof himself and was sure the problems were again purely aesthetic. He could not understand how 'a man of the Dean Rural's age and presumed experience could, with any regard to truth, or unless he [had] taken leave of his senses, deliberately state' that the chancel roof was being supported by the screen. He said that in 1869 Karslake had reported the church to be 'in satisfactory repair', and he remarked somewhat sarcastically that 'the Dean Rural's sight [appeared] to have improved with age'. Having received this lengthy reply from Southcomb, Temple set up a local commission to look at the survey report and at Southcomb's response. In March 1877 the commission reported that with judicious repair the chancel roof would last many years. Southcomb however was still not satisfied. He wrote again to Temple hoping that Karslake would be required to repair his damage.[23] He received no reply but still continued to pursue Karslake. The dispute finally came to an end when Karslake died suddenly in October 1878. Three years later Southcomb himself resigned from ill health.

The living of Rose Ash then passed to his cousin, Henry Granger Southcomb. In 1882 a church restoration account was set up and fund raising was started. In 1885 John Matthews the rural dean noted that 'nothing short of a general restoration of this pretty village church can be recommended',[24] and in 1888 a public meeting resolved on a full restoration.[25] This was completed in 1889 and was followed three years later by the building of a new chancel.[26]

Why was John Southcomb apparently so reluctant to restore his chancel when as rector he was responsible for its upkeep? Was it simply due, as it seems, to an unwillingness to back down? The answer may lie partly in an article published in 1884 signed 'R. L. B.' and probably written by Robert Lewis Bampfield, Vicar of West Anstey.[27] The article (see Appendix) contains a wonderful description of Rose Ash church when visited by Bampfield some years earlier, and gives fascinating detail of what Bampfield calls 'peculiarities of arrangement' which he thinks are 'well-nigh unique'. This arrangement had been installed in the late seventeenth or early eighteenth century as a self-imposed penance by Lewis Southcomb, rector from 1675 to 1736. Lewis was the first of eight consecutive generations of the Southcomb family to hold the living. (John Southcomb was the sixth.) Lewis had been a non-juror but he subsequently recanted in order to retain his benefice.[28] His conscience then got the better of him. It seems that he regretted his lack of the 'heroick and Christian bravery of soul . . . that an ambassador, of the holy Jesus, ought always to be ready to shew, and . . . since his desire to retain his living had been the cause of his fault, he designed to spend a considerable portion of the proceeds on the poor and the adornment of his chancel'.[29]

Was a wish to protect this adornment one of the reasons for John Southcomb's reluctance to carry out restoration work? This would certainly tie in with the contents of his second letter to Gould in which he said quite plainly that he did not plan to alter the chancel but merely to repair what was already there. It would also account for his unexplained refusal to carry out the work recommended by Edward Ashworth, a much respected church architect, who had recently restored three local churches.[30] John Southcomb was no doubt aware, like Bampfield, of the historical significance of the chancel decoration. And as the sixth Southcomb rector to hold the living it is unlikely that he would want to be responsible for the destruction of an interior that had been preserved by his family for two hundred years. Whatever his reasons, his long drawn-out dispute with Karslake kept the restorers at bay for nearly ten years. But ultimately, despite his efforts, his ancestor's remarkable chancel interior was swept away and the church was reduced to the 'monotonous level of Victorian "restoration"' that Bampfield had so eloquently warned against.[31]

Notes and References

1. The school is now the village hall.
2. Cherry and Pevsner 1997, p. 703.
3. NDRO, B678A/PW/2/c/1. This contains the reports (in chronological order) made by the various rural deans after their annual inspection of the condition of the church's fabric and fittings.
4. Southcomb quoted this letter from Karslake in his (Southcomb's) comments to the bishop on the Archdiaconal Survey of St Peter's, DRO, Faculty Petition, Rose Ash 1,4 (1-15).
5. NDRO, B678A/PW/2/c/1.
6. DRO, 4131M/F11, p. 45.
7. Ibid p. 46.
8. Ibid.
9. Diary of J.L.H. Southcomb (JHLS Diary), photocopy in possession of Andrew Jones, the original in the Osborn Collection, Beinecke Rare Book and Manuscript Library, Yale University.
10. DRO, 4131M/F.11, p. 48.
11. JLHS Diary.
12. DRO, 4131M/F.11, p. 49.
13. Cherry and Pevsner's incorrect statement that St Peter's was heavily restored in 1874 suggests that they found a record of Ashworth's recommendations and that these were for a substantial restoration.
14. DRO, 4131M/F.11, p. 50.
15. DRO, 4131M/F.11, p. 74.
16. Ibid.
17. DRO, 4131M/F.11, p. 75. The 'Ordinary' was the court of the archdeacon and the bishop.
18. DRO, Faculty Petition, Rose Ash 1, 4 (1-15).
19. DRO, 4131M/F.11, p. 77.
20. Ibid.
21. Ibid.
22. DRO, Faculty Petition, Rose Ash 1, 4 (1-15).
23. DRO, 4131M/F.11, p. 208.
24. NDRO, B678A/PW/2/c/1.
25. Jones, 2010, p. 184.
26. Some of the woodwork was re-used in the north aisle roof including a number of unusual figural bosses. The screen at the east end of the north aisle (described in the Appendix) was re-used in the new building. The unusual painted texts and royal arms still survive but

sadly not the colour on the other parts of the screen. Some parts of the old rood screen also survive. They were restored in the 1930s when an exquisitely carved new top was added. Again, sadly, no colour survives.

27. The article, reproduced in the Appendix, appeared on 19 April 1884 in the *Weekly Mercury* and was reprinted in Vol III of the *Western Antiquary*, April 1884, pp. 252-254 under the title 'A non-juror's church'. The *Weekly Mercury* was printed in Plymouth from 1881 to 1888 when it became the *Western Weekly Mercury*. It survived under this title until 1921.

28. Nonjurors were Anglican clergy who refused to swear allegiance to William III and Mary. They felt bound by their oath to James II who, although deposed by Parliament, was still alive.

29. Saunders 1900, pp. 219-220. She gives her source as *Life of Kettlewell*, N. Ferrar. This possibly refers to *The Life and Times of John Kettlewell: with details of the history of the Nonjurors / by the author of Nicholas Ferrar, his household and his friends*. It was edited by T. T. Carter and published by Longmans in 1895.

30. St Rumon's, Romansleigh was restored by Edward Ashworth in 1868, St Mary's, Bishops Nympton in 1869 and St Michael's, East Anstey in 1870–71.

31. Appendix, final paragraph.

Bibliography

Cherry, B. and Pevsner, N. (1997) *The Buildings of England: Devon*, Harmondsworth: Penguin Books Ltd.

Jones, A. (2010) *Victorian North Devon: a social history*, privately published by Andrew Jones, The Rectory, Bishops Nympton, South Molton, EX36 4NY.

Saunders, H. (1900) 'Notes on the history of a North Devon Parish. Aissa, Rose Ash', *DAT*, 32, pp. 212-228.

Appendix

A Nonjuror's Church

Church restoration, unless conducted in a thoroughly conservative spirit, is always fraught with serious danger to much that is interesting from local associations, or that is important on ecclesiastical or historical grounds. Sometimes the gain does not at all counterbalance the loss. We are therefore anxious to call attention to a church, now about to be "restored", possessing peculiarities of arrangement well-nigh unique. Some of these peculiarities must, we fear, disappear, but many of them, we trust, may be spared as rare illustrations of a period in our Church and Civil history. In any case, a careful record of their existence should be preserved.

The Church of Rose Ash, in North Devon, stands embosomed in trees, on a conspicuous eminence, about five miles west of East Anstey station. On entering this church some years since, the writer's attention was immediately caught by details of adornment and arrangement that were new to him, indicating a care for the sacred building and an attention to reverential ritual, at a period often supposed to have been sadly wanting in such care and reverence. The thought at once occurred to him, – "This church has been in the hands of a non-juror." His suspicion proved correct. In the "Life of Kettlewell" we have a list of non-juring clergyman, and among them we find "Mr. Lewis Southcomb, Rector of Rose Ash, Penitent."

The term "Penitent," appears to apply to one who having taken the Oath of Allegiance to William III and used the new State Prayers, afterwards made a retraction, and was admitted, by an authorized form, to the non-juring communion. Whether Lewis Southcomb was able to retain his benefice is a point we cannot without further inquiry, determine. But he was evidently of the school which produced Sancroft, and Ken, and Kettlewell, and Spinckes, and Hickes.

The church consists of nave, chancel, north aisle, north chancel, aisle, tower and porch. On entering, the screen first claims our attention. The mediæval work has been carefully preserved across the chancel, and is composed of four arches, with a door in the centre; massive upright posts run up from the ground. The arched openings are filled with good "Perpendicular" tracery of the best period, and

207

the whole is tastefully decorated with vermillion, blue and gold. There are closed panels below; and above the screen an open space, through which pass three upright posts supporting a beam; above which all is closed up to the roof, and on this real "East end of the Church" are inscribed, as the Canon of A.D.1603 directs, the Ten Commandments; an arrangement which may be noticed in some other churches in the district, where remains or traces of the screen are found, as at Molland. The doorway of the rood-loft existing in the north aisle shows that the screen once extended across the whole church; but, from decay, or some other cause, the portion separating the chancel aisle, and also the "return" running eastward on the north side of the chancel, disappeared and were replaced in the days of the non-juror, as it would seem, by screens which, while they cannot vie with the mediæval work, are yet very praiseworthy, and deeply interesting from the period to which they evidently belong. There is neither arcade nor tracery; the open space is divided by rails ornamented with knobs or mouldings, baluster-fashion, and decorated with yellow, red and blue. The panels below are ornamented with the rose, half-circles, and similar devices, and would almost seem to have been taken from some secular building. Above the rails are inscriptions in Old English lettering, which certainly seem characteristic of "non-juring" principles and times. Looking west, we have from the 72nd Psalm: – Give the King Thy judgments, O God: and Thy righteousness unto the King's sonne. Then shall hee judge Thy People according unto right, and defend the Poore. On the inner side facing east, is the text, from "Esai: 49" – "Kinges shal be Thy nursyng Fathers, and their Queenes Thy nursyng Mothers: They shall fall before Thee with their faces flat upon the earth." We must notice that this is not from our present version, but from Coverdale's translation of A.D.1535: and this may have some bearing on the question of the exact date of this Post-Reformation screen. A small triangular board, surmounting the screen, above the door, bears on its western side, the Royal arms (including the white horse of Hanover), and the letters G. R.: on the inner side it bears a shield emblazoned with three black lions, surrounded by hearts, and with angels for supporters, and the letters Q.A. Can this mean Queen Anne? The screen running eastward between chancel and aisle has this inscription on its north side, from I. Timotheus, 2nd chap,: – "I exhort that, first of all, supplications, prayers, intercessions, and giving of thanks, be made for all Men; for Kinges, and for all that are in authoritie." On another triangular board above this is painted a shield containing the Prince of Wales' crest and motto, and the letters P. G. {or C}. Whether we detect in all this a spirit hesitating between loyalty to an exiled prince and submission to a *de facto* sovereign, we must leave it to others to determine; it is not easy now to guess the exact course of thought which directed this remarkable combination. The text on the chancel side of the screen is of another kind. "Quench not the spirit: examine all thynges: holde fast that which is good abstayne from all appearance of evyll." On the triangle we have, "Pray continually: In all things give thanks: for this is the will of God in Christ Jesus toward you." These are from I. Thess. v., and are not from any present translation, neither do they quite agree with any preceding one. The obliterated sentence is no doubt, "Rejoyce ever." These texts from versions earlier than the authorized of A.D. 1611, militate against our supposition that the later screens are the work of the non-juror, and would rather pronounce them to be Jacobean, though with some much later additions. The altar rails are handsomely turned and carved, and would seem to be of the time of Queen Anne. They are "re-turned" eastward, with gates admitting into these side partitions, so as to allow communicants to assemble on three sides of the Holy Table. The floor of the sanctuary is laid with squares of black and white marble. Behind the altar, as a reredos, is painted, in gold, a cross on three steps, above which are the words, "So God loved the world;" up the stem runs, "Let my Disciple take up his Cross, and follow Me," which is not a quotation from Holy Scripture, though conveying the import of one. Across the arms is "We preach Christ crucified," above this, on the north, "I am the living Bread which came down from Heaven"; on the south, "This cup is the New Testament in My Blood;" beneath which is a chalice. The east wall is painted to represent red curtains, the lower portion looped up above the Holy Table, and, above all, just beneath the ceiling, is a large eye, with beams of light proceeding therefrom, which, from its position is really a striking and very significant feature. Throughout the church, the ancient barrel roof, with its host of bosses, remains perfect, and (we will hope) in good condition. In the chancel the ribs are painted gold, red, and blue, and the square spaces between are plastered.

These compartments, sixteen in number, contain a brief history of the Twelve Apostles, S. Paul, S. Stephen, S. Mark, and S. Luke. If, of dire necessity, these legends must be destroyed, it will be a pity; as, probably, they do not exist in any other church in England. Of these we give some of the most remarkable:-

"St. Bartholomew, August 24, – He was also called Nathanael, and stil'd with the High & Honourable Character of an Israelite indeed, in whom is no guile by our Blessed Saviour Himself, St. John i, 47. He preach'd the Gospel in India, and endeavouring to reclaim the people of Albanople from Idolatry, he was flead alive and then crucified." Beaneath is his emblem – a cross.

"St. Andrew, An Apostle, November 30. He was born at Bethsaida in Galilee, a Brother to Simon Peter. As they were both fishing together, our Blessed Saviour passing by bid them to follow him. After which St. Andrew preached the Gospel in Scythia, and converted numbers. He was the first Bishop of Constantinople, and at Patrae he was condemned to be crucified by being bound to his Cross." Beneath is a St. Andrew's cross.

"St. Peter, An Apostle and Bishop. He was born at Bethsaida, and a Fisher Man. He was converted by the Miracle of the great draught of Fishes. St. Luke, V.9. After which he preached the Gospel through Pontus, Galatia, Capadocia, Asia, and Bithynia. He was first of all Bishop of Antioch, afterwards Bishop of Rome, where he was crucified with his head downwards." Beneath is an inverted cross.

"St. Mark, – An Evangelist and St. Peter's Disciple, – He preached in Lybia, and almost through all Egypt. It is thought he wrote his Gospel at Rome, A.D. 43. And suffered Martyrdom April 25, 62. His Body was translated from Alexandria to Venice, whereof he is the Patron." Beneath is a spear.

Of S. Simon it is told that he "came here into Great Britain where, for preaching the Gospel, he was crucified & here buried."

S. Luke is erroneously called "An Apostle." We are told that he was "born & bred a scholar at Antioch, where he studied and practiced Physick." His emblem is the trunk and branch of an olive tree, on which he was hung. The emblems of the martyrdom are given in each case, as S. James the Great, a sword; S. James the Less, a club; S.

Philip, a pillar: S. John, a cauldron on a fire; St. Matthias, a hatchet; S. Stephen, a heap of stones.

The chancel-aisle would almost seem to have been used as a school. A large round-backed arm-chair, fixed, occupies the centre of the east wall, looking west, and in front of it is a capacious desk, such as schoolmasters use; and, against the north wall are two rows of forms and desks, seemingly for children. The holding of a day-school in the church was a practice not unknown at the beginning of the last century. The arrangement seems almost too much for the mere holding of a vestry in a country parish.

The Canon of A.D.1603, which orders "chosen sentences" to be "written upon the walls of the churches," has here been carefully obeyed. Every triangular space between the heads of two arches has its well-chosen text. On the wall on each side of the door are the suitable words, "Blessed are they that dwell in Thy House: they will be always praising Thee," and, "I had rather be a Doorkeeper in the House of my God: than to dwell in the tents of ungodliness." And on the west wall of the aisle is a painting, not badly executed, of our LORD seated on the Mount, with the Benedictions inscribed beneath. Above this is a date which may, or may not, belong to it – A.D. 1767. Around the various seats are painted red curtains, and not to be admired as a matter of taste. There are other remarkable inscriptions on the walls in various parts of the church on tablets formed of raised plaster, with a moulding or frame of the same. The following are admirable lessons for all who enter the house of prayer. – 1. "Our duties to God are, – Faith, Hope, Love, Fear, Trust, Humility, Honour, Worship, Repentance. 'Thou shalt love the Lord thy God,'" &c. 2. "Our duties to ourselves are, – Humility, Meekness, Constancy, Chastity, Diligence, Temperance, Consideration. 'We are not sufficient of ourselves to think anything as of ourselves,' &c." 3. "Our duties to our Neighbours are Justice, Charity. And both these to be shewn to their Souls, to their Bodies, to their Goods, to their Good Name. 'Thou shalt love thy Neighbour as thyself.'" 4. "The three Theological Graces are Faith, Hope, Charity. 'Every good Gift,' &c., S. James, i., 17." 5. "The four Cardinal Virtues are Justice, Prudence, Fortitude, Temperance. 'As we have therefore opportunity,' &c., Gal. vi. 10."

There is a well-made, handsome screen of oak, under the tower arch, quite closed up, with the inscription: – "John Doidge, Churchwarden,

1730." There is little to be said of the structure itself. The east window and tower window may possibly be of poor "Decorated" design. The other nine windows (all – save one – being of three lights) are great square-headed openings, with mullions running to the top, but totally void of tracery or cusps, and such as the most conservative restorer need not care to retain. Such windows are, however, the most common variety in the neighbourhood, as at Knowstone, Molland, and others. There is a square Norman font. The tower is very plain and poor, and has no staircase, being ascended by a ladder. The large Bible, not in very good order, is what is called the "Vinegar" edition, of A.D. 1717: so termed from a misprint in the heading – "The Parable of the Vinegar," instead of "The Parable of the Vineyard." It is quite worthy of some care with a view to its being preserved and used. In the neighbouring church of West Anstey is a very perfect copy, in its old binding, still in use.

Outside the church, the only noticeable feature is a queer, mysterious, rough stone in the wall above the porch roof, which looks like a bracket for an image. In the churchyard, near the chancel door, still stand the parish "stocks," in very fair repair; and, as they are now becoming almost as rare as a pillory, it is hoped that this specimen will be preserved to satisfy the curiosity of future generations.

We feel that many Post-Reformation peculiarities preserved in this remote church, may well be counted of sufficient interest to save it from the complete sweeping-out too common in the process of "restoration". Many of those interesting features could be easily retained, the handsome screen especially, and others, as inscriptions, could be copied, and so replaced in their old well-chosen positions. For these things are precious links, connecting us with times often spoken of as dead and cold; but concerning which there is proof that they were not wanting in high faith, pure piety and devotion, love for God's house and worship, and many a noble Christian grace and deed.

Better to treasure up such instances where we find them, than to make all brand-new and so reduce our churches to a monotonous level of Victorian "restoration".

West Anstey.   R.L.B.

Source: *Weekly Mercury*, 19 April 1884.

The Religious Controversy in Nineteenth-Century Woodbury

Gillian Selley

After the Reformation in England the religion of the country fragmented into a variety of conforming and non-conforming versions of Protestantism. In the 1830s the unity of the Church of England was challenged when a group of men in Oxford, both clergymen and students, published a set of *Tracts for the Times* defending the Established Church and its doctrines from political interference. Many of these tracts introduced ideas akin to certain Roman Catholic doctrines, which, in a country that was strongly anti-Catholic, antagonised clergy and laity alike. This group of men who sought a catholic revival in the Church of England were known as the Oxford Movement and its members as Tractarians. John Henry Newman and Henry Manning were two promiment members of a number of Anglican clergy who became Roman Catholics. High Anglicans who remained within the Church of England continued to emphasise the heritage of the apostolic succession and the doctrines of the early church fathers.

The Evangelical Protestants, originally in agreement with upholding the doctrines of the Established Church, were alienated by the move towards the Church of Rome, and became fiercely anti-Tractarian. Any hint of ritual or connection with Roman Catholicism was abhorrent to them. If their own parish church was of a High Church persuasion they either worshipped at a church out of their parish which had a

Figure 1. William Spreat's drawing of Woodbury church. Reproduced courtesy of Westcountry Studies Library, Devon Libraries.

minister with more evangelical views, or in many cases, built their own churches and appointed their own minister.

This is the background to a long standing religious controversy which divided parishioners in the Devon parish of Woodbury in the nineteenth century. The following letter, written from Woodbury, appeared in *The Times* newspaper in October 1845 from 'A Member of the Church of England'.

Sir, – May I venture to request your kind attention to a subject of which many persons feel as deeply as I do the importance, and which through your kindness alone, by inserting this in your valuable columns, will be made known to the parties for whom it is intended, viz., the priest vicars of Exeter Cathedral? These gentlemen are the lay impropriators of the parish of Woodbury, the population of which is above 2,200; its tithes amount annually to 1,100£; it is a perpetual curacy, and not under the control of any bishop; they abstract from this unfortunate parish the above amount, with the exception of 110£ a year, which the clergyman here receives. He has been 36 years the curate, and is now really unable, from infirmities both of body and mind, to perform those sacred duties which devolve on him with justice to his parishioners; the result is, the parish is most dreadfully neglected entirely from want of an active and religious minister; and, although only seven miles from the city of Exeter (a city renowned for its strict observance of religious duties, and attention to the wants of the poor), scenes of the most disgusting depravity and immorality are daily being enacted here from the bad example children have shown them by their parents – they of course follow in their wake, and even children of the most tender age are frequently heard in the streets uttering oaths of the most shocking character; and it is a well-known fact that in the whole county of Devon there is not a parish where so little respect is paid either to religion, education, or morality as Woodbury. I will only mention one circumstance that will sufficiently show, I trust, the dreadful state of this parish – that is with regard to the sick poor. Information some time since having been forwarded by a number of the parishioners to that excellent body of Christians, the Wesleyan Methodists, of the total want of Scriptural advice, they at once nobly responded to the call of their afflicted fellow mortals by sending down a missionary, who now resides in the parish and performs our minister's duty with the exception of preaching in the parish church. His whole time is devoted to instructing the poor and affording comfort to the sick. Yet with all this there are so many abuses still existing that one scarcely knows how to reform them, neither will it be of the least use to attempt it till we have an efficient clergyman; therefore I, on the part of my fellow-parishioners, claim that prompt attention from the Priest Vicars, which the case so justly deserves, and which has so long been denied us.[1]

This letter led to a chain of events which turned the parish of Woodbury into a battleground for twenty-five years and altered the way of life and attitudes of many of its inhabitants. Whether it was due to the publication of this letter in *The Times* or not, the Priest Vicars suggested to the incumbent, the Reverend John Edsall, that a curate should be sent to assist him with his parochial duties. A young clergyman, the curate of St Thomas in Exeter, called John Loveband Fulford, was sent to Woodbury in 1845 and took over many of the duties of the vicar.

Figure 2. The Reverend John Fulford on his tricycle.
Reproduced courtesy of Roger Stokes.

A few months after Fulford's appointment a young doctor from Wiltshire, Robert Brent, arrived in Woodbury to take up the medical practice there. Robert was the son of Isaac Brent, a master scribbler from Trowbridge, who had leased a mill outside Westbury and sent his son as an apprentice to a doctor in the town.[2] As the Brent family were staunch Baptists, Robert was excluded from going to university or medical school. At the end of his apprenticeship he had travelled up to St Andrews where he was examined by the authorities at the Medical School there, and awarded his MD on 1 July 1845.[3] The Reverend John Loveband Fulford had been the curate to the Reverend J. Medley, who was thought to favour some of the practices of the Oxford Movement and was therefore a suspect clergyman in the eyes of some Woodbury parishioners.[4] Dr Robert Brent was an opinionated, convivial, energetic and impulsive man, but also a charismatic one who gathered an influential group of parishioners around him to hound Fulford and make life unpleasant

Figure 3. Colonel Dr Robert Brent in uniform.
Reproduced courtesy of Roger Stokes.

for him. Brent was a staunch Tory who had a finger in every pie in Woodbury, and was well known in Exeter and the surrounding villages as a military man and an agriculturist, who involved himself in any cause or interest that reared its head.[5]

When the Reverend John Edsall died in August 1846 the churchwardens (one a Unitarian and the other an Evangelical Protestant) suggested that a Mr Clarke should be appointed as the new Vicar, ignoring the fact that John Loveband Fulford had applied for the ministry in Woodbury. After much consultation amongst the clergy in Exeter the Reverend Joseph Corfe, Custos of the Priest Vicars, appointed the highly recommended Fulford to the position of Vicar of Woodbury, raising the hackles of the Brent coterie. When it became known that Fulford had been chosen 'nightly meetings were held at a public house in the village where profane and obscene songs, with inflammatory harangues were used to excite the parishioners against their new pastor and the Priest Vicars'.[6] The churchwardens subsequently requested the organist to refrain from attending in church and urged their domestic staff to absent themselves too.

On Sunday 11 November 1846, Mr Fulford, accompanied by the Custos of the Priest Vicars, proceeded to the church to read himself in. They discovered that 'near the churchyard on a conspicuous part of a wall were publicly exhibited profane caricatures and exciting addresses, tending to bring into contempt sacred ordinances and Ministers of Religion'.[7] A crowd of disorderly persons had congregated near the spot with the intention of obstructing the curate but this was prevented by Thomas Porter Esq., who had continuously supported Fulford, whom he considered to be the victim of a wicked and organised system of religious persecution.

> Divine Service proceeded as usual, marked only by the absence of the usual singing and organ playing, till the Curate and the Custos proceeded to read the service at the Communion Table, where on a signal given by a person in the Gallery, about 25 young men and boys suddenly rose from their seats and in a tumultuous manner quitted the church.[8]

A similar attempt to disrupt the service was made in the afternoon. Neither the churchwardens, sidesmen nor the eight-strong choir attended the services, and thereafter the choir sang at the Evangelical Protestant church at Woodbury Salterton.[9]

After such an 'auspicious' start to his ministry, Fulford endeavoured to bring some spiritual order to the parish without bowing to the threats and insults of his opponents. The accusation that he was a 'Tractarian' was quite inaccurate in that he was not an Oxford man but an alumnus of Cambridge. There he had been influenced by the architectural views of Pugin and stated that his desire was that the interior of churches should return to the arrangements of the period after the Reformation. He was opposed to the Evangelical movement, which had certainly crept into Woodbury parish, and had destroyed or concealed many of the old features of the parish church.[10] Several of the leading parishioners were of this persuasion and some of the most influential attended the Unitarian Meeting House at Gulliford.

Dr Brent and his friends drew up a petition to send to the House of Lords to ask that Mr Fulford should be removed from the parish. Many of the working men and their families were bullied into signing this petition, and since many of Brent's supporters were farmers and employers their support would have been easy to obtain. When the Reverend Joseph Corfe heard about this petition he prepared a 'Statement' to give to a Member of Parliament if Brent's petition were to be sent. In this he explained the history of the Vicars Choral and its Rectory Manor of Woodbury.[11] He also gave details of how, when he had suggested to the Reverend John Edsall that he should have a curate to assist him, Mr Edsall admitted that he should never have taken Holy Orders, and that he preferred to socialise with the local farmers. This 'Statement' of about 3,500 words undermined Brent's assertions regarding Mr Fulford's unsuitability. Neither the petition nor Mr Corfe's 'Statement' appear to have been sent.[12]

Robert Brent was a frequent correspondent to the editor of *The Western Times*, a noted Nonconformist, whose editorials were full of invective against the Anglican Church and the Bishop of Exeter. Brent, or one of his cronies, fed the newspaper with a variety of stories about the absence of any congregation in the church, about Fulford's 'papist' practices, and of how much Fulford was despised by the parishioners. He also accused Fulford of writing the 'famous' letter to *The Times* newspaper, which rebounded on him as he was eventually forced to admit that he himself was the anonymous correspondent.[13] An instance of the spiteful actions instigated by Brent was the difficulties that Fulford had in finding a house in the village for his family. There was not a parsonage in the village and an allowance was made by the Priest Vicars towards the rent of a suitable property.[14] The wife of an earlier vicar had left a sum of money in her will to augment the incumbent's salary as long as he lived in the parish.[15] Fulford attempted to lease or buy several properties but obstacles were put in his way and he was obliged to live in Harefield Cottage in the parish of Lympstone. Estates owned by the Priest Vicars in the parish were hung onto grimly, until eventually one tenant was prepared to end his lease and make the land available for the building of a Parsonage.[16]

Brent was churchwarden for several years even though he did not attend the parish church. The churchwardens were elected by the parishioners alone, the Priest Vicars having no say in the candidates,

Figure 4. Parsonage House drawn by Fergus Kyle 1966.
Reproduced courtesy of Roger Stokes.

and so the Brent group was able to keep its own men running the affairs
of the church in Woodbury regardless of the wishes of their vicar.

During the late 1840s and early 1850s there was a flurry of correspondence concerning 'Papism' and 'Tractarianism' in Devon. There
were two newspapers with opposing views, *The Western Times*
for the non-conformists and *Woolmers* which was described as the
mouthpiece of the Bishop of Exeter. Correspondents wrote long
diatribes, Brent being one of these, with letters full of invective
against Fulford. Occasionally Brent sent for publication a set of letters
he had exchanged with the Priest Vicars and Fulford, and on another
occasion a series of letters between himself and the Bishop of Exeter
and the Woodbury churchwardens. These letters triggered off more
correspondence from clergymen and laity in Exeter and its environs,
writing under pseudonyms such as 'presbyter', 'looker-on', 'lover of
truth and honesty', 'anti-idolatry', 'an enemy to usurpation', or just 'a
protestant parishioner', and so on.

Since Fulford held firm and refused to be driven away from the
parish, Brent and his friends decided to entice his congregation
away by building an alternative church. In July 1847 the following
advertisement was placed in local newspapers:

APPEAL TO ALL GENUINE PROTESTANTS

Especially those of the Established Church on behalf of a NEW CHURCH at WOODBURY, 7 miles from Exeter. The inhabitants of Woodbury deeply regret that any necessity should have arisen for such an appeal. But on the decease of the late Incumbent, Mr. Edsall, the Priest Vicars of Exeter, who are Patrons of the Living persisted, in defiance of the respectful remonstrances of the parishioners, to intrude upon them their present Tractarian Incumbent, Mr. Fulford, the most objectionable appointment that could be made both to high and low, rich and poor, in Woodbury. Since the Reverend gentleman's entrance upon the living, the Church, previously filled has been deserted, and the inhabitants of a large Parish in which union prevailed, (and there were not half a dozen Dissenters), have been virtually ejected from the venerable fabric, in which they and their forefathers have long worshipped. They have found shelter in a small building in which the Services of the Church are duly performed by the Rev. W. Wippell, but which is much too small, (accommodating only 150 to 200 persons), for the large Congregation, very many of whom are unable to obtain standing room. Two inhabitants therefore have decided on building a commodious Sanctuary, to be used as a FREE CHURCH OF ENGLAND, till such time as it *may please God to send a faithful Protestant Minister* to the Parish Church. The New Church will be vested in Trustees sincerely attached to the Church of England, who will be empowered whenever so desirable a return can be conscientiously effected either to convert the Free Church into a Chapel of Ease or School-rooms to be used in connection with the Established Church, or in any other way as circumstances may decide, with the approbation of the incumbent and the Parishioners. The Inhabitants are not able to raise the entire cost of this undertaking without the aid of their Protestant Brethren, whose Donations they earnestly and respectfully invite to be forwarded to the account of the Treasurer of the Woodbury New Church at the Devon and Cornwall Banking Company, Exeter, and Messrs Hanbury and Co. London.[17]

Having had this appeal published, Brent then sent a copy to the Bishop of Exeter, requesting him to remove Fulford from office. He then wrote to the Archbishop of Canterbury with the same request. In September 1847 Brent wrote to *The Western Times* asking the editor to publish a series of nineteen letters that passed between him, the Archbishop, the Bishop of Exeter, the Reverend Joseph Corfe, and John Loveband Fulford. The Archbishop declared that the affair was nothing to do with him, and the Bishop of Exeter could find no legitimate reason, either doctrinal or personal, why Fulford should be relieved of his ministry in Woodbury. With regard to the above 'Appeal' sent by Brent, the bishop replied that 'I have no hesitation in saying, that to such a document I cannot permit myself to give any consideration whatever'.[18]

The appeal itself was full of spite and exaggeration, and the comment that there were only a handful of Dissenters was quite wrong as the parish had had a Unitarian Meeting House in Gulliford since the late seventeenth century, and from the middle of the eighteenth century a variety of houses in the parish had been licensed by the Bishop of Exeter to hold religious meetings.[19] The appeal was ultimately successful, and enough money was raised to build a new Free Church which opened for worship in May 1851,[20] with William Wippell as its free minister.[21] At least with the troublemakers worshipping in their own church Mr Fulford was free to hold his services without interruptions. Even so the 'true Protestants', as they described themselves, continued to write malicious articles about Mr Fulford and his congregation in St Swithun's. The vicar was a patient man who bore with Brent's behaviour without resorting to retaliation, though he did gently chide the doctor in some of his letters. At the end of a series of letters which Brent had had published in *The Western Times* Mr Fulford concluded his letter to Brent writing, 'you have been and it appears are ready to express your opinion, when I think it worth having I will not fail to seek it'.[22]

The Western Times revealed its bigoted stance on the issue when the following doggerel, penned by a Woodbury hand, was published in January 1848:

'We May Be Happy Yet
   Oh! Pray as thou were wont to pray
      Within that ancient pile;
'Ere Fulford came, alas! the day,
      and crushed our hearts awhile.

Some thought perchance 'twere best to quell,
    Some insults to forget,
On which could memory cease to dwell,
    We may be happy yet.
Departed Edsall never praise,
    His doctrines clear and plain,
Round those too sad a feeling plays,
    To think of them again.
Such recollection off we cast,
    As if we ne'er had met;
And thus unmindful of the past,
    We may be happy yet.[23]

In 1850 the Reverend John Fulford wrote a letter to the 'Inhabitants of Woodbury' setting out his beliefs and aims for the parish of Woodbury. Where it was published or how many copies existed is not known as the original text has vanished. It is known of though because Robert Brent, on reading it, retaliated by writing 'A Running Commentary' on this letter, quoting large extracts from it and giving his criticisms of the vicar's views. His 'commentary' was published by Trewman and Company of Exeter, the publishing company of the *Exeter Flying Post*.[24]

In 1855 the following rather strange advertisement appeared in the local newspapers:

'WANTED'

By some English Members of Ye society, "De propagandi fide", a zealous supporter of Ye common cause, sufficiently well-versed in Ye Latin and English characters of Ye Medieval ages, to give "free translations" of Ye Golden Legend of Ye Christmas Carols and Ye other Monkish poetical compositions of the *most enlightened* period, in order to give more effect to Ye Legends of "Good King Wenceslas" now first introduced for congregational use into this diocese. A member of Ye Society, direct from Rome, would have a decided preference; but any gentleman, who can procure a certificate of competence from Cardinal Wiseman, will be accepted. The utmost secrecy will be observed.
Address: Mr. SAMUEL SLY, sign of Ye Mitre, Oxford Street
January 13th, festival of St Hiloriers. [25]

What was the significance of this? In December 1854 Mr Fulford had bought several copies of the Reverend J.M. Neale's book of hymns for Christmas, some of which he had introduced to the congregation at St Swithun's. And what was wrong with this? Everything, according to his detractors. They were horrified that some of these hymns used Latin words, and other unacceptable words such as 'holly', 'ivy', 'laurel' and 'bay'. The phrases 'ox and ass before Him bow' and 'ox and ass adore the King' were also considered quite unsuitable to be sung in a Protestant church. The author of these hymns was also quite unacceptable since he was an Oxford man and had been accused of Tractarianism. The two carols considered to be most obnoxious were *Adeste Fidelis* and *Good King Wenceslaus*, though neither of these was sung in St Swithun's. Robert Brent was so incensed by the introduction of these hymns that he wrote to the Bishop of Exeter asking him to prevent Mr. Fulford from allowing them to be sung. As usual, Brent had his correspondence with the bishop published in *The Western Times*. This resulted in a flurry of amusing correspondence about Woodbury farmers needing to be taught Latin and the history of King Wenceslaus. The bishop did not forbid Mr Fulford to sing the hymns but he did admit that he thought they were not suitable for a Protestant congregation.[26] The Reverend J.M. Neales's book also included hymns to be sung for Eastertide, the use of which caused another surge of letters in the press.[27]

Brent continued to snipe at Mr. Fulford until in 1859 he had acquired another cause. In that same year he formed the first Company of the Devon Volunteer Artillery, and promptly fitted out his men with uniforms, set up a drill hall and acquired two eighteen-pounder guns.[28] Though there were still disputes with the churchwardens when Mr. Fulford altered arrangements in the church without their consent, on the whole life was much easier for him. However he was accused of going round the church with a chisel disclosing old features which had been carefully tidied away. In his 'prying' he discovered a sedilia and piscina in the chancel which had been boarded and painted over. He also removed whitewashed boarding from the walls to disclose the staircase to the rood cross and an entrance to the chancel on the south side.[29] The boarded-over pulpit was revealed to be a Jacobean one which had been carved by a Woodbury carpenter in 1635.[30] Mr Fulford was strongly criticised for moving the choir from the gallery at the back of the church and the organ into the chancel, and also for placing a cross or vases of flowers upon the communion table.[31]

Robert Brent had one more triumph to his name when he funded the building of a Masonic Lodge at Topsham which was opened in 1870.[32] He died on 26 February 1872 following an epileptic fit. Brent had experienced fits over a period of ten years, purportedly caused by an explosion resulting from the premature firing of an eighteen-pounder gun at a military exercise.[33] Even in death he shunned St Swithun's and his funeral was held at Woodbury Salterton where he was buried. Mr Fulford continued his ministry until his death in 1898. By this time he was much loved by the parishioners. The church in Woodbury was restored in 1894, his son Robert Medley Fulford being the architect for the internal work.[34] In 1893 Mr Fulford wrote an article explaining in what state he had found the church when he became its vicar, and what alterations and major repairs he made to it during his ministry. He had fulfilled his dream of turning the clock back for Woodbury church to reveal a post-Reformation building, removing all the evangelical coverings which masked the old features.[35] Although the terrible disputes of his early days must have been a burden and worry to him, his strength of character and determination allowed him to achieve what he had strived for in restoring St Swithun's Church in Woodbury. Christ Church always remained a free church with no links to the parish church. After Robert Brent's death it was used by a variety of denominations and had fallen into a dilapidated state by the 1970s. It has now been fully restored and enlarged and is occupied by a very active membership of Free Church men and women.

Notes and References

1. *The Times*, 30 October 1845.
2. 1841 census for Westbury in Wiltshire.
3. St Andrews University, Degrees of MD, 1 July 1845.
4. Reverend J. Medley was appointed Bishop of Fredericton in Canada in 1845.
5. Robert Brent's interests were wide ranging. He was Chairman of Clyst Farmers' Club, Secretary of the Devon and Exeter Protectionist Society, Chairman of Exeter and Exmouth Railway, Trustee of Exeter Turnpike Trust, steward at the Bath and West Show, member of the Exe Salmon Fisheries, and so on.

6.   ECA, Miscellaneous papers of the Vicars Choral (VC): draft of the Reverend Joseph Corfe's *Statement* intended for the House of Commons.

7.   Ibid.

8.   Ibid.

9.   Ibid.

10. Fulford 1854; Fulford 1883; Fulford 1893.

11. ECA, Archive of the Vicars Choral. The church of Woodbury and its estates (amounting to about 300 acres) were given to the Vicars Choral of the Cathedral in 1205 by Bishop Marshal as an augmentation to their income, having previously been held by the Abbey of Mont St Michel. In 1401 The College of Vicars was established by a royal charter of King Henry IV. The Priest Vicars were the impropriators of the church of St Swithun and were responsible for proving the wills of Woodbury parishioners. They were the lords of the Rectory Manor of Woodbury for which they held regular manor courts. The minister of Woodbury was the curate to the Priest Vicars who were the rectors of the parish church.

12. Fortunately Mr Corfe left copies of all his correspondence so a very clear picture is given of what was occurring in Woodbury. These are held in ECA in boxes of miscellaneous papers of the Vicars Choral.

13. ECA, VC, miscellaneous papers (*Statement* of Reverend Joseph Corfe).

14. Ibid.

15. DRO, 53/6 box 66/31 (miscellaneous papers including the will of Mary Davy, widow of the Reverend J Davy, dated 10 September 1808).

16. ECA, VC, Miscellaneous papers, a copy of a letter from Mr. Joseph Corfe to the Dean and Chapter, 1847.

17. *Exeter Flying Post*, 15 July 1847, p 2.

18. *Exeter Flying Post*, 2 September 1847, p. 4, publication of the letter of 10 Aug 1847 from the Bishop of Exeter to Dr Brent.

19. DRO, Moger 1 PR 109-111.

20. *The Western Times*, 24 May 1851, p. 5.

21. *Exeter Flying Post*, 26 June 1851, p. 8.

22. *Exeter Flying Post*, 2 September 1847, p. 4, published letter of 14 August 1847 from Fulford to Brent.

23. *The Western Times*, 22 January 1848, p. 5.

24. DRO, 3726/Z/Z1 (A running commentary . . . on 'A letter to the inhabitants of the Parish of Woodbury . . .').

25. *Exeter Flying Post*, 18 Jan 1855, p. 8.

26. *Exeter Flying Post*, 25 Jan 1855, p 5, letter dated 15 Jan 1855 from the Bishop of Exeter to the churchwardens of Woodbury.

27. *Exeter Flying Post*, 22 Feb 1855, p. 3.

28. *Exeter Flying Post*, 1 Sep 1859, p. 7.

29. Fulford 1893, pp. 63-72.

30. DRO 4344A-99/PW1, Woodbury Churchwardens' Accounts.
31. Woodbury Vestry Book 1848-1885, 25 Oct 1870 (this book is privately owned).
32. *Exeter Flying Post*, 1 Jun 1870, p. 7. Brent Lodge still exists in Topsham, though in a different building. There is a large portrait of Brent as a Colonel in the Volunteer Artillery hanging on the wall.
33. TNA, C 16/699/B306, C 16/711/E72 and C16/768/B53 – the medical evidence was recorded in a hearing in the Court of Chancery in 1871–72 brought by the Exeter Sewage Company against Robert Brent.
34. DRO, Rural Dean's Reports on the parish of Woodbury, 6 March and 15 June 1894.
35. Fulford 1893, pp. 63-72.

Bibliography

Fulford, Reverend J.L. (1854) 'Church Worship and Chancel Arrangements', *TEDAS*, 5, pp. 124-130.

Fulford, J.L. (1883) 'The Future of Gothic Architecture ', *TEDAS*, 2nd series, 5, pp. 60-65.

Fulford, Reverend J.L. (1893) 'Notes on the Church of St Swithun, Woodbury', *TEDAS*, 3rd series, 1, pp. 63-72.

Anatomy of a Parish: Parkham 1841/1842

Arthur Dark

Introduction

The fortunate coincidence of the 1841 census and the 1842 Tithe Map and Apportionment enables us to reconstruct the North Devon parish of Parkham in great detail. In 1841/42 it was a large coastal parish of 5,330 acres of which 1,426 acres were described in 1842 as 'waste'.[1] This large area of waste, representing twenty-seven per cent of the total land surface, mainly took the form of a belt of moorland occupying the middle and southern end of the parish. Comprising Ash Common (enclosed by 1850) and Melbury Moor further south, it was a significant source of rough grazing and fuel (furze) to those who had access to it. Today, much of this land has been afforested. The population in 1841 was 995, having risen from 584 in 1801.[2] The settlement pattern was a dispersed one of a few scattered hamlets with isolated farmsteads and cottages lying between them. Farmsteads would have been instantly recognisable by a substantial farmhouse with various ancillary buildings comprising barns and housing for animals. Four of the farmsteads in the parish are described in the Apportionment as Bartons,[3] belonging to four of the fifteen largest farms in the parish.

The hamlet of Parkham, after which the parish is named, was grouped around the parish church of St James, and contained the rectory and two of the three taverns, the Bell and New Inn. In the census it is described as Parkham Town village and had a population

229

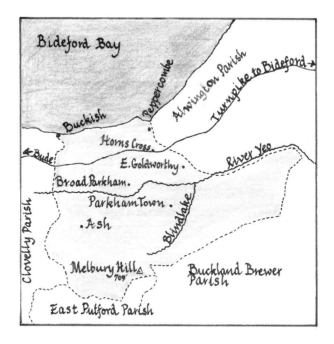

Figure 1. Parkham 1841: The seven largest hamlets. Arthur Dark.

of approximately ninety-nine. The third tavern, the Hoops Inn, was situated on the turnpike road to Bideford. Parkham Town village lay on a spur between the deeply incised River Yeo and its tributary, the Blindlake, which fed into the Torridge. The Parkham Hamlets are shown on Figure 1.

Buckish Mill was a recent settlement in the early nineteenth century, mostly comprising a single line of cottages on the eastern side of the stream that powered Buckish mill. The mill, which was situated on the western side of the stream, was the oldest building in the hamlet, and had become part of the Cole estate by 1808.[4] The other element in the name, Buckish, was the name of a small manorial estate belonging to the Coles of Woolsery.[5] The stream marked the boundary between Parkham parish to the east and Woolsery to the west. The small population living on the Woolsery side of the stream would have brought the total population of Buckish Mill to above 100 in 1841. Nearly all the cottages on the Parkham side belonged to the Pine-Coffins of Portledge in Alwington parish who owned most of the land between Buckish Mill and Portledge.

Figure 2. Parkham looking from the north across the Yeo valley.

Social and Occupational Structure

Farmworkers represented by far the biggest occupational group in Parkham in 1841, although this is not immediately evident in the census, which identifies agricultural labourers (eighty-two of them, and all male) and a group simply described as servants (seventy-five males and fifty-one females). The vast majority of the male servants were living on farms in Parkham, and were undoubtedly farm labourers. The term agricultural labourer is never used to describe them. Most of the female servants were also living on the farms, or at the few gentry houses, and some would also have worked on the land as well as in the farmhouse. The group described as agricultural labourers, on the other hand, would have been day labourers available for hire. In general, the living-in farm servant was better off than the day labourer, since his food, drink and clothing were provided by his master. There were also fourteen apprentices of both sexes living and working on the farms. These were 'apprentices to husbandry', poor children who had been bound as apprentices for seven years to local farmers in return for a premium (financial incentive) paid by the parish, and later by the Poor Law Guardians (after 1834). The latest apprenticeship for a child of seven in Parkham occurs in 1813, but even in 1842, children as young as nine were still being apprenticed to husbandry.[6]

One occupation that depended directly upon farming was corn milling. There were two millers in Parkham, at Boccombe and at Old Mill, both of them utilising the water of the river Yeo. As we have seen, a third mill operated at Buckish Mill, on the Woolsery side of the boundary stream between the two parishes. There were also two limeburners in the parish, Samuel Paddon at Peppercombe and John Harris at Buckish. The two mile stretch which was the Parkham coastline formed a solid rampart of cliff. Only at Peppercombe at the eastern end, and Buckish at the western end, was it breached by two small streams running down narrow valleys (combes) to the sea. In both cases limekilns had been built on the beaches where the valleys reached the sea, and coal and limestone could be landed from South Wales. Only three fishing families can be identified in the census. John Prance and William Baglole [sic] operated from Peppercombe and James Braund from Buckish Mill. There may have been others operating part-time but clearly fishing was less important in 1841 than it became later. The catch was hawked from door to door in the parish by itinerant fishmongers called jowders, one of whom was the author's great-great grandfather.

The day-to-day needs of the parish were met by a whole army of artisans and craftsmen which made the community largely self-sufficient. Building work could be done by eight masons and nine carpenters (plus two apprentices), with the help of one glazier and a thatcher. There was also one local joiner. Three blacksmiths, each with an apprentice, could make and repair any of the ironwork on the farms and shoe the many horses. Fresh meat was provided by eight butchers, and there were two woolcombers. Clothes and shoes could be purchased locally from one shoemaker, four cordwainers (shoemakers) and an apprentice, two tailors, one dressmaker, one milliner, one bonnet maker and four glove makers. Glove makers steadily increased in numbers in most North Devon villages throughout the nineteenth century.[7]

What is perhaps most notable about the list are the occupations that are absent. In this community of nearly a thousand people there was no doctor, dentist, midwife, or any other member of the medical professions. Childbirth and death would all have been dealt with by experienced women from within the community. Critical illness or serious accidents were crisis situations for poor families in relatively isolated rural communities. The average age of the sixteen individuals who were buried at Parkham in 1841 was only 46.3 years, dropping to 34.7 years in 1842. The burials in 1842 included 'a stranger found drowned', whose age was estimated at twenty-two. Such burials were commonplace in the coastal parishes of North Devon.

Surprisingly, there were no retailers listed in the census, not even a general store or post office. Everyone baked their own bread. Most retailing was done by itinerant pedlars, like the fish jowder's referred to earlier. A notable absentee from the list of artisans is a wheelwright. This may reflect the fact that until 1840s, much of the work of transportation in rural Devon was still done by packhorses, and panniers borne by donkeys; such was the frightful state of the roads. There was no resident policeman; indeed no police force. Law and order was maintained by the part-time parish constable who was chosen by the Vestry from amongst the strongest and most dependable members of the community. Normally he would indicate his presence by hanging his elaborate constable's stave outside his front door. The sole representative of national government in the parish was the coastguard who lived at Horns Cross. Although the local landed gentry owned by far the greatest part of the land in Parkham, none of them lived within the parish.

Mary Passmore was the village schoolmistress and lived at Cuckingstool [*sic*] Cottages, but she would not have ranked as a member of the professional classes. There is no evidence to show that she was anything other than a Dame School mistress, striving to teach the elements of reading, writing and arithmetic to a motley group of children who gathered around her kitchen table for a few pence a week. A National School, financed by the National Society for the Education of the Poor in the principles of the Established Church, was not built in Parkham until 1849/50.[8] This, and a smaller number of schools financed by the Nonconformist British and Foreign School Society, became the most usual mode of education for rural working class children in the nineteenth century.

The professional class was uniquely represented by the rector, the Reverend Richard Walter. He was seventy-seven years of age. His seventy-four year old widowed sister lived with him. They were attended to by no less than seven servants. As rector of Parkham (rather than a mere vicar or perpetual curate) he was entitled to the entire tithe income of the parish, which the 1842 Tithe Apportionment valued at £730.[9] In addition to his house, the living included 129 acres of glebe land, a substantial part of which he could rent out or farm.[10] He also owned the freehold of a forty-two acre farm in Parkham, known as Hodiland or Hadiland. Walter was buried at Parkham on 17 July 1842.

It is very difficult for us today to envisage the standing and prestige enjoyed by a man like Richard Walter. Quite apart from his wealth, he was as a university graduate, by far the best educated individual in the parish. He was also the ex-officio chairman of the Vestry, the committee responsible for both church and secular affairs in the parish, and was therefore a rating authority. Vestries were either closed or open, and in the latter case Vestry members were elected by a gathering of all the parishioners. In the closed Vestry, of which Parkham was one, the committee was a self-perpetuating oligarchy in which existing committee members elected others to fill any vacant posts.

Until 1834 the Vestry had the responsibility of appointing two Overseers of the Poor who, together with the two churchwardens, were collectively responsible for collecting and dispensing the poor rate. The loss of responsibility for the relief of the parish poor in 1834 significantly reduced the power of the Vestry, and was the beginning of a slow process by which the Vestry lost its civil powers. Nevertheless, in 1841 the Vestry still had to appoint a parish constable and a Surveyor of the Highways. It was not until 1856, and the compulsory creation of county constabularies, that the parish constable became redundant. The Surveyor of Highways was eventually replaced in 1865 by Local Highway Boards responsible for highways in a group of parishes. The Vestry was also responsible for electing the parish clerk. He and the Rector were the only paid officers of the parish. Non-conformity had not taken hold in Parkham by 1841, although a small Wesleyan chapel was built at Holwell under the terms of a Trust Deed dated 22 April 1823.[11]

Thirty-two individuals declared themselves to be of independent means. However, there appear to have been only three other families who might qualify as being of similar social status to the rector. One of these was Matilda Hucks, an elderly widow of independent means, who resided at Foxdown House, with four servants. Her late husband had been responsible in 1820 for a diversion of one of the two roads which connected Parkham Town village to the turnpike road between Bideford and Clovelly.[12] In diverting it further away from Foxdown House, which was his purpose, he widened and improved it. But his assertion of private ownership, through the erection of gates at either end, was to result in controversy and vandalism for decades to come. A young Irish woman called Mary Kelly, also of independent means, was living with Matilda Hucks, and was one of only seven people within the parish not born within the county.

Charles Bruton Esq. was the owner of Tuckingmill and South Yeo in Parkham. His wife, Frances, was one of the two daughters of the rector. Charles Bruton lived at South Yeo with three members of his family, including his son Walter Meddon Bruton, then a law student, who later became rector of West Worlington. Five servants were employed by the family. In 1846 Walter Bruton married Mary Kelly of Foxdown House and later named his daughter after Matilda Hucks.

The widowed Elizabeth Caddy was living with her family of six at Bowden, with four servants. Her husband John was consistently described in the parish registers as a gentleman. No other gentry families are discernible at this time. All in all Parkham was a society of very little wealth, and a significant proportion of the population were living perpetually on the margin of pauperism. In 1841 this meant entry into the Union Workhouse in Bideford (built 1837/8). The post-1815 economic depression was forcing many to emigrate to Canada, which might account for the twenty-three uninhabited houses revealed in the 1841 census.

Bideford was the only market town within realistic walking distance of Parkham (six and a half miles), and in 1841 had a population of 5,211.[13] The quickest route to Bideford was probably along the coast road from Bude, which, because it was a turnpike, was better maintained than any other local road. There was a tollgate known as the Waytown Gate at Lower Waytown, manned by Elizabeth Croscomb. Markets were held in Bideford on Tuesdays and Saturdays as well as three annual fairs. The town had a post office, banks, solicitors, auctioneers and valuers, seedsmen, saddle and harness makers, insurance agents, physicians and surgeons, and a wide range of shops and taverns. Its busy quayside was one where coastal shipping, fishing boats, and the occasional arrival of ships bringing timber from Canada, or taking emigrants to North America, could be observed. Local potteries supplied the district with coarse domestic ware (Sgraffito) and there were several basket makers.

Land Ownership and Tenancy

No single landowner had a monopoly of land ownership in Parkham, unlike nearby Clovelly parish where Sir James Hamlyn Williams Bt. had almost total ownership of the land.[14] Clovelly was a classic example of a 'closed parish', where the resident landlord at Clovelly Court wielded immense power and influence over what went on. Parkham, by contrast, with some forty-one different landowners, was an 'open parish'. Land continually changed hands and there was nothing fixed about the pattern of land ownership. None of the five principal landowners (Table 1) lived in the parish.

Table 1 The five principal landowners in Parkham in 1842, listed in order of importance.

Lord John Rolle of Stevenstone near Torrington (59 landholdings).

Reverend John Thomas Pine-Coffin of Portledge in Alwington (49).

Samuel Trehawke Kekewich (MP for Exeter 1826–1830) of Peamore near Exeter (27).

John Lee of Ilminster, Somerset (12)

Lewis William Buck (MP for North Devon 1839–1857) of Moreton House near Bideford (3)

(Lewis Buck's son George changed his surname to Stucley in 1858 and became a baronet in 1859.)

Figure 3. Limebury Farm.

The rector's 129 acres of glebe (church owned land) was a life interest only, but he also owned the freehold of a forty-two acre farm, which made him one of the major farmers in the parish. Amongst the forty-eight people described as farmers, only fifteen had holdings of over 100 acres, of whom only four farmed holdings above 200 acres. The largest was Melbury, at 547 acres, and farmed by William Pridham. The largest group of farmers were the forty-six individuals occupying holdings between ten and 100 acres, with a further group of twenty-four occupying holdings of between one and ten acres. All told, eighty-five people were occupying land holdings greater than one acre in extent. In other words although forty-eight described themselves as farmers in the census, an additional thirty-seven other individuals were also occupying land from which they were obtaining economic benefit.

The twenty-four people occupying land between one and ten acres in extent included four who described themselves as farmers, seven who were artisans (including Ann Heydon the bonnet maker), one butcher, one miller, five agricultural labourers and one of independent means.

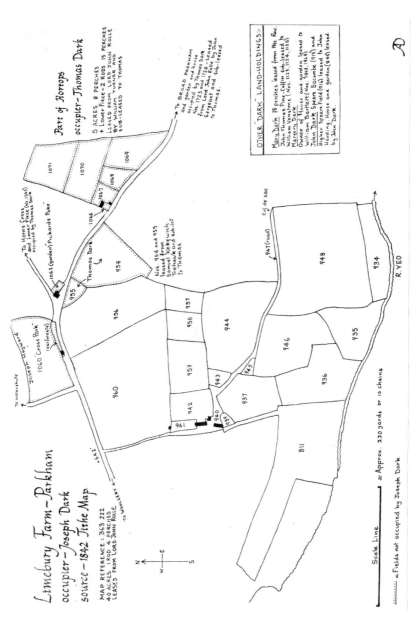

Figure 4. Limebury Farm, Parkham, on Parkham Tithe Map 1842.
Courtesy of the Devon Record Office.

The parish registers habitually use the terms yeoman and husbandman in order to distinguish between the bigger and smaller farmers, but these terms are never employed in the census. The term husbandman is clearly used in the registers to distinguish a small subsistence farmer from a landless labourer. Yeomen are the larger farmers, employing labour and able to generate large or small surpluses. Indeed the term farmer, as used in the census, should always be checked against the parish registers and Apportionment in order to assess its significance. Those occupying holdings of less than an acre are mostly occupying dwellings with gardens attached. Although these gardens might be tiny they were of enormous importance to the occupants because they provided the opportunity to grow vegetables and keep a pig.

The author's paternal great-great grandfather Thomas Dark, and his younger brother Joseph Dark, would have been typical Parkham farmers at the time.[15] Joseph is described in the census as a farmer of Limebury. The 1842 Tithe Award shows Limebury as comprising forty acres, one rod and four perches, leased directly from Lord Rolle, plus seventeen acres, three rods and twenty-one perches (Moleshill), sub-leased from John Sergeant. Joseph had inherited the farm from his father, Thomas senior, who had died in 1835. Why Joseph inherited, rather than his elder brother, Thomas junior, we have no way of knowing. Joseph belonged to that middling group of forty-six farmers working a holding of between ten and a hundred acres. Indeed, his fifty-seven acres was probably about average for this group.

Like Joseph, Thomas Dark is described in the 1841 census as a farmer, although Thomas's seven acres put him squarely in the middle of the twenty-four individuals with the smallest holdings. The 1842 Tithe Award shows him to be occupying a compact small-holding close to Limebury, comprising a house and six small fields. The farmhouse occupied the south-western corner and lay only a few hundred yards east along the road from Limebury. In the census it is named as Linebury Cross Park. A seventh field, known as Lower Piece, lay about three-quarters of a mile away on the road to Horns Cross. In 1842 all seven fields were in pasture and totalled five acres, eight perches. This little holding was described in the Tithe Apportionment as 'part of Hortops, Broad Parkham' and was sub-leased from William Turner, who was in turn a tenant of Lord Rolle. Additionally, Thomas occupied two more fields given over to arable, and adjacent to Joseph`s fields.

Both fields lay very near to the farmhouse on the opposite side of the road. They belonged to Samuel Trehawke Kekewich, and Thomas sub-leased them from Thomas Lemon.

Although Thomas is described as a farmer in the census it is important to note that at the baptisms of his seven children he is usually described as a husbandman, except at the baptism of his fourth and his seventh child, when he is described as a farmer and a labourer respectively. The term husbandman is almost certainly the term that would have been used within the parish to describe his economic and social status. It was a term habitually used in North Devon at the time. Thomas eventually gave up farming in Parkham. He moved to Woolsery, and then to Bideford, where he became a publican and fisherman.

Whilst Thomas struggled, Joseph's son John (born 1836) expanded Limebury by incorporating Thomas's smallholding, and ultimately (in 1889) bought the freehold of eighty acres from the trustees of Lord Rolle for £850. John survived the great agricultural depression at the end of the century and retired to Bideford in 1901, leaving a tenant behind at Limebury. John's story demonstrates that it was possible for some farms to survive into the twentieth century, and the period of agricultural prosperity that preceded the First Word War. His Uncle Thomas's story is that of the many husbandmen who did not survive the 'hungry forties.'

As we have seen, the fifty-seven acres or so farmed by Joseph, and the seven farmed by his brother Thomas, were typical of the Parkham farmer at the time. What was also typical was the fact that they were tenant farmers. The vast majority of the land in Parkham was farmed by tenants. Even the biggest of the farms, Melbury, was sub-leased from Henry Downing, who leased the land from Lord John Rolle.

In Devon the traditional terms on which land was leased out by the freeholders was ninety-nine years, or two or three 'lives', whichever was the shorter. The three lives might be the farmer's wife, a son and a grandson, for example, in order to ensure that the farm remained within the family. The terms of the lease usually required the payment of a lump sum or 'premium' at the beginning of the term, followed by a yearly rent. Sub-leasing can make the picture of landownership and occupancy very complicated.

The Parkham farms were overwhelmingly family affairs, where

much larger families than we are used to today, lived with one or two farm servants who were very likely to be related. There were no less than thirteen Downings living at Goldsworthy Barton in 1841. There were also nine Pickards at Ash, nine Heals at East Stone, eight Mays at Babeleigh, and eight Moasts at Halsbury, to name but a few large family groups. No wonder Bartholomew Pickard, a single farmer of 13 acres, named his cottage 'Robinson Cruso [sic] Cottage'!

There were no less than four female farmers named in the Parkham census of 1841 and three more women are listed in the Apportionment as occupying land. Three other women would have been well known in the parish, Elizabeth Stanlick who was running the Bell Inn, Elizabeth Croscomb who was manning the toll gate, and Mary Passmore the Dame School mistress. The 1841 census does not record marital status, but more often than not women assumed these responsibilities as a result of early widowhood. The experience of the Dark family shows how this situation could come about, and how common it was. On the 17 December 1846 Joseph Dark of Limebury died, aged only forty-three, following a two year decline (the then universal way of describing tuberculosis). Joseph's eighty-three year old mother died two years later, to be followed by the death of his widow Rebecca, at a mere forty years of age. She too had died from tuberculosis (phthisis on her death certificate). Ironically, Rebecca's name occurs in the list of Parkham farmers included in Whites *History, Gazeteer and Directory of Devonshire*, in 1850. The decennial census of 1851 shows that the farm, which by then extended to fify-nine acres, was in the sole charge of Thomas's daughter Mary, aged nineteen and unmarried. Mary was, apparently, running the farm with the help of her sister, Louisa, aged seventeen, her brother, John, aged fifteen and two farm labourers. One of the labourers, Samuel Johns, lived in. John Dark was listed in *Kelly's Directory* of 1856 as a 'Farmer of Limebury'. Mary's younger brother had taken charge earlier, when his sister married John Collins, a Parkham blacksmith, in 1852.

Kith and Kin

Another characteristic feature exemplified by the Dark brothers was that they were both married to daughters of Richard and Grace Dunn of Nethercott Farm in Parkham; Thomas junior to Miriam

(1827), and Joseph to Rebecca (1831). It is impossible to exaggerate the extent and complexity of the network of blood relationships and inter-marriage that bound the people of the parish together in an all pervasive network of mutual obligation and support.

Two cottages lay very near Limebury Farm and Thomas Dark's smallholding (see Figure 4). In 1841 one of the nearby cottages, later known as Pickard's Poke, was occupied by a carpenter named Jasper Pickard, his wife Ann, and an old lady called Mary Bailey. The other cottage was occupied by Jasper's son Thomas, an agricultural labourer, his wife Susanna (formerly Dark) and their three children. His mother-in-law, Mary Dark, and another labourer called John Lee, lived with them. There were actually nineteen other Darks living in the parish in 1841, all related and connected by marriage to other families. Opaque from the outside, Parkham parish could have had few secrets within it.

Such then was Parkham in 1841/2; a rural community poised between two worlds. One looking back to the eighteenth century and earlier, when yeomen, husbandmen and agricultural labourers relied on oxen, donkeys and pack horses, and used scythes, sickles and flails to bring in the harvest; self-sufficient, secretive and withdrawn. The other, the second-half of the nineteenth century, increasingly mechanised, with fewer farm labourers, secularised local government and a growing range of horse-drawn vehicles as roads improved, becoming increasingly literate and open to outside influences, but with the shadow of the workhouse always in the background.

Notes and References

1. DRO, Tithe Map and Apportionment of Parkham, 1842.
2. Decennial Census Reports 1801 and 1841.
3. Parkham Town Barton, Halsbury Barton, Goldworthy Barton and Cabbacott Barton. Barton 'signifies a farm much larger than the average' [and] 'nine times out of ten, one with a long and interesting history . . .' Hoskins 1966, p. 30.
4. Buckish is a name derived from Bochewis, a Domesday place name meaning land recorded in a book.
5. Few R. & Few, J. 2003, p. 9.
6. DRO, 1892 A-Z/PO510.
7. In the 1861 census for Parkham there were twenty-one glovers and one

glove collector who distributed glove parts for sewing, and returned the completed work to Torrington.

8. White 1850, p. 775.
9. Ibid.
10. The rectorial glebe comprised twenty-six different holdings and included the churchyard and rectory. By 1850 the glebe had declined to 119 acres (see White 1850, p. 774).
11. Charity Commission copy 10395.
12. *The North Devon Journal*, 10 August 1876, p. 8.
13. Pigot 1844.
14. Apart from the glebe only three other individuals owned land in Clovelly: William Cole Loggin, the Impropriator of Woolsery, owned 103 acres, William Ching sixty-nine acres and John Squire sixteen acres. Everything else was owned by Sir Charles Hamlyn Williams.
15. Dark 2009.

Bibliography

Dark, A. (2009) *Dark of Parkham*, [CD-ROM] Arthur Dark.

Few, R. & Few, J. (2003) *Who Lived in Cottages Like These? the inhabitants of Bucks Mills*, Sandown: The Braund Society.

Greenhill, B. & Gifford, A. (1967) *Westcountrymen in Prince Edward's Isle*, Toronto: University of Toronto Press, 1967.

Hoskins, W.G. (1966) *Old Devon*, Newton Abbot: David & Charles.

Hubbard-Fielder, D. (1989) *The Story of Bucks Mills and Bucks Cross*, Barnstaple: Aycliffe Press.

Jacob, G. (1970) *Looking back on Parkham and Bideford Years Ago*, Bideford: Bideford Gazette.

Pigot (1844) *Pigot's Royal and Commercial Directory and Topography of the county of Berkshire, Buckinghamshire, Cornwall, Devonshire . . .*, London: I. Slater.

Vancouver G. (1808) *General View of the Agriculture of the County of Devon*, London: Board of Agriculture.

White, W. (1850) *History, Gazeteer and Directory of Devonshire*, Sheffield: White.

Whitlock R. (1991) *A Victorian Village*, London: Robert Hale.

The Great Exodus: migration and Victorian Devon

Greg Finch

The infant River Taw, rushing northwards from the edge of Dartmoor, still powers the waterwheels at the Finch Foundry in Sticklepath. When the founder of the edge tool works died in 1862 his eldest grandson William Finch, whitesmith (tin worker) and Methodist lay preacher, could have been forgiven for entertaining hopes that he would take charge of the business. However, it ended up in the hands of two of his uncles, and William moved away to London, following in the footsteps of his brother George. Their two other brothers took the same path during the next few years, and all ended up in various metal working trades in the eastern counties.[1] Three dozen Finches had lived in the adjacent parishes of Sampford Courtenay (which includes Sticklepath) and South Tawton in the 1780s: farm and road labourers, paupers, craftsmen and tenant farmers, and all descended from a single South Tawton family established nearly a century before. By 1851 their number had risen to forty-seven, but there were just thirteen left in 1881. Many other Finches joined William and his brothers in the great stream of migration from Victorian Devon.[2] Their individual paths are used throughout this article to illustrate various aspects of the county's migration experience.

   The scale of this exodus was unprecedented in the county's history. Devon probably accounted for around 3.7 percent of the national population in the late seventeenth century, a share it still held at the time of the 1801 census.[3] A reasonable estimate of the net balance of

245

births and deaths suggests no net migration away from the county during the eighteenth century, and possibly even a slight net inwards flow. The scales seem to have tipped in an outwards direction from the 1820s.[4] By 1841 Devon's share of the national population, at 3.3 per cent, was starting to slip behind, and by 1881 had fallen sharply to 2.3 per cent. By 1911, at 1.9 per cent, its share had halved in just over a century, reflecting Devon's adjustment to a marginal role on the periphery of an industrialising nation.[5]

Table 1 Net Migration

Decade	Devon		'Urban' Devon		'Rural' Devon	
	Net migration	Migration Rate*	Net migration	Migration rate*	Net migration	Migration rate*
1841-51	-29,300	- 0.54%	11,600	0.47%	-40,900	- 1.35%
1851-61	-53,000	- 0.93%	1,200	0.04%	-54,200	- 1.85%
1861-71	-55,400	- 0.95%	-8,200	- 0.27%	-47,200	- 1.69%
1871-81	-59,200	- 0.99%	-7,200	- 0.22%	-52,000	- 1.97%
1881-91	-36,600	- 0.60%	2,600	0.07%	-39,200	- 1.58%
1891-01	-22,700	- 0.35%	13,900	0.34%	-36,600	- 1.56%

*Migration rate expressed as a percentage of base population in each decade

Sources & method:

Devon: Finch, 1984, p. 174, rounded to nearest 100. Net migration is the residual between censal population totals and natural increase during the intervening decade. Natural increase rates for Devon 1841-71 have been revised based on adjustments for under-registration calculated by Wrigley & Schofield, 1981, App 8, pp. 631-7. All Census and Registrar-General reports published between 1801 and 1936 are now available at the University of Essex Online Historical Population Reports (OHPR) website: <http://histpop.org/ohpr/servlet/Show?page=Home>.

'Urban' and 'Rural' Devon: aggregated from 41 districts into which parishes were regrouped to separate growing towns from the rest of Devon, and thereby overcome the limitations of contemporary Registration District (RD) based summaries. The most geographically contiguous RD natural increase rates have been used in net migration calculations for each district: Finch, 1984, pp. 185, 282-5, 288. The 'urban' districts were Plymouth, Exeter, Torbay, Teignmouth/Newton Abbott, Barnstaple/Bideford, and growing resort towns of the North and East Devon coasts.

Table 1 shows migration to have originated mainly in the countryside. Across the county as a whole, the three decades from 1851 saw the heaviest losses, at nearly one per cent of the population each year. But whereas there was something of a recovery in the towns thereafter, the rural migration rate remained high until the Edwardian period. At between 1.5 per cent and 2 per cent of the population in each year, the migration rate was between a third and a half higher than the average for rural southern England as a whole, and even on a par with Ireland from the 1860s onwards.[6] Contrary to the perception that change came slowly in the South West, Devon's population reacted rapidly.

As ever, it was mainly the young who departed, illustrated in Figure 1 by the experience of South Tawton in the 1870s. The actual population in 1881 was thirty per cent lower than the level one would have expected based on the 1871 level and prevailing age-specific mortality rates. Migration 'hollowed out' the parish's population structure in just ten years. Great gaps appeared in the ranks of those in their late teens and twenties during the 1870s, with reductions of upwards of forty per cent. The number of girls between the age of eleven and twenty was low compared to boys in both 1871 and 1881, reflecting an established pattern of moves away to work in service, a feature noted in other rural areas with limited employment opportunities for women.[7] The removal of young adults of marriageable age also reduced the overall birth rate compared to that which the 1871 age structure is likely to have generated, resulting in the shortfall of children below the age of eleven. Across Devon as a whole the removal of young adults therefore also contributed to low population growth. The county's rate of natural increase was thirty-five per cent lower than the national average by 1900, mainly because of a reduction in the crude birth rate.

Low rural wages might have provided a strong incentive to migrate but contemporary opinion was sceptical. The view of the local gentry, concerned at the all too evident depopulation of their own districts, is to be found in the address to the Devonshire Association by its president in 1902, the Reverend W. Harpley of Clayhanger, in the hills west of Tiverton. Farm labourers in his neighbourhood, he said, 'have argued that, all things considered, they are better off with their 14 or 15 shillings a week and concomitant advantages than their brother townsman who is earning 20 or 22 shillings a week.'[8] Rather,

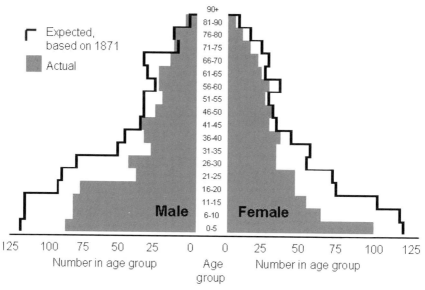

Sources & method:

Actual: reconstituted from 1881 CEB for South Tawton, via <www.ancestry.com>.

Expected: 1871 CEB South Tawton, adjusted by 'survivorship ratios' derived from age specific mortality rates 1871-80 for Okehampton RD, using method given in Hinde, 2004, pp. 15-20. Population aged under 11: projected from Okehampton RD fertility rate applied to expected female population and reduced by child mortality rates. Further details on these and all other calculations are available from the author on request.

Figure 1. South Tawton parish population structure 1881.

he laid more stress on the advance of education, cheap travelling, cheap postage and the Press, which all helped to reduce inertia. Of these, one suspects that the post had more impact than the newspaper, conveying the personal experiences of those who had gone before. As more people left, few remaining villagers would have been without a family member or neighbour relaying news to break down any ignorance of those dark continents which lay beyond the woods on the horizon.

Limited employment opportunities rather than comparatively low wages were of greater importance in motivating people to leave. The harsh regime of the Victorian Poor Law which awaited able-bodied paupers will have been readily understood by the young and energetic

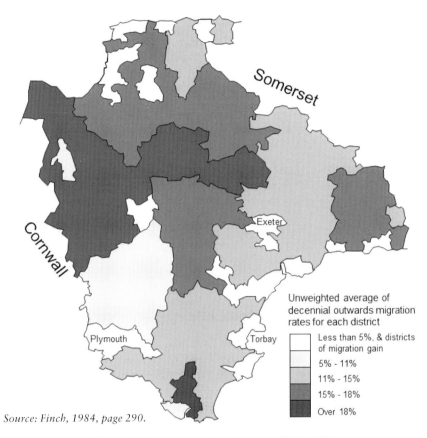

Source: Finch, 1984, page 290.

Figure 2. Devon net migration rates 1841–1911.

without work, and prompted them to move. Cornwall suffered greatly from the collapse of copper mining in the 1870s, and this had some impact within Devon too. South Tawton was certainly affected, with many men still employed in the mine at Ramsley in 1871. Across Devon as a whole, however, mining was far less important than farming as a source of employment. Over 81,000 people were enumerated in farming employment in 1851, but there was a dramatic reduction to less than 44,000 by 1901.[9] Figure 2 shows the variation in the rate of net migration from across the county. Losses were particularly heavy from the poor farming country of West and North Devon, where 'all green things lie crushed between the hammer of the west wind and the anvil of the yellow clay.'[10] A third of this area's population was lost between 1841 and 1901. The more fertile farmland of the Exe Valley and South Hams fared better, as did the Tamar Valley north of Plymouth, sustained first by copper mining and then by the rise of market gardening.

Confronted by large numbers of redundant farm labourers at Halberton in East Devon on his arrival from Lancashire in 1862, Canon Edward Girdlestone directly orchestrated the migration of some 400 families in the reverse direction over the next ten years. It seems that Girdlestone's personal endeavours opened a channel of migration along which others travelled later. Lancashire attracted perhaps 1,500 migrants from Devon in the 1850s, but this rose to over 2,000 in the 1860s, when Girdlestone was at work. The number of migrants then increased to around 4,000 in the 1870s, before dropping back again thereafter to around 1,500 per decade.[11] If people moved between relatively backward to advanced regions in the course of industrialisation, Lancashire might seem a natural destination for those leaving Devon, but other domestic destinations were actually far more popular, as shown in Table 2.

Some tentative conclusions can be drawn. Given that a reasonably high level of local movement between parishes which lay either side of county boundaries might have been expected, gross migration from Devon to its neighbouring counties was surprisingly low. At a time when they too were losing population Cornwall, Somerset and Dorset would not have had much to offer. London and the South East, on the other hand, were far more popular as destinations, and much more so than the industrial districts of the Midlands and the North. The capital city was but a few hours journey by train and its growth was relentless.

Migration from Devon to the Glamorgan coalfield ran at over 4,000 per decade, an average which conceals an apparent surge in the 1870s and 1880s. This was readily visible to F.W. Knight, MP and owner of Exmoor, who observed in 1882: 'The North Devon farm labourer well knows that the great Welsh coalfield lies only a few hours sail from any of the little harbours that dot the coast from Bideford to Watchet, and that among the teeming gangs that work among its mines, docks and railroads, he can at a day's notice get work at higher wages than at home.'[13] It is likely that Bristol was the destination of most of those moving to Gloucestershire, and Portsmouth (thanks to

Table 2 Migration from Devon to the rest of England and Wales, 1851–1901

	Average per decade	%
Total	50,000	
Adjacent counties		
Cornwall	3,200	6%
Somerset	3,000	6%
Dorset	1,300	3%
Non-adjacent counties		
London	11,900	24%
Surrey, Middlesex, Kent	6,000	12%
Glamorgan	4,100	8%
Hampshire	3,100	6%
North West	2,700	5%
Gloucestershire	2,200	4%
W Midlands (excluding Gloucestershire)	1,800	4%
South East (excluding London area)	1,800	4%
Essex	1,700	3%
Yorkshire	1,600	3%
Northern Counties	1,300	3%
Wales & Monmouth (excluding Glamorgan)	1,200	2%
South Midlands	1,100	2%
North Midlands	1,000	2%
Wiltshire	600	1%
Suffolk, Norfolk	400	1%

Sources & method:

English and Welsh county populations by birthplace are available at each census from 1851-1901, giving the 'lifetime migrants' at each census. The number of Devonians assumed to remain alive in each county by the next census date is arrived at using national survivorship ratios (Baines, 1985, Table 4.2, p. 105, and see note 12), and is deducted from the Devonian birthplace count in that next census to leave an estimate of migration between the two dates.

These figures must be used with caution. For example, the migration of Devonians to Hampshire between 1861 and 1871 depends not only on the mortality rate amongst Devonians already in Hampshire in 1861 – the survivorship ratio – but on how many might have moved on or moved back in the meantime. Furthermore, the numbers at any one census date could have been affected by the presence of temporary workers engaged on railway or other major construction activities. The figures thus derived for each decade have been averaged here to avoid the temptation to read too much into the calculation for any one decade.

County groupings: North West: Cheshire, Lancs; West Midlands: Hereford, Shropshire, Staffs, Worcs, Warwicks; South East: Kent, Surrey, Sussex, Hants, Berks; Northern Counties: Durham, Northumberland, Cumberland, Westmorland; South Midlands: Herts, Bucks, Oxon, Northants, Hunts, Beds, Cambridge; North Midlands: Leics, Rutland, Lincs, Notts, Derbys.

its naval dockyard) within Hampshire. One suspects also that some element of the migration to Kent was to Chatham, the third great Victorian royal dockyard, after Devonport and Portsmouth.[14] In all, some 50,000 people in each decade left Devon for other domestic destinations in the second half of the century, and we still need to consider those who left Britain altogether.

The level of emigration by decade is estimated in Table 3. As a residual calculation, the effects of any errors introduced at the intermediate estimates of inflows and outflows from Devon will be compounded, but there is some reassurance to be had in comparing the decade to decade movements with other estimates.[15] But even allowing a margin for error it is quite clear that, compared to migration within England and Wales, a remarkably high percentage of those leaving the county went abroad. Nearly half of those leaving Devon in the 1850s emigrated, and around a third until the 1890s. Approximately 12,000 went to London each decade, but double that number went overseas. Since it is thought that up to a third of emigrants later returned, the gross outflow is likely to have been higher still. From England and Wales as a whole, the rate of net emigration peaked at around twenty five per 10,000 population per year in the 1880s but in Devon the rate apparently came *down* to 40 per 10,000 in that decade.[16]

Emigrants from Devon were not necessarily more enterprising than those who moved shorter distances, for the kind of opportunities available overseas were often less different to a country dweller than those on offer in the crowded towns: 'emigration to rural Canada might leave a countryman in more familiar surroundings than migration to Manchester'.[17] Some created more domestic excuses for leaving: Joseph Finch of Charleton, near Kingsbridge, (whose family had left South Tawton in the late eighteenth century) left his wife and young children for another woman in 1843, with whom he went to America, and ended up as a hotel keeper in Ontario.[18] Whatever the intrinsic attraction of the Empire's great Dominions, the level of emigration was surely also influenced by the operation of a busy national emigration trade from Plymouth throughout the Victorian period. According to the officially gathered statistics, nearly half a million people emigrated from Plymouth between 1840 and 1900, the third most important port of departure from the UK after Liverpool and London. From 1842 it was one of the ports from which those given free or assisted

Table 3 Devon migration flows by decade

	(1)	(2)	(3)	(4)	(5)	(6)
	Net outwards migration (from Table 1)	Gross outwards migration to Eng & Wales	Gross inwards migration	Net Emigration (col 1-2+3)	Emig-ration as % of total	Emig-ration rate*
1851-61	53,000	40,300	25,100	37,800	48%	66
1861-71	55,400	51,300	21,200	25,300	33%	43
1871-81	59,200	61,900	28,300	25,600	29%	43
1881-91	36,600	45,800	33,800	24,600	35%	40
1891-01	22,700	50,700	39,000	11,000	18%	17

*Emigration rate expressed as number of emigrants per 10,000 population per year

Sources & method:

Column 1: see Table 1. Column 2: see Table 2.

Column 3, Gross inwards migration, is calculated in the same way as outwards migration, using census birthplace data for Devonian residents.

Column 4: based on simple arithmetic to balance the gross domestic flows in columns 2 and 3 with the estimated level of net outwards migration in column 1.

passages were directed to depart. Knight, quoted above, went on to say that 'no parish is without its representative in Canada and the United States',[19] yet eighty-seven per cent of those leaving Plymouth were bound for Australia and New Zealand. Assisted emigration was actively encouraged to develop the antipodean colonies in preference to the closer ports of North America.[20] With a national departure port and all the supporting emigration related services on the county's doorstep, it seems reasonable to assume that many of those emigrating from Devon in the latter half of the nineteenth century were bound for Australia.

Jacob Finch, the absconder's younger brother, was a farmer of 190 acres at Charleton in the 1870s. His eldest son James remained as a farmer in the neighbourhood but three younger sons left for Ballarat, Victoria, during the Australian mining boom of the early 1880s. William Jacob Finch sailed out with his wife and family of five young children on the SS *Potosi* in 1882, a name to conjure dreams of great mineral riches to emulate the fabled Bolivian 'mountain of silver'. William's brother Herbert followed two years later, setting off soon after his wedding. A year after Herbert's departure Jacob also went out to Ballarat, where he continued his life as a shepherd.[21] All were in their twenties. Once again a personal connection opened a migration channel, this time from one side of the world to another.

So emigration ran at a higher rate from Devon than from most other counties, and the rate of outwards migration from rural Devon was also significantly higher than from the rural south of England as a whole. It is tempting to conclude, therefore, that the attraction of colonial destinations, the relative ease of passage, and a stream of enticing news from pioneering friends and relations was responsible for the particularly high overall level of migration from the county. This could not have been simply a rural phenomenon. Table 3 shows that some 75,000 to 85,000 left the county each decade, far more than the 50,000 or so leaving from rural districts alone (see Table 1) and some of the latter remained within the county anyway. As a young man, tenant farmer William Finch of South Tawton moved to Cheriton Bishop.[22] Of his ten children only the eldest son John remained at the farm. In 1860 brothers George and Charles made the short journey into Exeter, where they set up as grocers. Over the next decade they branched out into wine and spirits dealing, and then also into brewing in the 1870s. As their business expanded they drew their siblings into the city to run shops and pubs. With the onset of the agricultural depression in the mid 1870s, John and his parents gave up the farm and also moved into Exeter.[23] Over the Victorian period as a whole, however, the attractiveness of the ancient county town could not match the rise of Plymouth and the resort towns of Torbay, which accounted for over eighty-five per cent of net inwards migration to Devon's towns between them.[24]

Following the arrival of the railway Torquay and Paignton grew so rapidly as tourist destinations that they relied heavily upon migrants to work in the booming service sector rather than on those born in the towns. Three daughters of Charles Finch of South Tawton were in domestic service in grand houses in Torquay in the 1880s and 1890s. Rapid though its growth was, Torbay was overshadowed by Plymouth (which is taken here for convenience to mean the administrative districts of Devonport, East Stonehouse and Plymouth). Whereas the

Torbay area had a population of around 50,000 by 1911, Plymouth had reached 220,000, making it by far the most important settlement west of Bristol. Its share of Devon's population doubled during the nineteenth century to reach a third of the county's total and it accounted for virtually all of Devon's population growth after 1841. The port, the Navy dockyard and related industries dominated Plymouth's Victorian development. It was the most important Devonian destination for migrants. The city's birth rate was also stimulated by the arrival of large numbers of young adults in the 1840s and 1850s, the converse of South Tawton's experience.

The Charles Finch whose daughters went into service in Torbay had two younger brothers who ended up in Plymouth. John moved there around 1850 as a builder, a good trade for a young man to learn in a growing city. He had his own firm employing two dozen men by 1861, and it had doubled in size by 1881. His brother Samuel moved first to Ottery St Mary in 1857 as a machine maker. Ten years later he was employed as a millwright at the new steam dockyard of Keyham, north of the original Devonport yard, and there he remained for the rest of the century.

The scale of migration from the Devon countryside into the towns cannot be quantified from the published census summaries for they do not distinguish by birthplace within the county. However, sampling work undertaken at the University of Plymouth from the original 1851 and 1871 census schedules allows a reasonable estimate to be derived for the city, and this is instructive. At least 16,000 Devonians moved to Plymouth between those dates.[25] The census report summaries of birthplaces of Plymouth's inhabitants by county allow an estimate to be made of the number moving in from outside Devon. However these are complicated by the presence of the Army and Navy, with its large and fluctuating numbers of young men stationed in barracks and on ships in port. For the purposes of this article an estimate of their numbers has been removed from the analysis.[26] Other than active servicemen it is likely that another 11,000 people moved into Plymouth during the 1850s and 1860s from outside the county, adding up to at least 27,000 in total.[27]

However a calculation of the decennial net migration balance to and from the city, based on the census population totals (again ex-cluding servicemen) and the rate of natural increase, suggests a net

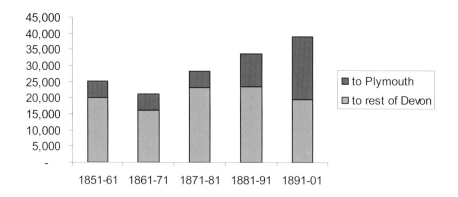

Sources & method:

As for Table 2, and applied to Plymouth detail in census summaries as well as county-wide data. Note: Plymouth data for 1861 and 1881 interpolated from county-wide trends.

Figure 3. Inwards migration to Devon by decade

exit of 1,500 people in these two decades as a whole. This means that if 27,000 people moved into Plymouth during this time, nearer 29,000 must have left for domestic and overseas destinations. A small net balance therefore hid much larger flows in each direction. Some individuals moved in and moved out. As with Samuel Finch moving to Plymouth via Ottery St Mary, the migration experience of individuals often took the form of a series of moves rather than a single lifetime event. This is a pattern easy to forget when faced with the aggregate figures derived from the censal snapshots. Many must have moved to the towns and then onwards to London or overseas. One of the Finch brothers who moved into Exeter to help with the family wine and spirits business had moved on to London by 1878 to run a pub. His married sister and her husband were at another pub just a few streets away in 1881.

Devon's towns and cities were, therefore, apparently not always that attractive as final destinations, but the county continued to attract a flow of inwards migrants from the rest of Britain and from abroad, (as shown in column 3 of Table 3). The inwards flow rose significantly from the 1870s. After 1881 this increase is accounted for by the resurgence of Plymouth, (see Figure 3) and was particularly influenced by a sharp rise in defence spending in the 1890s, with its impact on the dockyard and related secondary industries and services.[28]

Table 4 Source of inwards migrants to Devon 1851–1901
(itemising counties that sent more than 1,000 per decade)

	Approximate inwards migrants per decade	%	Inwards migrants per 10,000 source county inhabitants
Total	28,300	100%	12
Cornwall	6,800	24%	200
London	3,600	13%	10
Somerset	1,900	7%	40
Ireland	1,600	6%	3
Hampshire	1,300	5%	23
Gloucs	1,100	4%	19
Elsewhere	12,000	41%	5

Sources & method:

As for Table 2, using birthplace data for residents of Devon at each census, and census population totals for each county to calculate inwards migrant ratio.

In contrast to the outgoing destinations of Devonians, nearly a third of those coming inwards were from the adjacent counties of Cornwall and Somerset, a quarter from Cornwall alone (see Table 4). London and Ireland were also prominent sources of migrants, but when the numbers arriving are considered as a proportion of their home population the importance to them of Devon as a destination was far lower. Seen in this light Cornwall's importance as a source of migrants to Devon was greater still. Over the half century from 1851 to 1901, inwards migrants from England and Wales as a whole to Devon represented around twelve per 10,000 inhabitants per decade, but from Cornwall the ratio was around 200 per 10,000, and most of them went to Plymouth. It was much higher than the rate at which Somerset-born migrants came to Devon (forty per 10,000). While Plymouth was an obvious local destination from Cornwall, nowhere in Devon was attractive enough to entice a corresponding share of Somerset's population westwards, especially with Bristol not far away in the other direction. The ratio of those leaving Dorset for Devon was similar to Somerset's, its domestic migrants drawn perhaps to Southampton and Portsmouth. The majority of those born in Cornwall but living in Devon in 1901 were women, which dovetails with Deacon's surmise that much of the young female migration out of eastern Cornwall during this period was likely to be into domestic service in Plymouth.[29] Thus it seems that much of the inbound migration to Devon was local in nature, and might have been lower had the one large city, Plymouth, not been right on the county border with a neighbour which experienced very high outwards migration.

Other migrants to Devon came in relatively small numbers from right across Britain. The pages of the 1871 census enumeration books for Plymouth list the shipwrights and engineers born as far apart as Sunderland, Birmingham and Portsmouth.[30] Those stationed in the armed forces in Plymouth were perhaps also drawn from across the country. In 1901, however, only a third of those enumerated in Devon but born outside both Devon and Cornwall were in Plymouth or Devonport. The presentation of the printed census population summaries does not allow the location of the others to be determined, but it is reasonable to expect that an examination of the detailed schedules would find many of them in the coastal resorts, principally in Torbay. Any such demographic study of Torbay would add greatly to our knowledge of Devon's Victorian development. The census was typically taken in the first week of April. While this would exclude any distortion in resort populations that would arise from the inclusion of summer visitors, it is likely that the number of permanent residents was still overstated through the inclusion of people of independent means yet to move away after spending the winter in fashionable resort hotels. The Reverend John Johnson probably spoke for many when he told his land agent in the autumn of 1888 that he intended to move from his draughty Leicestershire rectory to a comfortable hotel in Torquay for the winter in order to safeguard his health.[31]

The census figures therefore probably capture a degree of seasonal migration in addition to an underlying flow of moneyed retirees to the coast, a trend followed for much of the ensuing century. A key aspect of Devon's integration within a maturing industrial economy was emerging. In addition to a benign climate, the attraction of scenery unspoilt by industrialisation drew many of those with resources generated by commercial and industrial development in the nation's heartland. William Wykes-Finch, enriched by his wife's inherited proceeds of the Cheshire rocksalt industry, returned to his ancestral home of South Tawton in the 1890s to act the part of the country gentleman.[32]

At the risk of some simplification, the overall experience of Devon's towns and cities was of inwards migration from the emptying countryside and, to a lesser extent, from elsewhere in Britain. But – with the conspicuous exceptions of Torbay and Plymouth (later in the century) – the towns did not grow significantly, and at least as many people left as arrived, moving on to the South East of England, to the South Wales coalfield from North Devon, and – in large numbers – to the Antipodes and North America. A lack of urban dynamism is also reflected in the patchy evidence on urban wages. Although they rose in Devon during the Victorian period they remained at around a fifth to a quarter lower than the national average.[33] Plymouth's size, its role in the defence industry, and the unique attraction of Devonport's industrial dockyard, set it apart from this migration pattern to some extent but not entirely. It is likely that many of those arriving in large numbers from Cornwall subsequently emigrated from the city's Baltic Wharf depot.

The great exodus from rural Devon must have helped to improve relative incomes for those who remained. In contrast to the urban wage pattern, farm worker wages rose sharply between 1870 and 1900, and reached the national average. Profound change in the county's agriculture, specialising rapidly towards pastoral farming, were mainly responsible for this but had a large pool of unemployed casual labour remained in the countryside the benefits would surely have been diluted.[34] Remittances might also have improved rural incomes. The flow of remittance income is a common feature of contemporary international migration from the poor to the rich world. It would be worth investigating whether a similar pattern developed in the quiet and half empty Devon villages from which the industrious young left in search of a better life, leaving their ageing parents behind. The effects of several decades of net outwards migration are seen in the overall population structure by the turn of the century. In 1901 there were relatively fewer children and young adults and more old people compared to the nation as a whole, a trend that was to become more pronounced during the twentieth century. At 29.5 the average age of Devon's inhabitants was already two years older than the national average.

In 1901, just over half a million native Devonians resided in the county. More than half as many again, some 270,000, lived elsewhere.[35] A sentimental image of Devon was fostered by those gathered together at a distance. The yearbook produced by the London Devonian Association in 1913 lists more than 100 corresponding associations around Britain and the colonies. Membership was based upon 'birth or parentage' and (it is safe to assume) respectability.[36] Whether the proud heritage of Devon idealised by the exiled professional classes was an image shared by the much larger number of ordinary migrants is unclear. However, their influence on shaping the county's image surely helped to reinforce the growth of tourism and retirement to Devon into the twentieth century, not to mention the historical profile of Drake and Raleigh. Its expression might not always have achieved literary distinction, but the image endured. This example, one of countless in the same vein, is from a contribution to the 1930 edition of the *Devonian Year Book*. It was penned by a lawyer long settled in London, the grandson of Charles Finch, the farmer's boy who made his way on the carrier's cart to set up as a grocer in Exeter.

> Exiles of Devon, the home of our fathers
> United we stand by the bond of our birth
> Sons of the West with the pride of our lineage
> Though scattered we be to the ends of the earth
> From the tors and the combes, from the cities and hamlets
> From manor and homestead and cottage we come
> Lifting our voices in songs of our Westland
> Bridging the distance that parts us from home . . .[37]

Acknowledgements

I appreciate the review comments of my wife Julie and of Liz Sobell to an earlier draft of this article, and the editorial suggestions of Jane Bliss.

Notes and References

1. Barron, 1983, p. 37; unless additional citations are given all biographical illustrations used in this article are derived from Census Enumeration Books (CEB) obtained via the indexes available on the <www.ancestry. com> website. Specific details are omitted here for brevity.
2. See Hoskins, 1972, pp. 174-5, and Alexander & Shaw, 1999, pp. 119-124 for overview. Finch estimates: Devon Record Office, Sampford Courtenay and South Tawton parish registers; 1851 British Census, Church of Jesus Christ of Latter Day Saints (LDS) CD, 500096000; 1881 Census of England and Wales surname index, LDS CD, 50169000.
3. Devon: The seventeenth-century comparison uses the 1674 hearth tax (Stoate, 1982, viii) and a household multiplier of 4.5, giving an approximate population of 190,000; 1801 census: 338,000, Finch, 1984, p. 174. England: Wrigley & Schofield, 1981, Table A3.3, pp. 532-4.
4. Finch, 1984, Table 2.1, p. 24.
5. Devon: total county population has been aggregated from parish level data to avoid the periodic inconsistencies which arise from changes in administrative boundaries: Finch, 1984, Table 6.1, p. 174; national: Mitchell & Deane, 1962, pp. 29-37, nineteenth-century population shares.
6. Migration rate from the southern rural residue is taken from Cairncross, 1949; Ireland: Carrier & Jeffrey, 1953, p. 14.
7. Hinde, 2004, p. 26; Deacon, 2007, pp. 42-3.
8. Harpley, 1902, p. 51.
9. Finch, 1984, Table A1.1, p. 266, from census figures for 1851, 1901 (OHPR website).
10. quoted in Hoskins, 1972, p. 311.
11. Curthoys, 2004; Heath, 1874, chapter 5. For derivation of estimated migration to Lancashire see notes to Table 2.
12. Without knowing the age structure of the 'lifetime migrants' in each county at each census the survivorship ratios can only be crude estimates, and will have varied from county to county. Those provided by Baines, 1985, p. 105 are probably more reliable than earlier offerings.
13. Quoted in Little 1882, p. 21.
14. Hilditch, 1994, Table 21.2, p. 216.
15. The decennial emigration trend thus revealed for Devon broadly matches the data provided as part of Baines' national survey after 1861

(Baines, 1985, p. 289), and also bears comparison with the trend of official emigration from Plymouth (see Brayshay, 1994, p. 109).

16. Thomas, 1973, p. 124.
17. Pollard, 1978, p. 124.
18. *ex inf* Mary McKeown, private communication.
19. Quoted in Little 1882, p. 21.
20. Brayshay, 1994, pp. 108-18.
21. *ex inf* Sue Vickery of Melbourne. Digitised records & powerful indexes placed into the hands of researchers by the internet, researchers who can now find each other and collaborate across the oceans, have opened up many such examples over the past decade or so. They allow further reflection on the nature, motivation and experience of migration to complement and illustrate the otherwise dry statistical analysis.
22. An example of circulatory movement between nearby parishes, a consistent feature of English small areas studies throughout the early modern period, and which continued in Victorian times. See for example, rural South Devon: Bryant 1971, pp. 136-41, and Kent: Perkyns, 1999, pp. 52-5. See also Pooley & Turnbull, 1996, pp. 50-71.
23. *Exeter Pocket Journal*, 1861; *Exeter Flying Post*, 7 April 1875; *Exeter Flying Post*, 11 Feb 1905.
24. Finch, 1984, Table 6.4, p. 181.
25. Ten per cent samples for Plymouth and Devonport in 1851: Brayshay & Pointon, 1984, p. 5, and for Plymouth and East Stonehouse 1871: Brayshay 1991, p. 55. I am grateful to Professor Brayshay for clarifying details regarding the source data. I have scaled these to reflect the city-wide population at each date, and allowed for intervening deaths based on 1851–61 and 1861–71 survivorship ratios. East Stonehouse was much smaller than either Plymouth or Devonport. Since the 1851 sample counts Devonport as 'rest of Devon', unlike the 1871 sample, the calculated level of local migration to the city between the two dates (16,000) is likely to be understated.
26. Derived from published census reports for Plymouth giving occupational detail. Some interpolation has been used to overcome reporting deficiencies (e.g. city data given for Plymouth only in 1881, and for over 20s only in 1871) based on ratios observed in prior and subsequent census reports. Estimated active service personnel in Plymouth: 1851–4,000, 1861–10,500, 1871–9,800, 1881–6,800, 1891–10,000, 1901–11,000.
27. Calculated as shown for Table 2.
28. Hilditch, 1994, pp. 216-7.
29. Deacon, 2007, p. 42.
30. TNA, RG10/2112, Plymouth St Charles parish.
31. Northumberland Record Office, Johnson papers, 3453/2/17.
32. Finch, 2006.

33. Finch, 1984, pp. 242-8.
34. Finch, 1987, pp. 97-8.
35. The 1901 census reports enumerated 220,000 Devonians in the rest of England and Wales. Those abroad are conservatively estimated at 50,000, based on estimated emigration flows by decade (in Table 3), allowing for a return flow of a third (Baines, 1985, p. 126) and a reasonable allowance for deaths.
36. Chope, 1913, p. 130.
37. Finch, 1930, quoted in *Western Morning News*, 6 May 1930.

Bibliography

Alexander A. and Shaw G. (1999) 'Population Change 1811–1911', in Kain R. & Ravenhill W. (eds), *Historical Atlas of South-West England*, Exeter: Exeter University Press, pp. 119-124.

Baines, D.E. (1985) *Migration in a Mature Economy: emigration and internal migration in England and Wales 1861-1900*, Cambridge: Cambridge University Press.

Barron, R.A. (1983) *The Finch Foundry Trust*, Okehampton: Sticklepath Museum of Rural Industry.

Brayshay, M. (1991) 'Plymouth's Past: so worthy and peerless a western port', in Chalkley, B., Dunkerley, D., & Gripaios, P. (eds) *Plymouth, Maritime City in Transition*, Newton Abbot: David & Charles, pp. 38-61.

Brayshay, M. (1994) 'The Emigration Trade in Nineteenth-Century Devon', in Duffy, M., Fisher, S., Greenhill, B., Starkey, D., Youings J. (eds), *The New Maritime History of Devon*, London: Conway Maritime Press in association with the University of Exeter, vol. 2, pp. 108-118.

Brayshay, M. and Pointon V. (1984) 'Migration and the Social Geography of Mid-Nineteenth-Century Plymouth', *TDH*, 28, pp. 3-14.

Bryant, D. (1971) 'Demographic Trends in South Devon in the Mid-Nineteenth Century', Gregory K.J. & Ravenhill W.L.D., *Exeter Essays in Geography*, Exeter: Exeter University Press, pp. 125-142.

Cairncross, A. (1949) 'Internal Migration in Victorian England', *Manchester School of Economic and Social Studies*, 17, pp. 67-87.

Carrier, N. and Jeffrey, J. (1953) *External Migration: a study of the available statistics*, London: HMSO.

Chope, R.P. (ed.) (1913) *The Devonian Year Book*, London: The London Devonian Association. [Online] Available at: <http://www.archive.org/details/19131915devonian00londuoft>.

Curthoys, M.C. (2004) 'Girdlestone, Edward (1805–1884)', *Oxford Dictionary of National Biography*, Oxford: Oxford University Press [Online] Available at: <http://www.oxforddnb.com/view/article/10773>.

Deacon B. (2007) 'Reconstructing a Regional Migration System: net migration in Cornwall.' *Local Population Studies*, 78, pp. 28-46.

Finch, E.C.T. (1930) 'Devon Exiles', *Devonian Year Book*, London: The London Devonian Association, p. 23.

Finch, G. (1984) 'The Experience of Peripheral Regions in an Age of Industrialisation: the case of Devon, 1840–1914', unpublished DPhil thesis, University of Oxford. [A copy is held in the Westcountry Studies Library, Exeter].

Finch, G. (1987) 'Devon's Farm Labourers in the Victorian Period: the Impact of Economic Change', *DAT*, 119, pp. 85-100.

Finch, G. (2006), 'A Victorian obsession: William Wykes-Finch and North Wyke', *TDH*, 72, pp. 24-30

Harpley, Revd W. (1902) 'Presidential Address', *DAT*, 34, pp. 40-58.

Heath, F.G. (1874) *The English Peasantry*, London: Warne.

Hilditch, P. (1994) 'The Dockyard in the Local Economy', in Duffy et al. (eds), *The New Maritime History of Devon*, London: Conway Maritime Press in association with the University of Exeter, vol. 2, pp. 215-25.

Hinde, A. (2004) 'The Use of Nineteenth-Century Census Data to Investigate Local Migration' *Local Population Studies*, 73, pp. 8-28.

Hoskins, W.G. (1972), *Devon*, (2nd edn), Newton Abbot: David and Charles.

Little, W.C. (1882) 'Report on Devon', *Royal Commission on Agriculture*, Parliamentary Papers 15 (c3375).

Mitchell, B.R. & Deane, P (1962) *Abstract of British Historical Statistics*, Cambridge: Cambridge University Press.

Perkyns, A. (1999), 'Migration and Mobility: six Kentish parishes, 1851–1881', *Local Population Studies*, 63, pp. 30-70.

Pollard, S. (1978) 'Labour in Great Britain', Mathias, P. & Postan, M.M. (eds), *The Cambridge Economic History of Europe*, Vol 7, Part 1, Cambridge: Cambridge University Press, pp. 289-312.

Pooley C.G, & Turnbull, J. (1996), 'Migration and Mobility in Britain from the Eighteenth to the Twentieth centuries', *Local Population Studies*, 57, pp. 50-71.

Stoate, T.L. (1982) *Devon Hearth Tax Return Lady Day 1674*, Almondsbury: T.L.Stoate.

Thomas, B. (1973) *Migration and Economic Growth*, Cambridge: Cambridge University Press.

Wrigley, E.A. and Schofield, R. (1981) *The Population History of England 1541–1871: A reconstruction*, London: Edward Arnold.

The 'Great Fire' of Kenton and the Victorian Rebuilding: the making of a distinctive architectural heritage

Ann Bond

Teignbridge District Council's Conservation Area Character Statement for Kenton describes the village's most characteristic feature as its nineteenth-century architecture which 'sets it apart from other villages'.[1] This character statement suggests that the Gothic styled architecture is late Victorian, giving a date of 1888 for the almshouses. The character statement goes on to suggest that the nineteenth-century buildings are the result of rebuilding following a fire in the village in 1856, but also that there was a significant delay before rebuilding began.[2] Many of these buildings are listed as being of special architectural or historical interest and the register entries give identical dates – late nineteenth century for most of the buildings, with the almshouses specifically dated to 1888.[3] Possible reasons proposed in the character statement for the presumed delay in rebuilding are the economic situation and ownership issues.[4] The parish of Kenton adjoins that of Powderham, and has a long association with the Courtenay family at Powderham Castle. White's 1850 Directory of Devon records that 'The Earl of Devon owns a great part of the parish and is lord of the manor'.[5] However, during the nineteenth century an inheritance dispute relating to the will of the ninth Earl, who died in 1835, resulted in the estate being administered by the Court of Chancery. Even urgent restoration work at Powderham Castle itself required petitions to the

Court of Chancery in 1842.[6] This situation continued at least until the eleventh Earl succeeded to the title in 1859 at which time his legal advisors were counselling that 'William Reginald now 11th Earl of Devon, then Lord Courtenay, was Protector of the Settlement and not his late father William 10th Earl of Devon'.[7] Nevertheless, research for this article, which has examined the circumstances and influences that led to such a distinctive village landscape, has also identified that the Victorian architecture is, in fact, of an earlier date than currently posited.

The Reverend John Swete writing in 1799 had described '. . . the town of Kenton, stretching itself a mile in the most picturesque manner . . .'[8] The Reverend Richard Polwhele was rather less kind and had written just a few years previously complaining about the whitewashed houses which he considered to be 'unpleasant to the eye' and that that the 'only decent houses in Kenton-town are those in the possession of Mr Collyns . . . and of the Rev. R. Polwhele'.[9] Polwhele, one time curate of Kenton, and Swete of nearby Oxton House were both writers on Devon's history and topography.

The 1840 tithe map of Kenton shows a village of densely packed cottages typical in Devon, arranged around the parish church and alongside a number of lanes radiating from the village centre towards neighbouring settlements and farmsteads. Opposite the church there was a line of mostly thatched cottages divided by the road to Mamhead, with the Dolphin Inn forming part of this line. Behind the Dolphin Inn was another thatched cottage. At around midday on 16 April 1856 a fire broke out in this cottage. It was suggested at the time that this may have been caused by ashes which had been thrown out near the Dolphin Inn, and which had been caught up in the wind, and then landed on the thatch. A high wind quickly spread the fire through the many thatched properties in the vicinity, bypassing others with slate roofs. Eventually some twenty-four houses and cottages were alight, the fire having spread to the cottages opposite the church (present day Church Street), cottages on the left hand side of the road leading to Mamhead (Mamhead Road) and cottages on the road leading to Oxton (High Street). A telegraph sent to Exeter resulted in the arrival at about 1.30 p.m. of the West of England fire engine, followed shortly by the Sun fire engine. Other engines from Powderham Castle and the Exminster Lunatic Asylum, as well as the Kenton parish engine, joined them. Efforts were mainly directed to preventing any further spread of the fire, rather than extinguishing the fires that had already taken hold. It was not until nightfall that the fires were finally controlled, by which time twenty-four houses and cottages had been destroyed and ninety-nine inhabitants had been left homeless. All but two of the houses destroyed belonged to the Trustees of the Earl of Devon, nearly all of them let on lease. The following day *Trewman's Exeter Flying Post* reported that: . . . 'the village of Kenton was yesterday the scene of a conflagration which resulted in the destruction of a large amount of property and deprived many poor families of the homes that were dear to them and of the household furniture which has taken them many years of arduous toil to accumulate'.[10]

By then the village known by the Reverends Polwhele and Swete and seen on the 1840 tithe map had been changed beyond recognition. The following day, a subscription fund was launched with the purpose of 'alleviat[ing] the distress occasioned by so great a calamity'. It was later stressed that those who received relief from the funds were 'of the most worthy and industrious of their class', and that they 'bore their losses uncomplainingly, and received the relief afforded them with gratitude'.[11]

By the morning after the fire news had also reached Lord Courtenay (William Reginald Courtenay (1807–1888), later eleventh Earl of Devon) in his office in Whitehall where he was secretary to the Poor Law Board. He immediately wrote to the steward of the Devon Estates at Powderham, suggesting possible accommodation for poor villagers who had been left homeless. 'With regards temporary accommodation, it has occurred to me that the upper rooms at the Belvedere might be made available for the use of two families and one or two of the rooms at the stables, and possibly, the unoccupied room in the N. gateway for an individual'.[12] He also added 'I trust that we shall never thatch again any cottage built . . .'[13] This view was endorsed by the *Flying Post* which, in a report a week later stated 'for the safety of property and the protection of human life we hope that steps will be taken, where practicable, to remove thatch from dwelling houses, and not to build any more houses with thatched roofs'.[14]

Perhaps the most obvious course of action would have been to quickly rebuild on a like-for-like basis in the vernacular style. Such dwellings were relatively cheap to build at perhaps an average of around £60 per house. Keeping building costs down also meant that rents could still provide a reasonable return on investments. As seen, however, the traditional village cottage constructed of cob and thatch was out of favour, both in public opinion as evidenced in the newspaper editorials, and with Courtenay himself. Further, as an aristocrat moving in the circles that he would have done, it is likely that Courtenay was influenced by the model village movement. After all, another prominent aristocratic landowner in Devon, the Duke of Bedford, was a well known advocate of such schemes and had provided model housing for his tenants in and around the Tavistock area as well as on his Woburn estates.

During the 1840s, and largely as a result of Edwin Chadwick's *Report on the sanitary condition of the labouring population of Great Britain* (1842), influential people became more aware of the appalling housing conditions endured by the poorer classes. Although Chadwick's report is often thought to concentrate on the problems of urbanisation, living conditions in rural areas were also examined, highlighting a lack of drainage, sanitation and fresh water. Overcrowding was also a concern. Many cottages had only one bedroom and the moral concerns associated with shared sleeping accommodation were also stressed. A desire to improve the standards of convenience and hygiene in cottages led to the establishment in 1848 of the Society for Improving the Condition of the Labouring Classes (SICLC), whose president was the Prince Consort. Prince Albert began to provide model cottages for his tenants at Sandringham and on other royal estates, and other wealthy landowners including the dukes of Bedford and Devonshire followed suit.

Initially, the most popular architectural styles for this type of rural model cottage were picturesque and eclectic. Revised classic and Gothic styles were expensive to construct and were thought to be too grand for workmen's cottages. An alternative, inspired by Henry Roberts's designs for SICLC was an unadorned utilitarianism, which notably influenced developments on the Duke of Bedford's many estates throughout the country. The Bedford cottages were built to a common plan or 'estate style' which was widely publicised in architectural and agricultural journals. Each cottage had two ground floor rooms consisting of a kitchen fitted with a range, and a scullery fitted with a boiler, and two or three bedrooms, one of which

Plate 16. Corbelled chimney stack, gabled roofs and cranked arched doors and windows, High Street.

Plate 17. Polychromatic brickwork detailing and Bath stone key and corner stones, Church Street.

Plate 18. Gabled dormer. Church Street.

Plate 19. Brick porch, Church Street.

Plate 20. The old piggeries constructed re-using stone from fire damaged cottages.

Plate 21. Wooden veranda, gothic tracery and tall chimney stack, The Almshouses.

Plate 22. Oriel window and carved bargeboard, Devon Cottages.

Plates 16-22 – Ann Bond.

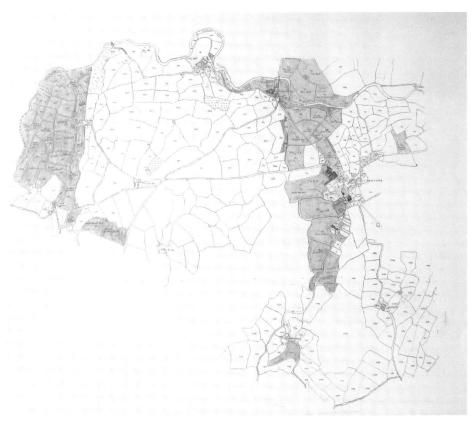

Plate 23. John Berry's land in 1841 shown on a tracing of Chagford Tithe Map
(held at the Devon Record Office).

Plate 24. Lower factory Chagford.
Chagford Local History Society Collection.

A former catch meadow leat follows a contour around a Branscombe hillside

Plate 25. A Branscombe stream below Pitt Farm flows close to the road but a leat is led off just below the farm to follow a contour of the hill.

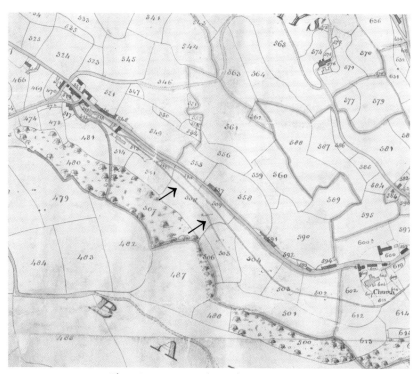

Plate 26. Branscombe Tithe Map 1840.
(Arrows indicate the position of the catch meadow leat).
Reproduced courtesy of the Devon Record Office and 'Parishscapes',
East Devon Area of Outstanding Natural beauty (AONB).

Patron and Architect

Figure 1. Statue of William Reginald Courtenay, eleventh Earl of Devon. Northernhay Gardens, Exeter. Photograph: Ann Bond.

Figure 2. Joseph William Rowell, Architect. Reproduced courtesy of Newton Abbot Town and GWR Museum.

had a fireplace. There was also an outbuilding for a privy and there was an oven shared by each block. The cottages were substantially constructed but the inside face was whitewashed rather than plastered and the only ornamentation was a slab bearing the ducal crest. These cottages were estimated mid-century to cost between ninety and one hundred pounds each to build and to show just a three per cent return, well below what was considered necessary to cover repairs and provide a return on investment. This low return, given the economical building method and that there were no site costs tends to support other landowners' claims that building cottages for labourers was not a viable proposition.

Lord Courtenay evidently considered some re-building to be a matter of urgency and commissioned J.W. Rowell to design new cottages. Less than a year before the fire at Kenton, Joseph William Rowell (1828–1902), a young architect in Newton Abbot, had been appointed surveyor to the Devon Estate after the death of the previous incumbent. At the time of his appointment, Rowell was just twenty-seven years old and clearly very ambitious, advertising his services to the 'Nobility and Gentry'.[15] Rowell was already engaged in preparing the development plan for the Wolborough Hill area of Newton Abbot and the completion of Devon Square and Courtenay Park, all for Lord Courtenay. By early June, plans for Kenton were well under way and on 12 June Rowell wrote to Mr John Drew, the estate steward, enclosing a tracing for two groups of cottages, one group of three cottages and another of four.[16] By 23 June detailed plans and specifications were ready with a ground map showing the proposed positions of the cottages.[17] Three days later, Rowell was writing that tender documents would be completed and ready to send to London within days.[18] On the same day an advertisement appeared in *Trewman's Exeter Flying Post* inviting tenders for the contracts to build the first two groups of cottages.[19]

In the meantime, Rowell was writing yet again to Drew that he would 'get the plans and elevations for the row of cottages opposite the Church at Kenton ready to forward to you for Railway on Saturday Evening in order for you to submit to Lord Courtenay as you wish'.[20] Detailed specifications for all three groups of cottages still exist and are held by the Devon Record Office. Each cottage was afforded a parlour with a fireplace and the bedrooms were also fitted with fireplaces. Cast iron galvanised furnaces were fixed in the sculleries, and the kitchens had cottage stoves with ovens and boilers. In a village with no sewerage system or piped water supply it would be reasonable to

---

THE FIRE AT KENTON.

PERSONS willing to CONTRACT for the erection of Houses at Kenton, in the place of those recently destroyed by fire, may see the Plans and Specifications of the first and second groups at the DEVON ARMS INN, in the Village, on and after TUESDAY, the 24th instant.

Tenders for the same are to be delivered to Mr. JOHN DREW, Jun., at Powderham Castle, on or before the 30th instant.

Dated Powderham Castle, June 21st, 1856.

Figure 3. *Trewman's Exeter Flying Post*, 26 June 1856.
Reproduced courtesy of Westcountry Studies Library, Devon Libraries.

provide earth closets. However, each cottage was to be provided with its own privy with syphon pan, connected to new sewerage systems and with a slate cistern covering the privy to collect water for flushing. For the third group of nine cottages, externally each house also had a piggery and wood store. No detail of the construction was left to chance with every material, fixture or fitting to be used was specified in great detail.[21]

These cottages were extremely forward thinking in the facilities that were provided. They appear to have drawn on the principles of the model cottage schemes advocated by Prince Albert, but also developed the ideals by affording additional conveniences such as front parlours, individual ovens and water closets. They were also to break new ground architecturally. Although Gothic styles were generally considered to be not suitable for workmen's cottages, the first two groups do show many elements of the style. The cottages are constructed of red brick and have steeply pitched and gabled slate roofs, cranked, or elbow shaped, arched windows and doors, and tall chimney stacks with one front stack corbelled out over the central door (see Plate 16). The groups are both built to a symmetrical plan. The contract prices for these new houses amounted to £423 15s 6d for the three[22] and £525 for the four[23] – average costs of £141 and £131.

By the time Rowell came to design the row of cottages opposite the church, a terrace of nine houses, he was much surer and confident in the Gothic style which he adopted. Clearly this would not have been possible without the support of his patron, Lord Courtenay. It is interesting to note that at the same time that both men were developing a strong and distinctive Gothic style in Kenton, their work in Newton Abbot, as commissioner and as architect, continued to be influenced by the villa rustica movement with its characteristic Italianate detailing and stucco terraces, though later work by Rowell in Newton Abbot, such as The Avenue, shows distinct similarity to his work in Kenton. For these two men, at least, there seems to have been less of a 'battle of the styles' and more of an accommodation of all styles.

The influence of the High Victorian movement of Gothic architecture for this terrace of nine houses has resulted in perhaps the most striking of the Victorian buildings in the village. Alongside All Saints Church, Court Hall and Church Cottage, these houses are identified as making an outstanding contribution to the architectural character of the Kenton conservation area. The High Victorian style, championed by members of the Ecclesiological Society, had as its most important element what was referred to as constructional polychromy. The development of the railways meant that transporting materials from further afield than the immediate local vicinity became perfectly feasible and so bricks of different clays and different colours along with other varied materials could be combined to great effect to produce a structural polychromy. Along with the contrasts of colour, contrasts of texture were encouraged and could be achieved by combining rough stone with the brickwork. This style was popular amongst those architects and patrons who had been influenced by Augustus W. Pugin's *True Principles of Pointed or Christian Architecture* (1841). It was Pugin's contention that Gothic style was the most appropriate style because it was English and Christian, whereas classical style was foreign and pagan. Gothic architecture represented the 'true' faith of an earlier Christianity. Structural polychromy in particular carried religious connotations as it could be seen as an exhibition of God's creation. Little use was made of polychromatic detailing before the 1850s, but from 1850 onwards some prominent examples began to appear, perhaps the most notable of which was William Butterfield's All Saints, Margaret Street in Marylebone (constructed 1850–1853). However, one of the leaders of the High Victorian movement, George Edmund Street had, in a lecture given in 1853, commented that 'our style' had found limited application to street architecture.[24] Possibly the scale required to show the style to its best effect was thought at that time to make its use in the small scale domestic hard to accomplish.

A terrace of nine houses might perhaps have provided the scope for Courtenay and Rowell to adopt the principles of polychromy for a domestic street scene. These cottages, which were constructed between 1857 and 1858, utilise the elements of the High Victorian style at a time when their use was mostly confined to church and country house architecture. The predominant building material is red brick, but structural adornments are achieved by the additional use of yellow and black brick banding and detailing (see Plate 17). The plinth is constructed of limestone and Bath stone has been used for the cills of the windows, abutments, key stones of the arches and the weathering of the plinth. The caps, corbels and weathering of the chimneys are also of Bath stone. Purbeck or York stone was specified for the entrance steps. Although not as clearly visible now, the use of ground Blue Lias lime and coal ashes for the pointing material would have also added to the polychromatic effect. The terrace is mainly constructed to a symmetrical plan, with some asymmetrical detailing, another typical High Victorian Gothic feature. The cranked arched windows and doors are accentuated by the use of Bath stone for the key and corner stones. The terrace is gabled at the ends and has two large gables to the front and rear at each end of the terrace. There is also a half hipped centre bay, gabled dormers (see Plate 18) and deep eaves and verges and brick porches (see Plate 19) to the cottages at either end of the terrace. The roofs are constructed of Delabole slate and have crested ridge tiles.

The cost of such dwellings was clearly going to be high, as quality materials were specified, but attempts were made to reduce the costs by re-using materials where possible. For instance the foundations, yard walls and back walls of the piggeries and wood sheds were constructed from the old stones of the fire damaged cottages previously on the site (see Plate 20) and oak timber used for lintels, wall plates and elsewhere was obtained from the estate free of charge. Cheaper materials were also specified for the back elevations of the properties which would not be visible from the street, including the use of rough hard bricks rather than best bricks at a saving of 4s 6d (22½ pence) per thousand. The back of the terrace also has no polychromatic detailing and windows and doors are simple openings without arches. Even so the lowest of the six tenders received for the construction was for £1,173.[25] The average cost per cottage was therefore £130, actually slightly lower than the previous cottages, despite the additional decorative elements included. Work began in May 1857 and was completed by April of the following year.[26]

Whether any more building work took place during the next fifteen or so years is unclear, but in 1875 four almshouses were constructed by the Devon Estate's own staff and specialist tradesmen. Detailed accounts for the construction of these properties show that work started in April 1875 and that the construction was completed in December. The total costs of construction amounted to £479 14s 6d.[27] These almshouses and also two cottages alongside all have attractively carved bargeboards with gothic quatrefoil detailing.

Similar bargeboards can also be seen in the villas that Rowell was at that time designing for the continuing development of the Wolborough Hill area of Newton Abbot.[28] They are also demonstrably of a type with the earlier cottages clearly indicating that Rowell was continuing to act as the architect for the ongoing rebuilding in Kenton. The almshouses with their wooden gabled verandas with Gothic timber tracery are again constructed of red brick with yellow brick and Bath stone dressings. As with all the other Kenton cottages designed by Rowell, the chimney stacks are prominent features (see Plate 21). Adjacent are Devon Cottages with many similar details and one with an oriel window on its street elevation, perhaps suggesting some influence from the Queen Anne revival style, then beginning to gain favour (see Plate 22)

The three cottages in High Street have been listed and appear to be little changed externally. The group of four has not been listed as a result of which one has been significantly altered. The cranked arches of the windows have been infilled and the windows replaced with uPVC windows, and the original brickwork painted over. One other has also has its brickwork painted. The terrace of nine cottages and the almshouses are all listed and are remarkably intact, with the exception of the loss of the original tall chimney stacks at either end of the row.

Figure 4. Early 20th century photograph showing Devon Cottages, the Almshouses and Church Street grouped around All Saints Church.

All these groups of cottages and almshouses have combined to give the village the distinctive character referred to in the conservation area character appraisal. They show the work of a partnership of patron and architect who were influenced by the cultural and moral mores of the time – the desire to improve the lot of the poorer labouring classes, particularly those who were worthy, industrious and importantly, grateful, and to improve their moral condition by providing separate sleeping accommodation for parents and for children of each gender. However, it would not be unreasonable to conclude that the architectural devices employed and the degree of ornamentation were not intended for the benefit of the occupants of the cottages, rather that they were a public display of taste and modernity. After all, poorer quality materials and lack of ornamentation had been specified for the elevations not visible from the street, even to the extent that although brass window catches were itemised for the front and side windows, those at the rear of the properties were to have iron catches. Although Kenton could not, in any sense, be described as a 'model village' elements of the model village influences can be seen in the planned nature and the high quality, both architecturally and functionally, of the Victorian housing. Courtenay became the eleventh Earl of Devon in 1859 and became known as 'the good earl' for his many charitable and philanthropic activities.[29] Rowell was to have a distinguished architectural career and in addition to his work for the Courtenays, accepted commissions from both the Palk and Rolle estates, and went on to restore All Saints, Kenton; St Mary, Kingskerwell; and St Michael, Trusham, amongst others. He also designed new churches, including St Paul, Newton Abbot and St John, Leusdon; schools, for example at Alphington; and many other buildings which can still be seen today.[30]

The question remains as to why the whole of the Victorian architecture has been attributed as late nineteenth century and the almshouses dated to 1888. One possible explanation could be that the first identified references to the almshouses are in the directories of the late 1880s. The entry in Kelly's directory for 1889 for instance, reads '. . . there are four almshouses, erected by the Earl of Devon (*d.* 1888), occupied by aged widows, who live rent free'.[31]

It is entirely feasible that the date which if fact refers to the date that Courtenay, then eleventh Earl of Devon had died has been misinterpreted as a construction date for the almshouses. Once attributed in this way it appears to have been repeated and accepted as a 'fact'. Apparently adding credence to this putative dating might be the commonly expressed belief that architectural creativity took longer to reach the provinces resulting in a time lag before local buildings reflected ideas expressed by the innovators in the field. The evidence in the records, however, is clear. There was no delay after the fire before rebuilding began and the architectural heritage is not just distinctive but is also innovative and progressive.

Notes and References

1. Teignbridge District Council (TDC), 2009a, p. 7.
2. Ibid.
3. See for example Listed Building Schedule numbers 85888; 85894; and 85905.
4. TDC, 2009a, p. 7.
5. White 1850, p. 409.
6. Presswell 2007, p. 19.
7. DRO, Courtenay of Powderham, 1508M/London/Court & Estate Papers/Court 29, 28 September 1859.
8. Gray 2000, p. 134.
9. Polwhele 1977, p. 160.
10. *Trewman's Exeter Flying Post*, 17 April 1856.
11. *Trewman's Exeter Flying Post*, 8 May 1856.
12. DRO, Courtenay of Powderham, D1508M/Estate Correspondence/ Box 2 , 17 April 1856.
13. Ibid.
14. *Trewman's Exeter Flying Post*, 24 April 1856.
15. *Trewman's Exeter Flying Post*, 6 September 1855.
16. DRO, Courtenay of Powderham, D1508M/Estate Correspondence/ Box 2 , 12 June 1856.
17. DRO, Courtenay of Powderham, D1508M/Estate Correspondence/ Box 2 , 23 June 1856; and Courtenay of Powderham, D1508M/Maps and Plans/Kenton/Plans/23.
18. DRO, Courtenay of Powderham, D1508M/Estate Correspondence/ Box 2, 26 June 1856.
19. *Trewman's Exeter Flying Post*, 26 June 1856.
20. DRO, Courtenay of Powderham, D1508M/Estate Correspondence/ Box 2, 27 June 1856.
21. DRO, Courtenay of Powderham, L1508M/London/Estate/Building Contracts/Kenton/3; Courtenay of Powderham, 1508M/London/ Estate/Building Contracts/Kenton/4. DRO, Courtenay of Powderham, L1508M/London/Estate/Building Contracts/Kenton/6.

22. DRO, Courtenay of Powderham, 1508M/London/Estate/Building Contracts/Kenton/4.
23. DRO, Courtenay of Powderham, L1508M/London/Estate/Building Contracts/Kenton/3.
24. Muthesius 1972, p. 42.
25. DRO, Courtenay of Powderham, L1508M/Estate/Building Contracts/Kenton/6.
26. DRO, Courtenay of Powderham, D1508M/Estate Correspondence/Box 2 , 5 April 1857.
27. DRO, Courtenay of Powderham, 1508M/London/Legal & General Correspondence/Kenton Papers 1835–1925/1875–6.
28. See for instance TDC 2009b, p. 31, figure 54.
29. Courtney 2004.
30. For further information on buildings designed or restored by Rowell see Cherry and Pevsner 1989, p. 944.
31. Kelly 1889, p. 280.

Bibliography

Cherry, B. and Pevsner, N. (1989) *The Buildings of England: Devon*, London: Penguin Books.

Courtney, W.P. 'Courtenay, William Reginald, eleventh earl of Devon (1807–1888)', rev. H.C.G. Matthew, *Oxford Dictionary of National Biography*, (eds) H.C.G. Matthew, Oxford University Press, 2004; online edn, Oct 2006 [http://www.oxforddnb.com/view/article/6459, accessed 21 April 2010].

Gray, T. (ed.) (2000) *Travels in Georgian Devon: the illustrated journals of the Reverend John Swete (1789–1800)* vol. 4, Tiverton: Devon Books.

Havinden, M. (1989) 'The Model Village' in Mingay, G.E. (ed.) *The Rural Idyll*, London: Routledge.

Kelly (1889) *Kelly's Directory of Devon and Cornwall*, London: Kelly.

Muthesius, S. (1972) *The High Victorian Movement in Architecture 1850–1870*, London: Routledge and Kegan Paul.

Polwhele, R. (1977) *The History of Devonshire*, vol. 2, reprinted edition, Dorking: Kohler and Coombes.

Presswell, D. (2007) 'Charles Fowler: architect, 1792–1867', *TDH*, 74, pp. 11-24.

Teignbridge District Council (2009a) *Teignbridge District Conservation Area Character Appraisals Draft Consultation Dec 2009: Kenton*.

Teignbridge District Council (2009b) *Wolborough Hill Conservation Area Character Appraisal*.

White, W. (1850) *History, Gazetteer, and Directory of Devonshire*, Sheffield: William White.

Letters from Victorian School Children at Rousdon: a unique record

Nicky Campbell

As young men, three brothers walked to Liverpool from the village of Watcombe, near Torquay, to find work. The first, in 1807, was Richard Peek and he was followed by his brothers William and James. Richard found work in a tea warehouse in Liverpool. In 1810 the three brothers set up Peek Brothers and Co. in Liverpool, and at 5–7 East Cheap, in London. They traded as wholesale tea, coffee, cocoa and spice merchants. The Peeks became very wealthy. The firm sold good quality tea at reasonable prices as long as all accounts were settled within the month. The success of the company can in part be attributed to the fact that after 1833 the East India Company no longer had a monopoly in the tea trade. The increase in tea drinking, by both rich and poor alike during the second half of the nineteenth century no doubt also helped the company, which became the leading tea merchants in the country. James Peek also founded a biscuit making business in conjunction with his niece's husband, George Hender Frean, and the company became Peek Frean. William's daughter married into the Drew family, founders of the Home and Colonial Stores; they built Castle Drogo, near Drewsteignton in Devon. All the Peeks endowed schools and churches.[1]

James Peek married Elizabeth Master in 1824. They had eight children. Their eldest son, Henry William Peek (born in 1825) became senior partner in Peek Brothers and Co. of East Cheap, from 1847 to 1895. His income was said to be in the region of a guinea a minute –

five million pounds a year. Henry married Margaret Maria Edgar on 20 July 1848 at Clapham. (Her father was one of the founders of Swan and Edgar's department store.) Their only child, Cuthbert Edgar, was born in 1855.

Henry Peek was active in politics. He became a Justice of the Peace for Surrey, and was elected as the senior Tory MP for the Wimbledon constituency from 1868 to 1884. He founded the Movement for the Preservation of Open Spaces and, in 1871, succeeded in preventing Wimbledon Common from building development, saving it for the enjoyment of local people. He sold Burnham Beeches and East Burnham common (374 acres) for a nominal sum to the Corporation of the City of London on condition that they should be opened to the public in perpetuity.[2] On 13 May 1874 Henry Peek was knighted, for services to science. As a devout evangelical Christian he saw it as his duty to help those in need. He advocated education for all, the removal of slums, the eradication of child labour, the provision of public health, and decent wages for reasonable hours of work. Henry Peek's family had emerged from a very humble background, which may explain his desire to help those in a similar situation.

Figure 1. Henry Peek. Author's collection.

In 1869 Henry Peek purchased the Rousdon estate of 350 acres for £22,500. Rousdon was a tiny, cliff top parish on the Devon/Dorset border, just west of Lyme Regis, where a population of eighteen lived in the 'three habitable houses'.[3] A local journalist reported on Henry Peek's philanthropic project:

> He was a real philanthropist – one who had accumulated a vast fortune and was desirous of doing a lasting good with it. His one idea was to purchase a whole parish and devote his wealth in improving the condition of the people in it without pauperising them, a principle, which all true philanthropists work upon. He found Rousdon, a decayed village, with a dilapidated church, ready to his hand. This was in the very early '70s, and in making enquiries into the condition of things he was astonished to find that many of the farm labourers were only receiving 7s. or 7s. 6d. a week, with, of course, the perquisites common to them. To one whom he made a confidante of he said, 'I am going to give my labourers 15s. a week, and give them every opportunity of earning money and making themselves happy homes.[4]

Henry kept his word about paying higher than average wages. Records for 1883 show that he was paying his twenty three farm labourers between 10s and 16s, plus benefits such as very low rents, free milk and firewood.[5]

Henry also believed passionately in education. The order in which he built the estate was firstly the church, then cottages for the workers, followed by the schools. The mansion was the last to be built. He was actively involved with all aspects of designing and building the estate, and nowhere more than in the design of the schools. The schools opened in 1876. Sir Henry was very involved in setting up the curriculum, and the headmaster observed that he was 'equally interested in the Religious as well as the secular instructions' in the school.[6] Before the 1870 Education Act introduced compulsory, free elementary education, poor children sometimes attended 'dame' schools, or specialist schools which taught a trade. In East Devon many children attended lace school, where lace making was taught to both boys and girls to enable them to make a living. Men could increase their earning capacity by lace making in their spare time. Children often started full-time lace making by the age of seven. In

Figure 2. Rousdon school as an architect's drawing.
Courtesy of the Trustees of Combpyne Rousdon Village Hall
(The Peek Hall).

1885 Sir Henry's grandson's christening robe, was decorated with lace made on the estate.

At other coastal schools boys were taught navigation skills. If these schools taught spelling at all, it was often a phonetic spelling. Dame schools traditionally charged 3d or 4d per child per week, which must have put a strain on family finances. The children were expected to be neatly dressed. The schoolmaster at Burton Bradstock used to whip children who came to school barefoot. Children from working class families had high levels of absenteeism, as they would be kept off school to help with planting, harvesting, and bird scaring, or to look after a younger sibling. Compulsory secondary education, free of charge, was not introduced until 1902. Sir Henry introduced secondary education in his schools from the start. He wrote to a contemporary,

> The most successful of our works at Rousdon has undoubtedly been the church and schools . . . Six years have elapsed since an area of about 2,500 acres was taken in hand. No child outside our boundaries is admitted, but all within are systematically looked up. The number

Figure 3. The school today. Photograph: Phil Planel.

between the ages of 4 and 13 is about 90 . . . we are seldom more than 5 short of our full complement.[7]

The first headmaster, appointed in 1876, was thirty seven-year old William Burgess, whose wife Ann would later teach at the school. Three of their six children became teachers. Beatrice, born in 1879, became schoolmistress at Rousdon in 1901. The headmaster's house adjoined the school, and over the years his duties grew. In 1883 Mr Burgess became postmaster of the Rousdon Post Office, situated in the dining room of the school complex. He also ran the money order and savings bank (1890), and oversaw the library and reading room (1893).

Mr. And Mrs. Burgess being the first master and mistress, and they have remained at the head of the school, doing successful work ever since. Mr. Burgess naturally looks back over his long years of service with some pride and satisfaction, as excellent results have been obtained, and it is noteworthy that at the present time he has some 30 children under his care whose parents were educated by him in the same schools. They opened in 1876 with 95 children. Mr. Burgess recalls that day with pleasure, saying that afterwards all the scholars were supplied with dinner, which consisted of meat dumplings and vegetables, in the presence of the late Sir Henry and Lady Peek.[8]

One of the major innovations was the building of a school kitchen and the laying out of a vegetable garden. 'The food is cooked under the personal superintendence of Mrs. Burgess, and the girls in the schools help in turn, thus having lessons in practical cookery, cleanliness, laying the table, etc., one of Sir Henry's objects being to train up the girls to be useful housewives when they get a home of their own'.[9] The boys produced the vegetables. This may have been the first instance of children receiving a cooked lunch at school anywhere in the country, and was many years before the Education (School Meals) Act of 1906 was passed.

The occurrence of poverty of the inhabitants of this thinly peopled district first inspired Sir Henry Peek to institute school dinners. It was evident to him that the children must be fed as well as taught, and with this end in view Sir Henry resolved to give them, on the five days they attended school, a good meal at a penny a head . . . we have testimony of her Majesty's inspector that it has seldom been his lot to examine a more efficient school. Go there some school day at twelve o'clock, and at the sound of the bell you will see the children come trooping in from their games . . . a brighter, healthier-looking set of children it would be hard to find . . . all alike are as fresh and healthy and intelligent as you could wish to see. Once indoors they are all marshalled to their places in the dining room, the infants on a separate bench at a low table reserved for their use. The dinner cooked by the school master's wife and daughters, is brought in and served by the older girls, and whether it be treacle and suet pudding, boiled rice and jam, or the favourite dish of all, roly-poly and bacon, the slices disappear with marvellous rapidity. No one is stinted as to quantity, and the bigger boys often dispose of five or six helpings with ease. When the meal is over and grace has been sung, they go back to their games while the big girls clear the table and wash up. The school itself, including dining room and kitchen was . . . fitted up by Sir Henry, and tuition is free of charge, but beyond this the dinner scheme pays its way. No arrears are allowed, and the 5d a week is paid by each child on Monday Morning, a reduction being allowed where there is more than one member in the family. Thus, two children are allowed their dinners for 9d, three for 1/- and four for 1/3d. All articles for consumption are bought at wholesale prices, vegetables being grown in the garden attached to the school house, and charged to the dinner account at current prices. Strict account is kept of every penny spent and every item of food supplied, and it had been calculated that during seven years, from October 1876 to December 1882, 110,221 dinners were given to the children, at a total cost of 107,406 pence.[10]

Interest in this experiment in feeding the children in school spread, and was discussed in Parliament. The Right Honourable A.J. Mundella, MP, wrote of Rousdon school: 'I visited and examined these schools on 8 March, 1889, and found them the best rural schools I have ever seen; most honourable to Sir Henry Peek, and most creditable to Mr. and Mrs. Burgess and daughters.'[11] Mr Burgess supplied Mr Mundella with background information on the families of the school children. This included the number of dependent children per household, the occupation and income of the breadwinner, and the amount of rent paid (only fifteen households out of the thirty-four paid rent). As well as noting weekly family expenditure on meals, Mr Burgess also reported that there had not been 'not a penny' in arrears since the school opened in 1876.

There were three classrooms, one especially for the infants. Each classroom had a fire with a large brass fender around it that the children could sit on. The boys had a different entrance from the girls, as well as different playgrounds. There were even indoor toilets for the children – no separate cubicles but the traditional three-hole communal type. The school opened on 20 0ctober 1876, ninety five children on the roll. Sir Henry visited the school every day when he was in residence, and often joined the children for their penny dinners. He was clearly sympathetic to their needs, as the following extract demonstrates,

At first the old difficulty as to boots troubled us; [but to meet this a] club was easily established into which the children, on Monday morning with their school fee, bring a penny or tuppence for their boot card, in this way many total up in a year, say 4/6d or 5/-. A pair of strong boots costs 6/- to 8/-, so in order that they may have a pair once a year, I offer a maximum bonus of half a crown for poetry or verses, learnt and said out of school hours.[12]

Mr Burgess submitted a weekly report to Sir Henry, which included a weather report. He listed attendance figures and commented on reasons for poor attendance. Sometimes the weather was 'very bad' and the 'littlest ones' could not get to school, or 'Turnip harvest over ran'. Mr Burgess also made regular requests for new school equipment. He noted that 'The new code' of teaching required each school to have a set of history books, which he had ordered. The American organ was 'no good with so many voices' and he hoped that Sir Henry could be persuaded to provide 'a 10 guinea Alexandre Harmonium'. (Three months later Sir Henry had obliged, and the new harmonium was judged a great success at the Christmas Treat.) Food is often mentioned in the letters. Mr Burgess asked Sir Henry if he could get hold of some apples, which 'make such a good change in the Dinners and are much enjoyed by the children'. He mentioned that the children had enjoyed 'honey with suet for the first time', and on another occasion reminded Sir Henry that 'if all the children come to the Christmas treat we shall require 90 presents'. In 1882 the children were learning verses from 'Watt's Hymns', and Mr Burgess reported that Flora Holt, the shepherd's daughter (aged four), 'repeated the whole 109 verses without prompting and quite surprised my daughter and myself'. The infants were paid a penny for every verse they learned whilst the older children earned a penny for three verses.[13]

As well as receiving a weekly report, the children would write to Sir Henry every few months, at Mr Burgess' instruction. All the letters were immaculately written and spelt. These were often very 'chatty' letters, and the children were not totally in awe of him. They talk of rabbiting and ratting expeditions, trips to the beach, events that were happening in school and at home, as well as thanking him for their Christmas presents and the school treats. The following quotations are extracted from their correspondence. Edward Cleal (aged eleven) wrote: 'My father was a pall bearer at Mrs Symes funeral. Mr Draper of Combpyne made the coffin and it was a very nice one. Thank you for the raisins and figs'. Kate Anning, (aged twelve), reported that: 'My aunt Eliza who lives at Combpyne is gone to live in the house that Aunt Mary came out from, Harry Everett has been living there since. Mrs Woolmington gave mother a Christmas card and a threepenny bit for me'. Walter Wilkins, (also aged twelve), said that: 'Combpyne church was decorated with holly and flowers and it looked very pretty. Mr Pearson gave Combpyne choir some presents, he gave me a writing desk'. Henry Perry told of going into Lyme Regis. He had only been there once before, although he was twelve years of age. Louisa Burgess reported, 'Sir, We have fires in the school now because it is so cold . . . There aren't many apples about this year and there won't be much cider making. Lord Bridport came to look over the Mansion and a lot of people came on Saturday to look over the Mansion. They liked it'. Annie Pierce wrote: 'Mr Talbot's son came of age and Mr Talbot gave a supper to all the farmers and peasants and ringers. The Lyme artillery band were there'.[14]

The children at Rousdon, in common with many working class children, worked on the farm during their school holidays, and were very aware of the seasons and the farming year. The schoolmaster set the dates of the holidays in consultation with the farmers, as one of the weekly letters sent by Mr Burgess to Sir Henry illustrates: 'The corn still looks very green and I am delaying the start of the holidays until the weather is such that the grain is ripe'.[15] Sometimes he misjudged it. Annie Tolman (aged 11) wrote to Sir Henry:

Sir, at master's request I write this letter to tell you what I did in the holidays. The first two weeks I was in the house helping mother, because Mr Sloman had not taken up the wheat so that we could go gleaning. But the last week of my holidays I went out gleaning. Mr Sloman has finished harvesting and had the thrashing machine in on Saturday. Next Sunday we hope to have our harvest thanksgiving and I hope the church will be prettily decorated but there are not many wild flowers about now.[16]

John Spiller, an estate farmer's son, wrote several letters to Sir Henry. 'Sir, The crops have been very good nearly everywhere. The first thing we harvested was the peas, the next was the wheat and oats. The barley was left to last. My engagement was to load on the waggons. We have some clover to cut'.[17] Later in the autumn, he wrote: 'Sir, Some cattle have been washed away. The winter has begun very early and the stock has been taken in, the mangold harvest is poor but we have some very large turnips amongst our mangolds, some of them measure 36 inches around'.[18]

Edward French (aged fourteen) was working for Farmer Symes in 1882 to pull weeds out of the corn for eleven hours a day, and had been 'pulling turnips for a fortnight'. Mr Woolmington of Manor Farm Combpyne 'put' Henry Sansom to mind the sheep on Saturday out in the field to keep them from the wheat ricks, while Elizabeth Gapper and her friends had 'three fields to glean in'. 'We have dug our potatoes and I had to stay off school a day for it. Tom Clothier is lodging with us now his father and mother are dead,' wrote Frances Farnham. Ten year old William Sansom was keen to relate that James Start and the dogs went catching rats, 'They caught 11'. Edward French wrote in 1882: 'Sir, I am going to tell you that I am come back to school again and for the first time I write a letter to you. I have been away for six months to work for Mr Symes'. Rosa Mattocks had been absent from school because 'Mr Woolmington has finished harvesting. He finished last Monday and I had to stay home from school to look after the baby for my sister, because Mr Woolmington wanted her out at work'.[19]

The educational standard at the school was very high, as Her Majesty's Inspectors found when they examined the children in 1882: 'In writing, spelling and dictation here passed 100%, in reading and arithmetic each 90%, in geography 94%, in grammar 85%. Twelve children passed in literature and eight girls in domestic economy. These results must be very gratifying to Sir Henry and Lady Peek'.[20] The following year the results were even better, with 100 per cent passes in reading, writing and dictation, and geography, ninety-eight per cent in arithmetic, and eighty-seven per cent in grammar. Fourteen pupils passed in literature and nine in Domestic Economy. The singing was 'good'. The girls had had to make a pair of stockings and a nightdress for part of their Domestic Economy exam. At Prize Day, 22 March 1883, good conduct prizes were given to Emma Holt (aged four) who was presented with a workbox, and to Samuel Harris who was given

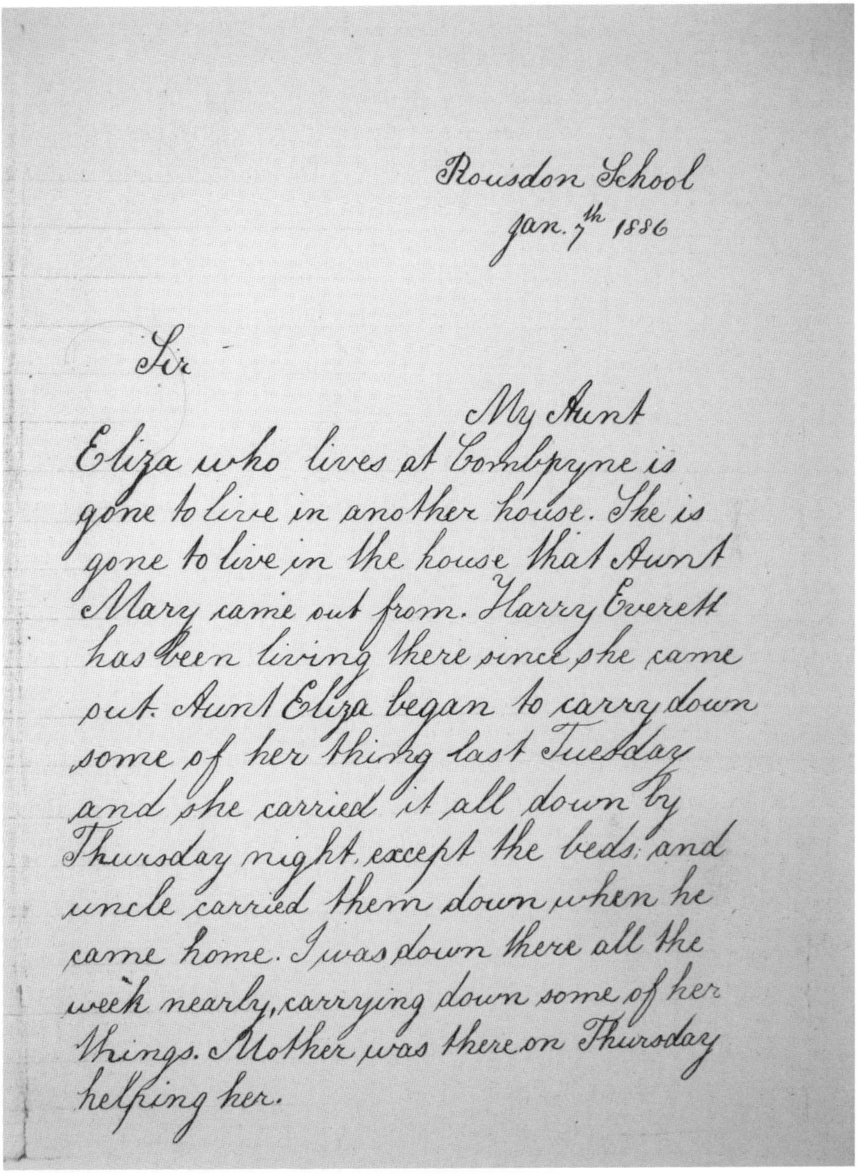

Rousdon School
Jan. 7th 1886

Sir

My Aunt Eliza who lives at Combpyne is gone to live in another house. She is gone to live in the house that Aunt Mary came out from. Harry Everett has been living there since she came out. Aunt Eliza began to carry down some of her things last Tuesday and she carried it all down by Thursday night except the beds and uncle carried them down when he came home. I was down there all the week nearly, carrying down some of her things. Mother was there on Thursday helping her.

Figure 4. DRO Reference: D1405M. A typical letter from one of the school children to Sir Henry Peek.
Reproduced courtesy of Devon Record Office.

a box of tools. Fourteen children in the Standard Class were given prizes of books for good attendance, as were four of the twenty-one children in the infant's class. The children also took part in concerts during the Christmas holidays, and were invited to parties and teas on the estate, 'We all of us went into the Mansion on Christmas Day to tea and supper', wrote Alice Cann in 1883.[21] Peek family celebrations, such as weddings, always included the estate workers, and the children had special treats then.

When Sir Henry Peek was widowed in 1884 he moved to Rousdon to live with his family. He continued in public service, and subsequently held the post of Deputy Lieutenant of Devonshire. Following his death on 26 August 1898, Sir Henry was mourned by all who knew him. At his funeral Rousdon school children 'were stationed on each side of the coffin in the large hall in readiness to convey the numerous floral tributes to the place of burial'.[22] He bequeathed 5,000 guineas towards the maintenance of this Church of England school, and Sir Cuthbert Peek continued his father's work at Rousdon School. During his time at Rousdon Sir Henry Peek had sought to implement a system of education, which was innovative in its holistic approach. His practical philanthropy included initiatives to improve both the health, and the housing conditions of the families living and working on his estate. He was successful in his endeavours, and gained the support of A.J. Mundella, a Liberal MP, and an early advocate of elementary education. Mundella was keen to publicise the merits of the Rousdon school 'experiment' to a wider audience, and the benefits of free meals in particular. When Sir Henry's great-grandson inherited the estate in 1935, an era of close community came abruptly to an end when the estate was sold. Rousdon School became a state school until it was sold in 1948. The mansion was subsequently bought by Allhallows school of Honiton.

Notes and References

1. Michell n.d., pp. 40-43.
2. *The Times*, 29 August 1898.
3. George 1921, p. 662.
4. *Bridport News*, 13 October 1905.
5. DRO, D1405M, Letters from Rousdon school children to Sir Henry Peek, 1882–6.

6. DRO, D1405M, Letter from Mr Burgess to Sir Henry Peek 1873.
7. Letter in author's ownership.
8. *Bridport News*, 13 October 1905.
9. Ibid.
10. Ibid.
11. DRO, D1405M, Letters from Rousdon school children to Sir Henry Peek, 1882–6.
12. Letter in author's ownership.
13. DRO, D1405M, Weekly letters from Mr Burgess to Sir Henry Peek, 1882–6
14. DRO, D1405M, Weekly letters from Rousdon schoolchildren to Sir Henry Peek, 1882–6.
15. DRO, D1405M, Weekly letters from Mr Burgess to Sir Henry Peek, 1882-6.
16. DRO, D1405M, Weekly letters from Rousdon schoolchildren to Sir Henry Peek, 1882–6.
17. Ibid.
18. Ibid.
19. DRO, D1405M, Weekly letters from Rousdon schoolchildren to Sir Henry Peek, 1882–6.
20. *Pulman's Weekly News*, 9 December 1882.
21. DRO, D145M, Weekly letters from Rousdon schoolchildren to Sir Henry Peek, 1882–6.
22. *Exeter Gazette*, 31 August 1898.

Bibliography

Dalrymple-Hamilton, Lady G. (n.d.) 'Rousdon and the Peek family', *Allhallows School Magazine*.

George, Sir R. (1921) 'An Architect's Reminiscences', *The Builder*, 12 May, p. 662.

Horn, P. (1989) *The Victorian and Edwardian Schoolchild*, Gloucester: Sutton.

Hoskins, W.G. (1954) *Devon*, Tiverton: Devon Books.

Johnston G. (n.d.) *Rousdon and the Peek Family: a miscellany*, Privately published by Allhallows School.

Mitchell, C. (n.d.) *Penny Dinners*, pamphlet.

The Contingent Career Path of the Young George O. May

R.H. Parker

George Oliver May (1875–1961), Devon born and bred, was a hugely influential accountant in the United States, one of only four recipients of the highest awards of both his professional body (the American Institute of Accountants, now the American Institute of Certified Public Accountants) and of academe (the Accounting Hall of Fame at Ohio State University). He was not only the senior partner of Price, Waterhouse & Co. (now PricewaterhouseCoopers) in the United States but also the author of over 100 articles and of a classic work on financial accounting published in 1943. The American accounting historian Stephen Zeff has written that May 'played an indispensable role in raising the standards of accounting and auditing practice [in the United States] in the critical decade of the 1930s, and he was one of the most incisive and most perceptive commentators on accounting principles during the first half of the twentieth century'.[1] According to the authors of the history of Price Waterhouse in the United States, 'His unparalleled expertise in accounting and tax matters allowed May to play a leading role as spokesman and theorist for the accounting profession as a whole'.[2] He is the only British accountant included in Zeff's 'fourteen who made a difference' in the first hundred years of the American profession. At the end of his long career he was regarded as literally the 'GOM' (grand old man) of American accountancy. But grand old men were once ambitious young men. May's career in the United States is well attested by Zeff and others. This essay looks instead at the young May's career in Devon (Teignmouth, Tiverton and Exeter) and asks how and why he was able to qualify as an English chartered accountant in Exeter, why he left Devon, why he migrated to the United States, and to what extent he maintained ties with Devon.

The main source of information for May's life in Devon is the first two chapters of his memoirs. These were written when May was in his eighties, and published posthumously in 1962 by the Ronald Press in New York, edited by his friend and Price Waterhouse partner Paul Grady. The memoirs are illuminating but lack detail. In particular, May tells us little about his extended family (grandparents, parents, siblings, uncles and aunts) and does not name people and institutions unless he has something complimentary to say about them. Grady was a conscientious editor who added some information about May's brothers and sisters, but he lacked local knowledge. He made mistakes in the transcription of personal names: Westron becomes Westrom and Wilfred Drake becomes Wilford Drake. This paper uses other sources (trade directories, censuses, parish registers, civil registration certificates, professional membership lists, and school archives) to fill in the details, give names and provide a context.

May's opportunity to pursue a successful career as an accountant in the United States was contingent on a number of pre-conditions. The first pre-condition was that of *class:* to be born into a family from which one could rise through the English class system, at a time when most Devonians were born into rural poverty. George Oliver May was born on 22 May 1875, at 6 Somerset Place in West Teignmouth, then as now in the central shopping area. Both his father (George England May, 1845–1927) and paternal grandfather (Benjamin Oliver May, *c.*1823–1890) were grocers. George Oliver was the second of six children borne by his mother Bessie (nee Goodland, the daughter of a butcher, born in Tiverton *c.*1846, died 1933). Round the corner at 3 Bank Street was another family business, a bookseller and stationers run by a Miss E.J. May. This was a respectable petit bourgeois background (shared by many English accountants, including Lord Plender, the first chartered accountant to be awarded a peerage), from which a clever hard-working boy could make his way into a profession.

The second pre-condition was that of *gender, ethnicity and religion*: that May be born male, white and Protestant. In the late-nineteenth century, most women in Devon, and the United Kingdom generally (as May himself comments in his memoirs in relation to his wife), had little opportunity of a good education. The professions were not readily open to them. There were no female chartered accountants (as distinct from bookkeepers) until after the First World War. This is not to say that there were no women in employment in the last quarter of the nineteenth century, but most of them were 'in [domestic] service' (including the servants employed in the May household in Somerset Place), working as shop assistants, or working on the land, especially in rural counties such as Devon.

Not only was May male, he was also, to use a North American expression that he would not have been familiar with when growing up in Devon, a WASP (a white Anglo-Saxon Protestant). So, of course, were most of his fellow Devonians and Englishmen during this period. Overt racism was common and Catholics and Jews still found some professions difficult to enter in both the United Kingdom and the United States. Although there is little evidence that religion played an important role in May's life, he was baptised, confirmed (in Blundell's School chapel by the Bishop of Exeter in March 1891) and married (1 January, 1902) in the Church of England, and was educated at an Anglican school to whose chapel he donated a sixteenth-century silver chalice (known as the 'May chalice') in 1951.[3]

The third pre-condition was the opportunity of a decent *education*. The standard of schools in late-nineteenth-century Devon was very variable and there were no universities.[4] What May called his 'first real school' was run by Thomas Sandercock at Orchard House in Teignmouth. May does not name the school or its headmaster but he describes the latter as a 'charlatan'. He is scathing about the staff with the exception of an inspiring mathematics teacher, a Mr Partridge, who was possibly related to William Partridge, the Tiverton solicitor who played an important role in the 1870s in ensuring a future for Blundell's School. In spring 1889 May successfully competed for an entrance scholarship to Blundell's, which he entered in the Lower Fifth form in September 1889 as a boarder, aged fourteen. The 1891 census return shows him in Westlake House, whose housemaster was a Mr Rooper (not mentioned by May). Noon's history of Blundell's includes an 1888 photograph of Rooper and his wife and what Noon calls 'some rather hard-boiled looking boys'.[5] At the date of the 1891 census there were thirteen scholarship boys and ten students boarding in the house. May had the good fortune to enter Blundell's when it was undoubtedly the best school in Devon and one of the best in England. May played rugby, won prizes in divinity and history, and was a member of the sixth form debating society. The memoirs do not mention the new buildings (opened in 1882) or Blundell's most famous headmaster (A.L. Francis, from 1874 to 1917) but May pays tribute to the inspiring and highly successful mathematics master, J.M. Thornton, whose many distinguished pupils included (after May's time at the school) the Nobel Prize winner A.V. Hill.[6] May does not mention that Blundell's was located in Tiverton, where two of his maternal uncles ran butchers' shops.

May was well aware of the debt that he owed to Blundell's and showed his appreciation of the education that he received there by a number of donations (not mentioned in his memoirs). Apart from the chalice already referred to, he donated £1,000 in May 1912, expressing the wish that the money be used to found a scholarship named after Thornton.[7] The donation demonstrates his desire to help boys such as himself to get a good education. In March 1914 the new playing ground at the School was designated the 'Mayfield'. He also donated money to set up a fund for the sons of Old Blundellians who had died in the First World War.[8] In 1948 he donated £1,000 in memory of his mother.

The fourth pre-condition was *choosing the right career*, from those open to him. He tells us that his family dissuaded him from an early interest in the Indian Civil Service. In December 1891 (aged sixteen), he was in the happy position of both being in line for the captaincy of the school Rugby First XV and being given the chance to work for a scholarship to read mathematics at Cambridge, followed by a career in mathematics, possibly as an actuary. By a combination of chance and financial exigency, neither eventuated. The chance was a visit to Teignmouth by John Milton Criddle, the son of a Somerset grocer and a relative on his mother's side, who had moved to Newcastle upon Tyne and been admitted as a solicitor in 1881. Criddle was accompanied by an (unnamed) chartered accountant. Criddle persuaded May of the advantages of accountancy to a boy who was both numerate and literate. To become a chartered accountant one had to serve an apprenticeship under 'articles': five years for a non-graduate, three years for a university graduate. Non-graduate entry was the norm. Moreover, three years at Cambridge, followed by three years' articles was apparently regarded by the May family as not financially feasible. It was, however, as May would have been aware when he wrote his memoirs, the option that Arthur Lowes Dickinson, the son of a London portrait painter who became May's boss in the United States and a leader of the profession in both the United States and the United Kingdom, was able to follow. Dickinson was educated at Charterhouse and King's College, Cambridge, obtaining first class honours in mathematics and qualifying also as an actuary.

The fifth pre-condition therefore was *to find a principal in a firm of chartered accountants* who would be willing to take May as an articled clerk for five years. There was little choice, if May was not to work a long way from home. Although by 1892 the Institute of Chartered Accountants in England and Wales had a national membership of 1,876, most of them worked in London and the big industrial towns. There were no chartered accountants in Teignmouth or Tiverton. The obvious place to look was Exeter, roughly half way between the two. Exeter was a cathedral city and county town, and the seat of the county court. It was still comparatively small, with a population of less than 50,000, and in 1892 had only two chartered accountants, Thomas Andrew and Charles Henry Fulford.[9] Since Fulford was Andrew's clerk, Andrew was the only possible choice. May's father paid a premium of 100 guineas (£105) and May began his apprenticeship on 15 February, 1892. He presumably commuted by train from Teignmouth to Exeter.

The choice of Thomas Andrew (1831–1902) meant that May was articled to one of the leading men in Exeter. By 1892, Andrew was well established and close to retirement. Born in the Cornish mining village of Illogan, he came to Exeter in the 1850s, became a Methodist preacher in 1855 at the age of twenty-four and continued to preach for nearly fifty years.[10] He obtained work as deputy chief clerk and later chief clerk to the registrar of the county court. In 1862 he became High Bailiff, at the same time practising as an accountant, and was one of the two elective city auditors from 1870 to 1878. He was mayor in 1881, certainly Exeter's first Methodist mayor and perhaps the first chartered accountant to be mayor of an English city. Active in the Devonshire Association, in whose *Transactions* his obituary was published in 1903, Andrew left a lasting physical mark on Exeter when in 1878 he and Thomas Rowe bought five old houses in Fore Street on behalf of the Mint Methodist church in order that they could be demolished.[11] By the time May was articled to him, Andrew was living at 18 Southernhay West, one of the best addresses in the city, and had an office in Bedford Circus, the centre of professional life in nineteenth-century Exeter.

Andrew's accountancy practice was adversely affected by the Bankruptcy Act of 1883 under which government officials took over a large part of the work previously carried out by private individuals. This Act, associated with Joseph Chamberlain, was not popular with the accountancy profession. Andrew was, however, appointed one of the new Official Receivers. May thus received a very good grounding in bankruptcy work (which helped him to obtain first place in his final examinations) but little practical experience of areas of accounting work such as auditing, investigations and taxation. Fortunately his bankruptcy skills were not completely wasted; an ability to apply figures to legal problems is transferable to many areas of accountancy.

Very important to May's subsequent career was his friendship with his fellow articled clerk, Charles William Westron, the son of an Exeter tea merchant. Westron set an example to May in three ways: by being placed fifth in the 1894 final examinations; by being the first person from Exeter to qualify as a chartered accountant by examination (Andrew and others had been admitted on experience alone); and by moving to London after qualification. May was the second person from Exeter to qualify by examination, surpassed Westron by coming first equal in his intermediate and first in his final and followed Westron to London. There were no other prizewinners from Exeter until the 1940s.

Both Andrew and Westron were committed writers, as May was to be. Andrew was the author of *Geological and Archaeological Papers*, published in 1875. Westron became a contributor to *Punch* and the author of four works of fiction set in Devon (*Salty*, 1919; *Combe Hamlet*, 1923; *More Salty*, 1924; *Salty Ashore*, 1929), plus a technical work entitled *The Bed-Rock of Double-Entry Book-keeping* (1924).

May and Westron shared their leisure as well as their work. Within easy walking distance of Bedford Circus, on the corner of Barnfield Road and Southernhay East, was Barnfield House, the recently acquired home of the Exeter Literary Society. The Society played an important part in the continuing education of the young George May. As a still existing inscription announces, the foundation stone of a new lecture hall was laid on 15 October 1890; the hall was officially opened on 23 July, 1891. The Society was at the height of its influence during May's five years in Exeter.[12]

The sixth pre-condition was *choosing the right firm after qualification*. May tells us that his first intention was to spend two or three years in a larger city gaining experience and then to return to Devon to open his own practice. Criddle obtained for him a favourable offer from a firm in Newcastle but May preferred London. Westron, who had joined the leading firm of Cooper Bros. in London in 1895, provided him with a list of suitable firms. Price Waterhouse was at the top of the list and after interview he was offered a job and started work on 15 February 1898 at a salary of £120 per annum. Westron, claimed May in the dedication to his memoirs, had led him in 'the only path that could have brought me to America'. He had been at Price Waterhouse for only five months when he was offered and accepted a post with Price Waterhouse's agents in New York, Jones, Caesar & Co. He sailed to America, reporting for work in New York on 28 July 1897. He was admitted as a partner in the American firm of Price Waterhouse in 1902 and became senior partner in 1911.

Although the 1890s was a top decade in migration from the United Kingdom, especially to North America, May's move overseas was not typical of English chartered accountants at that time. In 1898 only sixty-six (less than three per cent) of English chartered accountants were working outside the United Kingdom: twenty-four in the United States, eleven in India, ten in Australia, ten in South Africa, two in Canada, two in the Isle of Man and seven elsewhere. The attractions of the United States were the British investments there in need of audit and its relative closeness to Britain. Until 1891, India had been the most favoured overseas destination for English chartered accountants.

The seventh pre-condition was *not to have one's career disrupted or terminated by injury or death in war*. May was born in 1875, in what he called a 'placid era'. The many colonial wars, even those in South Africa at the turn of the century, were fought mainly by regular soldiers. May was not of an age to be called upon to fight in the First World War, although he registered for the United States draft in 1918 and worked for the United States Treasury. His family was not unaffected, however. According to Grady, May's younger brother Frank (who was about twenty-four years old in 1914) was seriously injured in the War.

May's eminent career as an American accountant was thus contingent on many things. In his memoirs, he puts it in terms of people: Partridge in Teignmouth, Thornton at Blundell's, Westron in Exeter, Dickinson in the US. He takes it for granted that he, like them, was male and white. Protestantism was important but not its form: Blundell's was Anglican, Andrew was Methodist, and Price Waterhouse a firm founded by Quakers. It was May's good fortune that his part of Devon possessed a good school. Blundell's gave him not only a good education but also increased his social status. He and his parents were right to favour a profession which, unlike the Indian Civil Service, readily accepted the sons of shopkeepers, which was experiencing rapid growth and which rewarded numeracy as well as literacy. Not going to university was not a handicap. Accountancy at this date was overwhelmingly a profession for non-graduates. It was fortunate that there was a firm of accountants in Exeter which

Figure 1. George O. May.
Reproduced courtesy of PricewaterhouseCoopers LLP.

although narrow in its work experience provided an encouraging environment and a colleague who acted as a role model. The move to London was perhaps inevitable, given the peripheral position of Devon in the British economy but the choice of Price Waterhouse was inspired.[13] All this said, May would still not have achieved his success as an accountant in the United States without his own considerable intellect, personality and ambition.

Many emigrants from England in the 1890s did not expect, or even sometimes greatly wish, to see their home country again. As a well paid professional, May was able to make frequent visits and maintain his strong family connections with Devon. He was back in England as early as December 1898 and January 1899, attending the wedding of his brother Henry (born 1873) to a local girl. May himself married Edith Mary Slocombe, the daughter of a retired builder, in Teignmouth on New Year's Day 1902, the same day on which he formally became a partner in the United States firm. His parents and siblings did not venture far from Teignmouth. After their marriage in Bristol, his parents lived in Teignmouth for the rest of their lives, latterly in Powderham Terrace. May's father died in 1927, leaving his estate to his wife. She died in 1933, dividing her residual estate among her surviving children, but bequeathing her jewellery to her daughters and to George such furniture as he wished to take. George and the three of his siblings who married (Henry, Frank and Winifred) all found their spouses in Teignmouth. Henry moved to Exeter where the trade directories record him as a hosier, hatter and glover at 1b High Street near the Eastgate, and later to Lymington in Hampshire, where he ran a shipbuilding yard. Frank (born *c.*1882), who married Florence Isabella H. Coe in 1905, became a hotel proprietor at the Rock House in Chudleigh. Winifred (born *c.*1878) married Wilfred Drake, a glass painter, (born *c.*1880) in 1905, moving to Exeter with her husband. Wilfred and his elder brother Frederick Morris Drake (born *c.*1876) carried on their business at Three Gables in Cathedral Yard. They were the authors and illustrators in 1912 and 1916 of books on stained glass and heraldry. Frederick Morris wrote in 1913 a brief centenary history of the Devon and Exeter Institution in Cathedral Close. He was also, under the name of Maurice Drake, a successful popular novelist.

What sort of man was the young George May? Arthur Lowes

Dickinson (1859–1935), himself a leading English chartered accountant, sixteen years older than May, wrote from New York in October 1902 to a London partner of Price Waterhouse that May 'was a very clever fellow & we all like him personally, but he has too high a opinion of himself at present and is very young'.[14] Eighty years later, another of Zeff's fourteen who made a difference to the history of the accountancy profession in the United States, Professor William Paton, who had grown up as a farm boy of Scottish descent in Michigan, recalled that he also had found May likeable but described him as 'a very conceited Englishman' (even though May had been an American citizen since 1909). At the same time, in Paton's view, he was 'a man of great courage, determination, and loyalty to his firm and his profession'.[15] May was also loyal to Devon, even if that county was not a place where he could have become a professional man of world-wide reputation.

Acknowledgements

I am grateful for the comments of C.W. Nobes, S.J. Sampson and S.A. Zeff and the unfailing helpfulness of the librarians of the Devon and Exeter Institution and of the archivist of Blundell's School.

Notes and References

1. Zeff 1987, p. 49.
2. Allen and McDermott 1993, p. 28.
3. Noon, 2002 p. 88.
4. Sellman 1967.
5. Noon 2002, p. 86.
6. Noon 2002.
7. Sampson 2004, pp. 287-8.
8. Noon 2002, p. 105.
9. Parker 2004.
10. Chick 1907, pp. 120, 137.
11. Chick 1907, p. 91, Le Mesurier 1962, pp. 27, 28, 31.
12. Hawkins 1920.
13. Havinden et al. 1991.
14. Allen and McDermot 1993, p. 49.
15. Paton 1981, pp. 91, 94.

Bibliography

Allen, D.G. and McDermott, K. (1993) *Accounting for Success. A history of Price Waterhouse in America 1890–1990*, Boston, Mass.: Harvard University Press.

Andrew, T. (1875) *Geological and Archaeological Papers*, Northampton: Dicey.

Chick, E. (1907) *A History of Methodism in Exeter and the Neighbourhood from the Year 1739 until 1907*, Exeter: S. Drayton & Sons.

Drake, F. M. (1912) *A History of English Glass Painting*, London: T. Werner Laurie.

Drake, F.M. (1913) *A Hundred Years with the Devon and Exeter Institution*, Exeter: Devon and Exeter Institution.

Drake, F.M. and Drake, W. (1916) *Saints and Their Emblems*, London: T. Werner Laurie.

Grady, P. (ed.) (1962) *The Memoirs and Accounting Thought of George O. May*, New York: Ronald.

Havinden, M.A., Quéniart, J. and Stanyer, J. (eds) (1991) *Centre and Periphery. Brittany and Cornwall&Devon compared*, Exeter: Exeter University Press.

Hawkins, S.J. (1920) *Exeter Literary Society: an epitome of eighty years work*, Exeter: Devon and Exeter Daily Gazette.

Le Mesurier, B. (1962) *A History of the Mint Methodist Church Exeter*, Exeter: Trustees, Mint Methodist Church.

Noon, C. (2002), *The Book of Blundell's*, Tiverton: Halsgrove.

Parker, R.H. (2004) 'Accountancy on the Periphery: the profession in Exeter to 1939', *Accounting, Business and Financial History*, March.

Paton, W.A. (1981) 'Recalling George Oliver May and Me', *Accounting Historians Journal*, Fall.

Sampson, M. (2004) *A History of Tiverton*, Tiverton: Tiverton War Memorial Trust.

Sellman, R. (1967) *Devon Village Schools in the Nineteenth Century*, Newton Abbot: David and Charles.

Zeff, S.A. (1987) 'Leaders of the Accounting Profession: 14 who made a difference', *Journal of Accountancy*, May.

George West: apprentice papermaker to American Congressman

Patricia Nash

In the Lady Chapel of St Disen's, the parish church of Bradninch, in Devon, there is a beautiful stained-glass window; beneath which is a brass dedication plaque. The inscription is as follows:

> TO THE GLORY OF GOD & TO THE DEAR
> MEMORY OF JANE WEST, WHO DIED 14th
> APRIL, AD 1854, THIS WINDOW IS
> ERECTED BY HER SON, THE HON: GEORGE
> WEST, MEMBER OF CONGRESS, US

Thirty-three years after his arrival in America, George West had not forgotten his mother, left behind in the church-yard in Bradninch. He had arranged for the window to be installed at his own expense, and erected a gravestone 'sacred' to her memory. George West, American congressman, had clearly prospered in his adopted country. His early life and apprenticeship in Bradninch, together with his own ability and ambition, formed the foundation of his future success.

George was born in 1822, the second of nine children. His father, also George, married Jane Blackmore in Bradninch in 1809 (see Appendix), where her family had lived for several generations. They had a daughter in the following year, who was baptised in Bradninch. Following the birth of their first child, the West's moved to the nearby village of Kentisbeare. The next five children, including their

305

son George, born in 1822, were baptised there. George West senior was listed as a papermaker each time. The family returned to live in Bradninch when George was four years old, and three further siblings were born. George senior had learnt the trade of papermaking following his father's premature death in Frome in 1795. This was not surprising as there were grist and flour mills in the majority of parishes situated in the river valleys of Somerset and Devon, and papermaking was started in some mills by the late eighteenth century, usually in redundant outbuildings.

Bradninch is a small town, ten miles from Exeter, situated in the low hills above the River Culm. In the early nineteenth century it was a compact entity with around 1500 inhabitants. It was typical of the time, with a population mainly of labourers and craftsmen. The surrounding farmland provided provisions for the town. Although daily life for the 'lower orders' meant constant hard work, long hours and low wages, not only for the breadwinner but also for the women running the home, Bradninch was nevertheless prosperous in comparison with the surrounding villages. Much of its security was due to the employment opportunities provided by local industries, including the paper mills beside the River Culm, where the inhabitants (including George West senior) sought employment in papermaking. The 1841 census shows that Jane West, her three youngest daughters, and two lodgers, worked as paper packers in the paper mill. Her two sons, Henry and George are listed as papermakers.

Young George West went to work at Kensham Paper Mills in Bradninch at the age of ten or twelve. Becoming a papermaker required a long apprenticeship; most boys who were taken on continued in low skilled work, or as labourers. John Dewdney, the owner of the Hele Mill, apprenticed George at the age of fourteen. He must have shown aptitude as sons of the resident workforce usually had preference. Over a seven year period George honed his skills with a renowned paper manufacturer. This was the height of the prosperity of paper-making in Devon, with Hele Mill at the forefront, due to its innovations. The mill was rebuilt after a fire in 1821, resulting in a modern structure which included gas lighting. A water turbine (for steam power) was installed, and the discovery of a spring water supply resulted in the production of better quality paper. New equipment enabled continuous rolls of paper to be produced, instead of handmade sheets. This opened up new opportunities and increased profit. John Dewdney invested in the latest industrial processes, and he invented the innovative system of 'glazing' writing paper, a superior product that found a ready market. The London to Exeter Railway (via Bristol) was laid by1844, and Dewdney was therefore able to improve the means of receipt of goods, as well as the despatch of his products. The new communication network passed through Hele, with a station and sidings next to the Mill. It replaced the use of horse and cart to the port of Topsham some ten miles away.

So George, as an apprentice, benefited from an inventive and positive management structure, and a reliable workforce to learn from. Being put in charge of the metal-works shop from the age of twenty-one meant that George learnt the craft of the papermaking process, as well as becoming knowledgeable about the machinery and the metal designs used for industrial watermarks. Watermarks had developed from producing handmade paper in wooden trays. When the wet-paper became thinner over the wooden slats, they showed up as lighter lines if the paper was held up to the light. Customers required individual watermarks (a recognisable image or pattern) that identified their product. These had to be impressed onto the paper during the manufacturing process using a device called a dandy roll. The dandy rolls were made of fine metal, and as the wet-paper passed over them it was compressed thinner. When the finished paper was held up, the design appeared as a lighter image.

In April 1844, George married his childhood sweetheart, Louisa Rose, whose family also lived in Bradninch. She gave birth to a son (see Appendix) in February 1845. George worked at Hele Mill until he was twenty-seven, and in February 1849 he emigrated to America with his wife and child. The reason why George emigrated is an interesting question. Living in a small Devon town, he would not have travelled far, and local events would have been of major importance to him and his neighbours. However his work in the paper mill had exposed him to innovations in industry, and business contacts brought him into contact with the wider world. In addition, George was no stranger to distress and hardship, and their impact on family life. In 1832, at the age of ten years, he had witnessed an extensive fire in the centre of the town, and at the same time, an outbreak of cholera in nearby Exeter which resulted in 402 deaths. The Bradninch burials records show

Figure 1. Portrait (engraving) of George West.
Reproduced courtesy of Douglas Mather Mabee.

that a third more people than usual died in the years 1832–35 due to outbreaks of cholera in the town, and George's youngest sibling James died in 1834.

The opportunities in the New World must have been compelling to a hard-working and highly skilled craftsman from rural Devon. It was however a major parting from the extended family, as news from either side would only be known long after any event. George, Louisa, and four year old George sailed across the Atlantic from Liverpool on a three-masted sailing ship, the *Isaac Wright*. The passenger list recorded a second child, 'Amber, female, an infant born at sea'.[1] Much later their traumatic early days in New York were described by George:

You see, when Mother [George's name for his wife Louisa] and I landed at Castle Garden from the old country in 1849 we were very poor. Our baby became sick and died. We had no money to bury the dear little baby and they took her from us . . . I have hunted the records many years and visited all the graveyards in New York City below Canal Street in the hope that I could get some trace of the dear dead baby's resting-place.[2]

It was a sad start to the new life and must have lowered their expectations.

At first, they lived near New York, where George worked in a paper mill in New Jersey, but within a year the family relocated over a hundred miles inland. George obtained employment in a paper mill in Tyringham, Massachusetts, that specialised in the manufacture of writing paper. He worked as a production papermaker, but was allowed to experiment. In February 1850, using skills learnt at Hele mills, he made a designed watermark. He invented a method of positioning the watermark against the dandy roll so that when the roll of paper was later cut to the required writing paper sizes, the image appeared in the centre of each sheet. This was the first such watermark produced in America. George's success demonstrates a determination to succeed in his new life through a combination of skill and energy. In the following year he took on the management of the paper mill of J.R. Smith and Co. at Russell, Massachusetts, and remained in charge until 1858. His time at Tyringham was consolidated at Russell, where he managed to save enough money to buy a quarter ownership of a paper mill in Cummington, Massachusetts, which included a full management role.[3]

During that time George suffered the loss of his mother, who died in 1854, but also joy at the birth of his son Walter, born in December of that year. His daughter, Florence Louise, was born two years later in July 1856. George's seventy-year old father left Bradninch following the death of his wife, and joined his son in America. George was prosperous by this time and able to support his father. He realised that there would have been no place for him in England other than the workhouse. George senior was accompanied on the journey by his eldest daughter, Elizabeth Mortimore and her family. Over the next few years three of George's siblings from Bradninch also decided to join them (Louisa Pitts, Martha Brown and his brother Henry and their families). Three married sisters remained in Devon.

George sold his shares in the Cummingtom Mill in 1860, and accepted an interest in the Empire Mill at Rock City Falls, Saratoga

Figure 2. Print of Empire Mill.
Reproduced courtesy of Douglas Mather Mabee.

County, New York State. Unwilling to undertake the venture blindly, he refused to go ahead with the deal until he had first worked in the mill for about a year. In June 1862, he purchased the Empire Mill outright for approximately $3,000 and conducted it with great success.[4]

George's purchase of the Empire Mill coincided with the difficult period of the American Civil War (1861–1865), and despite being a relative newcomer to the country he supported the abolition movement. There were at the same time opportunities to increase his prosperity and standing in the North. To quote from the Chronicles of Saratoga:

> the great scarcity of southern cotton during the Civil War period opened up a challenge to Mr West. Cotton for bags, so needed at the time as carry-alls for everything was at a minimum. Many cotton mills closed . . . leasing an idle mill, Mr West announced he would make bags of paper to fill the need. Doubt and scepticism were rife. Could a bag he made be strong enough to carry 50 pounds of flour? "No" said everyone, even Mr West's staunchest admirers. The young man who

had begun the manufacture of paper when very young was sure of himself and of his thorough training and he demonstrated it by producing manila paper bags that carried 50 pounds of flour.[5]

He was able to manufacture manila bags by using secondary fibres from the rope-making industry, which came from the stalks of the wild banana tree or plantain, imported from Manila in the Philippine Islands. Within weeks, orders were pouring in from all over the world. The bags were initially made by hand, but in an effort to speed up the manufacturing process George hired a designer who had come into his office at Rock City Falls with a plan to construct a machine which he maintained could do the work with great rapidity. Within a few weeks the machine was operational. The mechanical principles of the first paper bag machine, as used at the Empire Mill, are identical to more modern machines still in use today.[6]

George West was a pioneer in the manufacture of paper bags, which was one of the largest specialised industries in the decades that followed, continuing into the next century, long after his retirement. This was the foundation of his business and his fortune. By 1878 he had become the largest manufacturer of manila paper in the world, owning eight or nine mills in Saratoga County. He moved forward with innovation; he updated the machinery, introduced automatic steam pumps, had fire extinguishing systems installed, added electric lighting, and had the mills connected by telephone. He arranged the construction of a side rail-line from the Delaware and Hudson Railroad to some of his premises in 1878, combined with a freight house for storage at the railway depot. It made sense to find a local secure source of the basic material, so in the 1880s he purchased and maintained his own 8,000 acre spruce forest at Kaydeross Creek, Saratoga County. He perfected a new chemical sulphite process that made the wood-pulp mixture equal in strength and quality to the earlier manila paper.

George now ran his industrial empire from the huge Union Mill, in Ballston Spa, with the bag factory adjacent to it, and his own private residence opposite the site. It was estimated that his total output exceeded that of any other paper manufacturer either in the United States, or in Europe. He expanded to become a wholesale merchant of paper in New York City, and owned a store there with four presses

Figure 3. Union Bag and Paper Company.
Reproduced courtesy of Douglas Mather Mabee.

that produced personalised printed bags for grocers. It was said of him that he had at his command a thorough practical knowledge of every phase of the industry, executive talent, a genius for organisation, and tremendous energy.[7]

He also expanded into real estate, a creosote factory and mining; became a founder of the First National Bank of Ballston Spa; the owner of the 'Union' newspaper in Schenectady, and Director of the *Herald* newspaper in Utica. Later in his business life he saw opportunity in the need for 'carry-alls' stronger than bags, and expanded into the manufacture of cardboard boxes. In 1892 he was one of the Founders of The National Folding Box Company, formed with the patent for folded cardboard boxes which could be easily packaged and folded into boxes known as 'Tiffany', in that they were suitable for anything from packaged ladies' dresses, to nails, to soda pop, to light bulbs!

George finally retired from business in 1899, at the age of seventy-seven. He sold his paper production empire in its entirety to the Union Bag and Paper Co. for $1,500,000. Members of George's family were involved in this company, so there was a continuation of close practical family management.

During his long career George had become interested in wider political issues, and became actively involved with the Republican Party. In 1872 he entered public office as a member of the State Assembly from Saratoga County, serving five terms, from 1872 to 1876. During the last term he was Chairman of the Railway Committee. In his candidacy for the Assembly in the fall of 1872, not a single vote was recorded against him, a phenomenon that had never occurred before. His popularity in politics was remarkable. He was an able and practical man, and a convincing speaker. Thousands turned out to hear him, and he won them over with his frank and friendly manner.[8]

Three years later, in 1875 he was a candidate in Convention for the Assembly nomination against the Honourable Webster Wagner. The spirited contest attracted attention throughout the State, and the result was so close that on the final ballot George West was defeated by only one vote.[9] He remained out of office for four years. In 1880 George moved up the political ladder when he was elected to Congress in the United States central administration. He represented Saratoga County for the Twentieth New York District, completing three two-year terms (1881–1883, 1885–1887, and 1887–1889). During this period he served on several committees on manufactures and agriculture, and he enrolled bills.

George West advocated the value of protectionism due to his experiences both as a manufacturer, and as an employer. He also supported government ownership of the railways, and of the telegraphic lines that linked the whole country. As a legislator he was held in high esteem. He was considered upright in his principles, and was reported as saying 'I represent my constituents, not George West'.[10] In 1886 his re-nomination for the 1887 Congress was ensured, because when it was doubtful whether he would accept the Republican re-nomination, the chief Democratic leaders urged him to accept, declaring that no Democratic candidate would be nominated![11] They kept their word and he was elected without opposition. George was also a delegate to the National Republican Conventions in 1880, 1884 and 1886. He was the first to advocate Benjamin Harris for the presidency, and Levi P. Morton for the vice-presidency in 1888. In addition, he was a member of the Board of Trade and Transportation; of the American Geographical Society; and of the Republican Club of New York City.

He did not stand for re-nomination for Congress in 1889, but retired to resume his business activities.

George's personality was integral to his political success. He was honest, down to earth, and a gifted communicator. He was not a proud man and enjoyed jokes about his looks. In later life he was described as short, with an immense body, short legs, a large aggressive mouth, a large flat nose and a forehead that was round and high. His long grey beard added to his striking and original appearance. He was plain in attire almost to severity, 'but was known as Uncle George for all the world like the gentle, loveable old "Pickwick" that he was in heart and mind.'[12]

Figure 4. The George West Museum of Art and Archaeology.
Reproduced courtesy of Douglas Mather Mabee.

However, George's life was broader than just his business and political success. He devoted a great deal of his time to community projects in his home town of Ballston Spa. As treasurer of the Round Lake Association, he saved their camping grounds and donated $20,000 to build the George West Museum of Art and Archaeology, with a further $25,000 for its endowment fund. He was a deeply religious man, and covered one half of the cost of building the Methodist Episcopal Church, along with a fine parsonage. He supported other religious institutions, making large contributions towards the erection of the Baptist Chapel and the Roman Catholic Church in that same town.

David Walton Mabee, a grandson of George and Louisa, recalled being told, 'when there was no electrical call system within the Mill, Grandfather could put his two fingers in his mouth and you could hear his whistle clearly and distinctly above the roar of the machinery.' He also remembered that his grandfather George 'when he would return from Washington, his Victoria and team of horses would meet him at the station. There, mill employees would unhitch the horses and they themselves would pull the Victoria and Grandfather to his home; I saw that many times; then in the very late 1890's Grandfather George had a car.'[13]

George did encounter some problems towards the end of his career. There were several lawsuits against him in the late-nineteenth century regarding pollution of the Kayderosseras River at the site of his mills. These are seldom mentioned in the somewhat fulsome biographies of the time. Nevertheless, George West continues to be described in more recent research on Saratoga County as a larger than life personality.[14] He died in September 1901, aged seventy-nine, just nine months after the death of his beloved wife. It was estimated that his estate was worth $3,000,000 at the time of his death.

Even though he chose to emigrate to America, George West could have been called a Victorian entrepreneur. His devotion to Queen Victoria was unfaltering, and yet his loyalty to the flag of his adopted country was one of his endearing traits.[15] During his lifetime George returned to Bradninch for regular visits. He told friends that he wanted to help people on both sides of the Atlantic in a practical way. He had not forgotten the financial and social difficulties of his early years, and always carried a memento of those distressing days. This was a piece of paper made in southern England showing the watermark of 1837 that he had been involved with when apprenticed at Hele Mills.[16] As well as private help to individuals, the Bradninch Borough recorded three gifts of charity from George West. He donated £100 to the Church Schools, £100 to the Baptist School, and £100 for the benefit of the poor in the Parish. The latter was to help disabled children to learn a trade; to support clubs supplying coal and clothes; and to assist those in hardship with practical needs.

He also provided educational support through contributions to the reading rooms, the library and clubs for working-men in the parish. These were very practical aims and showed an understanding that ordinary working men needed support and encouragement in order to advance themselves.

An important public event took place in Bradninch in 1883 when, 'The Hon. George West, Congressman of the American Government was received by the Mayor and Corporation and greeted by the best people of the neighbourhood and given a public reception and banquet'.[17] Although George had by this time built up a vast business empire in his adopted country, he had clearly not forgotten his origins. If he had chosen to stay in England he would probably have prospered, and may well have been politically active in the latter half of the nineteenth century. However, George took on the challenge of American life and its expansive opportunities. He was as successful in politics as he was in business, and as a popular and industrious Congressman he had a wide-ranging influence both locally and nationally. George West had taken a creative leap forward in order to establish himself in America, and was hugely successful in all his endeavours.

Notes and References.

1. United States National Archives. New York Immigration Arrivals. The '*Isaac Wright*' Passenger list 26 February 1849.
2. *The Sun*, (New York) 1901, 'Reminiscences of George West'.
3. Ibid.
4. *The New York Times*, 20 October 1901; *New York Herald*, 16 January 1902, Obituaries of George West.
5. Anon. 1899. <www.onlinebiographies.info/ny/sara/west-g.htm>.
6. *The Saratogian*, 1951, 'Chronicles of Saratoga'.
7. Ibid.
8. *The New York Times*, 9 and 30 September 1884; 18 October 1886; 30 March and 18 April 1887; 1 August 1888; 17 February 1892.
9. Ibid.
10. Ibid.
11. Ibid.
12. *Ballston Journal*, August 1889, 'West, George – History of the Great New Yorker'.
13. Family records in private ownership; David Mabee (1924) 'My Grand-father George West'.

14. Starr 2008, p. 34
15. Croslegh 1911, pp. 34-62.
16. *The Sun Newspaper* (New York) 1901, 'Reminiscences of George West'.
17. Croslegh 1911, pp. 309-315 and pp. 340-341.

Bibliography

Anon. (1899) Biography of George West, [online] <www.onlinebiographies. info/ny/sara/west-g.htm>.

Biographical Directory of the United States Congress, 1774 to the present, [online] Available at: <http://bioguide.congress.gov/scripts/biodisplay. pl?index=woc>.

Croslegh, C. (1911) *History of Bradninch*, Alexander Moring Ltd: De La More Press, London.

Starr, Timothy (2008) *Lost Industries of the Kaydeross Valley, a history of manufacturing in Ballston Spa, New York*, The History Press: Brookside Museum.

Stone, William Leete (1880) *Reminiscences of Saratoga and Ballston*, New York: R. Worthington.

Appendix
George West's Family Tree

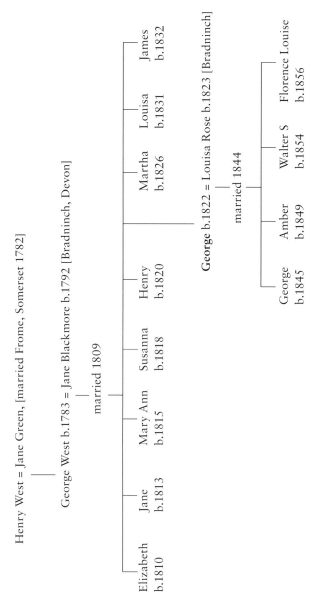

Henry West = Jane Green, [married Frome, Somerset 1782]

George West b.1783 = Jane Blackmore b.1792 [Bradninch, Devon]

married 1809

Elizabeth b.1810 | Jane b.1813 | Mary Ann b.1815 | Susanna b.1818 | Henry b.1820 | Martha b.1826 | Louisa b.1831 | James b.1832

George b.1822 = Louisa Rose b.1823 [Bradninch]

married 1844

George b.1845 | Amber b.1849 | Walter S b.1854 | Florence Louise b.1856

George's brother Henry and his sisters, Elizabeth, Martha, Louisa, with their families followed George to America. Jane and Mary Ann with their families moved to Exeter. Susanna and her family stayed in Bradninch. James died aged two. George's son, George, had three sons; and Florence Louise, his daughter, had four sons and three daughters. Walter S. died aged twenty and Amber died soon after birth.

318

From Wool to Electricity

Sue Price and Jean Rhodes

During the nineteenth century, the small Dartmoor town of Chagford prospered from the innovations of two remarkable men – John Berry, who is said to have built the woollen factory in the town in 1800, and George Henry Reed, who from 1889, used the water wheel of the disused factory for the generation of electricity. Chagford has a long history of innovation, which perhaps explains why it attracted these men of ideas who knew how to harness the power of its abundant water supply. Their efforts led to Chagford becoming, firstly, a wool manufacturing town, at a time when the Devon woollen industry was in decline, and secondly, one of the first small towns west of London to have electric street lighting. The South Western Electricity Historical Society places Chagford fourth in Devon: the much larger towns of Okehampton, Lynton and Lynmouth being earlier.[1]

W.G. Hoskins places the invention of the fulling mill in the thirteenth century.[2] 'Cloth mills' are recorded at Chagford Bridge in 1224.[3] The Churchwardens' Accounts of 1480–1600 show much profit from wool and tin. Chagford was made one of the four Stannary towns in Devon by Edward I in 1305. As such, it was the administrative centre for the assay and taxation of smelted tin, mined on Dartmoor by any person living in the area encompassed by the North Devon coast to the centre of Dartmoor, and from the banks of the river Taw in the west to the Devon–Somerset border in the east. Exeter was part of Chagford Stannary!

The history of the Berry family is confused, not least because of the frequency of naming Berry sons either John or Richard. There is no documentary evidence of 'John' Berry's arrival in Chagford, or exact dates and details for the establishment of the various mill buildings or their functions. Yet it is part of the town's oral tradition that 'John' Berry came from Ashburton in 1800 to build a woollen mill. It is sometimes claimed that a shortage of labour in Ashburton prompted the move.[4] Builders, by the name of Stone, came from the Tiverton–Thorverton area to construct the mill.[5] John Berry died in 1848. His tomb in Chagford churchyard records his age to be fifty-seven. Aged ten in 1800 therefore, the business would appear to have been started by older relatives.

From Land Tax Assessments we find, in 1784, a John Berry occupying 'part Town Estate' owned by Mr Leach. An Edward Leach was a sergemaker here in 1753, with house, warehouses, stable, barn, shop, linney and cellar forming a court;[6] a common arrangement in the domestic industry.[7] The name Leach is connected with the Berry family in the years to come. A more likely candidate for opening the

Figure 1. Berry's House. Rhodes collection.

mill in 1800 is one Richard Berry who owned 'Lawn House' in Mill Street.[8] This is next door to Moorlands, once a factory building, in the forecourt of which John Berry built a house in 1820.[9] This house was pulled down again only a few decades later but an early photograph and an etching exist with the title 'Berry's House'.

Pigot's Directory for 1822-3[10] lists a Richard Bury (misspelling of names is common in earlier documents), as a Chagford woollen manufacturer. In 1828 Richard Berry died and his son John Berry is among the beneficiaries of his will. Mill buildings are not specified among Richard's properties, although he is described as a serge manufacturer. He bequeathed 'the house wherein I now live'. On 21 August 1828 the *Exeter Flying Post* reported:

> Sunday evening at Chagford, Richard Berry Esq. age 71, for a number of years proprietor of one of the most extensive serge manufactures in the West of England. His strictly honourable and undeviating principles through life justly entitle him to be ranked among the most eminent and respectable manufacturers in the kingdom.[11]

Now thirty-eight, perhaps John was already an owner. Messrs. Richard Berry and Son at Chagford are listed as one of the principal woollen manufacturers of Devon in 1829.[12] Further evidence for the succession at the mill from Richard to John Berry comes from apprenticeship records: 1800 – 'William Aish age 8 apprentice to Richard Berry for Chagford Mill';[13] 1833 – 'John Jeffery age 9 apprenticed to John Berry for Chagford Mills'.[14]

By 1841 John Berry's family was well established in Chagford. He had married Susanna Bovey in Ashburton in 1816. The 1841 census lists John Berry as a 'Serge Manufacturer' with a son, Richard Leach Berry and daughter, Elizabeth Leach Berry. Another daughter Susan Bovey Berry is known. From the tithe apportionment and map of 1841 we can see how much property and land John Berry had acquired (see Plate 23). Springs and streams running through some of these fields augmented the water supply to factory buildings.

John Berry, woollen manufacturer, died in 1848. His will, apart from bequests to his wife Susanna and his three children, specified sale of his 'said Freehold, Copyhold and Leasehold Messuages, Tenements, Lands, Mills, Hereditaments and Premises by public auction or

Private contract'.[15] The manufacture of woollen goods includes many processes: wool sorting, scouring and combing; spinning, weaving, fulling, shearing, drying and the storage of finished cloth.[16] We can only assume that these took place in the several large factory buildings included in John Berry's estate.

An estimate from William Stone for building work at the Higher or Woollen Factory at Chagford Cross provides rare evidence for an 'engineers shop' and 'weaving and spinning shops' here.[17] At nearby Millpond, 'the ground floor was used as a fulling mill' (probably of much earlier date) and the louvred upper floor was a 'cloth drying loft'.[18] This louvred area also suggests a dye house which requires circulating air. The Lower or Blanket Factory at Rivervale Close (once known as Down Factory), had nearby a Rack Park for tentering and a 300 foot drying shed in Rackfield. It has been said that Lower Factory opened about 1820, on the site of an earlier corn mill (see Plate 24).[19] The undershot waterwheels of both these factories were served by a leat from the river Teign at Holy Street, augmented at Lower Factory by the Padley Brook out of Millpond. This brook is fed by springs rising between Meldon and Nattadon hills, some collected into a reservoir and the Town Leat, some crossing Padley Common as a stream. A large factory building, served by a branch of the Town Leat, was situated in Mill Street in the town. Now 'Moorlands', part of this was converted into a dwelling, perhaps when 'Berry's House' in its forecourt was demolished – date unknown – and perhaps for Richard Leach Berry.

The population of Chagford rose during the first half of the nineteenth century from 1,115 in 1801 to 1,836 in 1841.[20] Adult occupations in *Chagford Baptisms 1813–1826*,[21] and the 1841 census, list many woolpickers, woolsorters, woolcombers, fullers, abb spinners, serge weavers and packers. The most valuable contemporary evidence is provided by the Reverend T. Moore who, in 1829, recorded Devon manufacture of 'long ells' – unusually long cloths with combed wool warps and carded wool wefts in a twill weave – for the East India Company. He noted that of all Devon wool towns,

> the largest factory of this article is that of Messrs. Berry of Chagford. Here were made long ells or serges of various widths and lengths, blankets, miners' cloths etc. The number of hands included 115 men,

127 women and 98 children besides the weavers at Chagford and various surrounding parishes to the distance of 16 miles and upwards which exceed 800, amounting in all to 1140 operatives.[22]

The cloth was transported to Ashburton by wagon.[23] The Chagford to Ashburton road was constructed between 1780 and 1800.[24] The last military contract is said to have been for horse blankets for the British Army engaged in the Crimean War.[25] This success must be compared to the decline of the Devon woollen industry as a whole, due in part to the 'formidable competition of the Yorkshire trade which, by the 1780s, was turning to steam power based on cheap coal and organising itself in ever larger units'.[26]

An auction of John Berry's estate is known to have taken place after his death in 1848. Sadly there are no records to establish who bought his land and property holdings. We have no exact date for the closure of the business, but the 1851 census lists few woolworkers, and notes a population decrease to 1,557 persons which is attributed to the decline of the woollen trade.[27] Billings in 1857 notes the woollen trade 'entirely ceased'.[28] It is probable that the buildings fell into disuse. John Berry's son is not known as a wool manufacturer. Richard Leach Berry Esq., gentleman, had become a landed proprietor, listed second to the Earl of Devon in White's Directory for Chagford in 1850.[29] An estimate from W. Stone to R.L. Berry in 1867 for 'repairing the slate work on roofs of Higher and Lower Factories'[30] is the only evidence so far seen of Richard Berry's continuing financial interest after his father's death.

The business was later re-opened – the exact date is unknown – by John Fulford Vicary, a wool manufacturer from North Tawton, with a mill in Crediton. It is noted that 'one of the last Chagford serge manufacturers acquired a spinning monopoly for his mills within a sixteen mile radius while Crediton was obliged to range as far afield as Cornwall to find the necessary spinners and weavers'.[31] Vicary helped to set up the Chagford Gas Company in 1869, to supply the town of Chagford, the factories and the neighbourhood with gas and coke. The first mention of 'half time pupils from the factory' in the Chagford Parochial School log books, is also in 1869. They are 'absent a good deal' but the foreman did not dismiss them because 'he would have to stop the men whose engines they look after'.[32]

Power loom workers are first mentioned in the 1871 census. Although White's Directory notes 'a serge and blanket factory' in 1878-79,[33] we do not know the exact date of the factory closure. The last mention of 'Factory children' in the school log books is in 1878. [34]

It was indeed fortunate for George Henry Reed's later electrical enterprise that he was asked by Mr Vicary, in 1875, to provide two estimates for the repair or replacement of the old fourteen by fourteen foot waterwheel at Higher Factory. The repair included,

> new sets of arms; repair to all buckets, (80 in the whole); jointing backing planks and refixing; and all bolts and ironwork £84.15s [though he] could not guarantee the other part of the wheel [and the shaft was] 'also in a state of decay. [The cost of a new waterwheel], Fourteen feet diameter and thirteen feet in clear of shrouds made of all iron and hung on a wrought iron shaft 8" diameter to suit the waterway at the Chagford Higher Factory fixed complete would be the sum of Two hundred and eighty pounds three shillings this price does not include taking down the old wheel or any masonry that may be required.[35]

We do not know whether one of these estimates was accepted, only that some years after the final closure of the woollen mills Mr Reed took a twenty-one year lease on Higher Factory and used the waterwheel to establish a saw mill there.

George Henry Reed was the son of a naval captain from Portsmouth. The captain had lost his first wife – George Reed's mother – and remarried. The second wife, not wishing to bring up another woman's child when her husband was at sea, arranged for George to be sent to a boarding school during term time and then to his father's sister, Aunt Spencer, for the holidays. She was a kindly woman of whom George became very fond, later incorporating her name in those of some of his children, and she looked after him until it was time to begin his career.

In the early 1860s, George Henry Reed, aged twenty, came to Chagford to train as an engineer and machinist, working for John and William Dicker. They are listed in Morris' 1857 Directory[36] as wheelwrights, engineers and machinists and located in High Street, although Billings Directory[37] lists the firm as agricultural implement makers. In 1865, George married Susan Aggett, daughter

Figure 2. Rushford Works plaque.
Rowe collection.

of Henry Aggett, innkeeper at the Three Crowns Posting House and Commercial Hotel. The following year, their first child Lily Jane was born. By the end of 1869 he had established a business of his own at Rushford Works, in buildings he specially constructed on the fields above Rushford Bridge. This site is half a mile downstream from Lower Factory.

His enterprise grew over the next twenty years. An entry in Kelly's Directory of 1893 lists George Henry Reed merely as 'Engineer, millwright, and machinist; thrashing machine and traction engine proprietor; and manure merchant at Rushford Works' and also with 'saw mills at The Factory'.[38] But four years earlier, he had also established one of the first hydro-electric power stations in the country on this site. The Chagford and Devon Electric Light Company was formed in 1889 and incorporated on 18 November 1890, with capital of £2,000 in 2,000 shares of £1 each.[39]

The prospectus claimed that electric light would be cheaper, cleaner and healthier than the gas lighting in the town and expected 'a good margin of profit at £1 per sixteen-candle power lamp – a dividend

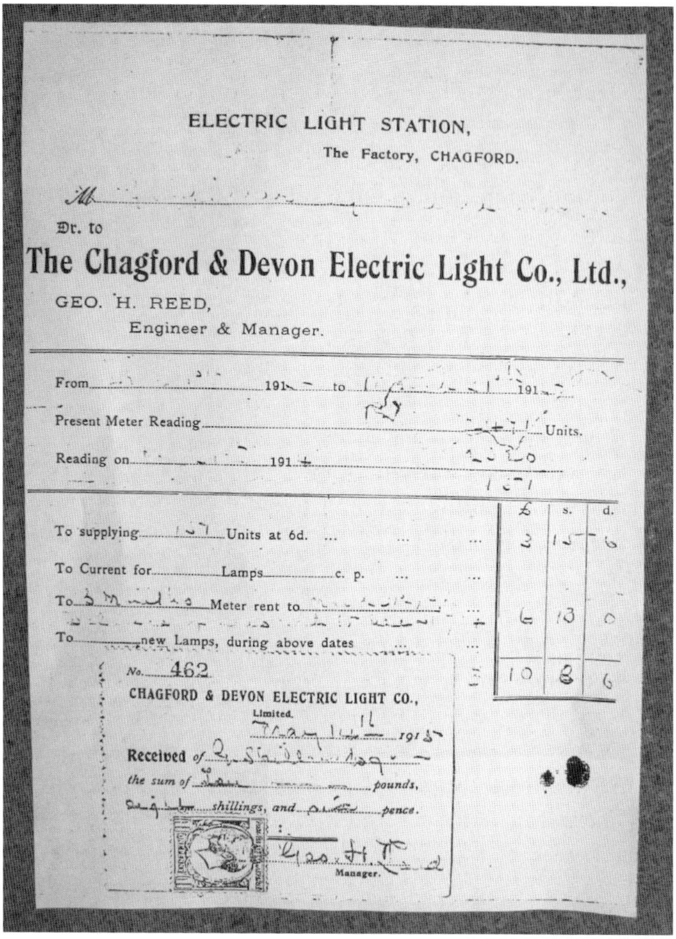
ELECTRIC LIGHT STATION,
The Factory, CHAGFORD.

M.

Dr. to

The Chagford & Devon Electric Light Co., Ltd.,

GEO. H. REED,
Engineer & Manager.

From ... 191 ... to ... 191 ...
Present Meter Reading ... Units.
Reading on ... 191 ...

	£	s.	d.
To supplying ... Units at 6d. ...	3	15	6
To Current for ... Lamps ... c. p. ...			
To ... Meter rent to ...	6	13	0
To ... new Lamps, during above dates ...			
	10	8	6

No. 462
CHAGFORD & DEVON ELECTRIC LIGHT CO.,
Limited.
... 1915
Received of ...
the sum of ... pounds,
... shillings, and ... pence.
Manager.

Figure 3. Chagford & Devon Electric Light Company.
Rowe collection.

of seven per cent, rising to fifteen per cent. Furthermore, 'many of the present consumers of gas in Chagford have guaranteed in writing to adopt the electric light, which will close the Gas Company'.[40] A contemporary poem, written by G.H. Hurrell, highlights this competition between electricity and gas. The poem was found by Dartmoor explorer and author Harry Starkey among old papers in an Ashburton bookshop in the 1980s. Hurrell was the blind organist at St Michael's Church, Chagford, and he lodged with the Reed family at Teign View.

The Chagford Electric Light

Dear Friends! The Electric Light draws nigh,
I hope you can see it with your natural eye,
Gas is a thing we can well do without,
For in Chagford they tell me its not much count.

Mr. Reed, McSweeney and Bartlett too,
I am sure they are trying their work well to do,
So I hope my dear people you will do what is right,
And take in the beautiful Electric Light.

Winter will come, yes after a time,
My words you will find I have put into rhyme,
No candles or matches, but turn on the switch,
Enabling the tailor to sew a fine stitch.

So now I have done and shall say no more,
These words I do mean to rich and to poor,
So friends pull together one and all with your might,
And bless good old Chagford and the Electric Light.

At Chagford the gaslight will soon be put out,
There is little to fear and nothing to doubt,
The Electric was lit on Wednesday night last,
There's nothing that glorious light can surpass.

Dear people you've seen the Light with your eyes,
If you do without Gas, I am sure you'll be wise,
So take my advice which I give one and all,
And very soon in Chagford you'll have no Gas at all.

Its cool, its harmless, it is free from all fire,
I'm sure you can touch the Electric wire,
One thing you can do and that you'll find right,
Just turn on the switch and there is the Light.

Goodbye my dear people! God Bless you dear folks,
My words I do mean and I'm sure they're not jokes,
Take heed my dear friends and read what I say,
And Chagford at night will be light as the day.

A parish magazine from 1891 expands on the entrepreneurial nature of George Reed:

There has been much talk lately about the electric light which it is proposed to introduce into Chagford. Mr. Reed has been showing off the light in the old factory which he has taken and many people assembled on two occasions to see it. The question of conveying it underground or overground by poles has been considered at a meeting of the ratepayers of Chagford. Some were in favour of wires being carried underground and not overhead. It was pointed out that to insist on this would practically defeat the scheme. On a show of hands being taken 25 voted for the wires being carried overground and 14 against. We hope that the electric light may find its way into Chagford, as there is such excellent water power existing, it seems a pity not to use it. We wish the promoters all success.[41]

An early edition of *The Electrician* records that Mr Reed:

installed two 20-unit 2,000-volt Siemens alternators, running at 850 revolutions, excited from two shunt-wound Crompton dynamos. The mains consist of two lead covered cables, $7/16$ B.W.G., manufactured by the Norwich Insulated Wire Company. The cable is laid underground in stout oak casing, tarred outside. A considerable part of the road had to be blasted before the cable could be laid. The 2,000-volt mains run to five distributing points, where transformers of the 'Hedgehog' type are fixed.[42]

The town was first lit by electricity on 1 September 1891. Parish Council Minutes of 1896 record: 'Chagford Electric Light Company offered to supply light of 32 candlepower for the sum of £2 per lamp per annum. Tender accepted'.[43] Another story from a 1935 edition of *The Western Morning News*, recalls that some forty years earlier, a young man hoping to secure the curacy in Chagford walked ten miles from Yeoford Station along the lanes: 'How reassuring it was to see, perhaps a mile away, bright lights on a hill and to know that Chagford was in sight'.[44] Today it is difficult to imagine the impression this made on him, when electric light in the countryside was unknown.

In 1906 George Reed continued to be listed as an electrical engineer

Figure 4. George Henry Reed with his son George Spencer (centre) and brother in law James Weeks. Rowe collection.

living at Teign View, near his Rushford Works.[45] Susan his wife was by then letting apartments there. His oldest son William had taken a job as an electrical engineer with the Marconi Company in Cornwall, leaving the family business. His second son George Spencer assisted his father in the family firm, whilst his daughter Bessie Spencer, helped her mother in the house with the boarding accommodation. Susan died in 1909. By 1910 Bessie Spencer Reed had taken charge of the Teign View apartments. She also cared for her father, who continued to employ several men, and run his engineering business and the electricity generating station with the help of his son George Spencer, now married to Lilian Mary Ellis and living with their baby son, Henry George Spencer Reed, at Ingledene in New Street. The family had a second child, a daughter Edna Mary, later Edna Rowe.

In the years following his wife's death, George Reed's engineering and traction business was gradually wound down. The introduction of farm owned tractors gradually replaced the use of traction engines, and new agricultural engineering companies such as Saunders and Rowe at Easton (later C.J. Saunders of Easton and Whiddon Down) and James Osborne in Chagford, provided greater competition. In addition, his son was spending the greater part of his time maintaining the electricity generating station. It is reported that:

> in 1911 the alternator was replaced with a DC generator, the AC system being changed to a 200 volt DC system. A gas engine was installed to operate in parallel with the waterwheel. The old waterwheel was struggling to support the new equipment, so in 1914 a 30hp turbine thought to be of American manufacture was installed.[46]

During the 1920s George Henry Reed sold the Chagford plant to W.G. Heath and Co. of Plymouth. Their bills were headed Chagford Electricity Supply Co., and by this time there were '80 consumers and 22 public lamps'.[47] In 1924 plans were made to extend the supply to Moretonhampstead. Mr Reed's engineering business was sold to William Denham of Swindonia, Chagford, who ran the traction engines with Fred Denham, his brother. George Henry died at Teign View in 1930. His son George Spencer Reed continued to run the family business.

Many small plants in Devon were amalgamated in 1931 when The West Devon Electric Supply Company was formed by Christy Bros. of Chelmsford. In 1933 when they were preparing to bring a modern AC supply to Chagford via a high voltage line:

> The firm brought with them their demonstration showroom, which was supplied from the old plant as Chagford was not then on the new supply. A cooker was connected for demonstration purposes, and the consternation on the face of Mr Reed was something to see, as his pet plant nearly went up in flames. The load was so considerable that the plant just could not cope with it.[48]

The Higher Factory walls were lowered for safety reasons in 1935 and extensive ruins remain to this day. The electricity plant carried on however. A three phase alternator was installed in 1940. In 1948 electricity generation was nationalised, and another new generator was installed. In 1967, J. Hellier wrote of Chagford's input to the National Grid:

> The truism about there being no sentiment in business does not apply here. The turbine only provides sufficient power to light about 20 houses – only one house if fitted with all modern appliances – but central authority is reluctant to dispose of its good and faithful servant, housed in a 15ft. square shed, which except for a dry summer when the leat level drops and a cold winter when ice blocks the turbine, still turns out about 20 kilowatts to help keep Chagford's houses bright.[49]

Electricity was reorganised again in 1989. At that time the gate to the small plant at Chagford bore the proud legend 'NATIONAL POWER plc'. Things changed again in 2000. Western Power became the new providers for the area, but by then Chagford Power Station had been sold to the South West Hydro Group based at Mary Tavy, where Mr. Reed's old turbine was taken for renovation and repair. At

Figure 5. Mr Reed's original 1914 turbine. Rowe collection.

this time it was seen by Gilkes of Cumbria who thought they might have made it, and considered it a most unusual design.

Unfortunately, just when the residents of Chagford wanted to restore and mount the old turbine as a memorial to its industrial past, it was judged beyond saving and sent to a scrapyard. Plymouth University recently used the station as a test site for a small hydro-motor. Will power ever be generated at Chagford's historic site again? This may depend on the growing interest in energy provision from renewable sources. It would be a fitting tribute to the energy and vision of Mr 'John' Berry and Mr George Henry Reed.

Notes and References

1. Lamb, <www.swehs.co.uk>.
2. Hoskins 1972, p. 124. Fulling is the process of cleaning, shrinking and thickening cloth using soap or Fullers' Earth and pounding with heavy wooden stamps powered by a water wheel.
3. Hayter-Hames 1981, p. 18.
4. Ibid, p. 89.
5. Personal communication, Alan Stone.
6. Chapman 1978, p. 11.
7. Stanes 1986, p. 69.
8. Lawn House Deeds in private possession.
9. Ormerod 1867.
10. Pigot & Co. 1822/23.
11. *Exeter Flying Post*, 21 August 1828, p. 2, Column D.
12. Moore 1829, p. 559.
13. DRO,1800/PO148/57.
14. DRO,1833/402-3.
15. DRO,1078/IRW/B/733.
16. Aspin 1982, pp. 17-26.
17. William Stone's Estimate Book. In private possession.
18. Department of the Environment, Listing Report on Millpond Cottage.
19. Rice 2002, pp. 41-42.
20. *Population Tables*, 1851, F20.18, Vol. I, Div. V, p. 50 [online] Available at: <census.customer services@ons.gov.uk>.
21. Devon Family History Society 2006, Chagford Baptisms, 1813–1826.
22. Moore 1829, p. 560.
23. Hayter-Hames 1981, p 89.
24. Harris 1992, p. 169.
25. Rice 2002, p. 69.
26. Hoskins 1972, p. 129.

27. *Population Tables*, 1851, F20.18, Vol. I, Div. V, p. 51 [online] Available at: <census.customer services@ons.gov.uk>.
28. Billings 1857, p. 96.
29. White 1850, p. 185.
30. Stone's estimate book in private possession.
31. St Leger Gordon 1950, p. 141.
32. Chagford Parochial School Log Books in possession of Chagford Primary School.
33. White's 1878/9, p. 207.
34. Chagford Parochial School Log Books in possession of Chagford Primary School.
35. G. H. Reed family papers in private possession.
36. Morris's 1857, p. 97.
37. Billings 1857, p. 97.
38. Kelly's Directory 1893, p. 106.
39. Prospectus in private family papers.
40. Ibid.
41. Chagford Parish Magazine, 1891.
42. *The Electrician*, 4 September 1891, p. 486
43. DRO, 2241A/PX/1/1/1 1894–1902.
44. *The Western Morning News*, 1935.
45. Kelly's Directory 1906, p. 130.
46. Lamb, P. <www.swehs.co.uk>.
47. Ibid.
48. *Express & Echo*, 19 January 1967.
49. Ibid.

Bibliography

Aspin, C. (1982) *The Woollen Industry*, Aylesbury: Shire Publications.

Billings M. (1857) *M. Billings Directory and Gazeteer of the County of Devon*, Birmingham: M. Billings Steam-Press Office.

Chapman, D. (ed.) (1978) *The Devon Cloth Industry in the Eighteenth Century: Sun Fire Office inventories of merchants' and manufacturers' property*, 1726–1770, DCRS New Series, vol. 23.

Gill, C. (ed.) (1970) *Dartmoor: a new study*, Newton Abbot: David & Charles.

Harris, H. (1992) (4th edn) *The Industrial Archaeology of Dartmoor*, Newton Abbot: Peninsular Press.

Hayter-Hames, J. (1981) *A History of Chagford*, Chichester: Phillimore.

Hoskins, W.G. (1972 edn) *Devon*, Newton Abbot: David and Charles.

Kelly's (1906) *Kelly's Directory of Devonshire*, Kelly's Directories Ltd.

Lamb, P., *History of Chagford Electricity Supply*. [online] South Western Electricity Historical Society. Available at: <www.swehs.co.uk>

Minchinton, W. (1974) *Devon at Work*: *past and present* Newton Abbot: David and Charles.

Moore, Revd T. (1829) *The History of Devonshire from the Earliest to the Present*, London: Robert Jennings.

Morris & Co. (1857) *Directory of Devonshire*.

Ormerod, G.W. (1867) 'Chronology of Chagford', *Parish Church Magazine*.

Osborne, F. and Lega-Weeks, E. (1979) *Chagford Churchwardens Accounts 1460–1600*, Trowbridge: Redwood Burn.

Pigot & Co. (1822/23) *Directory of Devonshire*.

Rice, I., (2002) *The Book of Chagford*, Tiverton: Halsgrove.

St Leger-Gordon, D. (1950) *Devonshire*, London: Robert Hale.

St Leger-Gordon, D. (1963) *Devon*, London: Robert Hale.

Stanes, R. (1986) *A History of Devon*, Chichester: Phillimore.

White W. (1850) *History, Gazetteer, and Directory of Devonshire*, Sheffield: William White.

Before the Mains: methods of water supply in rural East Devon

Sue Dymond

Before the mid-twentieth century, most water supply and regulation in rural areas was a matter for small communities, families and individuals. East Devon was no exception, with mains water arriving in some villages as recently as the 1960s. This article examines some of the methods used for water capture before this time and seeks to demonstrate how some of these methods linger on. Wells and village pumps were certainly used, but the focus here will be on several other methods that are perhaps less widely known. Although I have used traditional research tools, oral testimony has also played a large part.

Opposite, and just below the Fountain Head Inn at Branscombe, a column of water emerges from the hillside via a pipe, a feature from which the name of the inn is perhaps derived. This is one of the remaining shutes in the village that once provided water for the nearby cottages and was collected in a jug or bucket. This water was used for drinking, but it was often considered too precious, in terms of the labour needed for carrying it, for domestic use. Roof water was therefore collected for non-drinking purposes. This water was piped to storage tanks, some below ground, where it was either scooped out with buckets or a hand pump was fitted.[1] Houses some distance from shutes might use roof water for all purposes; Daws Weston, close to the coast between Branscombe and Weston, had no other water supply but that caught from the roof into the 1950s and probably later.[2] Similarly, the coastguard cottages at Weston Mouth, between Sidmouth and Branscombe, were also supplied with tanks for this purpose, although spring water was available nearby for drinking.[3]

Watering livestock in the past, in the absence of nearby water courses, led to the construction of dew ponds. Old maps, particularly tithe maps, often show them. The author conducted a survey of dew ponds, and compared to those shown on 1840 tithe maps of Branscombe parish and Beer parish; only a small number remain.[4] Dew ponds are naturally filling, man-made, large shallow saucer-like ponds with a lining of puddled clay to make them watertight. The base layers of the pond seem to vary, with the addition of lime in some instances to deter earthworms from burrowing through the clay layer. A layer of straw might also be included to add to the insulation, as any warmth was an unwelcome addition to a pond designed to keep cool in order to attract condensing moisture. Dew ponds were created primarily to water sheep, whose small feet acted on the clay, keeping it plastic and thus watertight, as they waded into the water. Cattle often damaged dew ponds with their greater weight and bigger hooves.

Dew produced water, even in the heat and drought of summer. Exactly how these ponds gather water, even in the heat and drought of summer, is debatable and may even seem magical! Certainly, rain water tops up the level, but it does seem that condensation on the cold water surface at night more than compensates for the amount that evaporates by day.[5] Although dew ponds have mostly disappeared, and been replaced by mains water-fed troughs, a few remain as wildlife ponds. Those close to, or straddling field boundaries, are most likely to survive as they do not interfere with modern farming practices.

So far, we have looked at fairly primitive, locally developed methods of water catching. Now we move on to something more elaborate and technological. Catching water for domestic and farming use, as described, could never meet all these needs. Another method that was very prevalent in East Devon exploited the local topography and geology. Where the topping of greensand meets the lower level of impermeable clay on the hillsides of East Devon, springs emerge. This spring-line provides gravity fed water for lower levels. Premises above the spring-line however, could also take advantage of this free-flowing water by an ingenious device known as a hydraulic ram.

A hydraulic ram (or simply a ram) is a pump which raises water to a higher level than its source, purely by using the power of the water itself. The water thus pumped is raised above to a farm or dwelling by pipes and stored in a tank which will then gravity-feed the water to where it is required. The components that comprise this pumping system are tailored to the individual needs of the site and the properties of the water source. I have spoken of springs providing the water source, but some hydraulic rams were pumping stream water and occasionally a ram would be using the power of stream water to pump water from a spring. As a generalisation, spring water systems are the least troublesome whilst those utilising streams can be more challenging. Problems arise from blockages caused by sediment, leaves and other debris, although a ram can tolerate impurities to some degree. To minimise intake problems, a spring is encased in a surround – a catch-pit – usually built of brick or concrete with a removable concrete lid. Water sourced from a stream requires different treatment and can be led off via a deep pool, fed by a weir, or even from a large pond constructed beside the stream which takes a proportion of the stream's water. Both methods are designed to allow settling of matter in suspension in the water.

I have already shown that a certain amount of water management and construction work is required, and hence some expense. The hydraulic ram itself is made out of cast iron and gun metal and therefore expensive. Yet, once properly installed and working, the maintenance is often minimal and within the capabilities of most users. Capital costs of an installation were traditionally met by the landowner, often an estate, as the majority of rams were linked to their tenanted farms and cottages. Whilst the motive for ram installation must surely have been to improve a farm by providing water for livestock and domestic use, thereby making it more attractive to lessees, no doubt rent charges reflected this. Having the same landlord, any pipes from one farm crossing the land of another would no doubt be less of an issue should problems arise. A letter written to the author from the present owner of Woodhead Farm, Branscombe, illustrates the succession of water supply methods and highlights how tenants were in this instance beholden to the landlord as regards water supply:

337

The ram situated below Watercombe Farm was installed just before World War II by the then landlord Clement Ford. Its purpose was to supply Watercombe Farm. The water was driven by the ram to a storage tank approx ¼ mile up the hill. One day when passing the tank Mr Ford noticed water running away from the overflow so he decided to pipe it to Woodhead Farm 'rather than go to waste'! Initially it supplied Woodhead Farmhouse and 3 wooden field-troughs but after the war more troughs were installed (about 12, I think) so that all the fields on the farm including Higher Barn were supplied. Approximately one mile of pipework was involved, all dug in by hand. The system worked very satisfactorily and made a good difference to the running of the farm as previously water was only supplied by one hand pump & 4 dew ponds. All ran successfully until the mains water became available (1960 approx) & the Ministry condemned the ram water stating it as unsuitable for milk production, i.e. the washing of the utensils & presumably as drinking water for the cattle. So at this stage the ram became silent – 'never to clack again'!'[6]

Figure 1. A ram which has pumped continuously for 90 years.
Just visible on the front of the ram vessel is the brass plate showing the model and unique installation numbers. Photograph: Sue Dymond

Whilst the majority of rams supplied farms and farm cottages, this was not exclusively the case; rural public houses and hotels could also benefit. Reputedly the Hare and Hounds public house at Gittisham had a ram, which would make sense, given its isolated situation. In a similar out of the way position the Three Horseshoes Inn near Branscombe, now near derelict, also had a ram which pumped water from a stream. Once a very successful hotel, with up to ninety guests at a time, the ram struggled to supply enough water to the Three Horseshoes in busy periods.[7] Were the guests aware of the water source? A local farmer laconically remarked, 'Yes, classy hotel and they were drinking muddy old river water.'[8]

Another example of the provision of a hydraulic ram comes from Awliscombe parish where, in 1926, the Church of England Bounty Office wrote to Reverend Romilly at the vicarage regarding provision for a hydraulic ram. However, by 1957 the Church of England was consenting to a loan and mortgage towards installing mains water supply there.[9] There is evidence in this case that the water was analysed for suitability for drinking before a ram was installed.[10]

This issue of sufficient supply shows the limitations of rams in high usage situations. The ram for the Three Horseshoes Inn was of Victorian origin and whilst the ram may have been perfectly adequate for its water needs at the time of installation, this would not have been the case after World War II. Unfortunately, although pumping steadily for twenty-four hours a day, a ram is unable to step up a gear in periods of high demand. Even before mains water arrived, rendering many rams redundant, in some cases there was an intermediate step of installing a diesel powered pump to provide an increased flow. This of course came with cost implications, the logistics involved in getting the fuel to the site and possibly higher maintenance demands.

I have argued that, from local inquiries, the interwar period was the heyday for ram installation. Information from a Ministry of Agriculture, Fisheries and Food (MAFF) booklet for 1934 indicates that landowners could apply for long term loans for rams from The Lands Improvement Co., the latter incorporated by Special Acts of Parliament (1849–1920).[11] The landowner could get a twenty-five year loan and Messrs John Blake, Ltd. (hydraulic ram purveyors) are quoted as having carried out water supply schemes financed by these long term loans, with the work initially sanctioned by MAFF

Perhaps, then, it is no coincidence that East Devon valleys were almost exclusively using Blake's Hydrams for water pumping.[12]

How does a ram work and what are the requirements for installing a successful hydraulic ram system? A sufficient flow of falling water, from a small height above the ram, powers it to lift a small amount of that water (as little as ten per cent) to a higher level. The waste water (up to ninety per cent), that is not lifted, runs away. Figure 2 shows the components of a typical system.

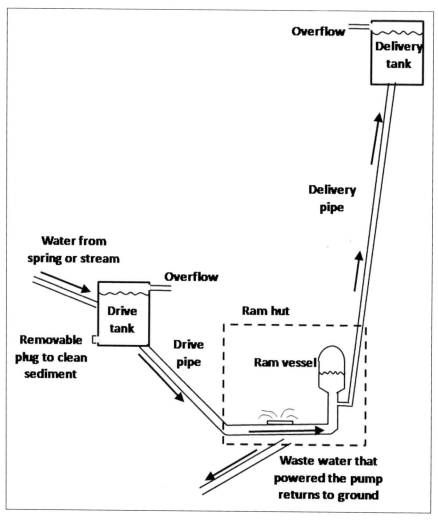

Figure 2. The basic layout of a hydraulic ram system. The distance from water source to delivery point can be several kilometres. Diagram: Sue Dymond.

The vibration caused by a working ram (the water hammer effect) could damage the ram, so they are set in a concrete base and situated in sturdy shed-like pump houses built of brick, breeze block or shuttered concrete; a wooden door is the usual means of access. These little disused huts are dotted across East Devon's valleys and vary in style. Some are certainly shed-like but many are only waist height.

As the height the ram will pump the water to is dependent on the height of the fall of water from the drive tank to the ram itself, on occasions it is necessary to increase this height. One way is to raise the drive tank as high as possible and to sink the ram housing itself into the ground to maximise the distance between the two. An excellent example of a raised drive tank and sunken ram housing can be seen on access land on East Hill, Ottery St Mary, although, sadly, vegetation has almost obscured the ram housing. Whilst the sunken Ottery ram housing is of small construction, another, serving an unknown farm, is of the proportions of an underground room and accessed by a metal cover and ladder.[13]

How old is this technology? The hydraulic ram, although invented in the last years of the 1700s, became popular in Victorian times. The oldest working ram I have seen dates from 1920.[14] There are others of similar age in the East Devon area. The years between World War I and World War II seem to have been the heyday of installation, but rams continue to be introduced up to the present day. It is unusual in our age of built-in obsolescence that ram manufacturers Green and Carter claim, 'Every pump is guaranteed forever. Most RAMs, installed prior to 1800, are still working as well as the day they were installed, and we still maintain a stock of all parts on the shelf'.[15]

Green and Carter are one of two companies who appear to have dominated the ram industry in this country. The other was Blake, from Accrington in Lancashire. Every ram I have examined in East Devon has been a Blake ram, known as Hydrams. The Green and Carter rams are known as Vulcans. Rams have a plate on the vessel (air chamber) which gives the model number and individual installation number. Plans of each installation are usually kept by the company responsible for the installation; hence the location of the ram, as well as its piping, can be identified should problems arise. A plan could also be lodged with the landowner concerned.

Understanding hydraulic rams in the landscape is not always easy.

The thumping sound of a working ram can be heard some distance away and I have been told this could be heard in many valleys in the past. Whilst a ram might show up on an Ordnance Survey (OS) map, its precise location is not so obvious. A further complication is that not all rams are shown on OS maps. Sometimes the surveyor has decided they are defunct devices and so removed them from subsequent maps, whilst some have never featured on a map. Using the knowledge of a network of local people will often be the most successful way to find rams, and also to discover which properties they were supplying with water and the various features and idiosyncrasies of particular installations. Access can also be gained this way; most people who use a ram take great pride in it and are happy to give a guided tour.

When a ram becomes disused and stops pumping, the pump-house, drive tank, pipes and other elements at the site may start to become overgrown. As the years go by it becomes increasingly difficult to see former ram installations as brambles and ivy cover such sites and trees grow up throughout the area. A ruined ram hut, chanced upon adjacent to a public footpath in Bovey Down woods, exemplifies the

Figure 3. A derelict ram hut beside a footpath in Bovey Down woods, Southleigh. Pumping stream water, this installation suffered blockage problems during its working life. Photograph: Sue Dymond.

difficulties in trying to make sense of a ram system without local knowledge. [16] Current OS maps do not indicate a hydraulic ram here, although it is indicated on an older map. [17]

A local farmer was able to tell me the derelict ram (Figure 3) had belonged to Bovey Farm across the A3052 road from Sidford to Seaton. The ram was pumping to supply stock troughs (via a supply tank in the vicinity) on either side of this busy main road. This involved pumping the water roughly forty metres uphill and then a distance of up to a kilometre horizontally to reach the fields. This is not the only installation where the pipes go underneath a main road.

Are hydraulic rams dead technology? Certainly not. The continued presence of ram manufacturers attests to that. Developing countries make much use of rams and high water rates in this country are causing resurgence in ram utilisation, with dilapidated ram installations being considered for refurbishment across East Devon.

Leaving aside methods of providing water for drinking and domestic use we move on to another system of using natural water sources for a different purpose. The system was known by a variety of names: catch meadow, catch-work water meadow, catch-water leat and field gutter, being the most common. [18] Although similar to the valley bottom water meadows that used rivers or large streams to lead water along constructed channels into adjacent fields, this system was used in hilly country, such as that found in East Devon. The purpose of watering hillsides was to promote grass growth to provide an early bite in the hungry gap between the end of the stored hay and the new spring grass growth. [19] Causing a flow of water to spill down a sloping field kept the ground temperature above freezing and allowed the grass to keep growing. The flow was achieved by diverting a stream, occasionally a small river, along leats and channels cut into a hillside above the area to be watered. The water was introduced along these leats in a controlled way, such that it moved steadily along, preventing pooling and stagnation, but not too fast, for erosion and breakdown of channels might occur. The water worked its way downhill by spilling over the cut channels, being directed to various areas of fields by the opening and closing of sluices, until eventually, it found its way back to the stream below.

Former catch meadows in the landscape differ little in appearance now from ordinary fields, but, from a distance, a level track or line can often be discerned following the contour of a hillside (see Plate 25). This would have been a leat or channel that carried the water, and can be easily confused with a farm animal track, which many have subsequently become. A blue line leading from a stream on the Branscombe Tithe Map[20] alerted me to the possibility of a catch meadow in the village (see Plate 26). The position of this brush stroke on the map, below Pitt Farm, matches a current cattle track which follows the contour around the hillside. Law's 1793 map of Branscombe also shows a similar line in the same position.[21]

I was fortunate to speak to a local man who confirmed this was indeed a part of a water meadow system. During childhood journeys to and from school he used to divert the water for his father (a farmer), in these very fields.[22] A labourer on the farm also used to manage the system. The stream was diverted to take away manure and urine from the farmyard (in some instances a temporary dam was created) and this found its way onto the field along the leats and channels. Road scrapings of animal waste might also be thrown in.[23] At Branscombe, before mains sewage was installed, the toilets at the Street area of the village were all in privies perched over the same stream, and so this human waste also found its way onto the fields below the farm. This particular stream was used to water fields belonging to several farms, and the farmers took turns with the supply.[24] When I asked how much of this source water was used by any farm in its turn I was told 'all of it!'

This seemed to have been an amicable affair but in some areas legally binding rules were necessary.[25] Again, like the hydraulic ram pipes, farmers having the same landlord might have led to more cooperation. Was a catch meadow out of commission during the watering period? No, but only sheep were allowed to graze there. Their lighter weight and smaller hooves were not as damaging as those of the cattle, who would have broken down the channels and leats.

The tithe apportionments for the area of Branscombe with these identified catch meadows, showed some of the fields were classified as meads.[26] Exploring further it seemed that mead fields were present in each case of positively identified catch meadows. The name mead does seem to indicate a strong likelihood that the field was watered by a catch meadow system, and mead fields are therefore a useful starting point in the search for catch meadows.[27] The next step is to look for a nearby stream where the water was taken off, and usually there is a farm nearby for manure supply. Confident in this approach I looked at a mead field on the side of East Hill overlooking Ottery St Mary and found no trace of likely leats.[28] Although the adjacent stream was a long way below the field, a local man who had been brought up on the nearby farm confirmed that it was indeed a catch meadow.[29] I had not considered that the take-off for the water was a good distance back upstream before it had lost height, and various hedges had obscured the sight line. The farmer revealed that this leat had been re-cut each year by a horse drawing a small distinctive looking plough, the only mention I have heard of such an occurrence.

The construction and maintenance of the catch meadow systems was labour intensive but felt to be worth the effort. Several men who remember this work in Branscombe, speak of fairly rough and ready methods of water diversion.[30] Whilst I have photographs of (fallen) stone slotted sluice gates from a former system near Axminster, those I spoke to emphasised lumps of wood and sacks of soil as the main stoppers and diverters of the flowing water. The catch meadow year started in about October when the watering and cutting or re-cutting the channels began.[31] The watering was not continuous, with different areas being watered in rotation, which also helped prevent stagnation. This watering carried on during the winter, encouraging grass growth. By about February grass was available for grazing.

So how prevalent were catch meadows in East Devon? The evidence suggests a similar situation to that on Exmoor, Devon, where 'Most of Exmoor's farms had a field gutter system, sometimes called a water meadow or catchwater leat system.'[32] Whilst oral history seems to be the main key to their discovery in the landscape today, there is documentary evidence of their existence in the early 1800s in Branscombe. Two entries in an account book of the Ford Family (copyholders of the Branscombe Estate from the Dean and Chapter of Exeter Cathedral, finally buying the estate in the late 1860s) concerning Charles Harding and water use, dated 21 January 1834, are almost identical in showing a charge was levied for taking water to fields that are being seasonally watered. One of the entries reads:

I have this day agreed with Mr John Ford for taking the water through his Field called round mead part of Pound tenement Estate into my

Field for the purpose of watering it from this time to the first Day of May next (when the said water is not wanted or used by the said John Ford) for which I agree and bargain to give him for the use of the said water as above stated for that period the sum of one shilling.[33]

Farm deeds from Branscombe during the 1800s and 1900s reveal precise instructions on operating the water meadows. When a tenant was coming towards the end of his lease he had to allow access to water the water meadows to the succeeding tenant or the landlord or someone under his authority. The wording on the leases for such permission for five Branscombe farms[34] from 1848 to 1923 is very similar, 'at any time after the last day of October in such last year to enter upon and gutter and water the meadowland and will not depasture such meadow with any cattle but sheep after the last day of October in such last year.'[35] Middlecombe Mill lease (1923) gives the last day of August, but other farms, the end of October.

Did the water freeze in catch meadows? Documentary evidence indicates that this is unlikely, but one hillside in Branscombe is remembered by two local men as being a sheet of ice in winter (local children slid down it on improvised sledges). The channels for this field can still be seen on the hillside. The water here was from a spring, not a stream, and did not therefore have the volume to maintain a good flow, and so froze during harsh winters.[36]

Asking those who remember catch meadows why they fell out of favour, the answer is often just one word 'artificials' (fertiliser). Whilst this is partly true, a combination of reasons was at work. Artificial fertilisers did become more accessible as they began to be imported or produced in this country, and grain and lamb imports led to a fall in demand for home production. Also, sheep farming became less profitable, as their dung was no longer required for manuring the arable land. The maintenance of catch meadows was labour intensive, and therefore expensive, and in addition mechanisation of farming resulted in the use of heavy tractors which damaged these fields.[37]

Perhaps we have come full circle with water, which was often seen as precious in the past when it often had to be carried by hand, through to the days of mains water and an endless supply at the turn of a tap, to present concerns over the cost and availability of mains water. Dew ponds and catch meadows are now largely things of the past, but the taste of water collected from a shute or provided by a hydraulic ram, is still preferred to mains water by some elderly country dwellers. Hydraulic rams have thumped away in East Devon's steep valleys for over a hundred years. They have provided a steady supply of water twenty-four hours a day, at a negligible cost, and with minimal impact on the countryside. For a few people that option still exists.

Acknowledgements

I am grateful to the many people who helped with my research; the list would be too long if I were to thank everyone individually.

Notes and References

1. Alan Gosling 2006, Personal communication.
2. Bert Warren 2006, Personal communication.
3. Daphne Sleight 2010, Personal communication.
4. Parishscapes Report 2006, East Devon AONB.
5. Martin 1907.
6. Edwin Purchase 2007, Letter to author (reproduced with permission).
7. Marie Dowell 2007, Personal communication.
8. David Hurford 2003, Personal communication.
9. DRO, 3020 A-1/PB 420.
10. DRO, 3020 A-1/PB 464-469.
11. MERL, TR MAF/P2/B3, p. 104.
12. John Blake established the company in 1858, trading from Accrington, Lancashire. Blake's hydraulic rams (Hydrams) are still available from Allspeeds, a company based in Accrington.
13. Grid ref. SY134946.
14. History of the hydraulic ram, 2010. <http://www.greenandcarter. com>.
15. Green and Carter's website product guarantee, 2010. <http://www. greenandcarter.com>.
16. Grid ref. SY205915.
17. OS 1:2500, 1958. Grid ref. SY205915.
18. Whilst most of these names are seen as referring to hillside systems, local people in East Devon do not seem to make a distinction, and call their hillside systems water meadows. The Devon Historic Landscape Characterisation Project viewpoint, designates a watermeadow as 'all types of meadow that were periodically inundated, whether by nature or design' (Turner 2007, p. 82). This does seem to accord with much oral and documentary evidence locally.

19. The early bite was extremely important but this was not the end of the usefulness of a catch meadow. Stanes 2005, pp. 127-8, comments on the water meadows' year are mirrored in other documentary sources – some vary slightly in stated timings.
20. DRO, Tithe Map, Branscombe 1840, shows Pitt Farm.
21. Law 1793.
22. Peter Gibbins 2008. Personal communication.
23. Vancouver 1969, writing in 1808, shows Sir Lawrence Palk's farmyard in a numbered illustration on plate XX1 p. 472, referred to on p. 474, and indicates no. 35 is a 'Receptacle for the liquid manure' with no. 37 being 'The main sewer, through which the liquid collected in the farmyard flows to the meadows below, over which it is regularly conveyed by channels cut for the purpose.'
24. Ivor Dowell 2008, and Peter Gibbins 2008. Personal communication.
25. Vancouver 1969, pp. 315-6 notes that many instances of dispute over watering rights came to his attention whilst surveying and he felt such troubles should be submitted to the Board of Agriculture to administer justice. Whitlock 1966, p. 76, whilst describing southern chalk streams, comments that dates and quantities for irrigating the water meadows were strictly enforced. In East Devon I have not found evidence of formal arrangements for water sharing, but possibly farmers with the same landlord had to follow a defined schedule.
26. Middle Moor – Mead, Higher Moor – Mead, The Meadow – Mead.
27. The Oxford Dictionary gives the meaning of mead as meadow, and the connection is obvious. Cutting & Cummings p. 163 describe the job of keeping the water flowing in the water meadows in the past as being that of the 'drowner', 'waterman' or 'meadman'. Despite the link between meadow and mead there seems to be a difference, which I suggest is that meads are invariably watered fields, and meadows only sometimes are. Mead can appear in the name of a field, or in its state of cultivation, in documents such as a tithe map. Further difficulties arise when a field is named a meadow but classified as a mead. Land use changes over the years and even within the farming year a watered meadow became a pasture; perhaps an interesting subject for further research.
28. Govetons Mead.
29. Peter Hill, 2008. Personal communication.
30. Peter Gibbins, 2008 and Ivor Dowell, 2008. Personal communication.
31. Vancouver 1969, p. 210, attributes more importance to the autumnal rains, than to any water falling after that time.
32. Riley & Wilson-North 2002, p. 128.
33. DRO, 1037M-0/E/3/3.
34. DRO, 1037M-0/E/1/5 (Higher House) 1892, 1037M-0/E/1/3 (Middlecombe Mills) 1869, 1037M-0/E/1/10 (Middlecombe Farm and

Mill) 1923, 1037M-0/E/1/8 (Pitt Farm) 1923, 1037M-0/E/1/2 (Taylors)
    1848, 1037M-0/E/1/4 (Lower Watercombe) 1885.
35. DRO, 1037M-0/E/1/5 (Higher House) 1892.
36. Stanes 2005, p. 12.
37. Stearne 2007, p. 113.

Bibliography

Allspeeds Ram manufacturers, 2010, [online] Available at: <http://www.
    allspeeds.co.uk/blake_hydram/index.htm> (accessed April 2011).

Cutting, R. & Cummings, I. (1999) 'Water Meadows: their form, operation
    and plant ecology', in Cook, H. & Williamson, T. (eds) *Water
    Management in the English Landscape – Field, Marsh and* Meadow,
    Edinburgh: Edinburgh University Press, pp. 157-178.

East Devon AONB (2006) Community and Landscape in Beer and Brans-
    combe, pp. 33-36, [online] Available at: <http://www.eastdevonaonb.
    org.uk/documents/Pscapesreport_Sept0806_web.pdf>   (accessed
    March 2011).

Fraser, R. (1794) (1970 edn.) *General View of the County of Devon*, Barn-
    staple: Porcupines.

Green and Carter Ram manufacturers, History of the Hydraulic Ram, 2010.
    [online] Available at: <http://www.greenandcarter.com> (accessed
    April 2010).

Green and Carter's website product guarantee, 2010. [online] Available at:
    <http://www.greenandcarter.com> (Accessed April 2010).

Griffith, F. (1988) *Devon's Past: an aerial view,* Exeter: Devon Books.

Jeffery, T.D., Thomas, T.H., Smith, A.V., Glover, P.B. & Fountain, P.D.
    (2002) '*Hydraulic Ram Pumps – a guide to ram pump water supply
    systems*', London: ITDG Publishing.

Law's Map, [online] Available at: <http://www.Branscombeproject.org.uk>
    (accessed April 2011).

Martin, E.A. (2011) {online} Available at <http://www.dewponds.co.uk/
    martin_dew-ponds1907.htm> (accessed March 2011).

Oxford Illustrated Dictionary (1962) London: Oxford University Press.

Riley, H., & Wilson-North, R. (2002) *The Field Archaeology of Exmoor*,
    Swindon: English Heritage.

Riley, H. (2006) *The Historic Landscape of the Quantock Hills*, Swindon:
    English Heritage.

Stanes, R. (2005) *Old Farming Days: life on the land in Devon and Corn-
    wall*, Tiverton: Halsgrove.

Stearne K. (2007) 'The Management of Water Meadows: four hundred years
    of intensive integrated agriculture', in Cook, H. & Williamson, T. (eds)
    Water Meadows: History, Ecology and Conservation, Macclesfield:
    Windgather Press Ltd., pp. 107-121.

Turner, S. (2007) *Ancient Country: the historic character of rural Devon*, Exeter: Devon Archaeological Society.

Vancouver, C. (1808) (1969 edn) *General View of the Agriculture of the County of Devon: with observations on the means of improvement*, Newton Abbot: David & Charles.

Watt, S.B. (2002) *A Manual on the Hydraulic Ram for Pumping Water*, London: ITDG Publishing.

Whitlock, W. (1950) *The Other Side of the Fence*, London: Herbert Jenkins Ltd.

Whitlock, W. (1966) *A Short History of Farming in Britain*, London: The Country Book Club.

Branscombe Postcards 1900–1950 as Resources for Local Historians

Geoff Squire

Introduction

Postcards in Britain came into being at the time of the 1870 Post Office Act. From 1902, senders of postcards were allowed to write on the same side as the address, thereby freeing the whole of the front surface for a picture. Of the various categories of picture postcards, topographical cards are of particular interest to local historians because they depict the features of a limited area or district. As a visual inventory of the first half of the twentieth century, these cards offer resources to local historians seeking to answer such questions as: What was this place or locality like? What did it look like? Why was it like that? Why and to what extent did it change during the period under consideration?

The postcards chosen here assist these enquiries because they provide visual clues and evidence to supplement the written, oral and other sources which promote our understanding of landscape change. The picture postcards of Branscombe which are discussed in this article are typical of the range available for many other places and for those studying other localities in Devon and further afield in this country. Large collections of topographical postcards can be found at the postcard fairs which are held frequently across the country.

Branscombe, a picturesque village and resort on the East Devon coast with a population of a few hundred, is well represented in

351

picture postcards. From the early years of the twentieth century, Chapman and Son of Dawlish and other postcard publishers visited the village on numerous occasions to photograph dozens of scenes which now tell us a great deal about the village in the first half of the twentieth century. The record they left us raises questions about the photographers themselves. How was their work organised? Why did they choose these views, sometimes photographed from unexpected positions and angles?

There are pictures of people, buildings and the wide sweeps of farm-land and woodland which emphasise the long established and largely unchanging rural character of the parish. On the other hand, some postcards show us things which no longer exist, while others reveal changes to houses, roads and land-use as time went on. On a broader scale the images show that by the late 1920s, relationships between parts of Branscombe and the wider world were gradually changing in ways which began to reshape the lives and prospects of some of those living in the village. For example, picture postcards from the 1940s and 1950s illustrate some of the changes associated with World War II and its aftermath.

Illustrating both continuity and change, the following examples suggest ways in which picture postcards could be used to develop topics in local history.

The Edwardian Village

In general, Edwardian postcards of rural Britain were intended to convey an impression of tranquil, rural charm. However, amenities were few. As some Branscombe postcards show, water had to be carried from shutes and wells. Mains drainage did not reach most of the village until the late 1950s. The poor state of the roads in the early twentieth century meant that horses and donkeys were the primary means of transport in the village (Figure 1). Later postcards show that the house on the left hand side of the photograph was demolished in the 1930s. Other Edwardian cards depict cob-walled cottages, thatched roofs, village shops and farmhouses.

The donkey (Figure 2) is being taken out to work on the south-facing cliff plats; these were plots of land where early potatoes and other crops could be grown in relatively frost-free conditions (Figure

Figure 1. Branscombe: rough roads.

Figure 2. Branscombe: countryside around the village church.

Figure 3. Branscombe: cliff plats.

Figure 4. Branscombe church: pre 1910.

3). Donkeys were able to cope with the slopes. These small cliff plats are now disused and overgrown. Local historians have researched the rise and decline of this unique cliff plat farming together with the associated land-use and employment changes. The hummocks to the left of the picture are the remains of old lime workings. Further brief comments on local lime workings are made below, relating to Figure 6.

Like many other churches, Branscombe church was restored (1910–1911) and picture postcards reveal what a church interior looked like before changes were made to furniture and architecture. The old horsebox pews (Figure 4) were removed at the time of restoration to be replaced by more contemporary seating. The unusual three-decker pulpit was moved from the position on the south wall of the nave to its present position. Other cards show a new boiler house and a new door into the south transept.

Local historians have shown that Branscombe, like other villages, was not completely isolated in the early years of the twentieth century, horse drawn carts and vans came regularly through the village to supply a variety of goods and equipment.[1] Picture postcards can sometimes challenge preconceptions. The leather containers protruding at the back of the trap shown on Figure 5 suggests that a travelling salesman was visiting on that day. Figure 6 shows the old coal-yard at Branscombe Mouth in its original form. The stone-walled yard was used to store coal for lime-burning, a small-scale local industry which came to an end in Branscombe during the 1860s.

The late 1920s and the 1930s

The postcards in this section (Figures 7-11) demonstrate the inter-war effects of tourism. In Branscombe the landscape changes were seen mainly at the eastern end of the village at Branscombe Mouth and the vicinity of the Square in the lower village. Similar inter-war postcards exist for other tourist areas in Devon and further afield, supplementing evidence from a variety of other sources about tourism in Britain at that time. By the mid-1920s Clem Ford, the major land owner in the parish, was living in the 'Lookout' (converted from the old coastguard cottages), which overlooked Branscombe Mouth and the old coal yard (Figure 6). Ford took advantage of the growing fashion for touring,

Figure 5. The Masons Arms in the lower village, *c*.1905.

Figure 6. The coastguard station, Branscombe. The stone walled enclosure was used to store coal for lime-burning.

camping and walking, and turned the coal yard into the Sea Shanty Café and Rock Gardens (Figure 7). This decision turned out to be a key factor for the future of holiday-making and, in turn, landscape change in this part of Branscombe. Picture postcards of similar tourist areas provide a valuable source for local historians researching the activities of local entrepreneurs who provided facilities and services for tourists.

The Sea Shanty still flourishes today, little different in appearance from that of the late 1920s when it was constructed. The distinctive appearance with tea rooms and rock gardens highlight an interesting contrast with the old coal-yard. With an adjacent car park, nearby spaces for camping and caravans and accommodation available in beach chalets, the Sea Shanty was well positioned to provide meals and other services for a growing number of visitors, including walkers on the coastal path.

Figure 8 gives an idea of the numbers of campers coming to Branscombe at this time – many of them in cars – as this picture shows. Other postcards from the period show tents on the beach and in other fields around Branscombe Mouth.

The beach chalets (Figure 9) were set up by the Ford family in the late 1920s and early 1930s. Situated on both sides of Branscombe Mouth, they did not have main drainage and water was supplied by standpipes and taps, seen at the top of the beach in front of the chalets. These chalets were replaced by more modern chalets soon after 1950.

The waterfall (Figure 10) at Branscombe, situated just around the corner from the Sea Shanty Tearooms, was surrounded by exotic plants and ornaments. Always an attraction, it was set up by Clem Ford on the site of an old gypsum mill. The waterfall no longer exists because the mill leat has been filled in.

The view of the Masons Arms (Figure 11) dating from the 1930s, shows that the Shell petrol pump is a new feature (see Figure 5). A garage in the Square nearby also catered for the needs of motorists. By this time the Square also had two shops and as other cards show, the Masons Arms and houses in this area were advertising accommodation and meals. There are also postcards depicting the buses that connected Branscombe to Seaton and Sidmouth. Many visitors travelled on the Southern Railway from Waterloo to Seaton

Figure 7. An early advertisement for the Sea Shanty Tearooms
and rock gardens, Branscombe.

Figure 8. Branscombe Mouth in the 1930s.

Figure 9. Chalets on Branscombe beach.

and then by bus to Branscombe. A period of around twenty-five years separates this view from the one in the Edwardian card (Figure 5). Comparison of the two demonstate changes in modes of transport, and indicate some refurbishing. Later cards show that the Masons Arms was enlarged following World War II.

In addition to providing evidence about the local landscape changes associated with inter-war tourism, picture postcards like those in this section raise questions about the wider context of these changes. They reflect some of the wider social and economic developments of the period, in particular the provision of holidays with pay and the growth of manufacturing and service employment in parts of south-east England and the Midlands where increases in income, leisure and mobility offered the possibility of holiday visits in new cars to the countryside and beaches. Branscombe, as an attractive seaside village, was able to benefit from these trends. Provision for summer visitors included accommodation, pubs, shops and garage facilities, thereby boosting local employment opportunities and income, albeit of a seasonal nature. There are many parallels to this example, and evidence from other picture postcards shows the scale and distribution of inter-war tourism in Britain.

Figure 10. The waterfall, Branscombe.

The Forge

Branscombe's forge dates from the seventeenth century and as one of the few remaining traditional Devon forges, it has long been of interest to local historians (Figure 12). This picture postcard of the blacksmith Harry Layzell shoeing a working horse in the 1920s can be seen as an example of how one or two cards can stimulate further enquiry in local history. This one could lead to consideration of wider social and economic change and how an individual adjusted to the vicissitudes of a changing working environment in the middle part of

Figure 11. Ye Olde Masons Arms.

the twentieth century. W.G. Hoskins constructed some case studies of this kind for an earlier period.[2]

As a specialist blacksmith and wheelwright, Harry provided essential services for farmers and other members of the community continuously from 1913 until well after 1950, apart from a break for service in World War I. The skills of the wheelwright and farrier were in constant demand while horsepower was the main form of transport. However, after World War II, changes in farming and transport led to some marked changes to his work and prospects because, at this time, there was a sharp decline in the demand for the traditional skills of wheelwrights and blacksmiths. There were fewer farm carts and implements to be serviced, fewer working horses to be shod, and little or no demand for new cart wheels. Consequently, the activity depicted in this picture postcard and repeated at forges across the country, was rarely encountered.

Faced with this changing environment Harry Layzell, like other blacksmiths, had to turn to other sources of income. From the author's knowledge, he was able to build on his experience of repairing water pumps and roofs, sweeping chimneys (much needed in the days before central heating), making ornamental metalwork and weather vanes

Figure 12. The Smithy, Branscombe.

and preparing shiny 'good luck' miniature horseshoes for sale to passing summer visitors. From the late 1940s he also delivered the mail. A man with immense practical skills, like other blacksmiths, he used them to adjust to his new situation in the post-war world.

World War II and its Aftermath

In September 1939 war broke out and holiday activity in Branscombe was brought to an abrupt halt. Evacuees replaced holiday makers and the beach, vulnerable to invasion, was mined and sealed by lines of concrete tank trap devices topped by barbed wire. Pill boxes on each side of Branscombe Mouth were manned by the Home Guard and scenic coastal walks became the pathways of armed patrols. The garage in the Square was turned into a munitions factory and photography for picture postcards was discontinued for the duration of the war. The trappings of war took a long time to be cleared. A postcard sent on 25 September 1959 shows the lines of concrete defences still in place, fourteen years after the end of the war. The sender's message says 'Walked over here (Beer) to Branscombe on Wednesday day, a lovely spot but a pity they have not cleared away the wartime concrete barrier from the beach'. Some of the pill boxes are still in place. In recent years local historians and archaeologists have taken an interest in wartime defences and it has been suggested that some of those remaining should be preserved for posterity.

Postcards from the late 1940s and the 1950s picture the area around Branscombe Mouth and reveal evidence of a gradual revival in the holiday trade. Parasols and queues for ice cream at the Sea Shanty and people relaxing on the beach, now cleared of mines, are strong contrasts with the stark realities of 1939–1945. Accordingly, local entrepreneurs responded with improved services and facilities for visitors, upgraded accommodation and increased provision for car parking in particular. The historian David Kynaston explains the wider context of this post-war recovery, which is evident in postcards from seaside resorts in many parts of the country. He points out that in the hot summer of 1947, with the benefit of paid holidays, about half the population of Britain took a holiday.[3] This period pre-dated the era of jet travel and package holidays, and there were severe restrictions on the amount of money that could be taken abroad. Most people holidayed in Britain and as the local postcards show, Branscombe had its share of that revival.

As these examples from Branscombe show, picture postcards can present an effective pictorial representation of change.[4] The images offer an interesting glimpse of life as it used to be, as well as highlighting changes in the surrounding landscape and buildings of an East Devon community during the course of the twentieth century. They also help us to understand some local effects of changes in the wider world, making a valuable contribution to the historian's picture of the past.

Notes and References

1. Farquharson and Doern 2000, pp. 51-56.
2. Hoskins 1971, chapter 6, pp. 206-216.
3. Kynaston 2008, p. 217.
4. <http://www.branscombeproject.org.uk>. Further examples of Branscombe postcards can be found on this website.

Bibliography

Farquharson, B. and Doern, J, (2000) *Branscombe Shops, Trades and Getting By*, Branscombe: Branscombe Project.

Hoskins, W.G. (1971) *Old Devon*, London: Pan Books.

Kynaston, D. (2008 edition) *Austerity Britain 1945–1948: a world to build*, London: Bloomsbury.

Postcard Archive, [online] Available at, <http://www.branscombeproject.org.uk>. (Accessed June 2011).

Francis Henry (Podian)

Margaret and Michael Wilson

In 1949 people in Woodbury would have been surprised to encounter a black person living in the village. Born in Colombo, Ceylon in 1888 Francis Henry, known to us all as Podian (pronounced '*Pojan*'), lived in Woodbury until his death in 1968. He became a much loved member of the village and he delighted in his English home. Why did Podian live in Woodbury? The Templer family take up the story.

Robert Shaw Templer and his wife Frances Ann lived in Colombo, Ceylon (Sri Lanka) in the latter part of the nineteenth century. Robert was working for Cumberbatch – a tea company – and spent the winter in Ceylon, taking his summer holidays in Ireland. Their children were Cecil Robert (better known as Bob when, as a Brigadier, he came to live at Parsonage House in Woodbury), and twins Geraldine and Norah.

One day a seven-year-old Tamil boy arrived at their house asking if there were any jobs that needed doing. He was employed to clean shoes and to look after their eldest son Cecil Robert (Bob). 'Podian' is Tamil for 'Boy' and the family knew him by that name until he died. Four more children were born and Podian was the nursery fetcher, carrier and general factotum.

Having made enough money to retire at an early age, Robert Templer and his family returned to England. Podian was asked to accompany them and help on the voyage, although there was a proviso that he could go back to Colombo when he wished. But if he did, he could return to England again if he changed his mind. After a while he did

Figure 1. Podian taking a very young Cecil (later to become Brigadier Templer) for a ride in Ceylon in 1903.

return to Colombo, his fare being paid by the Templers. He was at once besieged by his family who, seeing a 'rich' member returning home, were after his money. Within four hours he bought another ticket and returned to England! He never went back to Ceylon again.

It is thought that Podian had started life in a Catholic Mission School and had been baptised into the Catholic faith before he joined the Templer family in Ceylon. Later, living in England, he had to have a Christian name and, returning to his Catholic roots, was given Francis as his Christian name and Henry as his surname.

As the family dispersed and married, Podian moved to North Devon to help Granny Templer. A member of the family, Cecil's nephew Maurice, has fond memories. "My first recollection of Podian was at our house in Barnstaple where he acted as traffic policeman in the hall and corridor whilst I, aged three, rode my little tricycle. I also remember visiting Granny Templer in Bideford where I was started off on my love of gardening by Podian on his patch in the kitchen garden, and feeding his chickens. (He loved young children and animals.)" When his parents were in India, Maurice went off to preparatory

Francis "Podian" Henry
1944, No. 1 Platoon,
Camberley Home Guard

Figure 2. Podian wearing his Home Guard uniform.

school and, accompanied by Podian, spent holidays with his aunt
Norah and her son George in Wiltshire. Both George and Maurice
clearly remember sitting in the kitchen listening to Chamberlain's
broadcast announcing we were at war with Germany. Podian said,
"Massa Maurice, that's bad, very bad".

Podian joined the local Home Guard and that must have created
quite a sensation. George remembers him saying that he was nearly
invisible at night – a source of much merriment to his colleagues. They
called him 'Mr Henry'. He told tales of guarding bridges at night,
with no weapons at all for protection. He was very proud to wear that
uniform and even prouder to receive the Defence Medal from King
George VI 'for Loyal Service' to those who had served from the outset
of war.

Leaving Wiltshire, Podian went to live with Maurice's family at Winterbourne Houghton in Dorset where he taught Maurice's mother to cook, and continued to grow vegetables. What an asset in wartime he must have been!

Meanwhile Cecil (Bob) Templer had met his future wife Ann and by the beginning of the war they had three children – Hazel, James and Jenny. Their early memories of Podian include times when he entertained them with amusing stories, both real and imagined! He never learnt to read, write or drive but he was often found 'reading' a book upside down to amuse them. He played tricks on the maids mischievously tying their shoelaces together before they went off to church.

Figure 3. Podian wearing his Defence Medal.

Figure 4. The presentation of a clock to Podian at Parsonage House in recognition of his long service to three generations of the Templer family.

During the war Bob was posted to Hong Kong in the Royal Artillery with Ann and the children. Eventually they became Japanese prisoners-of-war and were separated. Not until the end of the war did husband and wife discover that the other was alive. Maurice remembers the momentous day when the family was finally reunited back in England at Winterbourne Houghton. Podian played a major role in the saga by covering Houghton with Union Jacks and wearing his medal with pride.

Podian rejoined Bob, Ann and their children, moving to North Devon, Gravesend, Sheerness and finally, in 1949, to Woodbury near Exeter where Bob (now Brigadier Templer) bought Parsonage House. Podian lived there with the family until his death in 1968. The members of the family were known to him as Master Cecil (Bob), Missie (Ann), Master James, Miss Hazel and Miss Jennifer.

Podian had been left two cottages in Robert Templer's will and

Figure 5. Podian in Woodbury. Reproduced courtesy of Roger Stokes.

some of his money came from the sale of these two cottages. He also received a salary for his work and spent a lot of it giving generous Christmas presents and buying Premium Bonds both for himself and other members of the family. He checked 'Ernie' regularly and filled in the football pools, circling the numbers in a haphazard fashion and occasionally winning – which made him very happy! Podian cooked for the family who loved his Indian curry, rice, popadums and, best of all, Bombay duck. He continued growing vegetables for the family on his own plot. A lady who lived in the village took him to Topsham's Roman Catholic Church every Sunday. He joined the 'Over 60s Club' in Woodbury very early in its existence, walking from Parsonage House to the Village Hall. He could be counted on to put up the Union Jack on Christmas and Remembrance Days and the Canadian flag when Jenny and husband Fergus returned to Parsonage House from Canada.

Podian always turned on the BBC News when he went to bed, but as he grew older would often get confused, one day coming down to breakfast to tell everyone that the Pope had landed on the Moon! He was part of the Templer family and well loved by them and by the people of Woodbury. He was mourned greatly on his death in 1968. Francis Henry was buried in Woodbury Cemetery in the village that he loved. His heather-covered grave can be found in the cemetery in Pound Lane. Beyond, are the green fields of Devon.

FRANCIS HENRY
BORN IN COLOMBO 1888
DIED 3rd JANUARY 1968
70 YEARS THE FAITHFUL SERVANT
AND FRIEND OF THE
TEMPLER FAMILY
R.I.P.

Figure 6. Inscription on Podian's gravestone.

Acknowledgements

To Jenny Kyle, Hazel Cripps, Maurice Johnston and George Medley for their memories and photographs.

Mrs Phillips and the Defeat of the General Strike

Tony Simpson

On 14 November 1925 Councillor Mrs J.M. Phillips of Honiton received the first of many 'confidential' letters from a private address in Broadway, Worcestershire. The unknown correspondent, a Colonel E.F. Strange, appealed for her 'valuable assistance and influence . . . in case of national emergency'. Although he identified himself as Divisional Food Officer, the colonel did not reveal either the name or the location of the organisation he represented. He had at this point already approached the Town Clerk of Honiton, who, he told Mrs Phillips, had 'intimated' that she might act as Food Officer.[1] The potential 'emergency' referred to by the Colonel occurred six months later, during 'nine days in May'.[2] This event would be known as the General Strike of 1926.

At first sight Juanita Maxwell Phillips does not appear to have been an obvious choice of candidate for recruitment by the imperious Colonel Strange. She was a Chilean born expatriate whose previous activities would hardly have been viewed favourably by the Establishment. Mrs Phillips was a feminist ahead of her time. She had been a militant suffragette who continued to advocate various causes, especially those which sought to improve the lives of women and children, including unmarried mothers. But unlike many of her recently enfranchised fellow activists, Mrs Phillips had successfully stood for election to public office, becoming the first female mayor in the South West in 1920 (and in 1931 the first female member on

373

Devon County Council). When Colonel Strange's letter arrived she was in her fifth year as Mayor of Honiton Borough Council. She was also a Justice of the Peace, a member of the local Poor Law Union and served on a burgeoning number of influential national and local bodies. Mrs Phillips seemed determined to prove herself equal to any challenge.[3] Whether he knew it or not Colonel Strange was recruiting an unusually powerful woman into his male dominated organisation.

After averting strike action in July 1925 by setting up an inquiry into the coal industry, Prime Minister Stanley Baldwin had sanctioned extensive preparations to cope with the threat of a general strike, thus explaining Colonel Strange's contact with Mrs Phillips six months before the crisis occurred. She would at this stage remain ex-officio, part of a 'voluntary combination of citizens' recruited by the Organisation for the Maintenance of Supplies (OMS). The OMS Council, located near Whitehall, was headed by ten prominent Establishment figures. They included the 1st Earl Jellicoe and Lieutenant General Sir Francis Lloyd, both ex-military leaders, causing Sarah Harris to describe the OMS as 'a sort of private volunteer army'.[4] On 3 August the Home Secretary William Joynson-Hicks spoke of a danger of England being 'governed by a handful of trade union leaders if a Soviet were established here . . .'.[5] Chiming with Joynson-Hicks' view, a confidential OMS memorandum left with Mrs Phillips by Colonel Strange warned of 'attempts by revolutionaries or extremist bodies to stop services and industries, [and the public] threatened . . . on a scale unequalled in the past'.[6] Though the trade unions saw strike action as defensive – to prevent cuts in wages and conditions – ministers' attitudes had hardened and the strike was viewed as an insidious challenge to government and communities.

On 30 September 1925, in response to rising concerns about the OMS in press and Parliament, the Home Secretary made his position clear. His letter was reproduced in the memorandum given to Mrs Phillips. As well as acknowledging that he had been consulted on the establishment of the OMS, the Home Secretary was clearly supportive:

> It would be a very great assistance to us to receive from the OMS . . .
> classified lists of *men* in different parts of the country who would be
> willing to place their service at the disposal of the Government . . . not
> only is there no reason why you should object to the OMS but that you

. . . would be performing a patriotic act by allying yourself with this or any similar body . . .[7]

Robin Page Arnot described this arrangement as 'entirely new in the annals of strike breaking societies'.[8]

While Mrs Phillips undoubtedly saw herself as patriotic, her correspondence with Colonel Strange suggests she would later experience a tension between her elected position as Mayor and her role in emergency government. She was not alone in raising questions about OMS. Several newspapers had been critical of the organisation, and on 19 November, the day after Mrs Phillips agreed to act as Food Officer, the Home Secretary was questioned by Mr Taylor, MP, about 'secret' letters being sent to Town Clerks concerning plans for a national emergency.[9]

Figure 1. An OMS Poster.

On 20 November 1925 the Ministry of Health issued Circular 636, detailing new measures that would apply under the Emergency Powers Act 1920 'for securing the essential life of the country'.[10] A government appointee would act as civil commissioner in ten regional divisions including a South Western Division, for which The Earl Stanhope would act as commissioner, based at Bristol. Divisional Officers had also been appointed for transport, coal, postal and food services, the latter post being occupied by Colonel Strange. Divisional Officers were instructed to work with local officers (hence the Colonel's recruitment of Mrs Phillips for East Devon), and with local voluntary services, whose activities would be coordinated by a chairman selected by the government. Although local authorities were supposed to be kept informed of the ongoing situation, it was considered desirable that they should 'keep aloof from any industrial dispute'.[11]

On the same day that Circular 636 was issued, Colonel Strange wrote to Mrs Phillips thanking her for agreeing to act as Food Officer. He told her that he would be visiting Plymouth and Exeter, apparently to establish local emergency centres. That he agreed to her suggestion to meet for a chance of discussing the details perhaps reflects her concerns. A subsequent letter from Colonel Strange indicates that she wrote to him again on the 11 December, concerning the memorandum and the role of local authorities. It is noteworthy that in her dealings with traders and local authorities Mrs Phillips was referred to (and indeed referred to herself) as 'Borough Mayor', but at no point during the correspondence between herself and the colonel was this designation used. Circular 636 made it clear that she would not be accountable to her own, or to any other local authority, but to the Government Civil Commissioner in Bristol.

On Boxing Day 1925 Colonel Strange wrote formally to Mrs Phillips from Tyndalls Park Road, Bristol – his new address near to the Regional Commissioners Office at Unity Street – to confirm her appointment by the President of the Board of Trade. She would not however be placed on the payroll 'until required'; the strike was still over four months away. A second (handwritten) letter addressed her concerns. Colonel Strange wrote, 'With reference to the OMS the Government has decided . . . that recruits shall be absolutely at our disposal as individuals not as an organization'.[12] His typewritten press release stated that the OMS would shortly be opening a branch in the

Figure 2. Councillor Mrs Phillips at Sudbury Lawn, Honiton.
Reproduced courtesy of Westcountry Studies Library, Devon Libraries.

neighbourhood where volunteers would be able to register. Regarding her concern about the role of local councils, echoing circular 636, he told her: it was not 'thought desirable that Local Authorities should give active official support as such'.[13]

Few women during this period could have envisaged so powerful a role at a time when most women did not have the vote. Her role would extend far beyond Honiton Borough Council to the Urban Districts of Axminster, Ottery St Mary, Seaton and Sidmouth, and the rural districts of Axminster and Honiton. In her position as Mayor, and therefore conscious of local authority protocol, Mrs Phillips would have been aware of the need to consult with other councils. However, Colonel Strange cautioned that 'Local Authorities concerned will be informed at the proper time of your position in relation to them'.[14] As to what the 'proper time' was, this remained uncertain.

For Mrs Phillips, protocol would also have also meant introducing the Colonel to her fellow councillors. She wrote 'I take it you would then like to meet the Chairmen of Urban Districts and Rural Districts in this area,' adding that her Town Clerk was 'quite willing that we should use his office in case of emergency . . . just opposite my house.'[15] Colonel Strange replied on 25 January, stating that all Local Authorities would be informed about the Food Officers covering their respective areas, and he appeared to concede to her desire for a meeting. However there is no indication that Colonel Strange or anyone from the Civil Commissioner's office attended such a meeting. He wrote again on 3 February (using official stationery of the Board of Trade Food Department for the first time) offering to clear up any outstanding issues, and referring to a meeting which probably included local OMS contacts. Details of this meeting are not known, but Mrs Phillips' confidential papers include a list of names, addresses and private telephone numbers of those serving on Exeter Centre Emergency Committee. Fifteen male appointments and one female (Mrs Phillips) were appointed to this committee, which may explain why the Civil Commissioner's Office often addressed her as 'Dear Sir'. Colonel Strange had appointed Hugh Lloyd Parry for Exeter and John Pugsley for Tiverton – both Town Clerks – along with Charles Wills for Newton Abbot, and County Councillor G.K. Blatchford for Okehampton. The Centre would be based at the Bishop's Palace, adjacent to Exeter Cathedral.

The confidential nature of these arrangements, and the failure to include local authorities in such plans, enabled critics to argue that they were 'designed to supercede or subordinate the whole tradition of local government in Britain.'[16] This, and any established rivalries between councils, was an issue which confronted Mrs Philips when she wrote to Council Chairmen in East Devon on 12 February asking them for details of local food wholesalers. She used her new title of Food Officer in addition to that of 'Borough Mayor'. The letter was again marked 'confidential', and used the address of the Town Clerk, E.W. Hellier, although during the strike she based herself at her home, or at her husband's office.

The Chairman of Axminster Urban District Council replied curtly, stating assertively that the Council had already appointed a Committee to deal with this subject. He informed her that 'a meeting was called in connection with the Civil OMS at which I was appointed Chairman', adding pointedly 'I have called the two organizations together with the idea of formulating a policy'.[17] Councillor Webster was clearly intent on asserting his own authority. He appeared to view Mrs Phillips' new role as a threat to his own position. If so, this was a view shared by a number of local authorities who viewed emergency regulations as a threat to their traditional powers, and undermined the independent delivery of services to their communities as they saw fit. Francis and Smith point out that Emergency Regulations and the OMS 'were hardly invoked in the mining valleys'.[18] Having confirmed details of only two local wholesalers, Mrs Phillips wrote directly to local traders, adding Colyton to her list and again signing herself Mayor of Honiton and Food Officer. She was sufficiently encouraged by their replies to establish an Area Advisory Committee of butchers, bakers and grocers from all parts of the borough.

By the time the Samuel Commission reported on 10 March 1926, the situation had reached an impasse. The unions had rejected any suggestion of lower wages, longer hours and district agreements. On 30 April 'lock out' notices began to be posted at pits. Following a Cabinet meeting on 1 May, which included the Chief Civil Commissioner Sir William Thompson, the Government announced a State of Emergency. Regulations governing food and other essentials were issued. Ernest Bevin, who saw OMS and the regulations as a 'declaration of war', once again assured the government that the Trades Union Congress (TUC) were 'prepared to distribute essential foodstuffs'.[19] Trades unionists were right to be apprehensive; the OMS became an official government organisation and handed over its register of volunteers to the Commissioners. Numbers were thought to be at least 100,000 strong, including many military reservists. The TUC voted overwhelmingly in favour of strike action (3.5 million for, and less than 50,000 votes against). As the unions started issuing strike orders Mrs Phillips received seemingly contradictory instructions via telegrams from Bristol, first to 'resume duty forthwith', followed at 3.33 p.m. by 'Staff not to be engaged till further instructions – Strange, Unity Street, Bristol'.[20] The probable explanation was a last minute attempt by the Prime Minister and the TUC to resume negotiations.

At 11.30 a.m. on 3 May, with the General Strike imminent, Mrs Phillips convened a meeting of her Traders Advisory Committee. They met in the Town Clerk's Office. This was the first use of her executive powers as Emergency Food Officer, to 'explain the course of action to be taken in the event of a national emergency and discuss

any difficulty that may be likely to arise'.[21] Local traders immediately
identified a potential problem. Reporting to Colonel Strange, she
told him they had all agreed that there should be no credit account
between traders for goods transferred during the emergency. Honiton
traders, fearing a long strike, were not prepared to supply goods on
account. She added 'they seemed to think this could be arranged by
the Local Food Emergency Officer. Would you let me know if in the
event of this necessity arising I could so act?'[22] There is no record of
a reply.

Shortly before the deadline Mrs Phillips received a further telegram:
'11.19 fr. Bristol OHMS to Foodwatcher Honiton: Engage Necessary
staff within limits already authorized. Foodminder Bristol'.[23] She
wrote to Colonel Strange: 'according to instruction received I have
verified that my telegrapher address has been registered . . . have taken
delivery of stationery. I have engaged a clerk at the rate authorized'.[24]
William Henry Davey would be paid £1 11s 6d per week. The General
Strike began at midnight. Three million workers were involved. In
expectation of a long strike Mrs Phillips began to recruit for staff and
volunteers.

In Exeter all police leave was cancelled as 3,500 workers came
out on strike. Transport workers like W.G. Chinn of the National
Union of Railway men were especially influential. On the first evening
Exeter Trades Council established a strike committee based at the
Labour Club. They awaited instructions from the TUC General
Council; few were forthcoming. Although Exeter Central, Exeter St
David's and other railway stations were largely without passenger
services, some Devon General buses continued to run. In the absence
of most national newspapers, *The Western Times* continued to
publish a slimmed down edition.[25] Kenneth Gatey, Managing Editor
of the newspaper, and Sheriff of Exeter, was listed as a member of
the Government's Emergency Committee. At Bishop's Gate, (the
committee headquarters) plans for Emergency Government were
up and running. Local JP Phillip Rowsell was acting as Voluntary
Service Officer and enrolling volunteers. The Head of the National
Insurance Audit Department, H.H. Reeks, was acting as Finance
Officer. He had transferred from Bedford Circus to Bishop's Palace
where volunteers were being recruited. Though normal mail services
were severely disrupted, Exeter's Postmaster, J.C. Braithwaite, served

as the Centre's Postal Officer. Exeter's Food Emergency Officer (Mr Lloyd Parry) was waiting for a reply from Mrs Phillips.

Although in Honiton and other towns in East Devon there were no reports of 'gloomy men gathering on street corners', as *The Western Times* had reported of Exeter,[26] business was not quite as usual. All train and bus services were either cancelled or severely disrupted for the next week. Without the trains there were no regular newspapers or mail, and the absence of freight trains resulted in fewer coal deliveries. Even a quiet market town in Devon could not escape the shortage of basic commodities, or the general feeling of apprehension experienced by communities across the country.

On 4 May 1926, the first day of emergency government in Honiton and East Devon, events did not run as smoothly as Mrs Phillips might have hoped. Before reporting to her office she visited Mr Hellier, the Town Clerk, who was absent from his office (apparently ill). However, a letter sent to him, had been left for Mrs Phillips. The letter from Mr Lloyd Parry reminded them of his appointment as Food Emergency Officer for the Exeter Area. He instructed Mr Hellier to, 'put yourself in touch with me in the event of any shortage . . . and let me have details of any appreciable fluctuations in food prices directly attributable to the emergency that has arisen'.[27]

Mrs Phillips wrote immediately to Colonel Strange at the Commissioner's Office, demanding a ruling on 'what my position really is which I can quote as an authority when in communication with other councils'.[28] The previous day (3 May) Colonel Strange had in fact sent her a formal contract: 'I have advised the Area Finance Officer of your appointment as Local Emergency Food Officer . . . on a salary of 20/- per diem so long as it is necessary to retain your services'.[29] Mrs Phillips may have wondered why her opposite number in Exeter was unaware of her appointment, which had been authorised in December 1925. After all, her name was listed in the Exeter Centre directory, and the Finance Officer was aware of her position. Perhaps in an attempt to correct any false rumours about her position, she travelled by car to visit traders and other contacts. As she was 'employed on the Government Emergency Organisation', Mrs Phillips later claimed 4d a mile for her forty-seven mile round trip. On the second day of the General Strike Colonel Strange replied to Mrs Phillips, addressing her once again as 'Dear Sir'. He told her that the

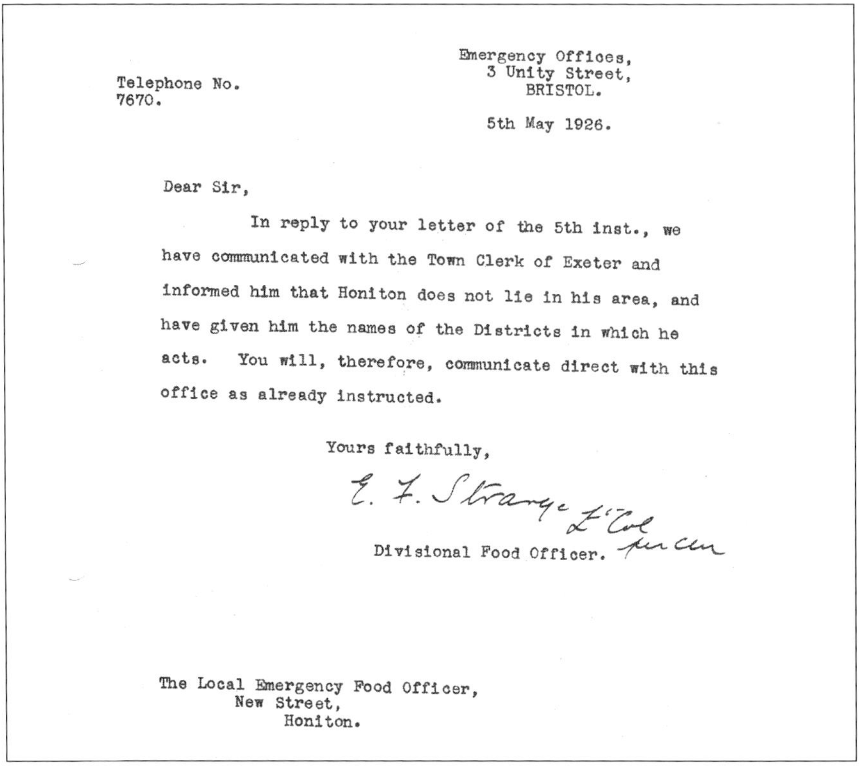

Telephone No.
7670.

Emergency Offices,
3 Unity Street,
BRISTOL.

5th May 1926.

Dear Sir,

In reply to your letter of the 5th inst., we have communicated with the Town Clerk of Exeter and informed him that Honiton does not lie in his area, and have given him the names of the Districts in which he acts. You will, therefore, communicate direct with this office as already instructed.

Yours faithfully,

E. F. Strange

Divisional Food Officer.

The Local Emergency Food Officer,
New Street,
Honiton.

Figure 3. WCSL Reference: OMS 14.20. Letter from 'E.F. Strange' to Mrs Phillips, addressing her as 'Dear Sir'. Reproduced courtesy of Westcountry Studies Library, Devon Libraries.

Commissioner's Office had 'communicated with the Town Clerk of Exeter and informed him that Honiton does not lie in his area, and have given him the names of the Districts in which he acts. You will, therefore, communicate direct with this office as already instructed'.[30]

In Bristol, the efforts of the Commissioner and OMS to maintain transport services had paid off and full tram and bus services were operating,[31] 'Blacklegs' (strike breakers) had also been recruited at Bristol docks.[32] Robin Stanes suggests that most Devonshire trade unionists (railwaymen in particular) 'were solid for the strike in the face of a hostile press and public opinion'.[33] In Exeter 'no proper newspapers were printed though management and blackleg labour did produce some truncated editons'. In a bid to maintain law and order the Chief Constable of Devon appealed in *The Western Times* on 7 May for men 'who set a value on loyalty to King and Country and to the cause of good and orderly Government' to enroll as special constables.[34] Mrs Phillips' husband, Tom, was one of 125 volunteers who signed up, along with twenty-four 'specials' signed up by Great Western Railway.

Planning for the long term, Mrs Phillips instructed her advisory committee to send a report by 11am on Mondays and Thursdays each week containing the following information, '1. Whether stocks are maintained 2. Any anticipated shortages with special reference to flour 3. Any fluctuations in price'.[35] Although in the next few days the TUC and the Miners Federation resolved to stand firm, leading members on the General Council of the TUC had clearly decided that the General Strike was lost. Mrs Phillips nevertheless continued to prepare for the long haul. She received a letter from Mr C. Bartlett, the local land agent, headed 'OMS' and listing fifteen clerical workers who would be available after business hours or before work.

The last day of the General Strike in East Devon on 12 May 1926 was again marked by mixed messages from Exeter and Bristol. At lunchtime news reached *The Western Times* at Exeter that the strike was over, 'The TUC leaders had capitulated . . . The few strikers around the London Inn Square were incredulous at first for their organization had barely got into gear'.[36] Mrs Phillips ('Foodwatcher') received an OHMS telegram from the Bristol Commissioners Office at 11.36am to 'continue acting till further instructions. No additional staff to be engaged'.[37] On the same day Phillip Rowsell wrote to her from Bishop's Palace, Exeter, instructing her to close her office with immediate effect. He had just received orders from Head Office to stop recruiting, and he instructed her to 'send . . . all the cards you have both filled in and spare', thanking her 'for all the hard and valuable work' that she and her staff had put in.[38] Five days later, a telegram to 'Foodminder' from 'Foodwatcher OHMS Bristol', instructed Mrs Phillips to send all records to the Bristol office.[39]

On 25 May she received a further communication from Colonel Strange, written on crested notepaper from the Civil Commissioner's Office, South West Division. In this request for comments on the working of the Government Scheme, and suggestions as to improvements, Mrs Phillips was once again addressed as 'Dear Sir'. Finally on 5 July he requested 'for purposes of record a list of the names and addresses of the *gentlemen* [my italics] who have assisted you as members of your Advisory Committee . . . the industries represented by them . . . as well as the Local Association . . . which nominated them'.[40] Whatever challenge of conscience she may have had during the nine days in May – and for almost six months before – Mrs Phillips had conducted her office with competence and efficiency. When her accounts were finally settled the General Strike in East Devon had cost less than £30.

The miners' lockout continued for a further six months causing considerable hardship in pit communities. Although Exeter Trades Council provided hospitality and took collections for miners' choirs, the Town Clerk (Hugh Lloyd Parry) told them that a City Watch Committee ban on Miners Lamp Day and the Ystrad Choir was 'definite and deliberate'.[41] In late November the miners returned to work on an eight hour day, accepting lower wages and local agreements, all they had striven to defeat. The Trades Dispute Act passed in 1927 made general strikes illegal. The membership of trade unions fell dramatically. Mrs Thatcher learned lessons from the General Strike of 1926 which she applied in the 1984 miners' strike.

Mrs Phillips' experience of the General Strike seems to have remained private. However she and her husband did support the local Miners' Relief Fund, and in 1937 she wrote to *The Times* suggesting that Coronation funds be sent to distressed areas such as Wales, where her sister lived.[42] On 26 January 1938 she became the first and only woman to be made a Freeman of the Borough of Honiton. Her brief experience as Food Officer during the General Strike would not be wasted. On the eve of World War II she was once again appointed Food Executive Officer for Honiton Borough, serving from the Little Theatre she had built at her home for the remainder of the war. In 1945 Mrs Phillips was elected Mayor of Honiton for the eleventh and final time, and subsequently awarded the OBE in 1951. She died at a Torquay nursing home in 1966, and was buried in relative obscurity at St Andrews Church, Awliscombe. A brief obituary in *The Times* stated that she was 'one time Mayor of Honiton.'[43] Juanita Maxwell Phillips has rightfully been identified by Todd Gray as one of the *Remarkable Women of Devon*.[44]

Notes and References

1. WCSL, OMS, 14.01.
2. Renshaw 1975.
3. Based on 'Celebrating Juanita', two lectures delivered by the author at Meadow View Chapel, Honiton (unpublished), 3 and 10 September 2009; *Viva Juanita: this is your life*, Honiton Players production, 23 April 2010.
4. Harris 1985, p. 41.
5. *The Times*, 3 August 1925, in Harris 1985, p. 40; Andrews 2009, p. 154, refers to 'the rabidly anti-Soviet Home Secretary William Joynson Hicks.'
6. WCSL, OMS, 14.01.
7. Ibid.
8. Page Arnot 1926, pp. 49-50.
9. Ibid., p. 57.
10. Ibid., pp. 59-62.
11. Ibid., p. 57.
12. WCSL, OMS, 14.03a.
13. Ibid.
14. WCSL, OMS, 14.03b.
15. WCSL, OMS, 14.19.
16. Page Arnot, p. 57.
17. WCSL, OMS, 14.07.
18. Francis and Smith 1980, p. 55.
19. Laybourne 1996, p. 43.
20. WCSL, OMS, 14.12.
21. Ibid.
22. WCSL, OMS, 14.14.
23. Ibid., 14.13.
24. WCSL, OMS, 14.14.
25. Kirby 1990, p. 34.
26. Ibid., p. 35.
27. WCSL, OMS, 14.20.
28. Ibid.
29. Ibid.
30. Ibid.
31. Renshaw 1975, p. 85.
32. Perkins 2006, p. 248. Perkins notes that 670 'blacklegs' were employed at Bristol docks.
33. Stanes 1986, p. 57.
34. Kirby 1990, p. 34.
35. WCSL, OMS, 14.23.
36. Kirby, p. 34.
37. WCSL, OMS, 14.27.

38. Ibid, 14.28.
39. Ibid, 14.30.
40. Ibid, OMS, 14.34.
41. Kirby p. 57.
42. *The Times*, 15 March 1937.
43. *The Times*, 'Deaths', 19 November 1966.
44. Gray 2009, pp. 143-144.

Bibliography

Andrews, C. (2009) *The Defence of the Realm: the authorised history of MI5*, Canada: Viking.

Francis, H. & Smith, D. (1980) *The Fed: a history of the South Wales miners in the twentieth century*, London: Lawrence and Wishart.

Gray, T. (2009) *Remarkable Women of Devon*, Exeter: Mint Press.

Harris, S. (1985) *The General Strike: how and why*, London: Dryad Press.

Kirkby, A. (1990) *In the Cause of Liberty*, Exeter: Exeter Trades Council.

Laybourn, K. (1993) *The General Strike of 1926*, Manchester: Manchester University Press.

Neville, J. (2012) *Viva Juanita!: Juanita Phillips, champion for change in East Devon between the wars*, (forthcoming).

Page Arnot, R. (1926) *The General Strike May 1926: its origin and history*, London: LRD.

Perkins, A. (2006) *A Very British Strike*, London: Macmillan.

Renshaw, P. (1975) *Nine Days in May*, London: Eyre Methuen.

Stanes, R. (1986) *A History of Devon*: Chichester: Phillimore & Co. Ltd.

'Noblesse Oblige': Dame Georgiana Buller and services for disabled people in twentieth-century Devon

Julia Neville

Farewell to Downes

When Sir Redvers Buller, Devon's greatest nineteenth-century general, died in 1908 his funeral was attended by mourners from the three worlds he had served: the estate, the army and the county. The two miles between his home at Downes and the church in Crediton were lined on either side by people paying their respects to 'the great soldier, the kindly squire, the good neighbour, the friend of all that were needy'.[1] His coffin was borne on a Field Artillery gun carriage, covered with a Union Jack on which rested his sword, his plumed busby and a wreath of yellow roses from his only child, Georgiana. Behind the coffin came Biffen, Buller's horse at the relief of Ladysmith, his master's empty boots reversed in the stirrups. Then came Georgiana, accompanied by her stepbrother and stepsisters. Buller's widow, Lady Audrey, as was the custom, did not attend. The church was full; simultaneous memorial services were held in Aldershot and in Exeter Cathedral; and a general's seventeen-gun salute marked his interment in the family vault.[2]

After the funeral, Georgiana Buller had to make a new life. When her father had retired in 1902 she was almost twenty and though, following convention, she had 'come out' and been presented at court, she had in practice become her father's assistant, helping him in the

387

administration of the estate where 'he knew every blade of grass . . . had planned every cottage and had known every labourer from his youth' and in his work for Devon County Council.[3] She had even taken a shorthand certificate in order to act more efficiently as his secretary. When he fell ill with the cancer that killed him, she had helped to nurse him. Nonetheless, although she was her father's only child, the Downes estate passed to the nearest male heir, her uncle Tremayne. She and her mother moved out of Downes into a house in nearby Newton St Cyres. They found some occupation in planning memorials to Sir Redvers and in discussions with his biographer, but neither these tasks nor her enthusiasm for hunting could provide sufficient occupation for an active and intelligent young woman.[4]

By a fortunate coincidence, the Territorial and Reserve Forces Act, incorporating the Volunteers and the Militia into a new Territorial Force based on county boundaries, had been passed only a year before Redvers Buller's death. Its implementation included the establishment of civilian organizations, also county based, formed under the aegis of the Red Cross and known as Voluntary Aid Detachments (VADs). The idea of volunteers 'behind the lines' who could carry out transport duties, provide rest stations and staff auxiliary hospitals in support of the professional medical corps had been Buller's own, first put in place during the South African War. Lady Audrey and her daughter had both attended the initial meeting for a Devonshire organization in July 1907: Lady Audrey became a Vice-President and Georgiana Buller the Assistant County Director for Exeter. The Devon unit became a major source of occupation for Georgiana Buller, involving her in fund-raising, recruitment and training, and by 1913 she had become Deputy County Director.[5]

'She simply worked like dozens of people rolled into one':[6] Georgiana Buller and the Exeter War Hospitals, 1914–1920

On 4 August 1914 Britain went to war. By 7 October the West of England Eye Infirmary in Exeter had been commandeered by the Red Cross, and by 14 October the first patients were admitted to its ninety-four beds. The flow of casualties was so great that a further four hospitals were established in Exeter, at the Episcopal Modern School, the Children's Home at the Workhouse, the barracks on Topsham

Road and in a student hostel in Castle Street. Eventually the beds in the Exeter War Hospitals totalled 1400. These were supplemented by a network of smaller units in clubs or houses lent for the purpose such as the Honiton Working Men's Club, the Crediton Liberal Club and the 'villa residence' at Chelston lent by the Mayor of Torquay.[7]

Georgiana Buller became the Director of the Exeter War Hospitals, which grew into an organization on a scale not contemplated before war began. As numbers of casualties increased it became evident that the task of caring for the wounded was more than a volunteer force could sustain. In 1916 the War Office took control of the VAD hospitals throughout the country. Only in Exeter was the existing Red Cross organization considered robust enough to meet the standards of the Army, and Buller was asked to stay on to manage the Exeter hospitals, the affiliated convalescent establishments, and other duties such as providing refreshments for the troop trains passing through Exeter and sterilizing and packing sphagnum moss for field dressings.[8]

The Devon author E.M. Delafield, popular in later life for her columns as 'The Provincial Lady', always denied that 'Miss Vivien' in her novel, *The War Workers*, was based on Georgiana Buller, but many people thought they recognized the portrait. Delafield had worked for the Exeter War Hospitals and although her fictional setting was called a 'Midlands Supply Depot' the account of Miss Vivien tackling her morning post sounds very much like Buller's daily task:

> Transport wanted for fifty men going from the King Street Hospital today – and they want more sphagnum moss. There ought to be five hundred bags ready to go out this morning . . . Hospital accounts – that can go to the Finance Department . . . The Stores bill – to the Commissariat. What's all this – transport for that man in hospital? I shall have to see to that myself. Look me up the War Office letters as to Petrol regulations . . . Here are some more of those tiresome muddles of Mrs Potter's. I told her about all those people on Monday . . . Why on earth hasn't it been arranged? Nothing is ever done unless one sees to it oneself. The Medical Officer of Health wants to see me. What are my appointments for today . . . ?[9]

Running hospitals for the War Office rather than the Red Cross proved a mixed blessing. Military discipline and organization meant that logistics became more straightforward, but this sometimes led to local friction. The Theatre Royal manager was aggrieved to find that regulations meant that wounded soldiers were no longer allowed out to attend a performance; three doctors resigned over criticisms allegedly made by Buller; the Surgeon-General's office interfered so much that on one occasion the nine Assistant County Directors all threatened to resign.[10] However by 1919 when the hospitals were decommissioned over 35,000 patients had been treated, staying on average twenty five days each. Buller was proud that their costs were below the national average: 'Not a penny was unnecessarily spent', she told fund-raisers at a fund-raising 'Monster Rummage Sale', 'but . . . they did not grudge anything, because their standard from the first had been to give to the men ... everything the public would want their nearest and dearest to have when wounded'.[11] Direct contact with the patients rather than administration and fund-raising was what she found the most enjoyable part of the job and although sometimes the soldiers chafed under the strict regime they did appreciate her for what one described as 'her great kind heart'.[12]

Figure 1. Georgiana Buller.
Reproduced courtesy of St Loyes Foundation.

It was not until 1920 that Georgiana Buller herself stood down. For her service she was awarded the Royal Red Cross and the new honour established by the King, that of a Dame of the British Empire. Local admirers raised funds to present her with a testimonial and a pearl necklace and, exhausted by her efforts and still in pain from a hunting accident before the war, she retired to convalesce at Sidmouth.[13]

'Broken Blossoms':[14] Georgiana Buller and the Princess Elizabeth Orthopaedic Hospital

During the summer of 1927 a small boy in a wheelchair pushed by his mother could regularly have been seen making his way towards the building site at Gras Lawn on the corner of Exeter's Wonford and Barrack Roads. He had been told that the new building was to be a hospital for people like him and he wanted 'just to be sure it's really there'.[15] Down to the site too, no doubt, came Georgiana Buller, now living at Bellair on Topsham Road, only a few hundred yards away. She had become the President of the Devonian Association for Cripples' Aid, the body that was developing the future Princess Elizabeth Orthopaedic Hospital.

Buller had become involved in this initiative after an approach by her own doctor, Henry Andrew, and a medical colleague from War Hospital days, Brennan Dyball, a surgeon at the Royal Devon and Exeter Hospital who had developed an interest in the new specialism of orthopaedics. Dyball's inspiration was the 'National Scheme for Crippled Children'. Its sponsors were practising orthopaedic surgeons who had published their proposal in the *British Medical Journal* in 1919. They described how 'the majority of children suffering from crippling diseases and deformities of all kinds' lay 'out of sight in their homes . . . in workhouses, or collected in homes for crippled children'.[16] Three-quarters of them, they claimed, could be cured by surgical treatment, and an even greater proportion enabled to be more active. The Chief Medical Officer rejected their proposal to make provision of orthopaedic hospitals a statutory requirement, and it was left to voluntary organizations to make the scheme work.[17] In 1925, at the prompting of Andrew, Dyball and Mrs Jessie Loch, a Crediton neighbour of the Bullers, a Devon and Cornwall Association for the Care of Cripples was established. It was then agreed that the two counties formed too large an area for a single service. A line was drawn from Bude to Torquay and at a meeting addressed by Georgiana Buller on 31 August 1925, the Devonian Association for Cripples' Aid (DACA) was launched to serve the eastern sector.[18]

For the next two years fund-raising was the principal activity. The target set for the hospital building fund was £15,000 (over £500,000 at today's prices), all to be raised from charitable sources, though local authorities were expected as part of their responsibilities for education for children with special needs to contribute substantially to the running costs. Buller spoke at fund-raising events such as the 'Fancy Fair for Crippled Children' held at South Molton and the 'Little Cripples Bazaar' (so called by the newspaper that had dubbed the children 'Broken Blossoms') organized by Exeter Rotary Club.[19] She wrote letters of appeal: one, published in the *Manchester Guardian*, urged the public to buy a brick. She was involved in selecting the site and in developing the plans. In an astonishingly short time, just over two years, the Princess Elizabeth Orthopaedic Hospital was opened by the Duchess of York, who graciously permitted it to be named after her infant daughter, the future Queen Elizabeth II. In fact on opening day the hospital was not quite finished and local children were recruited to play the parts of patients. Buller had refused to let the date slip, reputedly saying that the opening would go ahead, even if all they could open was a bathroom. The first patients were admitted on 16 December 1927.[20]

Rosemary Sutcliff, the author, was treated at the Princess Elizabeth Orthopaedic Hospital in the early 1930s. She remembered it as 'Mr Capener's kingdom'. (Norman Capener had been appointed surgeon-in-charge in 1931). She described its 'fresh-air' approach to treatment:

Two long wards, one for boys, one for girls, were separated in the middle by a glassed-in office . . . All down one side the wards were completely open on to a field, making no pretence of a garden. It was lovely in the fine summer weather, but murder in the winter, for staff and patients alike, worst of all in wild weather, when canvas screens had to be shipped all down the open side, blotting out the field and the sky along with the wind and the rain. But the rain spattered in over the top of the screens and the canvas bellied like the sails of a ship at sea, and the wind set the unshaded lights that hung on long flexes from the khaki-painted iron roof girders swinging wildly to and fro . . .[21]

After the opening Georgiana Buller continued to play a full part in the management of the hospital and the supporting outpatient clinics based in Barnstaple, Exeter, Honiton, Okehampton, Tiverton and Torquay, and later in Launceston and Kingsbridge. It was she with whom the county Medical Officer of Health crossed swords when he sought to exercise the right to agree which patients should be admitted at the county's expense, and she of whom the chair of the County Finance Committee once exclaimed in exasperation: 'A certain lady is trying to rule the County Council . . .'.[22] Buller and her committee, who knew that adults also could benefit from orthopaedic surgery, wished to extend the remit of the Orthopaedic Hospital to adults. This was not a development for which the county had budgeted. In March 1934 one of Buller's allies, Lord Mamhead, forced a debate on the issue within the County Council, prompting the Finance Committee chair into his exasperated exclamation, and, three months later, enough money was found to increase admissions. After this episode, however, Buller and her vice-chair, John Radcliffe, changed places. At the end of 1935 Radcliffe took on DACA and the hospital, and Buller turned her attention to a new project, one that the Association had been promising to tackle ever since its first beginnings, the broader welfare of disabled people, and in particular their training for employment.[23]

'No man is a cripple until he is crippled in spirit':[24] Georgiana Buller and St Loye's College

A Vocational Training Department (staffed by volunteers) had been established at the hospital from the very beginning. It made slow progress, however. Employers were reluctant to offer placements and there were limited opportunities for home working, although crafts such as 'Italian embroidery' were tried, and difficulties over arranging for sales. A first meeting about a possible project to create a training college that could run accredited courses to prepare people with disabilities for work was chaired by the Mayor of Exeter on 1

July 1930, but little had been achieved by 1935. Georgiana Buller had chaired the national Central Council for the Care of Cripples in 1932, and helped to establish the first training institute at Leatherhead. Once she took charge of the Devon project its impetus changed. A regional group representing the six counties in the far South West began to plan in earnest for St Loye's Training Centre for Cripples, later St Loye's College.[25]

As had been the case for the hospital earlier, an intensive period of fund-raising then took place. Millbrook House and its grounds on Exeter's Topsham Road was acquired, and a hostel and workshops converted or built. In a phrase to which Georgiana Buller was to return to sum up her life's work she described the college as 'transformed from a castle-in-the-air into a building of bricks and mortar'. The first trainee moved in on 8 July 1937 and the twenty-five places for trainees were rapidly filled. The college offered training in watch and instrument making and repairs, and in catering and gardening. Demand was so high that by June 1938 there was a waiting list of twenty four trainees from the South West and beyond.[26]

Trainees came with different backgrounds and disabilities. The first four who found permanent employment were a thirty-three-year old man who had had infantile paralysis, trained as a gardener; a thirty-two-year old man with a tubercular hip and a sixteen-year old with osteomyelitis who went into watch-making; and a twenty-year old who had lost a leg and became an instrument maker. One of the first graduates later reflected on his experience at St Loye's: 'I can only say that the training I received has been the greatest thing in my life. It has got rid of my inferiority complex, established me on an equal footing with other people, and given me a certain amount of independence, which is best of all'.[27]

Plans to develop the college accelerated. The neighbouring property, Fairfield House, came onto the market and, as Buller put it, it was 'now or never' to create space for women trainees, another 'castle-in-the-air' made real.[28] War came: the college's potential to help meet the need for additional labour was recognized and it was approved for work of national importance by the Ministry of Supply and the Air Ministry. Ernest Bevin, the Minister of Labour, reputedly after a personal appeal from Buller who remembered him as a small boy scrumping apples on the Downes estate, agreed to pay tuition fees for the students.[29] St Loye's College was confirmed on its seventy-year life as a specialist college.

A Woman of Great Gifts

Dame Georgiana Buller was a woman of great gifts. When she died in 1953, after sixteen years directing the work of St Loye's and after serving as a lay member in the new National Health Service, the St Loye's' Annual Report described her as 'a master of strategy and tactics with powers of persuasion which few could resist'.[30] Norman Capener, her long-term associate, said that:

> Whatever Dame Georgiana put her hand to she did superlatively well. She was a Justice of the Peace and she had a keen interest in music, drama and the arts . . . She was keen on gardens and had a great love of children. Her relatives saw this side of her at its best: she was charming with them. Equally was she with hospital children. Her rather stern face would light up with an unexpected happiness and interest . . . Dame Georgiana was a most able chairman of committees: orderly, coldly logical and quick in repartee. She was patient and kindly when working with those she liked or respected but ruthlessly direct and impatient with those who by foolishness, thoughtlessness, incompetence or obstinacy stood in her way.[31]

Georgiana Buller used her gifts to create three great twentieth-century services for people with disabilities in Devon: the Devonshire Association for Cripples' Aid, the Princess Elizabeth Orthopaedic Hospital and St Loye's Training College. All three were pioneering ventures which paved the way for their still-existing successors: the Devonian Orthopaedic Association, the Princess Elizabeth Orthopaedic Centre at the Royal Devon and Exeter NHS Foundation Trust, and the St Loye's Foundation. Nonetheless Buller was a child of her time, and the conventions of her generation shaped the way in which she used her gifts. As she was not, perhaps never needed to be, a radical, her work in Devon was bounded by the ideas, practice and attitudes of the times through which she lived. This shaped the expectations of what women could do; the way in which her voluntary organizations had to work; and the nature of the opportunities she was able to create for disabled people.

Georgiana Buller was born into a late Victorian world. She grew up in a well-to-do, well-connected county family. In her father she observed a devotion to service, a strategic grasp of direction and ruthless attention to detail combined with a personal interest in and concern for those dependent on him. Her mother was a great charitable patron in the way then expected of a lady, serving on committees and lending her name to appeals or fund-raising events to encourage others to give. Lady Audrey was also a conventional woman, president of the Exeter branch of the National Society for Opposing Women's Suffrage. Although Georgiana herself was unconventional enough as a teenager to write a play called *The Prude's Prejudice or The Triumphant Bicyclist*, in which she played a man,[32] she never sought to do anything other than to work within the framework of the county society into which she had been born. The Great War gave her an opportunity to learn what she was capable of and, like many other young women of her class, she took it. Her war service became a foundation for unpaid but full-time public service thereafter.[33]

The world of welfare in which she worked was itself evolving. The roles of voluntary organizations and of local authorities and central government were shifting along what has been called a 'moving frontier'. Responsibilities for the welfare of those who could not afford to pay for their care had once been sharply divided between the patronage of the charitable and the hated Poor Law. By the mid twentieth century a 'New Philanthropy' was emerging, a partnership between the state and the voluntary sector under which the state took greater responsibility for resourcing welfare services and voluntary organisations accepted state funding for some of the services they delivered. Voluntary organisations came to derive as much as a third of their income from statutory agencies.[34] This developing relationship frequently generated friction, with the statutory sector seeking to set policy for provision and voluntary organisations seeking to continue the freedom of action to which they were accustomed. Such tensions are evident in the difficulties that Devon County Council and the Devonian Association for Cripples' Aid experienced over the development of orthopaedic treatment for adults.

The services Georgiana Buller helped create at St Loye's College have been superseded by newer ideas about supporting people with disabilities to lead a normal life. As Borsay has described, the mid twentieth-century was still the period of collective solutions in shaping services for disabled people.[35] A philosophy of 'economic rationality' prevailed that valued equipping disabled people for economic independence as the highest goal and considered that this could be most effectively delivered in special institutions offering a narrow range of possibilities. St Loye's College fitted this now discredited model: but the limitations on what it offered were a practical response to the possibilities in a particular time and place. They illustrate Buller's pragmatism, rather than the limits of her imagination.

Georgiana Buller once described her talent as making a reality of castles-in-the-air. It was the very talent that her father had exercised to the full, comprehending the strategic objective and marshalling the resources to achieve it. She managed the War Office 'like toy soldiers', said one of her former colleagues.[36] Her obituary in the St Loye's' Annual Report stated that 'she worked unceasingly to persuade Government Departments, Local Authorities and private citizens that her ideas were practical politics'.[37] She herself modestly underplayed those roles. 'Nothing ever gets done unless you shout long and hard for it', she said, picturing herself as an 'agitator', and shout long and hard she did. The lives of many disabled people were the richer for it.[38]

Acknowledgements

Every attempt to contact the copyright holders has been made and the author extends her thanks to those listed below for their permission to use material reproduced in this chapter. St Loye's Foundation for the reproduction of the portrait of Dame Georgiana Buller, Extract from *The War Workers* by E.M. Delafield reproduced by permission of PFD (www.pfd.co.uk) on behalf of the Estate of E.M. Delafield. Extract from *Blue Remembered Hills* by Rosemary Sutcliff, published by The Bodley Head reproduced by permission of David Higham on behalf of the Estate of Rosemary Sutcliff. Extract from Norman Capener's obituary of Dame Georgiana Buller reproduced and adapted with permission and copyright of the British Editorial Society of Bone and Joint Surgery.

Notes and References

1. Melville 1923, p. 288.
2. *The Times*, 6 June 1908.
3. Melville 1923, p. 282.
4. DRO, 2065M add F357.
5. British Red Cross Archive (BRCA), 1293/1; DRO 2065M add F357.
6. Jones, *Express and Echo*, 16 November 1927.
7. DRO, 2065M add F357, press cuttings.
8. DRO, 2065M add F357.
9. Delafield 1918, pp. 29-30.
10. DRO, 2065M add F357, press cuttings; BRCA 1293/6, pp.30-31.
11. DRO, 2065M add F357.
12. *Express and Echo*, 10 November 1915 and 27 December 1915.
13. *Express and Echo*, 27 November 1921 and 22 February 1921.
14. DRO, 2065M add F357, press cutting undated and untitled.
15. DRO, Devonian Orthopaedic Association (DOA), (formerly Devonshire Association for Cripples' Aid), 1927, *First Annual Report*, p. 9.
16. Jones & Girdlestone 1929, 'The Cure of Crippled Children: Proposed National Scheme', *British Medical Journal*, 11 October 1919, p. 457.
17. Cooter 1993, pp. 155-158.
18. DRO, 2065M add F357. The Association later extended its work to South West Devon and North Cornwall.
19. *North Devon Journal*, 15 April 1926; *Express and Echo*, 17 November 1926 and 16 November 1927.
20. DRO, DOA (1928) *First Annual Report*, p. 9; *Exeter Working Lives: The Careers of Seven Exeter Women* 1987, Exeter Heritage Project, p. 24.
21. Sutcliff 1983, pp. 86-87.
22. TNA, MH 66-58, *Devon Health Survey*; *Express and Echo*, 8 March and 16 June 1934.
23. DRO, DOA (1936) *Annual Report for 1935*, p. 2.
24. WCSL, SF929/BUL U Buller, *G. Buller Scrapbook of Cuttings*.
25. *Express and Echo*, 16 November 1936.
26. WCSL, St Loye's College Annual Reports (1937) *First Annual Report*; (1938) *Second Annual Report*.
27. WCSL, St Loye's 1939, *Third Annual Report*, p. 3.
28. WCSL, St Loye's 1938, *Second Annual Report*, p. 8.
29. WCSL, St Loye's 1940, *Fourth Annual Report*, p. 3; Capener 1953, p. 674.
30. WCSL, St Loye's 1953, *Annual Report for 1953*, p. 1.
31. Capener, pp. 673-4.
32. DRO, 2065M add F357.
33. Pugh 1992, pp. 30-31.
34. Finlayson 1990; Macadam 1934.

35. Borsay 2005, pp. 129-133.
36. Jones, *Express and Echo,* 16 November 1927.
37. WCSL, St Loye's Annual Report 1953, p. 1.
38. Harvey 1998, p. 51.

Bibliography

Borsay, A. (2005) *Disability and Social Policy in Britain Since 1750,* Basingstoke: Palgrave Macmillan.

Capener, N. (1953) 'In Memoriam Dame Georgiana Buller', *Journal of Bone and Joint Surgery,* 35, 4, pp. 573-4.

Cooter, R. (1993) *Surgery and Society in Peace and War,* Basingstoke: Macmillan.

Delafield, E.M. (1918) *The War Workers,* London: Heinemann.

Finlayson, G. (1990) 'A Moving Frontier: voluntarism and the state in British social welfare', 1911-1949', *Twentieth-Century British History,* 2, pp. 183-206.

Harvey, H. (1998) *Towards a better Provision Fifty Years On: the Royal Devon and Exeter Hospital, 1948–1998,* Exeter: RD&E NHS Foundation Trust.

Macadam, E. (1934) *The New Philanthropy,* London: G. Allen and Unwin.

Melville, C.M. (1923) *Life of General Sir Redvers Buller,* vol. 2, London: Arnold.

Pugh, M. (1992) *Women and the Women's Movement in Britain,* 1914–1959, Basingstoke: Macmillan.

Sutcliff, R. (1983) *Blue Remembered Hills,* Oxford: Oxford University Press.

WCSL (1987) *Exeter Working Lives: the careers of seven Exeter women,* Exeter Heritage Project.

The Shearers and the Shorn Revisited: twentieth-century rural Devon through the writings of E.W. Martin

Andrew J.H. Jackson

Introduction

In 2005 the writer E.W. Martin died. Towards the end of 2006 a set of papers written by or belonging to him were acquired for the Special Collections library of the University of Exeter.[1] This is a short review of some of the contents of the papers, and a consideration of the national and regional significance of the work of Martin.[2] Ernest Walter Martin was born in the village of Shebbear in North Devon in 1912, and became a notable researcher and writer on rural life. Books written by Martin include: *The Secret People* (1954), on parish life up to the 1950s; *The Shearers and the Shorn* (1965), on rural depopulation and malaise in the county town of Okehampton and surrounding parishes; and *Country Life in England* (1966). Such texts feature among the literature published by other researchers and writers that considers rural change during the early to middling decades of the twentieth century. Martin, like other contributors to this body of work, gives the impression of rural society in peripheral regions in a state of decline.[3]

The writings of Martin are of interest to geographers, sociologists and historians concerned with rural change in the twentieth century. A number of key themes are of note in his research and publications: the course of twentieth-century decline, the endurance of community structures and sentiment, and contrasting attitudes towards the countryside. Such themes are of particular relevance for those assessing or indeed reassessing rural life in the early to mid-twentieth century. Was the economy of the countryside depressed, for example, the culmination of a long trajectory of decline; or is this overplayed? Did the self-contained rural community ideal breakdown, a process exacerbated by the circumstances of the inter-war years; or did communities evolve and adapt? How far can the emergence of the 'contested' countryside of today be traced back: to the 1960s, 1970s and 1980s; or, earlier, to the 1920s and 1930s? Martin's output, alongside those of a number of other influential writers, sustained a particular reading of change in the twentieth-century countryside. This interpretation is a potent one, and one that needs to be evaluated in any revisiting of the history of twentieth-century rural Devon and indeed Britain.[4] The survival of the Martin papers allows the development of his thinking to be more fully understood.

Revisiting *The Shearers and the Shorn*

An examination of the Martin papers in early 2007 took as its focus documents relating to one of Martin's most important works, *The Shearers and the Shorn* of 1965. It is of note that this is a volume in the rural sociology series that received the support of the Dartington Hall Trust and was published by Routledge. The series also includes, reflecting a broader agenda of the Trust, John Saville's *Rural Depopulation in England and Wales, 1851–1951*. The 'Dartington Hall Studies in Rural Sociology' also sponsored the classic *Ashworthy* by W.M. Williams of 1964. *Ashworthy* is the name Williams chose in order to mask the identity of the parish being studied in north-west Devon. *The Shearers*, meanwhile, is based on Okehampton and surrounding parishes, including that of Ashworthy. The Dartington Hall Trust had also supported earlier, similar research in North Devon by Mitchell.[5]

The Shearers and the Shorn is a work that deals particularly well with power and class in the countryside. The title itself is an analogy referring to the two 'them' and 'us' classes in rural society – the 'shearers' and the 'shorn'.[6] This study, like Williams' *Ashworthy*, considers the upheaval of the landownership and tenure structure in the context of depopulation and wider rural decline. Martin takes a similar, if not quite as melancholy-laden stance, as W.G. Hoskins in his county study *Devon* of 1954.[7] Neither Martin nor Hoskins mount a defence of the landed estate system as such, but both are in no doubt that the departure of the squire and instability in landed proprietorship had contributed to certain inter-related problems evident in the twentieth-century countryside, such as: out-migration, a loss of social cohesion and a weakening of economic well-being.

Beyond Devon, *The Shearers and the Shorn* falls into a group of texts concerned with northern and western Britain in the 1950s and 1960s, including William's *Ashworthy*, Emmett's *A North Wales Village*, Littlejohn's *Westrigg* in the Cheviots, and Nalson's *Mobility of Farm Families* in Staffordshire.[8] This body of literature looks back on the early to middling 1900s, and conjures up an image of decline, adjustment and uncertainty. Martin, of these writers, evokes especially empathetically a sense of times passing or lost, a gift also possessed by Hoskins. A prominent dimension in *The Shearers and the Shorn*, and in other like studies, is the departure of the squire – a central figure in the 'ceremonialist' regime, as Martin calls it.[9]

In the Martin papers is a cuttings file of book reviews.[9] Two reviews are quite striking. One is by the sociologist Ray Pahl. He wrote in *Town and Country Planning* on *The Shearers and the Shorn*, evidently impressed by Martin's discussion of the ceremonialism that had formerly held sway:

> Anyone who has attempted to put modern rural communities into their historical perspective will be familiar with the class oppression by which the rural elite maintained its power in the cosy communities of olde Englande. Mr Martin provides useful local evidence, and I particularly liked his chapter on 'the code by which the elite protected its interests' in the deferential society. [Quoting Martin:] 'Even now every twist and turn of contemporary affairs is affected by the ancient code . . . It has given a particular bias to class relationships, government, religion, culture, and all facets of borough and village life' . . . I welcome this study for the way it effectively scotches any notions of the 'good old days' in rural Devon. [Quoting again:] 'Pauperism, poverty, and the sense of inferiority were products of material and

spiritual misalliance. The social effects – rural depopulation, malaise and discontent – can't therefore be thought of as having an entirely economic origin'.[11]

Pahl is reflecting in particular here on Martin's account of the past, if near past. A second review turned more to Martin's findings in the context of the present. The review appeared in the *Sun* newspaper of 4 March 1965. The reviewer, A. Pottersman, in a piece entitled 'Cities where only the under-fifties may live', observes:

Britain in 1984 will be networked with industrial cities and their suburbs where nobody aged over 50 lives. In their factory-built houses the citizens will live off factory-bred chickens, cows and sheep; factory-grown wheat, vegetables and fruit. There will be patches of green belt, but just for the memory . . . Off to those areas of the country that cannot be reclaimed from their rural habits – Devon, Somerset, Wiltshire, Worcestershire – will be shunted the sick . . . Sociologist EW Martin wisely does not try to provide the answer. His job is to analyse and warn.[12]

The reviewer goes on, reflecting on Martin's interpretation of the aftermath of the undermining of the ceremonialist order:

It took all the might of social democracy, all the influence of the new bureaucracy, to break down this almost-feudal caste system . . . The vicious caste system of Devon life collapsed, says Martin, only when property-owning became a nightmare. Today, despite the invasion of mass society – newspapers, radio, television – the old isolation prevails. Now that families can be entertained at their fireside by the telly it may even increase . . . Farmers' wives may drive to town in their own cars to have their hair done. But the old social code, by which gossip can still drive young women to suicide, prevails . . . And as the young continue to move away because there is nothing to keep them, Okehampton and places like it retreat into further isolation and social death . . . We have been warned.

Such writings – of the likes of Martin, Pahl and Pottersman – have added to our perceptions of the countryside of the early to middling decades of twentieth century, and of the degrees of continuity and change in evidence.[13]

Other Writings

Following the examination of the papers relating to *The Shearers and the Shorn*, the inspection turned to documents in the collection identified as undated drafts of possibly unpublished work. One document, 'Rural society in Devon in the *c*.20th', was discovered to be that ending up in a much-abridged form in *Transactions of the Devonshire Association,* in a volume surveying the county at the Millennium.[14] A second file was found to contain drafts and a synopsis of a proposed book entitled: 'The deserted village: a study of rural poverty as a commentary upon English parish life circa 1800–1950'.[15] The work does not appear to have reached publication. Martin did, however, contribute a chapter, 'From parish to union: poor law administration, 1601–1865', to a book edited by him on *Comparative Development in Social Welfare* of 1972. His rationale for 'The deserted village', set out in a further document, argues that the book would be original in taking a view of rural poverty from the perspective of the rural community. The published literature, Martin points out, had become dominated by approaches centred on the national administration of poverty and the condition of the rural working class. There is some writing up of proposed content for 'The deserted village' within the surviving papers. Difficult to overlook, and certainly to speculate upon, is something that he wrote in his own handwriting across the top of the typescript synopsis of the intended work: '![*sic*] Problems of private utopian thinking'. This statement hints somewhat at a personal agenda, if a quite understandable one.

A third file, entitled 'The village today and yesterday', was identified to be a proof of what would be published as *The Secret People* of 1954, and later as *The Book of the Village* of 1962.[16] Although this file did not include an unpublished find, a return to the collection of book reviews, containing cuttings relating to *The Secret People,* proved fruitful. One review in the *Observer* is telling, by A.J.P. Taylor:

> This is an extraordinary book, bewildering to any reader who likes a clear simple impression. Yet the curious method of presentation does

not prevent this from being a good book. It has a genuine tang of the
earth in it; and the picture is all the more effective for being as over-
loaded with detail as a Breughel picture. The reader is made to feel
something of what village life was really like. And if he persists to the
end he will find a series of practical suggestions for reviving village life
and keeping it going in the future.[17]

This is possibly Martin best encapsulated. How do we categorise
him: rural sociologist, oral historian or country writer? His thinking on, and feeling for, the countryside appeared to motivate him to
become all three.

Conclusion

Martin had cause to reflect back upon his unravelling of the
complexities of rural change in *The Shearers and the Shorn*, and upon
subsequent oral history work in the 1970s, in preparation for an article
for the *Transactions of the Devonshire Association* for the year 2000.
Bringing his interpretations and conclusions up to date, he remained
hopeful. Despite all the change that had taken place since the great
watershed that was the First world war, he had held on to a faith in
the endurance of tradition and the capacity of rural communities to
sustain it:

> If we talk about tradition enough to try to understand what we really
> feel, what we really think deeply about our society, and about what
> we have done and what we are trying to do, then tradition will live.
> Tradition in the community in which I live still has life. It we fail to
> value tradition we shall be swallowed up by the engulfing power of
> world culture with all its bright technologies and false promises.[18]

The writings of E.W. Martin span a long period of considerable change
in Devon, a period still quite fresh and perhaps raw in the popular
consciousness. Martin's thoughts can stir emotion as much as yield
insight and prompt explanation.

The Shearers and the Shorn *Revisited*

Notes and References

1. EUL, MS 309.
2. This chapter is based on an unpublished seminar paper given to the Inter-war Rural History Research Group network on 7 March 2007. The author is grateful for the help of Susannah Guy and Charlotte Berry, then of the Special Collections, Exeter University Library. The assistance of Dr Tom Greeves is also acknowledged during the early evaluation process of the Martin papers.
3. Examination of the theme of decline features in more recent studies of the twentieth-century countryside, for example: Burchardt 2002, Howkins 2003, and Humphries and Hopwood 1999.
4. The findings of Martin were located within the context of twentieth-century rural change in a distance-learning course, co-authored with Lynne Thompson, for the Department of Lifelong Learning, University of Exeter; see, in an edited and abridged form, Jackson 2010. The emergence of a contested countryside has been explored by, among others, rural geographers such as Marsden et al. 1993 and Murdoch and Marsden 1994, and also came to be reflected in the findings of the *State of the Countryside* report (The Countryside Agency 2003).
5. Mitchell 1950 and 1951.
6. Martin 1965, xii.
7. Hoskins 1954, pp. 296-9.
8. For overviews of this rural sociological literature, see Harper 1989 and Wright 1992. Some of the rural social or 'community' studies of the 1960s have already been 'revisited', including, perhaps the most famous in this genre, Ronald Blythe's (1969) *Akenfield* (see Taylor 2006).
9. Martin 1965, pp. 8-11. The characteristics and fortunes of Martin's ceremonial regime were first considered by this present author in Jackson 1998, pp. 37-9.
10. EUL, MS 309/1/3/3/1.
11. The cutting from *Town and Country Planning* does not show the date of the edition, but the page numbers are shown, pp. 504-5. Pahl was not uncritical of certain aspects of Martin's work, drawing attention to particular theoretical limitations in *The Shearers and the Shorn*.
12. The cutting shows the date of the newspaper edition, but not the page number.
13. The Special Collections of Exeter University Library also contains papers of Henry Williamson. Williamson's writings have contributed similarly to interpretations of the twentieth-century countryside; for example, Jackson 1996.
14. EUL, MS 309/1/3/1/18; Martin 2000.
15. EUL, MS 309/1/3/1/10.

407

16. EUL, MS 309/1/3/1/25.
17. EUL, MS 309/1/3/3/1. The cutting does not give the date of the edition of *The Observer* or the page number.
18. Martin 2000, p. 247. See also Lane 2000.

Bibliography

Blythe, R. (1969) *Akenfield: portrait of an English village*, London: Allen Lane.

Burchardt, J. (2002) *Paradise Lost: rural idyll and social change since 1800*, London: I.B. Tauris.

Countryside Agency, The (2003) *The State of the Countryside 2020*, Wetherby: The Countryside Agency.

Harper, S. (1989) 'The British Rural Community: an overview of perspectives', *Journal of Rural Studies*, 5, 2, pp. 161-84.

Hoskins, W.G. (1954) *A New History of England: Devon*, London: Collins.

Howkins, A. (2003) *The Death of Rural England: a social history of the countryside since 1900*, London: Routledge.

Humphries, S. and Hopwood, B. (1999) *Green and Pleasant Land: the untold story of country life in twentieth-century Britain*, London: Macmillan/Channel 4 Books.

Jackson, A.J.H. (1996) '"The Serious Historian of the Village": rural tradition and change as recorded by Henry Williamson', *TDH*, 53, pp. 11-5.

Jackson, A.J.H. (1998) 'Rural Property Rights and the Survival of Historic Landed Estates in the Late Twentieth Century', unpublished PhD Thesis, University of London.

Jackson, A.J.H. (2010) 'Unit 11: Communities: new settlers and a new order', *The English Countryside, Rural Life and Cultural Change, 1900–75*, Exeter: University of Exeter, [online] Available at: <http://as.exeter.ac.uk/support/educationenhancementprojects/openexeter>.

Lane, J. (2000) 'Devon lost . . . Devon gained', *DAT*, 132, pp. 275-98.

Martin, E.W. (1954) *The Secret People: English village life after 1750*, London: Phoenix House.

Martin, E.W. (1962) *The Book of the Village*, London: Phoenix House.

Martin, E.W. (1965) *The Shearers and the Shorn: a study of life in a Devon community*, London: Routledge and Kegan Paul.

Martin, E.W. (1966) *Country Life in England*, London: Macdonald.

Martin, E.W. (ed.) (1972) *Comparative Development in Social Welfare*, London: Allen and Unwin.

Martin, E.W. (2000) 'Rural Society in Devon in the Twentieth Century: the fate of rural tradition', *DAT*, 132, pp. 233-48.

Mitchell, G.D. (1950) 'Depopulation and Rural Social Structure', *The Sociological Review*, 42, pp. 69-85.

Mitchell, G.D. (1951) 'The Relevance of Group Dynamics to Rural Planning Problems', *The Sociological Review*, 43, pp. 1-16.

Marsden, T., Murdoch, J., Lowe, P., Munton, R. and Flynn, A. (1993) *Constructing the Countryside*, London: University College London Press.

Murdoch, J. and Marsden, T. (1994) *Reconstituting Rurality: class, community and power*, London: University College London Press.

Saville, J. (1957) *Rural Depopulation in England and Wales, 1851–1951*, London: Routledge and Kegan Paul.

Taylor, C. (2006) *Return to Akenfield: portrait of an English village in the 21st century*, London: Granta.

Williams, W.M. (1964) *A West Country Village. Ashworthy: family, kinship and land*, London: Routledge and Kegan Paul.

Wright, S. (1992) 'Image and Analysis: new directions in community studies', in Short, B.M. (ed.) *The English Rural Community: image and analysis*, Cambridge: Cambridge University Press, pp. 195-217.

Index

Braunton Burrows 88
Bray, Revd A.E. 23–4, 25
Bray, Mrs 23–4, 25–6
Bread and Ale Assize (1280) 52
Brendan 'the Navigator', St 83
Brent, Isaac (master scribbler) 216
Brent, Dr Robert (d.1872) 216–25
Brentor church 137
Brewer, Emma 61
Brice, Henry 195
Bridestow 143
bridges 136, 137
Bridgwater 170
Bridport, Lord 287
Bristol 136, 139, 170, 250, 255, 258,
    379, 382, 383
Bristol Cathedral 133
Bristol Channel 167–80
Brithem Bottom 119, 120, 126, 127,
    128
British Association for Local History
    1
British Medical Journal 391
Brixham 21, 82
Broadhembury 56
Broke family 139
Bromlegh, John de 43, 44, 45
Bronescombe, John 26, 33
Brown, Martha West (b.1826) 309,
    318
Browne, Samuel 105
Bruton, Charles 235
Bruton, Frances 235
Bruton, Mary Kelly 235
Bruton, Walter Meddon, rector of West
    Worlington 235
Bryggs, Jane Sydenham 120
Bryggs (or Bruges), Sir Thomas 120
Buckish 232
Buckish Mill 232
Bucks Mills 86
Bude 235
Bude Canal 169
Budgen, C. 153
Buller, Lady Audrey 387, 388, 396

Buller, Georgiana (1884–1953) 387–97
    The Prude's Prejudice or The
    Triumphant Bicyclist 396
Buller, Sir Redvers (1839–1908) 387–8
Bully, Joseph 106
Burges, John 135, 138
Burgess, Ann 283–8
Burgess, Beatrice (schoolmistress)
    (b.1879) 283
Burgess, Louisa 287
Burgess, William (headmaster of
    Rousdon school) 283–8
Burgh Island 80–1
Burghley, Lord 105
Burn Woods 127
Burnard, Thomas 171
Burnham Beeches (London) 280
Burton Bradstock 282
Bush, Robin 87, 88
Butterfield, William 272

Caddy, Elizabeth 235
Caddy, John 235
Cadiz 171
Cadwallader 24
Caird, James 108–9
Calstock 134
Cambridge University 14, 15, 134, 139,
    296, 297
Camden, William 82
Candida (or White), St 138
Capener, Norman (surgeon) 392
Cardiff 172
Carew, Sir Gawain 144, 146
Carew, Sir Peter 143, 144, 145, 146
carols 223–4
Carpenter, Mary 62
Carter, Mary 194
Carter, William 194
Castle Drogo 279
catch meadows 343–6
Catherine of Alexandria, St 86
Central Council for the Care of
    Cripples 394
Chadwick, Edwin 268